The Bungle Book

Some Errors by Which We Live

G. V. Loewen

University Press of America,® Inc.
Lanham • Boulder • New York • Toronto • Plymouth, UK

Copyright © 2016 by University Press of America,® Inc.
4501 Forbes Boulevard, Suite 200, Lanham, Maryland 20706
UPA Acquisitions Department (301) 459-3366

Unit A, Whitacre Mews, 26-34 Stannary Street,
London SE11 4AB, United Kingdom

Library of Congress Control Number: 2015945854
ISBN: 978-0-7618-6642-8 (pbk : alk. paper)—ISBN: 978-0-7618-6643-5 (electronic)

♾™ The paper used in this publication meets the minimum requirements of American
National Standard for Information Sciences Permanence of Paper for Printed Library
Materials, ANSI/NISO Z39.48-1992.

To Jennifer Heller;

Sensible, Indomitable, Beautiful

Upon discovering a spike used to train elephants,
Mowgli asks the Black Panther what it is:

"It was made to thrust into the heads of them," said Bagheera.
"That thing has tasted the blood of many."

"But why do they thrust into the heads of elephants?"

"To teach them Man's Law. Having neither claws nor teeth,
men make these things, and worse."

From Kipling, *The Jungle Book* (1894)

Contents

Introduction

The Usual Suspects

Our language is full of clichés. The phrase in the title refers as much to itself as it does to a normative list. But what if we, as a simple thought experiment, make the adjective into a noun and the noun into a verb. We then have the usual, that is, what is normative, in action, suspecting something, perhaps of itself, but certainly of others. Indeed, in our society, and perhaps in every kind of culture that has ever been, it is what is the usual thing that is the source of all suspicion. Norms guard against deviance. So, the usual suspects now become something much better than a commonplace descriptor of a police line constructed in lieu of evidence. It is now a policed line, a guarded border over which transgression can be surveilled and its sources made suspect. The usual *suspects*.

There is something else to be gained by this syntactic sleight of hand. With the usual now known to be suspecting us and others like us, we can both guard against our more likely transgressions and call attention to "The Usual" as an inherent danger to all curiosity and the expectation of difference. Even the future itself may be said to have its day in court. Our experience of the day to day only marks time. It is the new that remarks upon it. We recall the time of a memorable experience, and tend to lose the routine in a formless fothering of living on and subsistence. What stands out, in other words, stands apart. By its very presence it defines itself as a transgression, even if the phases and cycle of a human life have conceded some apertures to the correct sequencing of new experiences, like a first love or a first child. A transgression is not necessarily a deviance in any correctional sense. Norms attempt to demand a certain timing of experiences, but they cannot dictate to us how it is we still face them with naivety and wonder. Now one might well be skeptical that wonder is also prescribed. Nevertheless, we are possessed by it and taken out of what had been ourselves. The experience of bewilderment, of alienation, of the diverse forms of subjectitude to which we are drawn because what is the usual thing carries nothing of this diversity within it, pronounce not merely the aleatory but also the transitory upon us. No matter the depth of feeling, joy or suffering, the apparently unending waves of either anomie or astonishment, this too shall pass.

This is why what is "The Usual" remains a beacon for us. It makes all journeys prodigal ones. Even the final movement, away from beings and toward the Being of what limits existence, is said to be a threshold over which an unusual usual has its shadowy place. Unusual only in the sense that its essence is difference and it is not living. So when we long to transgress the norms of the day to day, we do it with the full knowledge that we can always return if things do not work out as imagined. Unless the new takes us unawares—that is, we did not "expect the unexpected," another cliché of dubious merit—our stepping over this line or that always has a bit of the disingenuous about it. Like the one who walks away but turns her head back and slips us a sly smile, tossing her hair, the transgressor knows where home is and has been. We do not need the usual to suspect ourselves.

Since we both leave and return—perhaps the other has watched the lingering but diminishing figure of the first for a long time, willing her return and imagining that he could have some influence over the outcome of transgression with this too having the disingenuity of hoping to reinstate the same thing while stepping over the limit of another's freedom—it suggests that as an obvious corollary to The Usual suspecting difference and the new, that what is to be considered unusual is suspect. Not always discursively abnormative, not necessarily criminal, almost never evil, the unusual pushes it way into things through a combination of absences of experience which may even include the irruptive force of the uncanny. Experience of the unusual is absent by definition. We might sense the ending of a certain form of life—it may be adolescence or the ability to generally count on our consistently good health, or it may be a species on the brink of extinction or yet the twilight of gods—but when such a thing passes and oddly "becomes" fully absent, we cannot longer sense it at all. Like Carossa's "murmur of Gods' song," the passing of which is noticed only as a disquieting absence, the usual thing also has our genuine loyalty and good will. It is not at all as if the routine can only represent a grinding numbness. For the most part it presents itself to us as not only how we live, but also how we want to live. Quietude is found there. Solitude perhaps elsewhere. Even so, the unusual is always disquieting, simply because it also presents to us an absence of what has been the case. Now what is normative is no more, at least for the moment. We are lost in an awe that is always both awesome and awful at once. This is why the unusual is suspect, and not because it departs from a dictation. No one takes norms so seriously that she becomes their walking billboard. The only space where we cite the rules is when our children cannot or refuse to recognize them for what they are. Adults know that when those like them pretend to be nothing but the rules embodied, they are always up to something. Children, for a time, think that all adults are, are mobile agents of the rulebook, always ready to sanction transgressions. It is the realization that no one lives entirely normatively and that all of us transgress this or that rule when the time is right, that pushes the child into a more mature understanding of existence. Now Mowgli understands, for instance, that human beings desire to control the world even though they are not in themselves and by an inherent nature equipped to do so. Indeed, the shadow of the usual falls most heavily not upon our children but upon our non-human cousins.

To make our way through this tension of desiring difference and yet remaining loyal to the same, we must turn another patent phrase on its head. We must "unexpect the expected" in order to go beyond the usual while not remaining enthralled to the sense that we must at some point return. To experience difference is to be different and not to come back to the same, even in our imaginations. We do not leap without looking, but it matters what we are looking for. Just as when we gaze into an abyss, as Nietzsche famously warns us, we are bored into by whatever lurks there, monsters or perhaps lesser others that we have, in our efforts to get our successors to mind us, made into magic mountains, when we look across the gated fields what lies there is awakened. It returns our gaze and it too may wonder what will happen next.

Like opening an unfamiliar volume—we do not know how much it contains, whether we will sink or float let alone swim, is its liquid potable, are its contents fungible—what covers it over is the hinged limen of a portal, a way in and a way out. Though the adage about not judging a book by its cover has its merits, we can still afford to pause and listen to what it says . . .

As I approached the table abruptly a voice entered my head: "Hey . . . hey buddy! I lost my jaw. What a screw up! Just dropped right off. Can you? That's it, God, thanks. And can you relight that candle? Great. You know being dead is bad enough, but when you can't even see or speak! At least I wrote this book here, and now that there's light again it can be read. Like I said, being dead . . . oh, wait a second. . . ." As if a sudden realization had struck my new friend, he suddenly fell silent once again.

THE UNUSUAL IS SUSPECT

Something ends and another thing begins. The same for persons. That we do not know our specific ends does nothing to obviate the fact that we will approach and cross over, committing ourselves to the ultimate transgression upon which all of the usual things immolate themselves. Death is unusually usual in this regard. An unusual death provokes comment, media coverage, and chagrin, as well as perhaps a few chills. And just maybe, a little admiration. For after all, why not begin something in one's absence? A conversation piece, taking its place as part of a still life, still living on even though passed on. If something ends without a suspect, for instance, then the mystery and search for a source continue. This is the same thing as searching for an origin. Something has happened and we do not know what occurred to make it happen. An end has presented itself without a beginning, but to locate the source of the event, connect the start and finish as if their usually perpendicular lines did somehow connect on the far side of life's track, we need to run along backwards. The exiguous threads of complex tapestries aside, we need to trace the connections. We need also to realize that what once began as something has been radically altered, usually in a very normative but no less fatal manner, and thus has appeared in our view as something else, something quite other to its source. In this, we cannot take the end as a necessary clue to a beginning, even though it is certainly true that "something is only ever a beginning in relation to an end or goal. Between these two, beginning and end, stands an indissoluble connection. The beginning always implies the end. Whenever we fail to mention what the beginning in question refers to we say something meaningless" (Gadamer 2000:15 [1998]). The widest meaning of origins for human beings is the advent of consciousness. To be more specific, our own consciousness as set apart from nature must have begun imperceptibly. Some six million years or more are involved, a geological time scale that cannot be known in any detail, and stretches the limits of the very imagination that has evolved from it. But what is perhaps the most strange and wondrous part of this process is that it is unusual. Not sentience *per se*, as that is a shared feature of much life, perhaps all that we know so far. Intelligence, however that be defined, is also present in other animals, including sociality of a sort. Consciousness of the human variety includes both reason and conscience, and in this it appears to be unique. It is not natural but cultural, and yet it springs from nature. The hackneyed "man versus nature" narrative is seen as overdone, especially since we are still a part of the wider nature, beings who reside in the cosmos even if still parochial. Yet the connection between nature and humanity is of the same sort that embodies the connection between the beginning and the end. One might predict such an end as humanity, the probability of being correct increasing exponentially the closer to the present we can imagine ourselves observing, if we could take in the entirety of cosmic evolution. Not that this anonymous and universal process has anything to do with us, let alone producing us. Only that understanding that we are connected is what gives meaning to the process itself. This is the response that can be given to the question of the beginning.

Of course, such an early answer is no solution to the problem of connection, the bond that is at once "indissoluble" and yet also seemingly insoluble. All we know so far is that the source and the event are linked, but we do not know exactly how or why. One immediate implication of any concept of evolution is, however, the idea of change itself. As human beings develop, even in their own specific lives or selves, we change, and this change takes place over time as an inevitable result of living on. Animals develop, grow, age and pass away without the reflective sense that this is what is in fact happening to them. Human beings know, sometimes well ahead of the phenomena in question, what is happening and sometimes we also know why it occurs as well. Indeed, human consciousness allows us to predict the future without ourselves having lived it. Needless to say, such a faculty is often fallible, but the fact that it exists and can guess correctly the state of something that is not yet something is an extraordinary thing and sets itself apart from nature in an unusual and unexpected manner. It is *this* aspect of our character that can both suspect the unusual—some more rare occurrence may be seen to give us a clue of what is to come, especially if what we imagine as an outcome seems out of the ordinary—and provide the unusual with a list of suspects from which it can pinpoint the source of the event and perhaps also why it makes this abnormative or relatively unpredictable accounting of itself. All of this speaks of adaptability and change as concomitant parts of everyone, no matter how solid we feel ourselves to be in any one moment. The normative is relatively featureless to the one who lives and moves within its ambit. It is a series of trees. The forest is a consciously calculated construct that lends a sense of the whole to an assortment of parts. Human consciousness is the gestalt of nature, more than the sum of its natural parts.

Engaging through dialogue, confronting through dialectic, consciousness becomes not only the interlocutor of nature, but also of itself. It becomes quite precisely conscious of its own development and through memory, aware that it is has a history. This history differs from that of nature, which appears to know itself innately and remains aloof to its own evolution, perhaps most strikingly through its uncanny ability to adapt to any kind of change, even that catastrophic. Our history thus far shows us to be the scions of that self-same nature because we too have developed diverse adaptations in its face. More importantly, though less impressively, we have also begun to develop a suite of adaptations in the face of one another. Memory and anticipation are precisely what nature lacks. They are unusual and unexpected facets of a new "nature," that of humanity. Suspecting ourselves of a character that sets us bodily apart from everything else, we sometimes shy away from the fullest implications that such a character bears along with it. One of these things is the contrary notion of determination: "Strictly speaking, development is the negation of history. [ ] . . . discourse about an 'historical development' harbors something of a contradiction. As soon as history is in play, what matters is not what is merely given, but, decisively, what is new" (Gadamer, op. cit. 16). For something to develop out of something else, what is to be is already pre-given in what has been. Growth, yes, and the making of an appearance of what is not only to be, but what must be. In fact, this sensibility colors our perception of both custom and tradition as well as overshadows the authentic component of human history, the unexpected and not merely the unusual. Certainly it is more personally comfortable as well as more politically convenient to pretend that something has always been the case. All routinized traditions proclaim their eternal presence. Today, we moderns respond with at best a yawn in the direction of the rare and overcast specimen who trots out such a hoary chestnut as the negation of history. Even so, we have to be cautious as well as precise about reminding ourselves that what we can observe in our own age is also not an end-point even as it is also not a "development" in this looser sense of the term: "Traditions do originate somewhere, and they can form quite quickly. Often their origins are quickly forgotten and everyone assumes that they have always existed" (Thomas 1990:205). That tradition is history as it has been is one of Gadamer's specific philosophical points. This kind of pointing to while pointing at carries a specific injunction upon the present. Any kind of change must be accustomed to. The more comfortable we become with living in a new way suggests that we need not be wary of the history of the change to which we have adapted, and through which we have adopted the new in general, both within ourselves and externally in the surrounding world. It is rather the types of change that have come about against our will, or perhaps, with only our sullen consent, that tend to be reified. Their newly thing-like quality is a mirage, of course, but it does have the advantage of both brooking no dissent and having to demand no sincere consent, since it has become, willy-nilly, the only game in town.

Yet even here, such coyness is dissembling, because the arts it uses to prevaricate its eternal mask are themselves being crafted as we go. Biological or naturalistic analogies aside, it is reasonable to conclude that "Customs and ways of thinking are organic parts of human life, constantly growing, developing, changing and sometimes decaying like every other living thing. Much of this change, too, is due to our own action, to our deliberate working to change them" (Midgely 2004:66). "Developing" and "growing" make their expected appearance here as well, but the key to the entire endeavor rests in the sense that humans take conscious and even conscientious action to change things. Things, for human beings, do not change by themselves. This is another aspect of our unusual relationship to the norms of nature. Explicating this relationship has most often led to deity, divine creation or some subsequent intervention, or at the very least, a sage nodding of one's head at the presumed cosmic uncanniness of the presence of something "larger than life." Once again, we might flatter our present culture by stating that we do not fall into these romances as easily as did our ancestors, whatever their home culture and wherever they made their often violent ports of call. To append the extramundane to the expected and routine is, over time, to annex the uncanny and the oceanic to the normative territories of the day to day. For thousands of years, the other world of spirits and gods *et al* was contiguous with this world, that of humans and animals. Joined at the hip, shooting from the lip, two ships that met in the night but refused to pass along from each other, the religious worldview in its most broad sense was not a rejection of the pragmatic and naturalistic common sense view of the everyday world, but rather an extension of it. Indeed, like custom and tradition, expected and usual, it generated its own "of course" statements. It complimented the everyday language and the arts of subsistence with the more rarified, but still distinctly human languages of the sacred and of aesthetics. By doing so, our predecessors achieved a system that conjoined all forms of sense, however common or uncommon. None of this is technically part of common sense *per se*, as Natanson notes, but all of it stands as a collective interlocutor with the knowledge, local and pragmatic, of everyday life. The synthesis created through their dialogue and dialectic is Phronesis, or "practical wisdom." Any way of life can become parochial if it does not remain open to the history and development—the one representing authentically and sometimes radically new experiences, the other, as Gadamer suggested, surveying the landscape with a kind of predetermined propriety, the one transforming and the other possessing—as well as endangering itself by being jaded in the face of the mortal fact of not truly being able to possess one's property or otherwise. Culture and its attendant interior of common sense falls only on its inability to accept and understand the unusual. It is, in other words, what one suspects that frees oneself.

Getting beyond suspicion may be mandatory, but the pace at which we do so is not part of the demand in principle. Suspicion of unargued authority is, for instance, something that is an abiding virtue. A respect for the travails of one's ancestry, cultural or personal, helps me in the day-to-day put my problems into a wider perspective. That we are still more likely to extend our parochial worldview back in time rather than open it up through the encounter with our contemporaries in the space of the world as it is today still presents an ongoing challenge. But the homology of temporal perspective does, at least, provide us with a portable template by which to attempt the understanding of others who struggle like us but in their own way and with their own version of provincialism. These problems and challenges can, of course, be given dramatic and daunting voice in art and thought, but by far the vast majority of us encounter them in daily life. We do not necessarily have the ability to immediately appeal to culture with a capital "C" to evaluate them and pronounce a judgment to which we then can cleave our behaviors: "This sense of the importance of the everyday in human life, along with

its corollary about the importance of suffering, colours our whole understanding of what it is truly to respect human life and integrity" (Taylor
1989:14). And though cultures and societies can "suffer," we have made this
sensibility much more abstract than it may have been in the past simply by
reifying a new source and locus of the challenge of facing the everyday—the
individual. It is I who faces the challenge of living on and who is thus
astonished that mundane life can present so many problems. More so, that it
is I, ultimately, who not only has to deal with these problems and attempt
resolution of them, but, and all the more sobering, it is also I who is the
source of many, if not most, of my problems. Coupled with this new locus of
autonomous perception of life is the presence of a new narrative that chroni-
cles the work done and predicts that which is to be done. This narrative is
certainly biographical and often autobiographical and is quite different from
that of our ancestors: "We have passed from a pleasure to be recounted and
heard, centering on the heroic or marvelous 'trials' of bravery or sainthood,
to a literature ordered according to the infinite task of extracting from the
depths of oneself, in between the words, a truth which the very form of the
confession holds out like a shimmering mirage" (Foucault 1980:59). Not
only is it I who have problems and must then face them—perhaps the trials of
bravery have become personalized and each is now her own hero—it is also
myself who becomes the very center of the narrative structure, the epicenter
of events and the source as well as the terminus of whatever judgment must
be passed. The point of this new story is to suspect the unusual.

And this structure is mimicked externally as well. By the mid-twentieth
century at least, there occurs, corresponding to the rise of the modern confessional in psychoanalytical practice and now contemporary counseling and
"rehabilitation" of all kinds, "a notable change in radio, movie and television
programs, and up to an increase of fear and insecurity in millions of human
beings" (Sorokin 1956:170-1). Our society aids counselors and social workers in drumming up their own business, as it were. We are content with this
charade because we remain at the center of it, and it is a small matter if most
of the people who are willing to listen to our *recantation*—and not so much
"recounting," as in yesteryear—do so only because they are paid to. That
there is industrial scale employment to sit and listen to people's private
tribulations is remarkable in itself. After all, what happened to the core idea
that it was I who must deal with my problems? Not quite that, it seems, for
we can rely on the paid charity of others to at least push us in the right
direction. We cannot see ourselves objectively, so we are told, and the professional expert knows us better than we can know ourselves. All of these
comforts taken together produce a very odd situation. Perhaps the "malaise
of modernity" is not so much objective alienation, the wending and then
rending away from a transcendental source of order and purpose, as anomie,
or subjective alienation, and this not related to the world as it is but resting

within the interstitial crevasses of the shattered self. There are parts of ourselves that other parts have been trained to dislike or disdain. We are always of two or more minds about ourselves, and the counselor's job is not so much to put the egg-head back together again, but reconcile, in as democratic manner as possible, the parts of the self that sit upon the wall and glare down at the parts which have fallen off. The question regarding the status of the "higher" forms is disregarded—and it is *this* more than metaphysics in general that is a cause for alarm; what is the source and the purpose of social order duplicated in the interiority of the self?—it is the fact that they have not fallen that is predominant. They might well be the village idiot, sitting up there, but no matter. This dovetails with the response modernity has made to the loss of transcendental order and purpose: "We should strive to leave the world a more prosperous place than we found it" (Taylor, op. cit. 85). How do we define prosperity? Mostly through production and consumption techniques. But technique by itself, as we shall see later, is merely an epiphenomenon to a more occlusive sensibility. Not only hidden, it hides itself. It is reclusive. It shies away at the approach of the thinker and thus it is also elusive. It is one of those things that Nietzsche stated we must shoot at. For technical phenomena have their source in ideas and sensitivities inasmuch as they might rest in the sensible and the practical. The *moral* of the new story of me-centered confessional autohagiography is a resentment tinged belief that because I suffer, or apparently suffer, that others not only must, but also should suffer as well. It is not just, if at all, Taylor's sense of a "reasoned agape." Perhaps it is also present. We feel good and wish to share that feeling. But we also feel bad and wish, darkly, to share *that* with others as well.

Yet the messianic tendency of all feel-gooders and do-gooders in the world does leave its mark. Upon discovering a personal cure, we often take it to be a generalizable potion from which all can benefit. We undertake a mission to moralize and rehabilitate the world. From speaking tours performed by ex-addicts of all stripes, to inspirational speakers of the workplace and managerial "cultures," to the fading circus of evangelical orators, to the latest fad or crisis in politics, to those who write their so personal and intimate stories, or have them ghost-written, into best-selling memoirs, we are attuned to listen to the one who has suffered and recovered, in some Augustinian fashion—and with no doubt as much or as little sincerity as we can attribute to the one who started this angle—because all of them claim to not only speak as we would speak if only we could, but tell us in as bald a fashion as possible to bear, that we *should* and must do as they have done. We must become our own salvation.

Like all narrators, however, the transience of this or that crop of them gives way to the new. The structure of the narrative is perennial, but its actual locutors are merely annual. Speaking about oneself too long, it appears, can produce a self-conscious aspect of consciousness that trembles at the thought of yet another recantation. Note that this is not, as we might expect given the parameters of what counts as humane discourse today, a conscience trembling. It is not the shameless self-righteousness of it all that defies our continued participation in it. Rather it is precisely self-absorption, just as "the weariness of age, illness, and the fatigue of the long interview eroded his conscious controls, the censorship of rationality gave way to dreams and desires long buried in the unconscious, in a process greatly reminiscent of daydream" (Portelli, 1990:145). One begins to slide into the ineffectual pseudo-discourse of wish fulfillment, distraction and fantasy. Not that these are personal fables, the poignant and meaningful subjective allegories by which we live in the day to day. Nor do they participate in cultural myths. They are simply the vulgar jouissance of the platitudes of anywhere and anyone, what is sold to us as always something we lack. The annual character of this kind of auto-locution makes us the willing subjects of trend and fashion, just as much "small talk" contains the topics of the day, all of them passing and almost all of them passable. What constitutes a "serious" conversation must involve the self in a more naked manner. But even here, what occurs is mainly plaintiff and accusation, the confession of trifles, and the brandishing of the trivial as a set of norms upon which to hang one's previously deviant hat. Though there is something to be read between the lines, it is always the same thing. Before I was sinful, or I suffered, or both. Now I am cleansed, or at least on the up and up, and on top of this, as already mentioned, I am now a missionary for the more just society and the better person. Our heroes may have a tragic flaw, but the newer religions of the agrarian epoch stated that such a flaw could be transcended, unlike those of the Greek period, where fateful heels really did bring the various versions of Achilles down. With the advent of Buddhism, Christianity and Islam, this older and perhaps more realistic ethics was overcome, or given the opportunity to be overcome. This is also when interpretation becomes narrowed to a single-minded exposition, that of subjective soteriology, figuring out how one can be saved from suffering or gain wisdom through it. For then, implicit within the autographed world as text, were the signs that actually marked a path through the wilderness. The grand error of this schema was to have taken these signs not as meaningful, which they certainly were, but as the truth. No, truth and meaning are quite different, as different as is the forest and the path through it. We are literally lost in front of the truth, which is the wild, anonymous, and the impersonal forest of nature. Any path at all is something that we humans have constructed, perhaps based on otherworldly signage that is implicit in nature, perhaps not. Either way, such signs become errors when they are taken for truths. Signage points always away from truth, just as the path in the forest presumes to lead to a way through, in *and* out, and does not seek to strand us in the middle of nowhere, which is in fact precisely where truth is: "The principle of a viable hermeneutics is always to interpret a text in such a way that what is implicitly in it is made explicit" (Gadamer, op. cit. 102). Interpretation generates meaning. It is meaning that makes nature and cosmos comprehensible for human beings, we who must live within its envelope. Truth is rather and indeed a "pathless land."

Knowing the history of interpretation is a must. Insofar as it can be known at all is, of course, another exercise in interpretation as well as the involvement of the subject in the making of meaning. It is this correspondence between what I am as a living being and what I must to do to live that takes me away from and ultimately outside of nature. This may seem radical enough, but it is something that human beings have been doing for millions of years. Not exactly new, but ever vigilant, interpretation, the cutting of a path through the wilderness by reading whatever we can into it, cannot yet be simply brushed off as old hat either, mainly because the paths of our ancestors wear themselves out through long term use. The nature around us changes, and the meanings we can glean from it, or put on it, also change over time. But more importantly, interpretation takes us out of our own time in a partial, but crucial, manner: "The ahistorical thinker too is likely to be the unwitting child of the immediately prevailing climate of opinion" (Barrett, 1979:40). One could blame "science" for this issue and leave it at that, but this would be as unwitting in its simple-mindedness as is the actual circumstance of ahistorical research. We never leave our own age and we are always children of it. But we need not remain child-like in the face of it, and it is the confusion between the necessity of being born into a specific human moment and being limited to knowing only what that moment says of itself that is the root of the issue. To find oneself within this confusion, an error by which we both live and die, is to desire the thoughtless ease of correct responses to the already acquiesced sense of solution: "Here one is secretly at work abolishing questioning altogether and is intent on cultivating the modesty of blind faith. One declares the sacred to be an essential law and is thereby taken seriously by one's age, which in its frailty and impotence has need for such a thing" (Heidegger, 1999:4 [1988]). Not really any different than pandering to the popular, the concern for being "relevant" takes on a more shadowy countenance when the parameters of what constitutes "making a contribution" are increasingly defined by the state. Indeed, it is highly ironic that whom we recall as being "great" are all of those who have stood, not outside of the history of their time, but apart from the normative desires of those who live in that time. More so, for even those who stand alone might well desire to be followed or to be, at least, ignored rather than disdained, they have stood against what "everyone" and therefore no one has stood for. They have thought against it, their meditations untimely, but the first step in thinking is to take note of unthought, which colors our experience of the enact mentality of living-on. Heidegger uses the most common place of

terms to designate the manifestation of the attitude of unthought, that is
"talk" or "hearsay": "One even writes books on the basis of such hearsay.
This 'everyone' is precisely *the* 'no-one,' which circulates in factical Dasein
and haunts it like a specter, a how of fateful undoing of facticity to which the
factical life of each pays tribute" (ibid:26, italics the text's). The entire effect,
if not necessarily the entirely calculated purpose, of the fashionable distractions of consumer society as well as the melodramatic rhetoric of both politics and economics, is to obviate our existential situatedness. Our "being
there," the famous Dasein of Heidegger, is "undone" in this way. We no
longer can place ourselves historically, emphatically denying that we must
confront mortality and that we are beings of finitude. It could be seen as
another necessary error to deny these crucial aspects of the factical life. Even
so, the manner in which we negotiate them surely counts for something.
Denying them outright is not only an empirical and historical error, we must
ask whether or not it really does serve our purpose, as a species and as
individuals, to pretend that finitude simply is an illusion, that my mortality,
as well as the facticality of living on in the face of both an unspecified death
and within the immanence of an only partially known history, is something
that cannot truly effect me.

It was Nietzsche who in our times first began to discriminate between the
need to be future-oriented—we, as human beings need to bracket our finitude
for the time being and get on with life; indeed, this bracketing was classically
what allowed human life to become possible in the first place, the great gift
of Prometheus being the hiding of the true timing of our deaths from us—and
the equally pressing need to be aware that we are who we are, that is, finite
beings who live and who die. But even this was but a prelude to thinking
about living. Like all great thinkers, Nietzsche must himself confront the
perennial questions, one group of which is simply, what does it mean to live
a human life? How can such a life have meaning? If it does, where do such
meanings come from, and how are they interpreted in our time as opposed to
or juxtaposed with the interpretations that have been given these questions
and their compatriots in the past? This is the very same problem that we just
saw the early Heidegger take up and rail against. What does unthought do to
people and culture? Does it provide a new meaning through which people
can fulfill their humanity, or does it sabotage the ability to make meaning at
all, "abolish questioning," which is one of Nietzsche's favorite slings against
the modern age. And not all of the veils that obscure our relationship to
history and mortality come from the shallow fords of media and consumer-
ism. Some of them come from morality itself, and some, greatly against the
historical intent of such a discourse, even from science. The more serious the
source of the distraction—and the exponentially astonishing vistas given us
by the technical brilliance of our prosthetic sciences, both at the levels of the
cosmic and the microcosmic might well be taken as evidence of a growing

sensibility that the human future is ours simply due to the fact that we are here and we are "working" in this way—the more seriously it can decline the existential demand to both self-examine and to make meaningful the human community with a view to a general and collective future. I say, such sources *can* get in the way of these all-important tasks, but need they? For at the same time, both science and morality have provided the very building blocks out of which a human future can be constructed. Once again, there appears to be a choice before us, and not a fate surrounding us. Faced with such a choice, human beings do tend to split the middle, imagining that this is the best compromise and that one cannot possibly be so serious all the time about something that we cannot, in the end, have any certain control over, that is our individual deaths and the future of the species. Fair enough, but this rationale can quickly become a rationalization for inaction and unthought, and indeed this is what the great critics of modernity have stated that it mainly is. The error then becomes not one that is necessary for life, as the ethical pretense that we have a future and must live on in this constructive illusion - rather than the delusion that we will always have a future—but begins to serve the baser motives of denial, distraction, and pretense in general: "There is, after all, scarcely a good practice in existence whose name has not been borrowed at times to gild something disreputable. Hypocrisy is indeed the tribute vice pays to virtue" (Midgely, 2004:159). [1] There may well be a psychological structure to this relationship, whereby what is necessary becomes the source and force for its apparently equally necessary denial. Jung speaks of the cognitive archetypes that provide the foundations for our mythology and also for our more down to earth sensibilities, the shadow, the hero, the mother and the father figures. All of them must be lived with and lived through, including the seemingly subaltern shadow. They cannot be avoided, but the manner in which we engage with them often has the same element of rationalization and hypocrisy, as when men and women argue, for instance. The former pride themselves not on rationalization, but on their rationality, which, historically, women were said to lack. This is nonsense, and we have thinkers like Jung to thank for overcoming such patent bigotry. Patent, yes, but for men, and perhaps also for women of the past, a necessary error through which the encounter with the other major physical expression of humanity could be lensed and worked through. The latter pride themselves on their ability to "feel" and express emotion, which men are said to lack even to our own day. When they clash, men and women hang their hats on these errors of projection, embellishing the other with what is in fact for the moment absent but in reality fully present in themselves. With an apt description of many a domestic dispute, Jung (op. cit. 15) even goes so far to say that the solid rationality of the woman can only be sidetracked by seduction or worse, broken by beating or rape! Precisely so given that the solidly anti-social irrationality of the man leads him to potentially commit such acts. The irony here is not so much that we are changing epistemological partners and dancing, but that in confronting what and who we believe to be the other we take on the stereotypes we associate with them. It is almost as if we imagine that we must become like them in order to communicate at all. The man must get emotional, the woman attain rationality. Jung reminds us that what is really occurring is that the other brings out in ourselves what the usual suspects in us, in this case, the realization that gendered performances are something that we must keep up and that our primary gender identification is in fact a fragile and ambiguous thing.

This reality gets lost in our efforts to translate the imagined language of the other into what is supposedly our own and only our own. Emotion and logic, so we are told from the fictive but ubiquitously famous planet Vulcan, are like oil and water. But even in the fantasy, the two of them do co-exist. Perhaps just as apt as Jung's amusing description, the scripts of Star Trek continually have to remind us that it is we humans who see them as discrete and not Vulcans. The latter simply have their emotions under a more rational control and oversight than do we. It is perhaps testament to our human tendency to desire their separation that an element of a fantasy could attain such fame. Not that there is not a real difference here, both between men and women, who are socialized quite differently, as well as between emotion and rationality, which might even originate in different sectors of the physical brain. In order to translate the situation more clearly, to lose less of its authentic difference, we need to grasp the part of ourselves that already holds some sense of the knowledge of the language of the other. This, Heidegger, suggests, is related to the phenomenological notion of forehaving: "In the case of translation, this forehaving which needs to be critically appropriated so that it is fitting to the translated text includes not only the point of view of the translator's own language, but also the translator's initial philosophical understanding of the meaning of the translated text and of the intellectual period in the author's development to which the text belongs" (1999:94 [1988]). Here we can read "text" as any context, including that of the spoken word or even of an unspoken communication, such as in music or painting etc. Just as history does not restart itself out of nothing, I do not come into any human context knowing absolutely nothing about it. Even regarding or being confronted by nature, I can often judge correctly the level of danger I might be facing. Strolling on a path in a forest, or indeed, even off the path which would heighten the risk of being able to get away from a puma leaping out, for instance, is still not the same thing as being in an earthquake or charting the often apparently random course of an oncoming tornado. Still further, within the human ambit, I know that human beings are present and must have some desire and sense of purpose that is at least partially recognizable to me. They are not, after all, from some other planet, fictive or real. Some shared language may be essential to communicate the detail or finer nuances of both emotions and rationalities, but even in its absence I can rely, for the most part, on their sense that say, outright and sudden murder or assault is abnormative and I can be on my way.[2]

Another manner of defusing the reification of imagined opposites into concrete and sometimes violent opposition to one another is to diversify one's own sense of self. Imagining that the self is any one thing is, in any case, as we shall show below, an unnecessary error, and thus one that we do not need to live by. This must be done at the symbolic level, however, because material analogies are often ambiguous. Take the problem of commodity or product competition, a form of opposing interests in market and business: "It is hard to say [ ] whether product differentiation takes the edge of competition, as is so often asserted. It seems to me that it intensifies competition for the efficient and protects the inefficient" (Lösch, 1967:196 [1945]). Indeed, even in daily life, the person who is organized no doubt accomplishes "more" in terms of simple output per energy expended, but the character of this "more" as well as the manner to which certain forms of organization—rational or emotionally driven?—lend themselves or are bent to certain valued tasks like production and even consumption. We are all aware of the person who is said to be a "brilliant shopper," as if something like that could be called a form of genius. But in our market society, where consumption often is the pinion of the economy, such skills are not only real but also valuable.[3] One of the skills involved is being able to decide amongst competing brands and price-points over both the short and long terms, balancing a budget and calculating the consumption rates of others, such as family members. Both rationality and emotions are fully in play in these contexts, and however divorced from what the philosopher might prefer as an existentially authentic scene, shopping is part of the daily life of almost everyone, and thus, like cooking, "there too the Gods are present."

During the course of any mundane activity we may be suddenly impressed by our good fortune, or by the fact that our prior calculations have worked themselves out in a "brilliant" fashion. In this is held the kernel of something much more profound, and we cannot be sure that the difference between the mundane and the cosmic is merely an analogy. This is certainly a world-historical understanding, though surely some of the crucial moments in cosmic evolution rest primarily on potential and not necessity, as when, probabilistically speaking, the first proteins began to reproduce copies of themselves, a process later directed by DNA sequences, or the thresholds at which various adaptations to environment due to natural selection actually changed the form and behavior of this or that species. Given enough time, and here of course we are speaking not even of geological epochs, but of those cosmic in length, *all* events contained within any probability curve will eventually occur. This is what is calculatable in the sense Gadamer is suggesting, and not a history that can be taken in a predetermined way. Indeed, it was this very idea of a fateful and perhaps also fatal sense that history, and specifically human history, was given that was the hallmark of the *previous* way of thinking about origins, and colored the most famous cosmogonical narratives that spoke of the beginning as well as the end. What survives from this earlier period of thought is not so much its truncated sense of development or telescoping of history—though we are still a notoriously short-sighted culture in many ways—but rather and especially its sense that origins and indeed all forms of change occurred in the mists of incalculable time. This sensibility shows up today in our tardy concern regarding the environment and the human future in general. In some ways, the void left at our feet, as it were, by the concentration on the grand sweep of things allowed for technical discourses to proliferate. The language that these disciplines spoke was supposedly non-moral, sometimes seemingly amoral, and often, though they preached utility, also impractical or at least theoretical in outlook. The proliferation of these new ways of thinking about the content of human life and the reason within history, that is, what history was supposedly leading to - and here one could think of not only Hegel and Marx, but also even Nietzsche, where time is an eternal cycle and Freud, where a very Greek pessimism seems to reign—promoted the idea that "discourse" itself was an inherent good and could provide the intellect of humanity. Famously, Foucault has exposed the effect of this aspect of modern thinking with regard to not only the intellect and reason, with its attendant shadow of unreason and even madness, but also discipline as a conceptual and coercive apparatus, as well as sexuality. And it is speaking the language of discourse, constructing and abetting the construction of discourse that is key: "This is the essential thing: that Western man has been drawn for three centuries to the task of telling everything concerning his sex [ ] and that this carefully analytical discourse was meant to yield multiple effects of displacement, intensification, reorientation, and modification of desire itself" (Foucault 1980:23). If myth creates archetypes, discourse constructs objects. We are aware that each science has its privileged object that also contains within it the objective of this or that discipline. Psychology has mind, anthropology culture, sociology society, geography space, history time, and so on, and although all of these are patent reifications, each serves the purpose of focusing the energies of this or that discipline in a way most economically and technically well-adapted to its goals. Objects in this sense are not the same as things, but are more like social facts. Of course, unlike the usual social facts of shared belief, rates and the tables that contain them, concepts and the frameworks that support them, and laws and the principles that require them are mostly beyond the ken of the day to day. Thus there is another gap, kindred to that of the space between the time in which we live and the occluded space of origins, that comes to be filled up by discourse, this time, with discursive objects. Foucault gives us examples from within his own analytic of power relations for sexuality: "Four privileged objects of knowledge, which were also targets and anchorage points for the ventures of knowledge: the hysterical woman, the masturbating child, the Malthusian couple, and the perverse adult" (ibid:105). These objects concern us still, though the sources of their concern vary. Reproduction is the concern of the state, for population and economy walk hand in hand, as well as, more darkly, the sense that one must maintain a viable military force. Some countries have too many people, and some too few. Russia, at this moment of time, is in a demographic crisis, hence the concerted efforts to influence the diaspora of ethnic Russian speakers in the region. Western countries exhort their citizens to have more kids, especially those Caucasian because of the lingering ethnicism of Eurocentric elitism. One can easily find persons who speak at once of being delighted about observing the births of white children and being concerned that the aboriginal or black populations are burgeoning. Deviant sexuality amongst adults is still a hot topic of all voyeuristic psycho-therapy, and the sex acts of children, solo or in groups, are a perennial source of chagrin amongst parents of all stripes, who are most likely jealous, if nothing else, that the phase of life that affords the most sexual freedom, adolescence, is long past and that they must work for a living and on top of it all, may be long married to spouses who have no sexual desire for each other.

The teacher and the doctor, the parent and the politician, are all at least *moved* by sex, if not embodying the sexiest characters themselves. The nurse far outstrips the doctor, for example, in the stereotype of innuendo; as does the schoolgirl outreach the teacher. Son and daughter, pending puberty, are more interesting than good old Mom and Dad, and one does not need to refer to politicians and police. But the sources of authority about sexuality, or over sexuality, are moved in the direction of discourse more than repression. They attempt to move the objects of sex as well in a certain way, to bring them together in a willing flock or herd, or to cure them of their abscesses and their misdemeanors. These figures contain more than meets the eye (cf. Lingis, 1989:65). What is expected is no longer merely what is routine. Expectations have to do with what we idealize to be the best case as well as what we imagine to be taking place in spite of our uncertainties. We might like to think the worst of certain "kinds" of people, or even life phases, especially adolescence, but we are also often dishonest about what others are "up to," especially in middle class suburban single-family dwellings. To master both culture and nature requires not only a firm hand seeking to control both and even to push behaviors upon them, but also, because we are aware of our finitude and our limitations, a vivid and egocentric imagination that speaks to our own culture as if it was nature's favorite child. The abstraction of history and science as themselves both reified objects in the sense mentioned above, lends credence, if not credibility, to the idea that we can hold our own against the both of them at once. The weight of history is not necessarily a dead weight. The force of nature sometimes acts in our favor. Yes, both of these are true, but they are not always true and never necessarily so. In order to harness the presence and power of culture and nature we have objectified them. The main point of this objectification was to put ourselves at a safe distance from them, not only so that we could see them coming—in a way that we could not and cannot predict the timing of our own personal deaths—but that we could then step out of their way if they could not be halted altogether. Our relationship to culture and nature thence became one of increasing utility, and our sense of what morality is has followed along; "Morality is conceived purely as a guide to *action*. It is thought to be concerned purely with what is right to do than with what is good to be." (Taylor, 1989:79, italics the text's). It is commonplace to recognize that we almost always ask each other what we do—and that itself is almost always intended to mean what employment one has—upon meeting someone for the first time, than who we are. What to do instead of how to be is the order of the day. On the one hand, this makes sense. In sizing someone up it is handy to know what he or she does for a living. It gives us a rubric related to social class standing, and if single, how marriageable the other person is, or what kind of status authority they might carry with them, and so on. But in categorizing other persons along status and class lines alone is, on the other hand, the chief manner of paying tribute to the dominant mode of unthought that carries our culture forward. It is the expected thing to do and is in no way unusual. Even more to the point, many of us might well have difficulty responding to the existential version of the query, that is, "Who are you?." We would most likely simply give our name, but of course that is not the real intent of the question of "how to be" or "what is the good life." It would also strike us as strange if a more or less complete stranger desired to engage us at this comparatively "deep" level about our sense of identity and self in the world. Only someone shilling easy religion at us might do so, we might imagine. These kinds of conversations are, and sometimes justifiably so considering the probable sources of them on the everyday, to be avoided like the plague. At best, even if we had an answer to the combined challenge of the question of ethics and existence we might think that it is nobody's business with the possible exception of intimate friends and life-partners. After all, these are the persons with whom such conversation might possibly come up.

So far so good. We have not only been able to delineate the other person's occupation *et al*, but we have also been able to avoid the puzzling aporia of our own existence in relation to them. We simply share and share alike. They know what I do, and I know what they do, and nothing more is deemed necessary by either partner. This "sensate" understanding of otherness, however, presents a problem. In not needing to know anything important about the other person beyond the utility of what he or she can represent in the public life to and for me, it makes it very easy to not merely stereotype others but to also begin, if circumstances suggest, disdaining them. "The Jew" is of course the now canonical example of this suasion. And "Jews," of course, occupy certain employment niches, have a narrow range of personalities, and are always looking after their own interests *en bloc*. You see how this greasy logic slides along. Once we have identified someone as *something*, an element in the midst of like elements populating a category, rather than a human being first and foremost with highly individuated desires and biographies, than the process of objectification can take over and one simply fills in the blanks by virtue of a set piece of scripted rhetoric or ideology. On top of this, we have become increasingly cynical about the character of others. Many of our news items highlight negative things being done by people both far away or close at hand. It almost seems as if we are entertained by the idea that the other is an evil force in the world. At the very least, these media tend to confirm our suspicions regarding other people, especially large blocks of those hailing from other cultures strange in some way to our own. Both at home and abroad, we have developed the sense that we must constantly be vigilant about protecting what we have and indeed, even *who we are*, and it is at this moment that our bemusement regarding that second aspect of life is confronted head on and immediately by-passed, because we have been able to define it negatively as *"we are not them."* This definition by negation is much more convenient than attempting to construct an existential or ethical identity from scratch. It circumvents the need for any authentic dialogue, because our neighbors, more or less like us, can simply agree with one another that "we too are not like them." Such agreement mirrors another kind of cynical sentiment that is also quite pervasive amongst the usual suspects of our society: "We are prone to believe in the power of the struggle for existence, of selfish interests, egoistic competition, hate, the fighting instinct, sex drives, the instinct of death and destruction, in the all-powerfulness of economic factors, rude coercion and other negativistic forces. Yet we are highly skeptical in the power of creative love, disinterested service, unprofitable sacrifice, mutual aid, the call of pure duty and other positive forces" (Sorokin, 1956:302). We have rationalized as abstract forces the being of suffering and sorrow. The more abstract the better, just as in the case of the stranger or the other, because it allows us to declaim any personal responsibility for action in the world. Even though morality is increasingly only seen as a guide to action, as Taylor suggests, it is also clear that we would eschew as much of this action, of whatever content it may consist, as possible in order to feel "free" of both its constraints and its effects.

The question of being and what is good to be has been reduced to "not them" or anything but "how these others are and live." This patent response allows all kinds of irresponsibility and hypocrisy on our parts while also allowing the examined life to become a moribund feature of "philosophy" as merely an historical artifact. Philosophy, in other words, can no longer be about thinking and only concerns what has been thought by yet others who are also increasingly strange and marginal to us: "We have today become so pithless and weak-kneed that we are no longer able to hold out in the asking of the question. When the one philosophical medicine man cannot answer it, then one runs to the next. The demand increases the supply. In popular terms, this is called: an increased interest in philosophy" (Heidegger, op. cit:16, [1921]). It cannot be lost on us that, given the original dates of the last two citations, thinkers have been unhappy about this contemporary turn of events for at least a century or so. But has not each generation in its turn heaped opprobrium upon its successors? Have not the artists and thinkers, self-styled and otherwise, always sought to distance themselves from the fads of the day, seeing in them nothing but the vulgar "herd animal" message? Why should these thinkers, and even this writer, for that matter, be any different? What actually is the problem here? These would be reasonable exclamations if it were not for their source, and by this I do not mean the sense, equally a stereotype and a usual suspect, that only the cultured and gifted elites—however this category might be defined—are capable of thinking and there-fore must do everyone else's thinking for them. Not at all. The message here is that all of us are not only capable of thought, but that it is both our nature and our duty as human beings to practice to the utmost this capability. In-deed, this is the only way that after six million years or so, we have amounted to anything at all as a species. "Not having claws or teeth," as Bagheera reminds us, was originally a huge disadvantage, and a fatal one, as often as not. But it was "Man" who invented the Law that confronted and often contradicted the laws of nature. It was humankind that discovered that Nature was ordered and that that order was comprehendible by human beings through reason and experiment alone. These revolutionary ideas, and the abilities that have stemmed from them, were only made possible by human beings exercising their uniquely evolved and native faculties. To turn away from them in the slightest is an offense, not against culture or the cultured, and not even necessarily against the imagined gods or the possibility of any God, but to the entire cosmos that has, by probability and accident, brought such a consciousness forth. We have the strongest possible motives for think-ing, even in the day to day, about the widest and deepest topics. If the canny consumer can be recognized as an outlet for thought, than anything can. But instead we practice a distanciation from thinking because along with it comes the responsibility for action in the world, and it is this, rather than thought, that we are particularly anxious to keep our distance from (cf. Midgely, 2004:136). No doubt the challenges that modern society faces are not simply, or even primarily, from outside threats. After all, the entire world has more or less been globalized into various genres of modernity. If we still thought in nineteenth century terms, we would be convinced not only of the utility of this transformation, but of its inevitability. Further, such a world-historical change would be seen as the best thing for everyone involved, no matter the shorter term sacrifices. That there are severe doubts in some quarters regarding the last two of these variables represents a real alteration of Western attitudes. At the same time, now the issue is, in the face of these doubts that are also self-doubts, what exactly are our roles and responsibilities in these matters? "In today's highly complex and thoroughly organized society no one is in a position to believe they can completely master the problems which cause concern and anxiety in our civilization" (Gadamer 1996:159 [1990]). Yet there is still responsibility. It is something that we are forced to begrudgingly accept. If we attempt to exempt ourselves from the world at large we become "idiots" in the Greek sense of the person who thinks himself or herself as remaining fully human but yet able to become a fully private "citizen" with no public concerns or duties. The individuation of persons, carried out within the same ambit as that of mass culture, perhaps a corollary to the idea that "madness" as a concept arising precisely in the age of reason, as Foucault famously investigated, allows such persons, you and I included, to generally absolve our selves from global responsibility, specifically any duty towards those who have suffered or are suffering due to specific circumstances caused by obvious agents external to the West or to our respective nations. Yes, we can absolve our "selves," but what about ourselves? In a global society, the presence of geographically defined nation-states is a bit of an illusion. Yes, there are borders and boundaries, armed frontiers and even non-governmental gauntlets, but nonetheless, people and things move about more freely than at any other time in human history. Capital demands this constant motion regarding things and persons, for both are in essence commodities. One uses one's labor power to gain access to resources and objects. In so doing, one also becomes an object in the chain of objectifications and commodifications. It is a myth that we are somehow separate from these forces, in the same way that no fully human citizen of a classical polis could be private and maintain either his citizenship or his humanity. The myth that we are not responsible is our most scandalous irresponsibility.

Yet it is just as clear that we do not take on these kinds of obligations as individuals first and foremost. The way in which we live, quite literally, our lifestyle and quality of life expectations, gear much of the rest of the world into our service. But we do this as a society, and not as persons. So, any myth that attempts to assuage our collective bad conscience must address not you and I specifically, but how we live as a group, which is precisely what Taylor was implying our new morality *cannot* do: "Myth is a system of communication, a message with a characteristic structure which fulfils a specific social function: it offers a model of behavior. As an atemporal construct defining a partial reality, myth alienates the individual, taking him, or her, into a false reality at the same time as giving meaning to his or her existence, separating what is essential from what is accidental" (Cabezali et al, 1990:162). It is ironic that in our modern scientific and technical age, we are still content to trade morality for myth in this way. The "model of behavior" exemplified or allegorized in mythic narrative is a guide to action, and not a book of ethics. It tells one how to live but not what one is living for or why. It is thus a bearer of the greatest utility for a culture that lives well on the backs of others who do not. Even within our own national boundaries and social norms, there remain many marginals who do not themselves live much better than the marginals of the wider world. These subalterns are even more silent because they generally lack a political or an academic spokesperson. When immigrants arrive in the West, one of the most common themes of their ingratiatory discourse is to join the dominant groups in these respective nations by heaping disdain upon the native marginals. "You have grown up here and yet you still are poor and uneducated, while I grew up there and have made something of myself." This rhetoric, also completely and utterly mythical, ignores the reality that the vast majority of in-migrants to many Western states are from elite backgrounds. How else could they have afforded to come here? Their local status was the polar opposite of those whom they now, in classic Horatio Alger fashion, disdain. Their authority comes from the assertion of myth, and, because the new land also participates in this myth that is likely one of its own inventions, we generally have no problem with new immigrants and at least accept them into the folds of competitive labor and work ethic. But authentic authority does not come from myths that tell us how to live, but rather moralities, or better, ethics, which tell us why we are living this way and what is good and bad about it. Morality, seen in the light of ethics, is a *critical* discourse and not one passively set into stone. It retains its original Mosaic moment—in the Hebrew example the first function of the ten commandments is to literally and figuratively smash an idol representing the previous and therefore recidivistic age—and does not let itself become a monument, most importantly, to itself: "The word 'authoritative' precisely does not refer to a power which is based in authority, it refers, rather, to a form of validity which is genuinely recognized, and not one that is merely asserted" (Gadamer, 1996:119 [1983]). As Durkheim famously noted, even science maintains its authority only through the recognition of the wider society, almost like a form of popularity or at least something that is usual and not suspect in the normative sense that we have been discussing here. Authority based on power alone never has popular support, only that coerced in some means more or less subtle. The difference between the politician and the statesperson is brought to mind. Philosophy as a mode of being is authoritative, but as an academic discourse merely an authority on things, and increasingly, not even that: "The modern period might even be described as the one in which philosophy has become most uncertain of itself" (Barrett, 1979:10). This uncertainty has appeared and threatened to engulf thinking in general in large part because of the lack of a public critical discourse with which to challenge both norms and policies; more succinctly, we lack the authoritative position from which to suspect forms of authority. Indeed, we have preferred to cast our sense of something being a suspect and thus being suspect in the direction of thought, philosophical or critical, or more recently, scientific and historical. What we forget is that when we question the relevance of history, for example, we place ourselves along a dubious continuum that includes, amongst other characters, the holocaust denier. This is not a straw person statement. The disbelief in the authoritative inertia of what humanity has been misplaces our current accomplishments and allows us to become, ironically, too certain of ourselves. In this situation, philosophy's "uncertainty" is truly unhelpful to us, for it can no longer provide its own provenience: "Why the suspicion of philosophy, then? Perhaps the reason comes to this: [ ] It is, after all, profoundly unsettling to be forced to examine one's oldest and deepest beliefs" (Natanson, 1970:156). However profound or unsettling such an examination is, and surely this would vary according to just how "fundamental" any normative or cultural assumption is deemed to be—and in this there is increasingly little agreement due to the ever-increasing diversity of our massive national societies—Socrates' dictum, made appropriately in an "apology" that connotes nothing of the usual meaning, that the unexamined life is not worth living for a human being remains salient. Perhaps it is more salient than at any other time, even though we imagine the growing cosmopolitan atmosphere of the Aegean region must have impressed Socrates himself and perhaps led to such a remark. For it is within our own time that we, for the first time, confront the entire world as it is. All of its conflicts, diversities, uniquenesses, and disquieting practices are on the table in front of us. Technology brings these tensions to our senses, and the objects we consume are constructed out of the outcomes or resolutions of those same tensions. Yet that self-same nexus of technology and consumption do little to help us understand the tensions involved in creating how we live. Hence once again the convenience of having merely models of behavior to learn and adapt to and not a critical ethics or philosophy to have to explain ourselves to. We may even suspect a theory of human life to be lacking in this regard, that ultimately, theory cannot help us explain ourselves to ourselves, and, more pressingly, to others whom we rely on and exploit, simply because there is little popular support for critical thought in mass culture, including educational institutions and publications. It is certainly true to say that "there is a limit to our understanding, and this is where theory reaches the height of its development with its most important achievement by deriving from conditions that can be immediately understood propositions that, as dogmas, give a clue to the mastery of much more intricate cases" (Lösch, 1967:358 [1945]). Theory is not mere speculation. It rests upon the known while at the same time not accepting it as certain. Once again, the crucial difference between truth and knowledge is revealed as the hinge upon which the human sensibility either opens or shuts, for it can either upon the world or shut upon itself.

If Socrates is held up as the paragon of thinking or self-examination, itself a cliché, we also need to recall that he did not imagine that through the examined life one should ultimately reach the truth of things, only a better knowledge of the things at hand. For "Greek thinking holds in reserve a principal contribution toward limiting the illusions of self-knowledge" (Gadamer 2001:124). It is this limitation that fails to adhere when authority is asserted or invoked, but just as assuredly it remains in its vigilant position whenever what is authoritative is recognized. To open ourselves to self-examination is the beginning of knowledge. This knowing takes the form of self-understanding and has the character of a process and not a state. *Norms lie in state.* Our imagination of morality is merely the language on its headstone.

UNEXPECT THE EXPECTED

Exhortations to exhume what has been dead and buried have come from a great variety of places and times. The self-examination of culture must continue beyond the grave. From the body politic to the student body, the corpus of the corpse must be taken apart and investigated piece by piece. Perhaps there is something worth salvaging, or something that can be reanimated. Or perhaps there has been a premature burial. Perhaps some of the things that rest underground are in fact still restless. Norms and our adherence to them have a way of rushing the funerals of that which is inconvenient. What is critical is not in fact critique's own condition, but our own.

This critical sentiment that desires the removal of normative sediments carries a shovel rather than a spade. The latter was traditionally a symbol of the grave, the tool of the gravedigger and thus ultimately an emblem of death, which in the medieval hierarchy of symbolic values trumped even earthly love. Even today, much technology and scientific energies are harnessed in the search for immortality, or at least indefinite life. From artificial intelligence to cyber-organic implants and stem cell research there is a compelling movement away from degradation and decay, a movement thus also away from the signs of finitude. With the death of the old god of value-oriented morality came also the demise of eternal bliss and rest. The conception of paradise had to shift from an otherworldly one to one placed somehow, somewhere, here on earth. Could its new abode be that of our own organic consciousness, extended and prosthetized through high technology? Extending consciousness while still living is a good second best to bringing it back after its corporeal means of existence has been shuffled off. Indeed, with the rise of our contemporary anti-transcendental metaphysics, the summons of the Greek rite of *nekyia* could no longer be accomplished. The spirits can no longer hear us, even if they remain somewhere else, such a place also beyond our own disenchanted understanding.

The flight from finitude must be understood not only as a replacement part for something that is now historically absent in our culture, but also as an expression of the potency of our modern egos. The loss of god, the afterlife, the rites of recovery and communication with the dead, the general *Entzauberung* of our times, reveals only a co-extant set of variables to which we are not only responding with our own sense of prosthetic godhead, but also seeking to prove wrong in the first place. More fundamentally, we are trying to right what we perceive as an existential wrong, the greatest of wrongs—or perhaps it is merely a technical fault of an unfinished evolution, no matter— that such beings as us are still fated to die at all. Why should we not go on, given all of our own species' accomplishments? Why should there be inherent limits, insulting, even humiliating, because they are not only limits but also that they have not been set by ourselves? Perhaps this is in the end the source of the desire for relative immortality: that death reminds us of something that remains beyond our control and this in turn reminds us of the old way of thinking about things, where gods and the fates had power over us in this ultimate way. Getting rid of the bogeys of transcendental metaphysics did not rid us of their effects upon us, we might imagine. It is this kind of prejudice that lingers underground, and not any specific and personal spiritual desire. Our true limits lie buried in the historical sediments of cultural inertia: "Our own preconceptions are so deeply entrenched that they hinder us in our understanding of other cultures and historical worlds. To achieve a better understanding, we must try to become conscious of our own preconceptions" (Gadamer 2001:60). Other cultures include the history of our own. Even our recent ancestors lived and thought quite differently from us. We would have difficulty understanding their worldview and even more difficulty living in their world. The Victorian period, with its emphasis on order, its disdain of the comfort of children, its narrow labor market and lack of antibiotics, to list just a few alien circumstances, is a recent historical phase. Their imperial ambitions, corseting of women both literally and figuratively, and general public prudery might be more familiar to us, as these things have had a longer shelf-life than the items formerly mentioned. Even so, it does not take a very long "historical telescope" to note that as the past recedes from us, it does so at an increasingly rapid rate, not unlike the view of the cosmos commanded by real telescopes. So much is this the case that after a few centuries of looking backward, we are often unable to tell the difference between what is real and what may have been real but also may have been mostly, if not completely, an imaginative fiction or fantasy: "The most ambitious historical objective would be the study of changes over time of the very boundary between imaginary and real, as we know them today: of how generations of human beings have contributed to create our own notions of reality" (Passerini 1990:52). Indeed, we might not have the courage to face the results of such a study. So many instances of the ancient percolate through what we imagine to be our thoroughly contemporary consciousness. But all forms of consciousness were, in their own time, contemporary to themselves. And what does it mean to exist in one's "own" time? How can time itself be seen as being possessed in this way? Is this too part of a subterranean worldview, alive and well, if shady and cool, beneath the graves of the ancestors?

This is no mere historically interesting piece of ethno-archaeology. We are speaking not only of the history of what we take to be something that defines us as definitively different from all who have passed before us, but also of the things that lurk within us, ready to sabotage our boldest and brightest ventures. We have of late discovered the earth is not the same thing as the world. What is meant by this is that the idea of a world is defined by human beings as the projection of their cultural desires and anxieties, hence "worldview." The earth is its own thing, separate and anonymous and remains part of nature, and not culture. The two concepts clash most simply because of population load and the extraction of resources, but their tension is not limited to one at base material and demographic. Our very success at manipulating the earth in our favor also spells within it our demise. Something has to change, and since nature itself generally changes at geological or cosmic rates, it is we who have make the adjustment, and we clearly need to do it sooner rather than later. Culture is inherently adaptable, even though it also has an inherent inertia about it. Custom and tradition however, are not necessarily always the villains. There are many historical examples of challenges human beings have faced and overcome, most recently the history of microbiology contains a great many instances of this dynamic. The question then becomes how to convince the living that the dead may be still of some use to them. The anxiety about death, both personal and conceptual, retains its force even if we are asking those who preceded us for aid. We imagine, in our still living state, those who love life or at least tolerate it, that the dead, if still "alive" in some strange and perhaps even eldritch sense of the term, bear some great resentment for having died and yet being forced to remain conscious, or to be aware that they maintain, in spite of death, some form of consciousness of themselves and of the species as a whole. Why would they want to help us? It is in fact our own fears that prevent us from understanding our own history; hence the question may be more succinctly expressed as "how to use a memory to combat public myth when the person has already found a safe refuge within that myth?" (Thomson 1990:81). We need to own up to the reality that it is our construction of the dead that prohibits intercourse with them. In fact, books and sundry other documents, culture memory, monuments and archaeological discoveries all point to a great willingness on the part of our ancestors to share all they can with us, at any time and in any place. It is we who shun the dialogue to which they are perennially open.

But there is another anxiety that has more reality to it, even though the compulsion to give it its due is often premature. This trepidation asks a different question than the one above: What if, even after the dead have shared all their available insights with us, and we have understood and taken it all into account, that it still isn't enough for the challenges we are facing today? This is a possibility of course, even if we have hardly exhausted all of our sources of information to this regard. But even if such an outcome is rendered more likely the further we investigate any specific set of problems, we still have our own sensibilities, living, adaptable, and imaginative, to fall back on. Indeed, we should be as much using these faculties as those of the dead. They should be used in concert with one another, a *tutti* of human instrumentation and artistry. At the same time, unlike the usual orchestral ensemble of sounds, we should not necessarily expect harmonious order. This is the case because it is always so that " . . . reality is more various, less tidy than myth. Time and again real personal experience breaks through, at times negating the myth, taking the story in unexpected directions and finally giving its substance to every life story" (Burchardt 1990:249).[4] Speaking with the living tells us many things about content—the topic of conversation may be shallow or profound, but the sense that we humans are interested objectively in many different things never departs from us—but speaks quite narrowly and thus in a more ordered fashion about contentment. Human interests mask human needs, or at least can project them onto the worldly landscape of physical consciousness. Why do we have hobbies, for instance, or pursue aesthetic devices and designs? Contentment with a life that is finite in its ends and ambiguous along the way is the most obvious response. A diverse life gives the impression not only that one can live many lives at once, and perhaps even be many persons—hence the attraction of the anonymity of the internet—but also that this life might well go on indefinitely because we can switch up our interests at any time. We give ourselves the impression that we can control our destinies because we can, to a great extent, control what we put our living energies into. Of course, this freedom of interest and effort on the part of individuals, shorn from their wider community obligations, is a privilege of developed nations, and thus mostly still a Western sensibility. It is part of the ironic story of the concept of freedom that we will have occasion to detail near the end of this book. In pursuing diversity within one's own life, we can also, more shadily, appeal to all of the more dishonest aspects of human ability. We can, in other words, simply pretend that we are more things than we actually are. This not only has the advantage of impressing ourselves of our vital self-interest—I must stay alive and well at any cost, even at the cost of knowing who I am and what my limits are—but as well we can impress any and all others who might have

doubted our abilities to play the adept, to adopt any necessary mask to convince others of our virtuosity at living, and to adapt to any circumstance that
is suddenly foisted upon us: "Truth and untruth weave the seamless web of
human nature, and history is the arena of their struggle" (Barrett 1979:164).
So within the chorus of desire and ambition, there will always be those of us
who, in order to distinguish our own voice from the rest, do not follow the
conductor's baton and depart from the score. The dead have less control over
their shadowy but still ongoing destinies than do the living, but even here we
may find voices that refuse to sing along with the music chosen by contemporary culture. De Sade and Woolf might be two literary examples, but the
most obvious thinker who vexes us to this day with his unrecognizably
Dionysian song is of course Nietzsche. He is an irksome figure precisely due
to his doubting of our highest desires, including those of altruism and community, the idea of the "good society" and the responsible citizen. Nietzsche's untimeliness has been echoed by many other thinkers of great variety,
from Russell to Bataille, but because philosophers, artists, poets, writers and
others, have a penchant for all singing their *own* songs, they do not represent
an ordered counter-chorus to the one in which most of us continue to sing in.

And it is *this* idea, the sense that one human being has one's own song to
sing, that is perhaps the most self-evident hallmark of our self-conception of
modernity. Needless to say, we do not know how many of us, or how many
times in our own lives, that we have lived up to this new ideal of what
constitutes not only individuality but also human freedom in general. If we
all agreed that there should in fact be no chorus at all, than the very social
character of the desire for freedom would elude us. One cannot be free
without all of the social apparatus that appears to impinge on that very
freedom. There is no freedom outside of society and culture. If the "unexamined life" was, and remains, not worth living for human beings, and if the
ancients were able to recognize this, is our contemporary contribution on that
order and scale the idea that the unfree life is similarly not worth living for
humans? And what is the price of freedom for the one, or for this or that
culture, in a globalizing world where all are somehow interconnected, and
where my actions really do have an effect elsewhere, often out of sight and
thus out of mind? What is the character of a freedom that adheres only to
material privilege, most of which is inherited? The ability to be empathetic to
the desires of someone whose very existence contradicts our own wishes for
the good life seems rare in today's world. We can understand this, for most
of us feel at some deeply intimate level only our own needs and desires. Yes,
we can feel these in a lover, perhaps, or sometimes even in a friend or family
member, but such comprehensions, both apprehended in their ability to be
caught momentarily but also in their uncanniness, the aspect of their character that makes us apprehensive—how can it be that another feels the way I do
given the preconception that we are not only all different, but that we should

always try to be only our own person, sing our own song, like the elites of our cultural model?—can never be comprehensive. We must, in fact, desire the desire of the other in order to apprehend its presence, or open ourselves to it so that it apprehends us. And all of this must occur within an ongoingness that reconfigures temporality to suit the needs of the personal rather than the orders of the day: "It is only because we already have an intimation of something that we seek to bring it to mind and eventually discover what it was that we were actually looking for. In this way the dimension of the past is opened up to us, and we develop a sense of time itself" (Gadamer 1996:146-7 [1986]). This puts it rather phenomenologically, as if the glancing ray of the pure ego can cut through the overlapping Gordian veils, its signal at once clearing and also focusing the surrounding noise. Yet it is true that we do not wander aimlessly in the world. We imagine ourselves somewhere other than where we are. We construct potential projects, or at least toss their bare bones into the unknown to see what accrues to them. Fishing in this way both keeps the essential character of ourselves safe enough, while risking an appendage or a sensory node, risking only limb and not entire life. Even so, if this process is at work within the ambit of the personal, it encounters larger concerns such as justice and general benevolence, anxiety and the absence of historical consciousness only through an ethics. It has to have an "intimation," not of an object *per se*, but of a mode of being. And this mode of being is both recent and quite different from what had passed before as the just or the ethical (cf. Taylor, op. cit:396). However unequally applied and distributed, it is a little sobering to realize that humaneness as a cultural ideal is quite recent. It is likely also based merely on the material circumstances of population load and competition for resources, though this new ethic has not stopped us, any of us, from continuing to employ the much more ancient sensibility of kill or be killed to get what we want. Humaneness, which often seems to carry us in the direction of being kind to animals—"humane societies" and the like—is either an afterthought or a token, a gesture made to perhaps our awakening conscience but also perhaps to the sense that the victims or the losers could have been us. On May 3, 1945, the first Russians into the FuhrerBunker were female Red Cross nurses. Their prize was some of Eva Braun's lingerie, but not long after the Red Army replaced the Red Cross and began emptying the bunker of its living survivors. The Battle of Berlin had ended a few hours before and this was the moment of kindness. We can well afford to be skeptical about benevolence, even if its appearance on the cultural horizon suggests much promise as well as a necessary pragmatism. Necessary not only given the global nature of today's society, but because we retain the power to annihilate ourselves within a different few hours of the pressing of a few buttons and the turning of a handful of keys.

By the same token, we can equally not afford to become cynical about this new ethic or sensibility. It may well be what saves us, and it may hold the only hope of saving us in the face of our other proclivities and abilities. A combination of pragmatism and skepticism serves us well here, as it does in so many other human contexts, but there is something more that was added in our own time to the discussion of the good and the truthful, and that was the idea of art as the voice of the good and as the space of truth. Art has this power because its presence speaks for itself in a new way. It is art that provides the most humane outlet for the "accursed share" of humanity's prodigious imagination and excess energies. War is certainly another outlet, and just as truthful in a sense, but it is not a lasting outlet because it affirms itself only in its own destruction. The question of its inhumanity was re-solved the moment the species entered its first war, whenever that was and whomever it was between. It was Nietzsche, once again, who began our understanding of the new ethics in the light of the equally new ability to radically critique ideals and orders from a human perspective of individua-tion and innovation: "Nietzsche is the first philosopher to have put into question the supreme value of truth." (Lingis 1989:85). This questioning of the manner in which we had questioned things is different than historical or scientific investigations. This is because it questions the question itself. It is not simply a matter of stepping back and asking, "are we asking the right questions?," but rather a new mode of being that boldly and baldly states that the fact that we question as well as the way we question is now to be interrogated. One of the most important ways it can pronounce this radical verdict upon prior and more expected modes of questioning things is, to use Nietzsche's famous phrase, to "shoot at morals." Shooting at morals meant that we no longer take aim at the phenomena of the world as if they are effects of some other, higher, or deeper, source material. The idea of essence itself was declared a myth, and there was to be no difference between what one could question and the questioner, as well as nothing to distinguish between what was questioned and the question of how one could question it. At least at first. For in questioning the questions, in thinking skeptically about the ideal of truth and the good, benevolence included as one of the new expectations of modernity, there began a separation, not between essence and appearance or even cause and effect, but between the ability to question and the body of the questioned. Tradition is always immanent. It is the source of what is to be questioned, the expected that must be unexpected in order for the species to mature over time and to come to terms with its own historical limits as well as one's own personal finitude. But tradition also contains the heritage of being able to ask a question, even if Nietzsche now demands that we direct this enormous if still human power against the very structures of our lifeworld, morality and discourse being his two favorite marks. Gadamer tells us that to have an "effective" historical consciousness means to be aware of what makes us tick, in his words, "the constitutive prejudices of our understanding" (2000:46). This is really no different from Nietzsche's exhortation. Exhume the bodies of knowledge and moralities that in our unexamined prejudice we shrugged off as dead and gone. In reality, they are right underneath our feet, indistinguishable from the earth to which they have formed an amalgam and an alliance. They *are* the ground even more than is the world, "For these prejudices are nothing other than our rootedness in a tradition" (ibid). So morality, as an important part of any cultural tradition, can be exhumed and disassembled only by questioning the very tradition that has bequeathed the ability to question. In hermeneutics, tradition is not something ideological. It carries the entirety of culture, and each age must decide for itself which parts of this inheritance are of value and which parts dross. Indeed, the more questions we ask of the tradition, questions shot at it so that it does not have time to simply respond with a "just so" story, the more we excavate not only the position of what came before us—imagine an archaeology of consciousness, the kind of thing Foucault was piecing together, where slowly coming to light are the foundations of ancient structures, except that these are the structures of our ideals and our desires, our anxieties and our necessities, including our "necessary errors," as Nietzsche referred to them—but also where we currently stand on top of these generally unseen and subterranean foundations, the more our historical consciousness becomes "effective" in Gadamer's sense.

In doing so, we find we that we sometimes extend the very structures we might have originally thought we should depart from, or, more naively, that we had departed from. The instance of "God's death," proclaimed by the madman in Nietzsche's *Gay Science* of 1882, is something that was not so much premature but incomprehensible. Today, people balk at the statement only because they might personally believe in God, but this is not what Nietzsche was after. It was clear that the old morality of agrarian godhead in whatever cultural form it took was long dead by Nietzsche's time, let alone in ours, simply because what ruled the world was increasingly a form of instrumental praxis based on the new nation states' monopolies of competitive forces. This was the new order, to be questioned in turn, certainly, but brought about precisely by previous generations' shooting at morals. This shift of course, even though it is our own, provides an ample testament of another cliché, that of being careful what you ask for. But the real lesson that can be applied without limit is the necessity for an ongoing questioning of social structures, social facts, institutions, and the often unseen foundations of each—unseen because there are also those who desire to resist the question in principle, to rule without question, or, more commonly, to simply live without the never-ending doubt that can become a neurosis. The philosophical cliché of examining one's life is always salient, but one also does not want to hamstring the *vita activa* by making the *vita contemplativa* the sole goal of existence. There has to be a balance, and in action we can also find the most radical of questions.

Not necessarily at first, however. What we tend to do in response to the breakdown of previous sets of idols, their human form turning to humus underground, is to mimic their structure and apply it to other realms of discourse themselves generating similar sets of questions, similar if not the same, because although they have the same goals, their material and methods may be somewhat different. Think of the relationship between religion and science, or nature and human nature. In both of these tandems, we see that the same goals are being worked towards. Science has taken over the explanatory territory once reserved for religion, and even, in its grand cosmological form, science too has begun to ask the perennial questions of existence, the whys and not just the hows of our presence in the universe, while not presuming a specific answer from the start. Therein lies the chief difference between the two. Religion, at least from agriculture onwards, knows in its heart that there is a creator God or gods and it is simply a matter of finding out why the deed was done and thus what our place in creation is supposed to be. Science asks the same question without presumptions. Or at least, not the same presumptions. Order, that is "cosmos" quite literally, is presumed. It is also presumed that human reason can know this order, or at least come to approximate it in its own thinking. It seems to me that these presumptions could be seen as just as bold as that of the existence of a creator God, interested in our fates or no, purposeful or random. How do we *know* that what passes for human reason in any particular historical epoch can approximate the language of nature? Well, we can point to the material evidence that is in our favor, the advances of medicine and engineering most prominently, or the fact that mathematical designs function equally well across vastly different human cultures, even though we must admit that any person from any culture must learn the technical languages of mathematics beforehand. These new languages, not part of any original cultural socialization, are what provide the space for the more grand assumptions to be made. This in itself suggests that human reason is neither innate, which science does not argue, but on top of this, that it must be constructed to adhere to at least itself, while the speculation is that it also, in doing so, adheres to the wider nature that is anonymous and has nothing to do with human reason. It is this last suggestion that carries within it the most fragile logic and that cannot be definitively proven as a certainty. It relies rather on a hallmark of its parent religious discourse, and that is a leap of faith.

It is this kind of acknowledgement that is reached only after following the thread of the skeptic as long as we can. Here, the idea of faith, as well as the sense that human reasoning, even if it differs from the language of nature, can come to understand it at least in part, itself an article of faith in science, allows us to duplicate earlier forms of consciousness and give them new material. For example, "Moral sources can be sought not only in God but in the two new 'frontiers': the dignity which attaches to our own powers (at first those of disengaged reason only, but now also including the creative imagination); and the depths of nature within and without" (Taylor, op. cit:408). At a much more simple level, though still pragmatic with reference to its own cultural goals, the shibboleth of stating that science is the means to discover the handiwork of God that is taught in many parochial schools provides the missing link between the competing discourses. And indeed, it was never the sense that evolution *per se* had killed God. The offensive character of Darwin lay in his laying bare the structure of what linked humanity to other creatures and even to the smallest of organisms. The conceit of a culture that was newly emancipated from its dependence on what was traditionally seen to be above it, to be greater than it, was now plunged into an even better reasoned dependence on what was lesser and lower than it! This could fairly be called the result of an enantiodromian dynamic. Pulling so strenuously away from the higher pushed us irrevocably into the lower. The pendulum of balanced investigation, reason, skepticism, pragmatism alike, had overreached itself. At a more personal level, Jung suggests that his conception is as much obscured there as at the level of culture: "Most people do not have sufficient range of consciousness to become aware of the opposites inherent in human nature. The tensions they generate remain for the most part unconscious, but can appear in dreams. [ ] The greatest danger about unconsciousness is proneness to suggestion" (Jung 1959:247 [1951]). The absence, not of consciousness, but of being conscious and therefore both having a conscience and having the ability to be conscientious, both ethically and in a more normatively obligatory way—the difference between say, a moral scruple which might also be a folkway and the idea that one needs to show up for work Monday morning—is precisely its proneness. We must be asleep to dream, or hypnotized to be more malleable to suggestion. The pre-modern worldview held that demons might assail us in our sleep. This has become in our own time a cliché entertainment commodity of dubious artistic merit, but what remains of this anxiety is the simple sense that we are weaker when we are not awake, and thus susceptible to all kinds of forces that otherwise would not bother us in the slightest, from attacks by quite physically real dust mites to the nightmares of the recovering addict, also real in their own way. If sleep is the brother of death, as the Greeks had it, then life and death are not inseparable but at the very least, contiguous, and hence sharing much of each other in themselves. To absent ourselves from this kind of existential torus, its unity conferred by its form and by the fact that we travel from one end to the other only to reach the point at which we began, dust to dust and all of that, is to lose the ability to resolve the tensions between opposites. Historically, we see the effect of this loss in the running away from a perceived danger only to run headlong into another. At the same time, this dynamic may also, at the personal level, be said to be part of the expected (cf. Neumann 1970:405 [1949]). The idea of what is partial is suggestive in two

senses. First of all, we are clearly partial to the cause of disengaging ourselves from an authority which is seen as either oppressive or outmoded or
both. In our eighteenth century example, the authority of the old God and his
mandate is the villain for moderns. Fleeing this, liberating ourselves and for
the first time experiencing the authenticity of humanity alone and aloof to
superstition, no doubt generated a few good nights both asleep or awake. At
the same time, the other meaning of partiality, the incompleteness of this
emancipation pushed our culture into what seems now to be a permanent
residence within the envelope of anonymous evolution. We are just as unfree
as "pure" humanity there than we were under the old God's thumb. Similarly, even closer to our own time, the liberation of ourselves as sexual beings
from the confessional disdain and disgust of the body that the old religions
harnessed us to has led, in its partiality, to being sexually enveloped in a
pseudo-scientific discourse of psychopathologies, hallmark romances, deviant and alternative kinks and what have you, that makes everything about
human love and intimacy into an object for collective voyeurism: "We are
often reminded of the countless procedures which Christianity once employed to make us detest the body; but let us ponder all the ruses that were
employed for centuries to make us love sex, to make the knowledge of it
desirable and everything about it precious" (Foucault 1980:159 [1978]). The
"bio-power" of contemporary sexuality is of especial interest to the state
where, as stated, demography and economy go hand in hand. It is the love
relationship between these two social institutions that must be adored, and
our own frail couplings are simply the oblations and libations paid in tribute
to the overweening and neurotic sensibility of the always-threatened nation.
We have traded the jealous God for the jealous country, and how could this
possibly be seen as a liberation of any kind?

   This kind of blind repetition of historical tropes leads nowhere and, for
the Greeks, to nothing: "We must not forget to avoid the path of the nothing,
but we must also not forget the other path, the path upon which mortals
stumble about hesitantly, erringly, and in constant uncertainty" (Gadamer
2000:114). This other path is the actually the only one open to beings such as
we, given our mortality and the limits of our senses and even the extended,
pliable and brilliant but still limited scope of our technologies and our cultural imaginations. This other path might contain repetition or forms of false
consciousness, but it is still a way forward and is, most importantly, a path to
something. The "path of the nothing" does not carry us forward, but merely
replaces one form of oppression, neurosis, or compulsion with another, as we
just saw with the example of religion and the state. The way of stumbling, the
"path less trodden"—and therefore sometimes barely scrutable in its differences from either the alien objectivity of a nature that surrounds it due to its
lack of traffic—does make all the human difference in the world, because it
is not only a way forward but reflects the authenticity of being human. It is,

in other words, the path of experience. It forces us to unexpect the expected due to its serpentine and occluded course. Indeed, it may not even be a path at all, and we will find ourselves blazing the trail for others to follow in their own way. If this is the case, we can expect not merely historical inertia to resist our way, but also those around us. This is where we must state our case from our own perspective, not so much against the history of the species, but often against the way in which we think about history or what the grand narrative of history should aspire to be: "As soon as we recognize the value of the subjective in individual testimonies, we challenge the accepted categories of history. We reintroduce the emotionality, the fears and fantasies carried by the metaphors of memory, which historians have been so anxious to write out of their formal accounts" (Samuel and Thompson 1990:2). This official anxiety reflects the trepidation latent in any journey into the unknown. Aside from whatever politically convenient moment, where the entirety of experience or the "whole truth" of things cannot be told lest it expose the current emperor's nakedness, each of us is cast as a thrown project into an alien world, that of our own society, to which we must lend our ears and bend our backs. The meaningfulness of our own lives as a small part of living history is overshadowed by the cultural meanings given to history, as we can know it in our own time. No one writes his or her own story by themselves. No one is aloof either to the world or to the words of the world. We know, from Heidegger, that the world "worlds itself" in specific ways that obscure it from being-there. But how do words "word themselves"? How does the world, through translation into a human experience, "word itself" in human language? There is a trap set mutually by the cunning of those whose world it already is and into which we are thrown as well as by our own sense of proportion; that we are always smaller than life but at once we are asked to at least try to be larger than our own lives. Certainly, "Autobiography is one of several ways of getting the better if this trap and convincing oneself that the commitment, with all the lost time and wasted energy, had a meaning, either individual—in the building of an interesting life—or collective; that history as a meaning" (Peneff 1990:40). Meaning could not of course have existed at all without culture, and culture, in its turn, could not exist without a very specific lack of culture—the knowledge of the moment of individual death. This was seen, quite rightly, as the greatest gift by numerous ancient cultures, famously celebrated in the narrative of the Greek culture hero Prometheus to which we have already alluded: "Previously man had lived in a state of gloom and idleness, awaiting death, dwelling in caves, just like many other creatures. But once the knowledge of the hour of his death was taken from him hope rose up and with it the first great human desire to transform the world into a habitable place" (Gadamer 1996:156 [1990[). The actual historical content of such narratives has to be taken with a grain of salt. Palaeoarchaeology reveals a rather different chronology than the myth, but this is not truly important. It is the metaphoric content that is of note, and at some obscure point along the evolutionary path our primordial ancestors were in fact able to rise up from their animal natures and transform the world. Here, "habitable world" may be taken in its most broad sense to mean a human world, a world in which humanity can find a home and continue to make itself at home in the world. And much later, indeed, around the same time as the Greeks themselves became aware that they not only should have mythic narratives that described the origins of their state of comparative cultural grace but that they should begin to move beyond mythic thought into that of reason and science, humanity began to examine the character of what it meant to be human in the first place. This is a task that appears to be only about two and half millennia old, rather than say, six millions of years, but it is one to which we can immediately relate and one which is carried on in our own time: "Accompanying that investigation is a concomitant interest in the reality of the investigator—himself—and his connection with the object of analysis, a troubled fellow-man" (Natanson, op. cit:84). What "troubles" us is the uncertainty that ironically has been generalized from the absence of that piece of culture which in turn makes all culture possible. The existential uncertainty regarding the "hour of death" is not contained in itself. We realize, somewhat abruptly, that for human beings *everything* is uncertain, and not merely because we might die at any moment. Indeed, because of Prometheus and other culture heroes, this ultimate uncertainty tends not to figure into our plans, projects, and phantasms, and this is the whole point of its occluded character. But at the same time, the knowledge that we do not have the knowledge of our own deaths infiltrates itself into all other forms of knowledge. It colors what it means for human beings to know at all.

In response to this odd and perhaps ironic situatedness of being, humans must ascertain not what can be known without respect of finitude and uncertainty, but precisely what is knowable within the ambit of a consciousness that always seeks to transcend its current and contextual limits. We, in other words, try to set limits for ourselves and then overcome them. That this can be done only on the path to something, groping forward and hesitantly, is the reason why we should not "forget" this other path, the true path of human beings in the world. There was never a moment in the history of our species where it originated something about itself through the unemotional comparison of its own devices with those of the animals. There must have been millions of such comparisons made, on the fly, as it were, or even in the heat of confrontation where one as a human being had to outcompete the other as an animal or die. But the idea that we base our own nature on a simple negation of the wider Nature is too pat. Humans are both more interesting and more conceited than just that. For human nature not only is responsible for itself in a way that we are utterly unaware any other creature possesses or is possessed by—in that what we call a "conscience" is both held by us and yet also holds us by virtue of it being the seat of social norms and our sense of what is ethically possible or warranted—it is also a crucial aspect of our "nature" that we must, once again, ironically, interpret the intention to do so, that is, to be a human being by virtue not only of a consciousness that is differentiated in a number of ways from animal being, but through and by our conscience, individual and collective. And we exercise this human faculty in the light and shadow of our self-same ability to mislead each other: "Interpretation is concerned with the fundamental difference of the actor's intention, the meaning he bestows on his own act..." (Natanson, op. cit:39). In giving meaning to our own actions, a meaning that is constructed out of the amalgam of what we perceive others to believe about us and the world around us and the reactions we get after the fact, after the action to which we have attributed intentional meaning has taken place, we name ourselves as having a place in that very world which too is named. No intent can be justified in this way, but only approximated. Intent is mostly a rationalization for what has happened. The commonplace "I meant this" or "I didn't mean that" speak to the problem of linking up thought and action. No doubt a great deal of "intent" is post-hoc, that is, it gets constructed out of necessity to cover up our now apparent errors, when things did not go as we expected. The consistency and repetitiveness of this issue might make meaningfulness often appear to be disingenuous. But this is more a symptom of the whole character of the "uncertain path" rather than the planned obsolescence of our sincerity. In putting forward our take on things, we must expect some likelihood that this will not be taken by others in the same way, for better or worse. In this, all intentionality is "apophatic," it presents a name that unnames itself: "Apophasis is a naming which unnames itself: approximates then overcomes the guess while still retaining it because the truth lies through language in language's brokenness" (Lilburn 1999:30). We cannot assume, in other words, that how we think about outcomes will have anything to do with the actual results of our actions. This may be the actual case some of the time, and enough cases of this exist that we may begin to think that "the right attitude" is half the battle, or that some other self-help exhortation gives us a certain edge or even insight into the future. The risk that obtains with such a prognosticatory belief is that it may begin to become a self-fulfilling prophecy that we can do what we want to do and thus when we encounter the inevitable resistance to this sensibility that even over the short term the world and its others will present to us, we might be tempted to try to force our will on others through coercion and manipulation.

In discourse too this same problem is present. Science runs on its rails until enough data is accumulated that its weight of contradiction to accepted ways of thinking must be confronted. Belief is even more notoriously conservative in this way, sometimes lasting thousands of years before human beings decide that enough is enough. How these decisions are made is complex, but when change is enacted it is often violent, because even if most people agree that the old must be cast out, they seldom agree on what is to replace it. What had been taken as certain truths or unquestionable lifeways may collapse, but the momentary void that is left in the wake of this transformation gives rise to both speculation and dogma. In principle, cultural and personal change brings us face to face with the inherent nature of the uncertain path. Because it is through socialization and within the envelope of cultured being that we avoid facing uncertainty and finitude, changing or giving up on aspects thereof can appear to be a real existential threat. But conventions also serve another more mundane purpose. They allow us to speak to one another as if there is no distance between intent and behavior, thought and action. This is why Mannheim, amongst others, cautions us that regular people do not think like philosophers. They do not have to in light of the more certain sense that mundane knowledge, the facticality of living on, is in fact shared with others and thus so are most of my intents regarding it. This is fine in so far as it goes, but "it is clear that a philosophical tradition begins to enter into the conversation here as soon as the concepts it employs are no longer taken up as something self-evident, if the exertion of thinking is directed toward bringing to speech the discernable implications of conventional concept usage" (Gadamer 2000:80-1). Historical and personal transformations involve us taking up a new stance towards the expected. We have not yet gotten to the point where we can unexpect the expected, for this is a patently philosophical and critical form of consciousness, but we have entered into a transitional phase where what we expect of others and ourselves is called into question. We no longer can assume that what has been called conventional is in fact what it appears to be. We are made aware that change is what we can expect, though we know not the direction and force of such changes as there may be. What is at hand, then, is a combination of worldly change and our uncertainty about how to react to it. Intent, in these contexts, is reduced from the panoply of imagined projects and future-orientations we bring to the table denuded of the self-knowledge of its limitations, to a mere sense that we must survive another day. The locus of power which was to be found in the conventional has altered its epicenter, or has become diffuse in the way Foucault has famously suggested; "Power is everywhere; not because it embraces everything, but because it comes from everywhere. And 'Power,' insofar as it is permanent, repetitious, inert, and self-producing, is simply the over-all effect that emerges from these mobilities" (198:93). Equally so, and equally famously, power does not reign either unobserved or unrestricted: "Where there is power there is resistance, and yet, or rather consequently, this resistance is never in a position to exteriority in relation to power" (ibid:95). Like intent, the limits to action lie within the scope and character of the action itself. In general, the "possessing" or wielding of power is the modern equivalent to that of magic. Magic itself is not owned but used. It belongs to no one, but can be learned and "mastered" to the extent that one has access to it or it has become part of the "stock of knowledge at hand." Power functions in the same way as did magic, and may even appear to have the same effects if its sources are obscure enough. And just as neither magic nor power can be controlled over the long term by either individuals or cultures, the knowledge we gain from the experience of using both as tools in the world, tools to enact our intents and then perhaps to rationalize our errors pending the results of the original actions, ultimately speaks only to the contexts we have in fact experienced. It does not, so to speak, allow itself to be used in imaginary spaces of the mind's eye where no actual experience has taken place. Thought experiments are a sound pedagogic device if they are based in prior events, phenomena, and human experience thereof, but they cannot be equal in their force of suasion to what others know to have occurred. This "knowing" may be personal or it may be learned as part of a discourse, as we might know the dates of historical events, for instance, but unlike power and magic, such knowledge *can* be possessed: "Knowledge is a making available of experiences which accumulate more and more and awaken the question of the meaning all of this has for us. In a certain way we already know things through our experiences, and yet we would like to know what confers meaning on them all" (Gadamer 2000:98). This may well be a human desire, and hence the grand constructions of systems of thought and belief with which we have enriched but also aggrandized the human condition. Even so, experiential knowledge runs into the same kinds of limits that both magic and power do; none of these can be said to be indicative of more than relative and contextual applicability. Different situations call for different knowledge and experience, just as in the tradition, different forms of magic were reliable in this situation or that, and different forms of power, in our own age, must be utilized depending on circumstance, political or economic, military or commercial. Ultimately, knowledge is also self-knowledge, and as we will see below, the diversity of human knowledge not only implies the diversity of the self and other selves, but also requires it. In this way, we are all beginners, embarking on a journey of self-discovery that, in spite of its potential for adventure and diversity remains limited not merely by structures but by the imagination both personal and cultural. These limitations are not quite the same as the ones we might put on ourselves by walking the "path to nothing," but they are limits nonetheless. The professional thinker is in no different a circumstance than is the amateur: "The philosopher's 'materials' are inseparable from his own existence; he is his own subject matter" (Natanson, op. cit. 17). Though this might sound like it contains a healthy, or unhealthy, helping of Augustinian navel-gazing, the salient point is that we cannot divorce ourselves from our experiences and look at them with a pure objectivity that will then guarantee a clearer truth about them.

Indeed, the "subjectivity" of modernity has been cast as part of truth's guarantor, and to cast it aside in some behaviorist manner courts the nothingness
of the other path that is able to remain no thing precisely due to the absence
of humanity. No discourse or politics that pretends to stand aloof from human experience—the eugenics of racial superiority, the idea of a transcendental "Culture" or religion, for example—can enlighten self-understanding
or mature the species. Thinking itself, however revolutionary, betrays it's
calling by attempting to possess such ideals and then transmigrate its own
soul into their artificial host. "Unexpecting the expected" comes from the
experience of having to use knowledge in the most human, and perhaps also,
humane of manners, that of coming to terms with the fact that what works
here does not work there, what I think I know is always in the service of
some specific purpose or intent, its magic is momentary, its power temporary. This is so for even the most profound of human inventions and its
deepest thoughts. Just what that center is, and what will be found there by
excavating the subterranean caverns of personal and historical experience
remains to be seen.

Chapter One

The Singular Self

Restoring light and voice to the human condition is clearly a collective enterprise. No one person can claim to have the insight necessary for such a task. And although the dialogue with the dead is a crucial part of the puzzle, it is the conversation we have with our living fellow humans that must take ultimate precedence.

Yet what is the character of these others? Their make-up sometimes belies their reality. They cover themselves over with themselves, and so we also are veiled. But without this umbrella of selfhood, our very singularity comes into question. This is the question with which I want to open this investigation: a closer look at the presumption that who we are is any one thing at any one time and place, and that this is how it needs to be.

In the first section, "Narcissus," the sense that we can unduly admire ourselves comes under scrutiny. As well, when we do seek to behold our self-image, it is always a singular one. This is the case not only because we have taken a snapshot of ourselves—and perhaps the newly prevalent fad for self-shot images is an effect of our desire not just to constantly and consistently admire ourselves in all kinds of settings, mundane and exotic, with others famous or anonymous, but also, and more importantly for our argument here, a condition of the fact that we are not at all one thing and one thing only—freezing ourselves in one moment of time, but also due to the sense that we travel through time and space and thus are inherently transient, aside from our lives in their entirety being transitory. We will ask the questions "what am I?," as well as engaging in a brief history of selfhood. Alternatives within the being of the self will also be explored.

In section two we will come more squarely face to face with the question "why is I so important?." Though it sounds grammatically incorrect to posit the question in this way, we want to get the sense that the concept of "I" is not something personal and possessed by singular human beings as persons, but rather an object in the world projected by a specific kind of society in a particular historical moment, that of our own culture in modernity. Not only will this help us get some perspective on the fetish of the singular self, but it will also allow us to observe the "I" transform itself through differing social spaces and cultural contexts, migrating here and there and indeed becoming something quite different. We will find that the self does not need the "I" to be any one thing, but is reliant upon it to serve the task at hand by taking on the role or mask of something more or less the same for the moment. It is not that the idea of a plurality of roles alienates us, but rather the sense that role and self have no distance between them.

Finally, and most briefly, a synopsis of the sociological sensibility of the Cartesian problem is presented. In "They are, therefore I am," the position of the engaged and reflective ego is projected into the world of others, the social world of multiple and transforming selves that allow us to get a sense of not only who we are, but that we exist at all. It is not the thought of the "I," in other words, that allows existence, but that existence is pursued by the expectations we imagine others have of us as a person like them and perhaps also unlike them. In this pursuit, we develop ourselves according to the norms and forms of the day, the crucial one being the mistaken sense that we are and should remain one thing.

1.1 NARCISSUS

This one thing is no doubt attractive to us. It reassures us that we are still whole and can be framed as such. It stands alone and aloof to any apparent influence, real or imagined, and it takes our breath away, this imagined selfhood, because it stares back at us from a distance, and yet it is still we. The fascination of the mirror, only noted by a certain stage of cognitive development—and never, seemingly, noticed by animals such as cats—contains a kind of magical surface, the tain of which is the mortar that holds the loose bricks of complex lives together. Is it only an instrumentality, or yet a coincidence, that we use the mirror daily to check "ourselves," applying cosmetic or depilation where deemed normatively necessary, adjusting the detritus of the day to day, encircling the entropy of wear and tear? We note, usually with some dismay that we are getting older. Or we might think that we have aged well, though this does not necessarily include the idea of aging gracefully. The mirror lies to us in many ways, not the least of which reversing our images so that we ourselves are inverted. It reflects something that we are not—a singularity—and it dulls our sense of history. We are able, for instance, to keep reappearing as if nothing at all had changed in our lives or in our souls.

Even so, it is clear enough that we are something, if not one thing, and that this object that is also a subject stares back at us with more or less the glance we give to it. What is it that we are looking at, and how do we know that it is, after all is said and done, some kind of representation of what we know to be ourselves? What is the subjectivity of the object of the self? We are an object unlike other objects in the world. Or, we are also an object like these objects but with something else added. We are conscious of ourselves, not to say often also self-conscious in the vernacular sense of being ill at ease or uncomfortable. Perhaps these two faces of knowing we are present as a person are related. It is not an easy thing to imagine that we are in fact a living being, unlike the table at which I write or the chair upon which I sit. We are not interchangeable with others in the way that furniture may be exchanged for other versions of itself. Yes, mundane objects like chairs and tables may be designed from blueprints to look quite different from one another, much more so than human beings, in all their cultural diversity, can look. A table might have three legs or six, but human beings must normatively have two. Less than this is considered a disability, while we would not suggest that a table, unless unbalanced in some way, would be lesser than other versions of itself if the leg count were up or down. Obviously there is a point of no return with certain design. A one legged table must have a very broad base, for instance, in order to maintain its basic "tabular" function. But seeing a table in the mirror does not provoke comment. We do not see anything other than what we would see if we looked at the object directly. Indeed, we ourselves, this "one" thing, are the only objects that we cannot see for ourselves. It is this irony that does provoke all kinds of mixed feelings, as well as suggesting that we investigate the challenge of this reflection, which is not at once our own reflection in the sense of Descartes and others, poses to us: "This search, this quest produced ambivalent feelings: the need for truth and the difficulty in stating it; the personal urge to remember and also to forget; the wish to bear witness on the one hand and to remain silent on the other, as a protest" (Bravo, et al 1990:97). Our ancestors engaged in this quest somewhat differently than do we. In the absence of easily reflecting surfaces, the pool that appears in the Greek myth of Narcissus is generally thought to be the only mundane aspect of the entire narrative. Yet even here we get the sense that the pool, at first present in order for one to drink, is itself somehow captivating, turning the head of the very one which it then holds within itself. The "difficulty" of stating the case for the singularity of being is not held reflectively, as is the image of selfhood, however "attractive." The contemporary sense of the term "narcissus," and its attendant "narcissism" or "complex," at once does justice to the captivation of the self by its own image—an image that we understand today to be the imagination of what we think others think of us—as well as betraying the older sensibility that one can quite literally fall in love with oneself without needing that self to be any one thing a any one time. Like love in general, we are able to accept the foibles and distinctions of the other, her rough edges and her polished parts. In the "primitive" corroborrees as well as in the classical cults, we find two key historical moments in the history of selfhood. In the former, the collective conscience of mechanical solidarity is celebrated as a reality. There is no difference amongst the members of the group. Indeed, this notion was extended to the animal or natural totem from which the group got its spiritual power and its material sustenance, though the second was a resource that was indirectly acquired by alliance systems, kinship and otherwise. With the latter, however, something momentous in the evolution of our specific culture was occurring. The "corroborree" of classical cults begins the separation of the individual, the self-conception of singularity that acts as a symbolic prelude to Augustine's introspection. As well, and just as importantly for the history of symbolism in general, since these rituals were often orgiastic in nature, including that of the agape, the members of these voluntary and secret societies, mystery religions and the like, spoke, sang and danced their god into being present with them. Indeed, without being vulgar, we can say that these people also loved their god into being. This was the origin of the singularity of godhead quite literally "conceived." The birth of the god was the result of the intercourse of the cult members, given generalized consciousness, liberated from the norms of marital or other kin bonds, and pulled away from the narcissistic sense that they were a specific being in a world of beings.

This is a far cry from our modern sensibility, but it does show that the self-conception that we adore just as loyally as did Narcissus himself is not at all something primordial or unchanging. There may even be some regret that our modern benevolent associations and religious societies and sub-cultures cannot boast of either collective conscience or for that matter, great group sex! However this may be, and *pace* the sociological reports of swingers getting together under the guise of philanthropy and what have you, we are much more aware that the self must be somehow self-contained, including its sexuality, voracious or no (cf. Lingis 1989:21). This autonomy, famously characterized by Taylor as both liberating and disquieting, certainly has a "Lutheran" moment to it. The reformation of the self in the eighteenth century is kindred to that given the idea of godhead in the sixteenth. One needs to have a direct line to the newly emancipated god because it is not merely the German peasant and others like him that is now without institutional succor. The Protestant God no longer has his church. So God, as Nietzsche later recognized, needs Man as much as the obverse is true. But this time, it is not even so much "Man" that is required, but individual men and women. Believers make up what is lost in the newly absent institution of church and religious organization. Similarly, the even more recent belief in the self models itself upon the new God. The balance that must be struck between emancipation and emasculation is clear: the power of godhead is no longer a *patria potestas*, it cannot claim to own men as chattel and rely on its intercessionary device on earth to enforce this claim. No, with the reformation we understand our relationship with God to be voluntaristic. At first this must have been both a very broad claim and a heavy burden to believe in. Yet the proof of this new pudding lay in the apparent betrayal to its personal singularity of personality. The sectarianism of Protestantism, historically in evidence almost immediately, took quite seriously the personality of Godhead and made it context reliant and resistant. Its reliance on small but growing sects of believers reinforced the original notion that God was to be both personal and personable. If not quite a *bon vivant*, at least He was there when you needed Him. And hence the sense that myself, as a human being, should also be there, fully present, self-responsible, and transparently open, not before a confessional, but before God Himself, was given form. God and persons were now equivocal mirrors of one another.

Compare this with the starkness of the anomic self we start to find in the late nineteenth century and we may well be startled by the outcome of this earlier transformation: "They also gave a definition of 'the self,' a self in relation to survival, a sort of desiccated identity that seemingly represented a subjective element; overpowered by fate, no longer capable of action to influence events, it loses its causal but not its existential value" (Bravo et al 1990:103). This is almost a *volte-face*. The newly empowered rational action of the enlightenment individual, as well as the earlier conception of the dignity of the person and its self-responsibility with God as a willing back-up, riding shot gun, if you will, in the carriage of human agency, appears to have almost altogether disappeared. By the *fin de siècle*, with its attendant prescience of the European apocalypse just over the haunted horizon, not only is the old God dead but as well the newer God which, as Nietzsche immediately states, means that rational mankind also now must come to terms with the very interior of his irrationality without the help of non-rational symbolism and mythic narratives. In its anxiety, the pride of the reformers flew in the face not only of institution and tradition, but of itself as well. Luther cast a rather large stone in the pool of Narcissus in order to break free from the addictive attraction of mere self-love, but in doing so, shattered the human community of selves into so many disparate pieces—the sects—that it ended up being impossible to place them back together in any coherent manner. Ecumenicisms aside, we know we are both diverse but also conflicting in our senses of ideal existence and therefore also what constitutes morality. There exists rather a Humpty-Dumpty of post-paradisal parade. Falling off one wall suggests that the wall remains unbreached and whole, but our vision of where we had been perched is also shattered, and thus the wall too looks like it has become as us, a great diversity of unrelated things, hopelessly scattered and broken. Is this the simple result of an imbalance in human aspiration? "Hubris calls for nemesis, and in one form or another it's going to get it, not as a punishment from outside but as the completion of a pattern already started" (Midgely 2004:104). Peneff reminds us that most life stories are both apologies, either in the Socratic sense of defense or in our more recent sense of confession and rationalization, as well as being spoken as if they are one voice (1990:38). The "as if" factor is clearly indicative of a piecing together. We have all, through the simple act and fact of living on, fallen off various walls at various times and places, and are always spending some of our energy picking up the pieces. Casual chestnuts such as "picking oneself up and dusting oneself off" are testament to this existential situatedness. But the problem we now face does not lie in the task itself, but rather in the self-imagery we use to try to accomplish it. Not only is there a goal of resurrection—we need to put back together the shattered self in the ideal image of both the reformation God and the enlightenment human—but we imagine that such a resurrection does not entail, as it formerly did, any kind of transfiguration. We think we can go back to being the same way, whatever that was, that we used to be. We forget that whoever we were at that now past time was also just as unfinished and fragmentary as we are now. It cannot, historically or culturally, "stand in" for us as made out of whole cloth. And still further, we imagine ourselves as already whole, crouching over the shards of selfhood as if we were ourselves a kind of *deus ex machina*, sifting and sorting, assembling and gluing: "The really strange and disturbing thing about all these images is the alienation of the human operator from the system he works on. He appears outside the system." (Midgely 2004:114). Clearly, and in the same way that it is commonplace to say that one cannot step outside of history, either one's own or that of the larger culture, we also cannot excerpt ourselves from the context that we wish to take as an object, most specifically, our fragmented selfhood. Further to this, we cannot exempt ourselves from the ethical implications of our own acts. The action involved in piecing together human experience is perhaps the most obscure to us. It is at once intimate and yet reflective. It is action that requires ongoing thought, thought that prods us to immediately act. The situatedness of our being-in-the-world in these moments is not truly philosophical in the sense that we can sit back and ponder our predicament. The gathering of being, the mode of being that is "pulling together of itself" requires the most interstitial recognizance of both subject and object. The mirror has been shattered and cannot be replaced by the sum total of its own shards. We need rather to simply get a new mirror, rather than attempt a reconstruction of the old one. If we can no longer see ourselves as whole, it suggests that either our self-conception as a singular entity was in error or that we are in error in appraising the current situation; that is, even if the old mirror now lies scattered in shards, its individual pieces still reflect a part of our reality. We are forced to look at ourselves as we actually are, and this is the more disturbing thing about the images involved, precisely because the sense that we can operate "outside" any context is simply false.

Our modern mass culture belies this falsehood. We seek to either restore the old mirror or replace it, but either way the goal is to see ourselves as whole once again. We cannot dwell for too long in the vision of fragmentedness. This is an ancient fear, as certain Hebrew texts suggest that the "back of God" is made of clay shards and the sight of it is kindred with pure evil. It is likely, given the time period of these narratives that the metaphor had not to do with individuals, as we understand the concept today, but with groups. The fission of a cultural community was an evil thing. It meant death to its constituent members. Today, the presence of massive and anonymous societies give the undue impression that fragmented being is at last conquered and we have nothing to fear from ourselves as selves that undergo a great diversity of experiences as well as changing over time. The group, being so large and attaining normativity through institutions and laws, is something that cannot be broken apart: "But these developments tend to lower the significance of the group as a unit composed of persons consciously or unconsciously bound together, and exalt the mass as a conglomeration of unrelated individuals" (Neumann 1970:436 [1949]). The group, in other words, is no longer a group in any sense that can be meaningful for any particular member thereof. It has no solidarity in the social contract sense of the concept. It is simply a large mass of persons living in the same geographical boundedness. Ethnicity, kindred, caste or class, morality or culture—none of these things is necessarily shared by anyone living within this contiguity. Now, it can be said quite forcefully that these older ways of uniting human beings each have serious problems associated with them, none more so than inter-group conflict. Perhaps especially today, when nationality is no longer always the immediate response when citizens are asked what is the most important thing about who they are in relation to their neighbors, these older structures are reasserting themselves, awakening from their dormancy, and causing a renewal of archaic conflicts across the globe. People often do not wish to live with one another, or, because of empirically verifiable events over the course of time, rightfully distrust those others with whom they had been living, as would a subaltern culture mistrust the dominant one in their part of the world. The fissioning of an at once globalizing humanity is an odd and also disturbing thing, most especially because it has had the tendency to be violent. We seem to be resisting the enlightenment ideal of citizenship, and of being the "good citizen" in the Kantian sense. We are beginning to reject the idea that the force of the state—still a very recent phenomena in the history of social group cohesion and adhesion—is something that is reasonable for us to internalize and thence to dispense as a vehicle for a posited general morality. The famous idea that we can hold our freedom to be a private affair and behave only according to rational law in public is still generally what we aspire to in the so-called civil society of our own time. Sociologically, these ideals need not be set up on metaphysical pedestals. They are simply norms, legal or otherwise, that are the most pragmatic form of inter-association. The aggrandizement that Kant tends to give to the act that aspires to model itself always on these forms is perhaps overdone: "So act that the maxim of your will could always hold at the same time as a principle establishing universal law" (quoted in Lingis, op. cit:39), is something that, given the cross-cultural diversity of humanity as we know it, could never truly be the case in any case. The "universality" of principles is, and always is, something that itself comes out of a specific culture and culture history. The principle underscoring the idea of principles is simply another cultural artifact. This is not to say that it has no merit because it is relative and not something that can transcend—in much the same way as we cannot transcend any "system that we operate on"—its own cultural suasion. Indeed, the very globalization that is being abstemiously resisted in certain regions is tantamount, once it is in place, to the kind of universality Kant and others imagined was in principle part of the human condition *per se*. Even so, this can only be a bare analogy. Cultural systems have histories, and we are being made painfully aware that the history of our own time, spreading the gospel of enlightenment democratic principles and the concept of the autonomous individual more than anything else, is fraught with authentic difficulties that had these ideas been universal in the first place, as part of the human genome, perhaps, would never have occurred and all would live happily ever after.

Yet we have moved on from the eighteenth century notions of shared rational wills and such-like. Reality has forced us to do so, but on top of this, reasoned reflection about concepts themselves has pushed us toward a different take on how we might not only get along with the others who live with us on this planet, but also, and very much related to this first sense, how we can get along with the growing sense that the autonomous individual is not only not an individual in the enlightenment sense but that his very fragmentedness is in fact an ironic yet authentic testament to his individuality. Though "we still find it easy to think of political society as created by will or to think of it instrumentally. [ ] we no longer understand the origins of society reposing in agreement..." (Taylor, op. cit:195). Certainly it is more rare to have the former come to light than the latter. Even the oft acknowledged great leaders of history all rode on a much larger context of cultural suasion. Their arts of persuasion already had an audience, and it was this force that took the world by storm, for better or for worse. Indeed, one would be absolutely correct to assert that the availability of this force occurs to its greatest and thus most dangerous degree in our own modern massive society, where, precisely because of the absence of older forms of group cohesion, novel and sometimes quite artificial notions of what makes me like the other can be proffered and

promulgated. Leaders only take advantage of a situation already well ensconced in its potential. The social inertia of such contexts is potent and
powerful, and it has a forceful ally in the desire to piece ourselves together,
to either reconstruct the whole or replace it with a new, but still complete
vision of ourselves. The completion, the completedness of the group tends
towards a total vision; one that cedes nothing to either time or space; one that
is all conquering of any difference that remains between us. The desire to
conquer reality in this way, to pretend that human beings are only one thing
and indeed, should and must be this thing alone, is ontologically perverse:
"This perversity can be described as a drive to make ourselves the centre of
our world, to relate everything to ourselves to dominate and possess the
things which surround us" (Taylor, op. cit:138-9). Monomania or the *idée
fixe* is the most obvious candidate for inclusion on any narcissistic list, and
certainly gives rise to the psychopathological concept of narcissism as a
"complex," but for our purposes, the insight that can be gleaned is not so
much about the aggrandizement of an individual will said to represent that
general—the idea of a leader's "vision" is precisely that he or she can see
what the people desire, something that is hidden from them but nevertheless
resides within them—but rather that the desire for the individual himself or
herself to be seen as one thing is the paramount drive to conquer the world of
things, that is the singular overcoming the plural. Fortunately for all those not
included in this or that leader's vision—and there are always those who do
not fit in either structurally or even whimsically—it is the plurality of humanity that is the paramount reality. Of course it remains to be seen whether
or not this latest drive for the One as one world will succeed in finally
obliterating all traces of human diversity in that self-same world.

In spite of the force of social movements such as globalization or the
therapeutic propaedeutic of oneness at an individual level—to be healthy is
to have a sense of the whole that is greater than the sum of its parts, akin to
the equation of organic solidarity and its societal gestalt—there have been
some famous alternatives raised that recognize the fragmentedness of being
in the world as not only a reality but as a valuable and uniquely human
experience. For these options, the entire notion of the polis as well as the self
is both different and differentiated. This idea, associated most fully with
Nietzsche's ethics, seems at first to be a kind of fatalism. Enjoy the moment
of one's existence, none more full than any other, and none more meaningful
than any other. Yet the idea of an authentic autonomy does, at least, mean
being free from desire while at the same time being able to express the desire
to be free. More on this much later on, but for now, it is enough to note that
Nietzsche and others following his lead have noted that the sovereign human
being is only so because he or she expressly does not borrow their notion of
will from anything other than their own self and its experience of being itself.

Because this experience is itself diverse, the sense that one can be free only in this or that moment of bliss, or that bliss can be but a moment, frozen in time and so taken out of the flux of temporality—the love scenes in popular cinema have this as a sentimental trope, but the fact that we as an audience not only respond to this trope but have experienced it in our own lives, however sentimentally, means that it is a widely held cultural ideal—is taken as evidence that on the one hand, the self cannot be itself unless all other aspects of selfhood are bracketed out or even expunged, and on the other hand, that bliss means coming home to a self which is singular and that this is the most authentic version of being rather than diversity, takes Nietzsche's ethics down a path he would likely not have sanctioned. For this path, while not exactly leading to nothing, tends to push us once again in the direction of imagining ourselves as independent singularities capable of enacting our will as a principle in the world. The Spencerian statement regarding competition and "the best fit" is perhaps more current, as Midgely herself suggests. Even so, this hardly absolves us from the problem that for a person to bend his will to an internalization is to court a form of slavery, as Lingis further to the above mentions (op. cit:39). The whole idea of the social contract—not so much in the way Durkheim later framed it, as not merely the origin but the form of the original human group, but as one of the enlightenment's pet projects—contradicts the idea of the individual. For to have a contract, a covenant, a solidarity with others is to forsake one's selfhood and become part of a group. Perhaps the single most important *leitmotif* of the cultural reaction *against* the enlightenment was the emerging concept of the autonomous individual, and indeed Nietzsche carries through with this emergence to the nth degree. Its "discovery" is now associated with the Romantic movement, in direct contradistinction to rationalism, "born out of the opposition to rationalism," as the Nazi phrase has it, with shadowy portent but also with some historical accuracy: "The discovery of the individual was indeed, at that time, the great achievement of romantic culture. The famous catchphrase, that the individual is '*ineffable*' and thus there is no possibility of conceptually grasping the individual's singularity, emerges in the Romantic period" (Gadamer 2000:12, italics the text's). This newer idea is crucial for the understanding of the still more recent sense that the self is not only not a singularity because of its much vaunted "ineffability," but in reality a fragmentedness of strewn aspects or better, modes of being. Once the stones of Romanticism shatter the mirror of rationalism, there can be no question of returning to the social contract inspired limitations on human individuality. The tain of the mirror has also been broken up. Yes, it still reflects bits and pieces of not only persons but also the wider culture—this social fact is reflected in what Schutz referred to as the "social distribution of knowledge"—but it cannot give image to the whole which itself no longer exists. Our sense of wholeness comes from the fantasy of imagining ourselves out of the picture, of excerpting ourselves from the "system" and then operating upon it as only an object. We have neglected to acknowledge the fact that any mirror not only reflects, and, for that matter, can refract, but is itself part of who we are. It is, in other words, not an image but a self-image, for we are the primary receivers and perceivers of what is held on the surface of the mirror. The tain, the structures of culture and historical context, are the mirror's depths, and, just as they are unseen beneath the glassy surface, so their effects upon us remain for the most part semi-conscious or even unconscious. Hence the idea that in our fragmentedness we finally glimpse the truth of being and that, following hard upon this, the truly autonomous individual is the one who knows the effects of what has been internalized and manifestly *not* one who attempts to then turn that internalization into a "maxim" much less a universal law.

At the same time, as much as we might venerate the singular will that triumphs over both rationality and community, that stands aloof to that other "triumph of the will" where the mythical group is fetishized and reified, there still exists yet another side-track that sabotages any sense that we have attained an authentic freedom. That is, in a word, the problem of imagining that my current success and autonomy has always and already been my own work and contains neither the internalization of norms nor the force of forms, and yet further, contains none of the efforts of others. This is always a patent falsehood, and in order to overcome it, it must be acknowledged even if it seems to take away from the merit or value of the individual will and its conquest of the world and of its own history. Perhaps those who have become wealthy in some form in their lifetime espouse this sensibility more than others: "The myth of success through one's own efforts tends to minimize the work of a whole group for the advantage of one individual. In the same way, by attributing to themselves an exaggeratedly modest social origin, entrepreneurs make out their rise to be more spectacular" (Peneff 1990:38). Yet none of us, given the very cultural conditions we live within and live within us, is immune from such mythologies; the making individual of them through personal fable but one which is eminently recognizable to others as they too would like to be able, eventually, to use it for themselves and in the same manner. It is, at base, just one more way of attempting to reconstruct the whole as if it were cut from whole cloth, as if the present, in its presence, was always present and never absent, as if the sensibility I have of myself today was always there, latent or fully realized and continuous, or in some evolutionary combination of the two. The paradoxes that ingratiate themselves into the logic of anti-history are indissoluble to either a materialist or idealist conception of reality. That is, the self-made person cannot idealize his will beyond material considerations and real-time and real-life opportunity structures, nor can the avid materialist suggest that it was simply hard work in the "real world" that made him what he is today. Nevertheless,

to attempt to do so—and it does not matter which "side" we originally pick—
is necessary in the quest not only for wholeness and singularity, but also to
the sense that one *has* worked and *has* suffered, which almost all of us in the
world in fact have to do. Here, the rites of passage found as a hallmark of
traditional societies can be seen to also pervade, or at least resonate, through
the halls of cultural tradition in general. In totemism, for instance, the totem—force or animal or mythical being—is "reincarnated" in the one to be
initiated into that specific clan (cf. ibid:247). One is not only a vehicle for
this other form of being but one is precisely that form of being anew while
remaining undifferentiated from the kindred as a whole. This displaces the
idea that a human being, or even human beings in general, should be at the
center of things. Surely this metaphor, as we would see it today, is based on
direct experience of the world and of the nature that surrounded the social
contract societies on all sides. *That* experience was not at all metaphoric.
Even much later, but still well before the Renaissance and the distinctly
Western notion that humans are the measure of all things, including themselves, the sense that "man" could be the focal point of experience, a subject
about which other kinds of being were in orbit, would have been unthinkable
or at least, a gross error to reality: "This is a specifically modern state of
affairs and, in the context of Gnostic thinking, an obnoxious anachronism
that puts man in the centre of the field of consciousness where he had never
consciously stood before" (Jung 1959:255 [1951]). Jung immediately suggests that the historical effect of Christ's absence at the millennium was to
place Man irrevocably into the center of his own consciousness (ibid:256).
This was a regression of sorts, because it reduced or narrowed our sensibilities regarding our place not only in the cosmos but as well, and more importantly for everyday life, our place vis-à-vis our limitations as mortal beings.
The proliferation of diverse and conflicting ideas and ideals that first begins
to be felt during the archaic period of riverine empires also produced a
reaction that displaced the rites of passage for example, into marginal or
subaltern and mobile groups, and centered the power and authority of early
states into the new urban scenes with their bureaucratic and temple complexes. "Oriental Despotism," as Engels somewhat romantically called it, was
based on the idea that power emanated from a singular place, and even, in
some cases where there was believed to be a god on earth, the pharaoh, for
instance, from a singular self. This was only the beginning of a lengthy
historical pattern of such placements. Long before this, however, there were
similar reductions being practiced within the conflicting religions themselves. No doubt this served to reify key elements that could then be mar-
keted as against other competing sects or cults who in turn had to simplify
their own religious dogma in order to retain fragile and finicky franchises,
whatever doctrinal purposes it may have later served (cf. Jung, op. cit:202 for
an example). Of late, we have even taken to reducing ourselves, distancing

ourselves from the reality of our own complexity. The error of the singular self is just one example, as we shall see below. Most recently, the ethical overcoming of Nietzsche, the yes-saying to all things and experiences, has an ironic reductive temper. The ability to utter a final and essential "yes" to the world and to our being in it suggests that all experiences that human beings can have are worthy of our unmitigated acceptance. This would, by definition, include all that produces needless suffering and sorrow, and all the calculated evil we perpetrate against one another. Surely there is something missing here. The world in fact figures strongly as not merely an antidote to transcendentalism—Taylor suggests Dostoyevsky, even with his Christian vision, forces his heroes to "go through modernity" in order to affirm their dignity as human beings in the world (op. cit:452)—but also as the source of the very diversity that provokes or invokes diverse human reactions in its turn. But there is more to Nietzsche's singular vision than at first appears. It is just that, in proffering to his contemporaries the understanding of the power of life *per se*, its generative forces pushing us to say "yes" and to celebrate the eternal return of the same, the nth degree of a logic of yes-saying, we find that we no longer attain the center of things as a group at all: "Thus the Nietzschean valuation of the singular individual over the universal subject of classicism is a valuation of life as a creative force over the subject as a locus in which the order of the universe is reflected" (Lingis 1989:57). We have moved from being the essence of forces other than human, to being their creation, to being their model and reflection, to being their investigator, to producing in ourselves their effects as a people, to being the one who overcomes them as an individual. Though each of these "phases" in human consciousness is incomplete, it relates back to us only part of the story of what we are and what we have been, taken together they do present a fairly coherent historical whole. But their actual source remains in how human beings, as mortal forms of reflective and reasoning consciousness, have to live in the world that tells us little or nothing about how to make that life meaningful. The eternal and universal yes to all things is a powerful way of reducing the advent of meaning to the self's insistence on itself as the sole means of making meaning. There is something aleatory about this position, even though there are many times in modern life that specific persons, all of us who inhabit the West at least, or have immigrated to it more or less alone, when Nietzsche's dicta must be practiced. Yet perhaps what is really missing here rests more on an empirical level, where, free or unfree, the many forces of suasion whose sources lie outside the individual consciousness that I call my own impinge daily on my ability to say anything at all in response to the wonders and sorrows of the world.

Indeed, we can go farther. Aside from the empiricality of these forces—institutions, other minds, tradition, scientific and social fact—there is, facing us down and resisting reduction, the day to day life of the regular person who occupies a finite, but precisely still diverse and conflicting, set of social roles. We might say "yes" to the set of these over a lifetime, but we hardly can reiterate the affirmative to each of them all the time or in every circumstance. Whatever that we may say about our ethics, it simply is neither realistic nor possibly even ethical to do so: "The moral can be expressed this way: existential subjectivity transcends mundanity only by honoring it. Social roles are the necessary condition for the emergence of the identity of the ego and remain essential to its expression as a being within a world" (Natanson, op. cit:87). Given that it was likely Nietzsche himself that "invented" the idea of role theory—his masked Dionysian vision takes off from here though it would have little appeal for the average social scientist—this much more pedestrian version of the transcendental self might be said to be part of his architecture after all. If the concept of self is both a "highly complex idea with many different uses," as Midgely reiterates in the face of simplistic dualisms (op. cit:69), this too plays into any Nietzschean understanding of the modes of being in the world that both transport us to higher ground, where we can take into ourselves a more panoramic view of what human beings have created for themselves, and assail us as limitations to what we might think and do in our lives as they pass along with us but also before us. We are not merely selves, on top of this, but persons, and the persona we might play at or indeed use to save our very lives from the pillaging of others and of institutions—the straight-faced theater of social sanctioned role is generally the best solution to any social predicament one might find oneself negotiating—helps us move beyond the limitations of a lock-step society. But they never collapse upon themselves or lead us to a center where the true "me" stands up and overcomes everything while at the same time stating in the most avidly stentorian tone a resounding "Yes!" to that same everything. This person is immensely social; whatever his or her subjectivity might nag us about. This is so simply because "The individual who recognizes himself as both alone and lonely within a typified reality is already a person" (Natanson, op. cit:25).

Now all of this is not meant to suggest that the self-overcoming overman is either unreal or a mere cartoon. It is simply to state that what is being overcome is part of the force used to overcome it. We overcome ourselves, mostly in a mundane manner, and mostly with the help of the perspective of experience that includes that of others and that of the tradition, as well as of the discourses of science and philosophy. Indeed, we can be said to affirm all of this as the necessary suite of forces we use to overcome what we had been. "Dying many times in order to become immortal" suggests that we practice this not only in the world, but most of all in day-to-day life. Nor is this to suggest that overcoming—the maturing or moving on, the letting go, the taking up of a new position, the gaining of experience and thus perhaps also perspective; all of these elements remind us that the "über" word that is so suggestive of heroics is firmly and consistently grounded in the everyday—is a simple thing to accomplish. Mundane though much of it is, it still requires of us some kind of basic courage, the kind of which real heroics, rather than those mythical or transcendental, are moved by. The necessity for overcoming the self in its patent and static singularity appears "as soon as man becomes conscious and acquires an ego, he feels himself a divided being..." (Neumann, op. cit:122). This seemingly paradoxical demand, that, one the one hand, we avoid sequestering the conscious aspect of human selfhood, protecting it or insulating it in some way in order to maintain the pretense that conscious life is the only reality and so that it does not simply suppress or repress the unconscious that grounds and helps process that reality into an holistic subjectivity, and, on the other, that we remain struggling shadows of selves cast as simple reflections of unconscious drives, no doubt creates significant tensions. The lack of ego, in both anomic and altruistic suicide, is a well-known factor in so far as the people at risk have little faith in themselves as a social and conscious being. This person, in the anomic state, is at risk for needless self-immolation. But the extinguishing of the selfhood of the conscious life is already part of the more mechanical social organizations that render altruistic suicide a viable and valid option in times of cultural crisis, as when this or that society feels it must defend itself from external threat. So even suicide must be seen as not necessarily the negation of culture in the demise of the individual. It could very well be the exemplary moment of that culture, although one still sees the desperation in the act. For cultures that have invented and given rise to the ego-concept and then stated that it can only find its fullest form in the individual as a person and a self, the problem becomes much more subjectively dangerous. Even so, it is the *unconscious* that allows conscious life to function properly and to maintain such a balance that suicide is not within the ambit of its day to day imagination let alone action. If human consciousness is then made up of not only its two respective aspects, but must also contain and maintain a gestalt, a synthetic rendition of both of them at once, a kind of archiphonemic apparatus that is constantly using the interpreted insights of the dream-work for perspective on the waking world—dreaming sleep is necessary for life to be lived as a reality rather than a perverse and projected dreaming-state—then to be conscious is also to not only have an unconscious but also to understand it as part of the lived state of being-conscious. What this means is essentially the singularity of personhood that we carry around with us is already and always in fact not singular. What "one's own" can mean in this thrownness of the projected tandem of modes of being must then attribute any singularity to a synthesis and not to an amalgam. The former is dialectical in nature and recognizes the other in itself. The latter is a new singularity, born of the fusion of different materials, and remains in its new state without respect to its history or any possible future differentiation. This is not a mere question of semantics, for the terms we use to designate selfhood also play an important role in designing it. If we continue to imagine that we present to the world one thing and it is the world that divides us and even tears us apart at the seams this is an illusion. The world is certainly another party to the construction of the self, and most specifically, the world of social others and the generalized other, but it is not also a simple single monolithic agency that ranges itself against us in all quarters. We have the advantage of being a "nexus" for the production of thoughts and deeds, not necessarily directly linked with one another, but linked through the location of consciousness that partakes in both waking and sleeping life. In this way, the Greek metaphor of sleep as the brother of death becomes clearer for moderns: it reminds us that to participate in life we must walk along with death and that through the nocturnal hours we do just that.

What emerges from this nexus is thought itself. If it appears to be our own in some unique way, it is only because we have experienced the world without the knowledge of some other's experience, for we simply cannot know not only the experiences of our contemporaries, some seven billion of them, or the posited nine times this number of human ancestors who have ever lived. At the same time, even if such a theoretical perspective were possible, the bare fact that we could access it would itself be enough of a new thing that we might say that our experience is still our own. And it is not so much the vaunted Cartesian intellect that issues forth with these thoughts. Certainly it is present, at least as an apparition of the intellect itself, providing perhaps an obverse collegiality to the visitations of otherness that might bump us in the night or set themselves up as more or less formal or casual interlocutors in our dreams. But it is manifestly not alone in its giving voice to thought, either one's own or through the iteration of another's. Natanson suggests thinking about this nexus of consciousness in a way that emplaces emotion and intonation into the picture. In doing so, we might avoid the error of having to think that the thinking self must be one kind of thing and must in turn make one kind of statement to the world or about it: "The existential problem, however, arises at a different level and concerns a qualitatively separate aspect of the self. Instead of defining loneliness as a mood, it would be more appropriate to suggest that moods are ways in which the self discovers itself in the world and defines its way of being there" (op. cit:23). So it is no surprise, that when I awake groggily from a dream or worse, what I take to be a nightmare, and then have to get on with my waking day and its routines, my mood might not match the mundanity of the challenges that I face. Yet it is that very routine that often constitutes the run of the waking hours that removes me from the unconscious and prevents it from further acting on its own. The idea of a "bad mood" or a "good" one is so commonplace that it generally bears no other comment except to simply state that this is what I am "in," as if we can inhabit a mood as we would a dwelling, abide within it as a kind of existential abode, however transitory. Indeed, we go even further than the use of this weak metaphor by stating that people whom we deem to have frequent changes of emotion or tone are "moody" and thus might well be avoided, at least for any serious undertaking such as a marriage or even a shared work contract of some other sort. We also think that we should, if engrossed by a negative mood, free ourselves from it. So much so has modernity cautioned us against falling into what the pre-modern metaphysics of emotion called "melancholia," that we see our emancipation from it to be a heroic act of not merely that modernity, but its greatest and most sacred scion, the individual. This may seem sentimental, even romantic. But if we consider some of the great afflictions of our modern era, obsession, neurosis, anxiety and depression, addiction and compulsions of all kinds, we realize that it does take a kind of heroic courage to step away from these and commit oneself to a new life. It is, quite literally, the remaking of oneself into a new person, kindred to the older ideas of conversion and the "twice-born" as a soteriological advent. Indeed, stepping away from addiction, for example, is an act of salvation; we are saving ourselves from a much worse fate. The effect of not taking this momentous step is, at best, to place the problem into some kind of socially sanctioned scene, where one's co-participants could well be assumed to be suffering from something similar as oneself: "We then get apparently groundless phobias and obsessions—crazes, idiosyncrasies, hypochondriac ideas, and intellectual perversions suitably camouflaged in social, religious, or political garb" (Jung, op. cit:169). No doubt it is much easier to attain a modicum of sociality through the sleight of hand of institutions—specifically, sectarian versions of all kinds, whether political or religions, or even economic in terms of fashions of the day or the "must-haves" of this or that season—than it is to face up to one's own liberation. For, in order to do so, we must first have to admit to ourselves that we have a problem. And such problems as these are in fact already defined by the very society that we have fled from, escaping, we think, its order and surveillance. To return as one prodigal to the very arms that cast us out, in our own eyes, seems itself tantamount to another kind of death. Yet to turn further away, into the authenticity of being in the world in all its mortality and ultimate limitation - its reality of not being able to give safe harbor to endless fantasies and pay court to the repetition of obsessions - anonymous to most others and yet responsible to them all the same, might spark yet further panic that would be in essence the same kind of thing from which we had shied away into the problematic behavior in the first place: "Free for our death, we are freed from the tyranny of petty worries and diversions, and thus open to the authentic self that beckons to us" (Barrett, op. cit:258). Authenticity, perhaps. But what of the sense that death represents itself to waking life both as a shadowy partner and fellow traveller, but also, inevitably, as an end to consciousness? This limit cannot be reckoned ahead of time by the analogical sense of falling asleep, of losing the conscious part of being to that unconscious, or letting this alter "take over" its job in some occluded way. Quite so, as the uroboric quality of consciousness mirrors the mythological state of the cosmic egg, so falling asleep is simply the act of balancing what, in waking hours, must eventually become unbalanced. We can say the same thing of "falling" awake, as it were, for too much sleep as well does us no good. We are more apt to forget about the sense of balance simply because, in our over-worked society, we concentrate on getting just enough sleep for the self to function - and indeed, to get as much work done as possible— while awake.

More than this, staying busy is cited as the optimum way of healing the self from crisis. Bereavement itself can easily become unbalanced. It broods along with us while keeping us sleepless; it distracts us during the day unless we can find a more focused manner of distracting ourselves from its presence. Business turns grief into mere sorrow, and sorrow is in fact what holds the healing force: "It is what makes it possible for us to live with what we would know, a renunciation drawing us near. Sorrow disarms the passions so that the other life may live contiguous with human consciousness safely" (Lilburn 1999:65). The "other life" is that which would have occurred had not the object of grief originally objected to its ongoingness. We not only "would have" known this other life in its fullness and continuity, but we will, wish, and desire to still come as near to it as we can, in spite of the loss. Sorrow then moves our desire away from the dangerous place of obsession or even psychosis, and places it safely amongst the living once again. Coming out of grief proper is a process analogous to that of waking up. There is, squarely in front of one, new life, and more than this, life anew. Further, with each waking morning, there is this promise repeated, so that time, linear, instrumental, measured and endless, actually retains some of its subjective character of the cycle and harmony, with a different kind sense of the indefinite because ever-returning: "Expectation, care, hope, the future—all these are involved in the process of waking up. And corresponding to this there is sleep and the process of falling asleep, which are marked by a particularly mysterious and obscure character which borders on that of death itself" (Gadamer 1996:130-1 [1989]). Without the latter, that which appears to extinguish anticipation and hope as well as annul any possible future, none of these could in fact occur at all. It is thus the rehearsal of the finitude of the future, its opening and closing repeated, curtains rising and falling, veils lifted and dropped, its face revealed and concealed from us each day and night, that allows not merely grief to be relinquished but also sorrow transformed to expectant interest and finally joy.

1.2 WHY IS "I" SO IMPORTANT?

Yet this experience, so necessary for human life let alone the balance of human consciousness, is still seen to be primarily experienced by the singular subject. In fact, it is seen that it must be so, that it is all important for me, and only me, to experience these transformations as something occurring *to* me, almost as if they had their source entirely external from my senses and sensibilities. The nature of my soul is made for the nature of the world written into a gearing mechanism that is objectively linear and subjectively cyclical. This is based on a contemporary understanding of both time and history. I, as a subject, experience time as history, and not the other way round. That is, history can only be felt as the times in which I live, and not as something abstract. The "when" of my own history, my biography and my self-understanding, is also not time in any larger sense. It is simply my life, and not even "life" in general. At the same time, these two rather contrived definitions of general and specific experience seem made for one another, and historically may be seen to appear with the advent of measured hours, the mechanics of time and thus that of nature, mathematically redefined and ordered but still experienced subjectively and as having some sort of purpose beyond itself: "This new order of interlocking natures arises to take the place of an order predicated on an ontic logos" (Taylor 1989:276). The mechanism of nature is coming to be known for itself, in itself. But our experience of this order is still lacking in its fundamental relationship to it. We do not yet possess an insight that alleviates the even more recent feeling of alienation from the natural order. Indeed, we are most often assailed, especially in this period of gradually awakening sensibility regarding the state of the environment and world ecology, with the idea that we are villains, disturbing the orders of nature and causing their interlock mechanisms to fail. Clearly, there is an empirical element to this responsibility and such a source is being used with ever-greater effectiveness as a way to construct the blame for such failings as can be observed. On top of this, because it is our routine way of living, its assumed and aspired to standards, its need to consume as an economic force, its commutes and work hours, its lighting of its monuments and streets at night, its hot showers and warm bedrooms, is the ultimate source of the danger to the wider environment, if not to "nature" proper. So our focus, in examining why we think ourselves as a singularity appears all-important to us, must begin with how we live in the day to day, and not seek to find the order of our being within a cosmic order still only partially understood: "Mundanity requires a proper spokesman, one whose first loyalty is to self-examination" (Natanson 1970:89). Furthermore, though this first loyalty is utterly necessary, it is not sufficient. We must also bear in mind that what we are examining is not in fact a "self" *per se*, and only becomes such through the very analysis we subject it to. It is simply not the case that a solid object is as it appears to be: "The trouble lies in the exclusiveness, the either/or approach, the conviction that only one very simple way of thought is rational" (Midgely, 2004:21). In order to simplify things, as we saw in the above discussion of the reduced self, or the reductionist approach to selfhood, we not only distend the ability of the rational to cover all forms of human experience, we contend that no other form of experience, even if known or perhaps yet knowable in a non-rational way, is valid. That is, even if we experience something that cannot be explained or explained away, we notoriously, at least in our own time, either let it escape us or escape from its presence. This presence, in its turn, comes to be defined as surreal at best, annoying or even frightful at worst. Either way it has no value; it is "either" invalid "or" invalidated, and this is the only rational manner of thinking about experience. No wonder who we are becomes so all-important! There is simply so little or comparatively little, left over from such a reduction that we treasure it all the more, over-aggrandizing its value as a rare commodity.

But this is not in fact all that we are. It is what we have become given a certain way of thinking about ourselves. We could have just as easily, in principle at least, gone in a different direction entirely and come up with a self that is, if not fragmented and fragmentary, at least much more interesting in its holism. For example: "The 'soul' does not represent just one particular domain among others, but rather reflects the totality of the embodied existence of the human being. [ ] The soul is the living power of the body itself" (Gadamer 1996:173 [1989]). It may also be said that the soul is what is spoken by the voice of the body, the meaning of the consciousness of the embodied. If the eyes are "the windows of the soul," another thing Aristotle tells us, then in this way of thinking about the self, the self appears to be more than meets the eye. It is not an object which only acts and may be described rationally, but a subject that intends and such intentions may not at all, or mostly not be, or sometimes, perhaps, never be, wholly rational. It has its own way of seeing; its eyes are its own. Though the behavioral analytic, based on observable action and lacking an ability to attribute intent as well as meaningfulness to any action, is moribund in any humanistic sensibility, we do in fact practice a version of it in our own subjectivity. We take its eyes for our own when we have to engage in typical situations and try thus to define them. Sometimes this is accomplished ahead of time, but more often than not, the vicissitudes of others' behavior, not to mention their more occlusive intents and aspirations—hidden not only from the behaviorist but also from us as fellow-persons—we must define and then redefine on the fly, in the midst of action, without the stolid and stale apparatus of behavioral theories to study in the meanwhile. The idea that the "soul" animates but also establishes the whole which it then causes to be embodied, that the soul is the subjectivity of the world around it, is echoed in this much more recent sentiment that includes the possibility, nay, the probability that what the soul had once wrought will disintegrate. Indeed, we can go further and suggest that the idea that the body must be animated in the first place, and that further-more the source of such animation must be either a special part of itself that comes from elsewhere and is implanted in the body, or that it is a gestalt of all of the electrical and organic forces and dynamics by which the body constitutes its basic functions; its higher abilities thus being constituted in turn by this newly present gestalt. All of this is predicated on the sense that we are not only a complex of processes, most of which are unconscious in the most basic sense—that is, they do not give rise either to their presence or their "intents" even in the dreaming life—as well as the notion that in order for consciousness to know itself as extant, there must be some other kind of being that "knows" that we can exist and continue to exist, since this is precisely what we have the greatest difficulty in coming to know about ourselves on our own. What is the nature of this "other" being or space of knowing? "Experience shows that the unconscious processes are compensa-tory to a definite conscious situation" (Jung 1959:204 [1951]). Exactly what they compensate on a case-to-case basis might be the object for a more profound version of empirical psychological theory, the "behavior" of the "soul" or its contemporary stand-in, the unconscious, perhaps. But what is more important is the value we put on redeeming, at all costs, the sense that we are not only more than a machine or another animal, but also more than we can grasp in our self-understanding. It is this latter desire for the presence of what must remain ironically absent—we wish to know that the self, or at least part of it, cannot be known to us—that drives all other interpretations of being in the world that do not rest on brute empirical recording of action and the measurement of responses.

To rest on this means to posit other orders, interlocking or no, from which animatedness evolves to us, or descends upon us. The former is now certain-ly more in discursive vogue than is the latter. But examined in this way, looking at their purpose from the standpoint of the self, they are very much the same thing. Both of them absolve us from the predicament of being an organic creature in so far as we are unlike other creatures, even if we are related to them in an evolutionary manner or as a special element amongst the other elements of creation. Both of them present to us the "impossibility" of thinking another way than either purposeful and meaningful animation or purposeless and ultimately, objectively meaningless action. But is this truly correct? We are also historically aware that anything once deemed impos-sible has often been overcome and either proven quite possible and real, or discarded as without merit given the advent of new ideas and forms of consciousness previously unknown. "Why is it impossible then, to conceive a person or even a culture which might so understand this predicament as to do altogether without frameworks, that is, without these qualitative discrimina-tions of the incomparably higher?" (Taylor, op. cit:26). The situatedness of being in the world as it is and not therefore being elsewhere, such as within the envelope of either Being or non-being, or more to the point, in some other world where the precise character of the "soul" or for that matter, the unconscious, is fully revealed to us through the intervention of what is "higher," suggests a kind of "predicament" predicated on the desire to at once be in the know about the self and how it *works*—rather than simply how the body or even the brain functions—and, because this is a struggle and involves the disintegration of the self and the fragmentedness of being, to be content with the enduring mystery of consciousness; specifically enduring because it is so endearing to us. It is this mystery, however contrived, that makes us special in the world of nature and creature.

Similar to James' famous suggestion that all religious thought is merely a giant exercise in aggrandizing the human ego, the nursing and caretaking over the mystery of consciousness, or the nature of the soul or what have you, might well be seen as a rearguard action in the face of the overwhelming evidence that it is organic and evolutionary gestalts, inevitable and without higher purpose, that drive forms of consciousness, including our own. If this is really the case, the mystery of life is resolved and each must then find his or her own resolution to make meaning with and within the knowledge of the objectively meaningless. This requires on our parts a sea change, because our eyes are now the windows on to the world and do not project meaning *per se*, as they were once thought to do: "In the business of changing ourselves, each of us is ultimately on his own; and that can be one of the attractions in striking out on a new path" (Barrett 1979:333). Such a path may lead inward, toward the space once occupied by the soul but now home to a diversity of experience, memories, desires and anxieties, or outward, into the world of norms and forms and further, into the world of others to whom oneself is at first glance not a work in progress, not a mobile vehicle of transient consciousness, but a polished and finished product of action and behavior, predictable and measurable. It is *this* first sensibility that we have of other that has given rise to reductivist theories that purport to explain the full presence of consciousness. Indeed, both paths are taken at once, and we are continuously placed at their intersection. The everyday heroics of most persons partake at least nominally in the mythic archetype. One has to get on with one's life—the external world—while at the same time negotiating any inner demons one may have—the internal world. This is presumably why mythic tropes involving the hero "with a thousand faces" remain staples of popular entertainment. All of us are aware, in a society which expects us to be our own person while at the same time expecting our allegiance as citizens, that there will be some sort of ongoing tension between these loyalties. Given the current situatedness of being in the world, one of its chief lines of fracture involves precisely this tension; the order of its magnitude will depend on how far one's personal sense of self departs from the surrounding sea of

norms and institutions and how not only they work in the day to day, but the
continuing presence and relative strength of their historical inertia.

The most obvious manner in which we make distinctions between where
and to whom one's loyalty belongs—when do we render unto Caesar and if
so, exactly what is his, etc.—is by finding a niche in the larger picture of both
the division of labor and the social distribution of knowledge: "The individual will have to specialize everywhere, but it makes a great difference whether
in his sphere there are only associates who specialize in the same field, or
whether he is surrounded by men who live for him the other possibilities that
he has had to forego" (Lösch 1967:194 [1945], italics the text's). In organic
solidarity this is at least a possibility, but we should not forget that it is the
rise of the division of labor, coupled with that of religious ideas and tensions
amongst competing resource allocations and their associated clan-based kin
groups that begins the lengthy journey to modern individuality in the first
place. So the advent of the obverse ideas of self and person may appear to
hold within them the response to these other social forces—appear, that is, to
be their authentic and heroic opponents who, in essence, do not share anything with that which they come to confront—but it is actually more the case
that it is a cultural system itself presenting a new functional component by
and for itself in order to keep things going more or less as they had been.
This is where reality departs from myth. The history of the self is clearly
bound up within the history of those social contexts that seem to be out to
negate it. They are not, in this sense, true opponents but more like interlocutors. Certainly there is the tension and edge of dialectic; the synthesis that is
sought is one of the expression of personhood and autonomous individuality
within the architecture of institutions and social norms. Like the equally
famous issue of the mind and the body, the division between self and society
is to a great extent an artificial one, and underscores our contention that the
"I" cannot be as important as we moderns have made it out to be, even in our
own time. And the most common way of avoiding this schism is to see the
person as a refraction of the world. After all, it is our subjective sensibility of
objective norms and forms found to make up the social world that allows us
to individuate our experiences from others. We do not understand the world
in quite the same way as do our contemporary fellow-humans. Cross culturally, this is glaringly obvious, and still leads to much conflict. But closer to
home, the personalized West whose cultural consciousness is uniquely its
own in a way that demands of us to take it into ourselves with the express
purpose of being different, it is also clear that in order to respond to this
unique demand that we shun the idea that we should conform too closely to
what others appear to be doing with their lives. "Do your own thing" is still a
watch-phrase for Westerners, even though it sometimes seems that govern-
ments are always struggling to combat the loosest threads of this ethical
dictum. And not only the state, for there also exist, almost as cautionary

narratives in which the proposed and supposed hero is not in fact heroic and retreats into the cowardice of the system—the "sell outs" of all kinds, perhaps—persons who come to represent to us the very embodiment of institutional apparatus and social norms. These "rule-enforcers" and "rule-supporters" are disliked by all rebellious youth, who take them as their patent and stereotypical enemy. But in fact, like the false issue of the mind and the body, the self and society, these persons too are not entirely what they seem to be. They have perhaps a better public performance of a neo-Kantian morality—they act as if their maxims should become general principles for example—than many of us, but they too must occupy, usually in some more private space, the role of rebel or non-conformist in some small part of their lives. Martinets are always the most at risk for the enantiodromian dynamic and thus must find some safety valve to let off the built up pressure of always appearing to be part of the system and never standing up against it. But there are those who exist even at the margins of this status, and although few in number, their very presence strikes us as personifying the thing that we must most avoid if we are to live an authentic human existence. These are the people who have embraced Sartre's concept of "bad faith" and live it as if it could be lived in good faith: "To speak of 'bad faith' here means that the self has chosen both a temporal and a moral mode of being, has in effect decided to avoid transcension of mundanity by embracing the typical as a form of protection" (Natanson, op. cit:121). This "escape from freedom" has been analyzed almost to death by twentieth century critical thinkers. Suffice to say that it itself is far from dead, and that we must guard against participating in this mode of non-being, the "path to nothing" about which we are warned from the very beginning of Western thought. The sense that one can carve out a niche in the system of functional production and consumption is certainly a start. Most of our waking hours are spent partaking in this order in some way. It stands to reason then that most of our sleeping ones are spent processing this mundane and routine experience, and thus also helping us avoid the trap of bad faith in general. But our very actions betray us. Even if we avoid bad faith directly we still are immersed in it in the indirect way of supporting the very system to which we cannot lend our loyalty as persons. This is why we aggrandize the "I." We hope to make this version of ourselves, the true "me," if you will, larger than the life that surrounds us. We have to be forced to confront the bare fact that the life we lead is after all also our own. We cannot disown it, because the "I" is the one who is acting within it and taking it in to itself. "Still, connectedness is more generally the case than not. One fact does make a difference to the others" (Barrett, op. cit:37). This interconnection between intent, action, world and outcome, prevents any sense that we can, once again, excerpt ourselves from the cultural context in which we are ensconced in any complete and convenient manner, ad hoc and at will. Instead, parking our radical desire to be a self and only a self at the door of our family home, our workplace, or other community building or even community breaking contexts, we engage in the somewhat hypocritical production of theatrical pretense. If we see it that way, that is. For what pretense is there in living on as myself in various social contexts other than that which tells me I am "really" only one thing and this "true self" appears when I am alone with myself and my thoughts, or doing the things I love the most and be damned with the rest of humanity!

It now looks like we are beginning to understand where the actual theater takes place in our lives. It is more about surrounding the sacred ideal of selfhood with a cloak of occlusion, one that the daggers of the social cannot penetrate. All our other acts, those public and those private with the intent of making a public impression, are held to be in service to this ideal of the hidden authenticity of the true self. Self-realization, an ancient idea associated with Aristotle's notion of *entelecheia*, is then to be had only within the narrowest of confines; that of the absolute privacy of our innermost thoughts. But this is precisely what self-realization is not. The Augustinian sensibility may have been suitable for the one who regrets his own biography and has, in the typically enantiodromian manner, eschewed it for the extremity of its opposite, which thereafter must be defended to the hilt by running down in a transparently cartoonish manner all that was representative of the previous self—"We can certainly hand it to Augustine that all natures are good, yet just not good enough to prevent their badness from being equally obvious" (Jung, op. cit:52-3)—but it is not authentic to the reality of its history. Indeed, the presence of memory and the recollection of it are integral to thought, and are "permanently involved whenever we are engaged in thinking" (Gadamer 1996:146 [1986]). However conveniently we expunge how things really went for us—and all of us rewrite our own histories with some affect of Augustine and with the same desire to "convert" the past me into the new me of the present—we still must face the fact that who we are today is made up of the sum of our previous experiences as they were *when* they were, and not so much the whitewash that today's me wishes to paint over them. There is in fact another version of the heroic self that is closer to the "good faith" of becoming human in both an individuated manner and one that is immensely and intently social: "Characteristically, a protagonist passes from the secular, material, temporal world to a supernatural, timeless domain where that individual undergoes a unique experience, and then returns to the human community transformed by the event and—ideally—able to bring new knowledge to the human community" (Cruikshank 1990:177). It is still a person, and a self, which, even in mechanical societies, must undertake the temporary absence from the collective conscience in order to be his or her own undertaker. The previous life is now dead, and one must return to the life of the community by in fact becoming, for a moment an authentic self within the realm of the selfless and the mindless. The previous life was that of non-responsible childhood, which in social contract societies did not linger in the way it does for young persons today. To return to the human community transformed means shuffling off the coils not so much of mortality, but of the apparent immortality of being dependent on others for everything. The timelessness of childhood is echoed in the timeless character of the other world, but in the latter, the lack of history is a reality. It is this contrast that teaches the vision-seeker that what he or she had experienced as a youth was unreal, and the reality is, upon their return that they must take up the full and serious responsibility of mature being within the ambit of the collective. How different are our own cultural norms today? They have become polarized, certainly, in the figures of state and an individual who lives on as a person even after the extended and diffuse rites of passage end—the transition from student to worker is one such end, from single to "married" another, from the absence of one's own children to their presence still another—and they occupy a much greater length of life-phases than they did for our distant ancestors. But their *intent* is the same. We must, however daunting or perhaps only annoying as the prospect may be, take up the full and serious self-responsibility as part of something larger than ourselves. Increasingly this "larger" vista includes the entirety of humanity, which I think must count as the biggest difference between organic and mechanical societies.

There may be one other crucial difference, but it is one that today, in the world of prosthetic godhead, is easily passed over. This is the metaphysical difference between our maturity and that of our ancestors. For us, the body, mind, and "spirit" move together as a unity from inexperience to experience, from non-responsibility to social obligation. For the members of traditional cultures, it is only the soul that does so. To speak of vision and experience in these specific terms today renders us mute or at least moot, for "Here we speak of the problem of the body and soul. We are confident we know what the body is, but nobody knows what the soul is" (Gadamer 1996:96 [1990]). It is this sometimes misplaced or misapprehended confidence that allows us to speak highly of the heroic whole of being undergoing and undertaking the rites of maturity in our contemporary society. But the very absence of knowledge, or even discourse, about the "soul" et al renders this confidence a bit of a sham. Indeed, "both are so profoundly interrelated that every attempt to objectify either of them without the other in the end leads to absurdity" (ibid). It is fine for traditional mythic narrative to excerpt the soul from the body, because in fact this is what is occurring. The body dies. It is representative of the previous life, that of childhood and inexperience. The soul goes forth from the carcass of youth into the other world, receives some wisdom there, and comes back to a new version of the body that is waiting to be reintegrated with its spirit. This part of the dynamic allegorizes what *also* is actually occurring to the initiate upon returning from the alien wilderness of both nature and super-nature, to his or her village, to culture, in other words, armed with the now transformed knowledge of "super-culture." This term may have some overtones of Nuremberg, but it should be taken as simply designating the new knowledge that has been received from the world of spirits that has not yet been assimilated into the world of humans. Yet at the same time it is clearly a human being who both carries it and thus also is now in possession of it. This additional, "value-added" novel experience and the knowledge contained therein is super-cultural knowledge.

So there is no conflict in imagining that the soul by itself takes part in this journey towards super-culture. The body to which it returns with the novel vision it has had is indeed new. But our version of maturation has reduced the life force to the organicity of the body itself, which thus cannot die, either literally or figuratively, because it is itself the source of all life and thus all experience. It must mature by itself, and in so doing, it loses the very part of itself that actually does the maturing; that is, the spirit of the intellect and the subjectivity of its experiences. The implications of this shift in thinking are vast. They include, most importantly, the production of modern discourses about aspects of human being in the world that are forced together, almost as if in response to the forcible *disassociation* of body and soul. These coerced companions lead as well to absurdity, just as does the discourse separating living matter from its evolutionary gestalt: "For us, it is in the confession that truth and sex are joined, through the obligatory and exhaustive expression of an individual secret. But this time it is truth that serves as a medium for sex and its manifestations" (Foucault 1980:61 [1978]). The fact that sex and sexuality are not the same thing arises from this coercive union of truth and the acts of sexual beings, defined as having the master status of sexuality and not being. In fact we are beings who happen to have sex, more now so for reasons of pure pleasure and community making rather than for evolutionary reproduction or the need for labor power, as in the past. The "truth" of the matter has nothing to do with either the act or the discourse that envelops it, but rather the shift in mode of production and therefore reproduction as well as the shift in thinking about what one desires as an individual, which can now often be placed ahead of collective needs. But none of this enlightens us on the topic of body and soul, precisely because we have had to distract ourselves from this more salient question to unpack the problematic enclosure of other forms of living consciousness, modes of being or even routine activities such as sex from the truth of being, which in truth occupies all these realms and cannot be so displaced into just one of them. It is our own desire to escape the division of body and soul that leads to our overwhelming and overweening interest in sex, for it is one of the social contexts in which we imagine that body and soul are once again united in fact, as well as having the added bonus of feeling that we are doing the same thing with another who is experiencing the same thing as are we. Sex then lends itself to "the truth of things" because of this precise reason: we know that the body and soul are not separate entities and cannot be objectified in this way, so we flaunt all discourses of division by engaging in the most frequent coupling of sexual unions. The error we make is in talking about it so much, and it is thanks to Foucault that we at least are more aware of this issue.

But sex and its attendant sexuality—the former attempting to prove the truth of the indissoluble and the latter participating in the objectification of being—are hardly the only means by which we put pressure on ourselves to aggrandize the "I." And it is through the measuring tools of the instrumental and objectifying discourses that we attempt to categorize and divide not merely human beings from one another, but slice and dice up the individual human so that the general concernfulness that unites in our consciousness body and "soul" has to deal with a myriad of other more artificial distractions that fragment us along the cleavages of learned techniques: "At the present time in Western countries almost every individual is tested from the cradle to the grave, before and after the important events in his life" (Sorokin 1956:51). Since the "soul" cannot by itself be measured without measuring some aspect of corporeal being—the soul of intelligence is the closest measure we have and the foibles of all intelligence testing are well known—we test ourselves rather to isolate and then extinguish the presence of the soul: "We are wholly taken up by anger, completely shaken by fear. We are not angry or fearful in just one part of the soul" (Gadamer 1996:149 [1986]). We cannot take talk of the soul literally. Indeed, any ancient expression of the life of humanity must be understood as a metaphor for the very experience we have of ourselves and of the world. Yet the concepts of animus or psyche, the animatedness of being or the very "Being of beings" are direct predecessors to our own notions of consciousness and even mind. We seem to have no problem bandying these latter ideas around as if they contained no contradictions or yet mystical connotations. But clearly they are no better at encapsulating human experience than are those of our ancestors. They remain, in essence, metaphoric. The ears to which the ancient metaphors lent themselves to are also vastly different today, as Jung notes with some humor (1959:177 [1951]). Our own inventions—though based on ancient conceptions—sound better to us because they give the air of respectable objectivity. They seem to carry around little baggage from other now disdained discourses, no more so than those religious. Consciousness appears to be a value neutral term, as does mind. But we have seen that "intelligence," a concept intimately related to these other two, has fallen on hard times due to the reality of the relativity of forms of intelligence and what constitutes wit and wisdom across cultural contexts and for whom within these contexts. It may be true that from our perspective our ancestors were naïve to the reality of both cultural diversity and the material truths of evolution and genetics, but the cultural imagination they developed at once can appear more open-minded, at least regarding certain concerns and expressions of human experience that gave rise to the great mythological and religious systems and their attendant discourses: "We overlook the unfortunate facts that far greater demands are made on present-day man than were ever made on people living in the apostolic era; for them there was no difficulty at all in believing in the virgin birth of the hero and demigod" (ibid:176-7). Perhaps we are not giving the classical period enough credit here. Surely they were as aware of the metaphoric basis upon which human language communicates as are we. Perhaps they indeed were much more aware of it, given their work to interpret the pronouncements of the temples and of the prophets. None of these, taken literally, made much sense. It is more likely that such discourses as were given rise in the wake of such communications of the gods and the other world were as rationalized and routinized as are our own, following as these latter do on the revelations of cosmology, high-energy physics, and neuro-psychology to name a few instances. Not merely were ritual voices translated and made more widely known, the very sensibility regarding what conscious-ness meant in the world had to be continuously interested across varying traditions, many of which were beginning to encounter one another in the new cosmopolitanism of the Eastern Mediterranean in this period. Literal opposites were not to be taken too literally. The reality of the confluence of life and death was too present in ancient times to be ignored. Life expectan-cies on average were much shorter than today. Experience was accelerated, and injuries of even the slightest kind might be ultimately fatal. The making sense of this world corresponded in many ways to the manner we must make sense of our own. These two worlds are, on top of any analogous situation, still related in many profound ways, and this relation is not as one-way as it would appear to be at first glance. Aside from the material discoveries of advancing techniques in archaeology, there is the constant revisiting of our cultural histories in the light of new knowledge about ourselves. It is not accident that because we continue, for the time being, to be mortal beings facing a definite end—though in an indefinite way—that life and death are still of great interest to us. To live a good life while one can, would have been recognizable to many ancient credos, both those moralizing towards a "high-er" form and those purely Epicurean:

> This reminds us of the fact that the role of death and the corresponding under-standing of death within the Christian cultural horizon to which we belong is an extremely unusual and extraordinary one. The extraordinary role of death in this tradition still has an effect even today, when religious backgrounds are waning considerably in the modern world. (Gadamer 2001:60 [1999])

Because we can neither experience our own deaths nor take death as a con-ception with any literal and material referent—the "reality" of the world of death is a kind of contradiction in terms—this term retains all of its meta-phoric features that originally made it of such interest to our predecessors that their most important culture-hero myths had to do with its overcoming and assuaging, its delay and its opposition. With the control of fire some million years ago or so, according to recent paleoarchaeological reports, human life took on an extended meaning for the first time. More precisely, human consciousness became such that it was now able to imagine self-consciousness; a sense that one could live and live on to the morrow with a view to either self-improvement or the improvement of the quality of the life of the collective. Very probably it was both at once. Our ancient forebears now had the time, on average, to reflect on their condition, which had just so remarkably changed, and it was at this "instant" that death as a conception emerged from the dark foliage of a wider nature. We were, through con-trolled fire and many other bits and pieces of cultural evolution, gradually distancing ourselves from the other forms of life on our shared planet. The long-term implication of this at the level of the subject is self-consciousness and the experience of the world as an "I," and this history gives us another facet of understanding why this idea has such great import for us.

The "I" does not rest alone and aloof to the experience of itself, however. Our specific experiences run alongside the presence of our wills and desires. They often contradict one another, and at the very least, are not identical to one another. Thus intentionality as a project of consciousness travels along with personal experience, both of the ever-changing distance between intent and the outcomes of action in the world, and thence, and following from this in turn, the ever reinvigorated attempts on our parts to push intent and out-come closer together. We desire the world of others and even the anonymous world of nature to be more like ourselves, at least in reference to our goals. This was always the case, even though nature specifically was often feared and shunned as something that could not be won over to our wishes. In more traditional cultural contexts, the self-expression of individuated wills was also marginalized: "If 'we' was absent in their speech, then 'I' was even more controversial. Despite the individualism of their culture, self-praise was regarded as a serious fault." (Johanson 1990:137). In subsistence societies, where resource extraction required direct and daily "heroism" of a sort that belied its courage only because of the severity of its mundane setting, relying too much on the will of one would in the end court only disaster for the group. There had to be an ascendant sense of the intent of the singular will, which in these cases must be to ultimately attend to the welfare of the com-munity. Depending on how this was defined—and one of the great chal-lenges of our modern world is to redefine community so that it embraces a global constituency in the light of our shared need for survival—there did not have to be any conflict between the motives of the hero and those he labored for. The mythic allegory of the hero in fact could be play-acted on behalf of those that the hero worked for: "The low level of social interaction in the [logging] camps allowed for a 'pure' sociability where the self could be presented or expressed as a role acted" (ibid:141). Each of us today is torn between the social role expectations of maturity and citizenship and the sense that authenticity can only be found by eschewing social roles. But we can take a lesson from mechanical societies on this point. For them, "maturity" was the outcome of the heroic quest for a new vision of the self, but this outcome was only realized when that new self brought back its newfound knowledge to the community and began to participate as a full member of its covenant. So to be a mature being is also to be a mature role player in the society at hand. They are not in any necessary conflict, and it is our imagination that the "I" is eroded by playing any role the origin of which is not seen to lie in the self that is an error (cf. Neumann, op. cit:150). In this light, it is the obligation of the "I" to not only attend to its respective social role playing with all due seriousness, it is a mark of mature being that one can do so while remaining oneself. The key is to recognize the social not "in" oneself as if it were an interloper or an invader of some kind, rusticating against our will and partaking of the creativity and imagination of personality whilst giving nothing in return. The sociality of the "I" is what makes it function beyond its own imagination. To think otherwise is to participate in "uchronia," as defined above, to imagine the history of oneself not only differently than it occurred, but also to place that history outside of reality as if it had never "occurred" in the way regular events come and go. It is reified and idealized without remaining part of the dialectic of history. In this way it "recapitulates" the suprahuman idols of both the ancients and the moderns, when we as living beings think that our lives have reached some sort of climax, and it is only their mortal tenor that forces us to continue on after all purpose and meaning have been left in the past, the "glory days" of youth perhaps, or the novelty of this or that love relationship: "In almost every case, the uchronic turn is placed as to coincide with a peak in the narrator's personal life, with the moment where each played the most important role or was, at least, most actively involved as a participant" (Portelli 1990:151). Taking oneself out of the real context of ongoingness and outcome allows one to remain, ironically, in some idealized version of it. In this imaginary space, no results must be accounted for, no passage of time suffered through, no extension of the self in directions running away from the dreamed of goal need be pursued. The attempt at the preservation of the self in this static form actually destroys the self in its social reality of forms. Such conflicts that we are trying to avoid rest within us, and thus will only themselves be preserved by preserving the self in some unchanging space (cf. Midgely 2004:72, italics the text's). On top of all this, the attempt at self-preservation as an unchanging being has the ultimate goal of vanquishing the character of memory itself. It is ironic that memorialization and the building of monuments to commemorate significant historical events—or those seen to be so at various times in a culture's history, mostly of an official sort—freezes the event in time and thus defeats the sense that one can have a memory or experience of it. The difference between history and memory is sometimes couched in these kinds of terms. Memory is personal and experiential, subjective and about action in the moment. History is objective, discursive, and reflective upon itself over the course of intervening periods of time. The latter is built out of the former, of course, so that they are never unrelated to one another. It may be reasonable to practice this kind of rubric in terms of the narrative of cultures, but much less so when it comes to those of persons. For we, while alive, remain to experience anew all that we have "already" experienced in the past. We continue, in other words, to experience the experienced, while cultures only do so in the most abstract sense of the word. To divide ourselves by attempting personalized versions of the monuments that cultures erect to themselves is not only absurd in terms of its vanity, but also ultimately doomed to failure as a mnemonic, as a reminder that this was not only how it was, but also how it *is*.

Memory must rather be treated, like the soul, as part of a living being who lives on and experiences both the new and the old in a new way. Hermeneutic experience, the "negative" character of what is authentically new in our lives, rests upon the sense that our ability to recollect does not serve the purpose of either self-aggrandizement in the ways we have been discussing thus far, but also in the service of aggrandizing a mythical past self which no longer can, or should, exist: "Personal memory is a vital weapon against a myth they need to fight to keep the respect of both others and themselves" (Henkes 1990:236). As well, we cannot afford to pretend that our personal memory can simply take the place of a shared history or an objectifying discourse of historical analysis.[1] The experience of the subject needs as many other experiences coming from these others to rise to the occasion of combatting either myth in general—urban, political, ideological, or religious, alone or in combination with these other items listed, if necessary—or the inevitable loss of personal memory that accrues to all of us as we live on. We do not recall things the same way even if we once did share them intimately and powerfully. There is a politics of convenience that rests within our psyches as much as it is more apparent within the ambit of state-sponsored discourses. In confronting our own mortality, we have the tendency to fall back upon the sense that we have accomplished something or other in life. But in order for these accomplishments to resonate now that life has not only continued beyond the time in which they took place, but ever onwards toward death, their memorialization is at least understandable if vainglorious. We have become so enamored of the "I" that we are unwilling to attribute any of its distinctions to the memories of others. That we did not choose to be born does not mean we can forsake the choices involved in living. Once born, we shun the thrownness that is our own for the projectedness of the twice born. All auto-memory is an effort at holding the conversion experience to ourselves as if it could never be repeated, as if we can never fall in love again, for instance, or as if we can never think as well, perform as well, or be as good a friend to that which lies over the horizon of present-day consciousness. Cultures sometimes also have this problem, but it is individuals who embody it. If we reach out to the dying we do so because we too will die. This "extremity" is reflective of our own passions, yes, but also our own limitations. To depart in this way is to remind others of their own departure and not, ironically, to seal the victory of memorialization. It is rather to shed light on the most shadowy event given to human existence. If the mystery of birth is one that we share with all others—we live on in community of those who have also been born in the same way, coming out of non-consciousness and thus can share reflection upon this curious circumstance for as long as all of us live—it is the mystery of death that we must face alone and further face the possibility that no reflection on its "experience" will be afforded to us. To shine a light in this area is the purpose of dying in front of others, and is, allegorically, celebrated in all known mythological narratives: "The hero is always a light-bringer and emissary of the light" (Neumann, op. cit:160). Whether Raven or Prometheus, the culture-hero of myth is merely an emblem for each living person who must shine the fullest extent of their own light into the regions where consciousness begins to falter. We cannot accomplish this most important task if we are centered on the preservation of and the ululation about the "I." If it is deserving of praise, it earns those desserts by making courageous transit of the deserts of non-existence, by watching over the dying, by partaking in the memory that can be shared and not selfishly redrawn and possessed by the one, and ultimately, its own demise. This circuit can be run only by the heroic quality of placing what has been in the common archive of what needs to known in order to get on with the task at hand, and the challenges ahead. What is lit by the hero figure does not remain so lit. Light must be brought and brought again. Only the living soul of a self that is itself in community and alterity is worthy of meeting such profound demands.

1. 3 THEY ARE THEREFORE I AM

So far we have been painting a portrait of, without directly pointing at, a more or less sociological definition of what it means not merely to be a human being, but to be a mature being within the realm of the social world. This has import on at least two levels. The "epistemological" due to the problem of either the reciprocity of perspectives or their non-reciprocating situatedness, and the ethical, due to the challenge of understanding that other persons have no less right to exist than do I. The two levels are of course related. In order to understand the existence of the other—not necessarily how she sees the world, but how she is what she is in the world—we need to adopt a stance that is open to perspectives that are not our own; either those through which we became fully human in the first place, or those we have ourselves adopted as mature beings in order to fit into the world once we placed ourselves in it with a little more volition than we could as children. These other perspectives are, in today's world, increasingly impinging upon our own in any case, and it forces certain questions from us, different from those we have traditionally asked of ourselves: "Can it really be true that we bear responsibility for things that happen to people in countries so far away from us?" (Midgely 2004:8). Perhaps the second set of obligations is not as strange as the first, in certain contexts. Think of the money spent on pet food and care versus that spent for marginal persons even in our own developed countries. This is likely because we imagine the animals who live with us not merely to be our companions, a little dim-witted but loyal on the doggy side of things—dog owners value obedience and authority—and clever but disinterested on the catty side—cat owners value autonomy and laissez-faire— but also to be somehow human, if not exactly like us. Other animals that find their niche within the human realm, mostly vermin, are treated with either disregard or revulsion. But Midgely's general point is clear: we are not used to thinking beyond the scope of the day-to-day relations we have with other persons within a very narrow geographical confine. Even the exhortations of national politicians do not always work if the country is very large. Our notions of responsibility are difficult to extend. We simply are not convinced either of the humanity, common or uncommon, or of any specific value that distant others from exotic cultures might have. At best we might say, "well, they have their own to look after them, and we need to look after our own, at least first and foremost." At worst we might react like the Nazis. Yet even looking after "our own" has much ambiguity to it, and the uncertainty surrounding the question not only of responsibility but to whom one is responsible and for what reasons is a consistent fixture in our lives: "This implication would seem to be inescapable, but it remains disconcerting: what could be the responsibility, the quality or the virtue of responsibility, of a consistent discourse which claimed to show that no responsibility could ever be taken without equivocation and without contradiction?" (Derrida 1995:9 [1993]). The fact is that the definition of "our own" changes over time. The most common experience of this change is divorce, or its analogues, where one passes from a shared joy of intimacy and companionship to nothing at all, or at least, nothing that resembles what the relationship had been. Not only this, but as well, one is no longer one's own, in a sense, because the person we had been when we were with this once significant other has also dried up and disappeared. We might not even be able to recognize ourselves after the fact. The root cause of such radical personal change is, we imagine, that we had not been able to fully understand the beloved or betrothed before it was too late, and it was this misrecognition upon which we ultimately ran afoul. This is both plausible and reasonable, but it ignores a simpler explanation: people simply change over time. Generally we not only expect people to do so and are suspicious of those who seem to stagnate for years in one place or state of mind, so there is no apparent problem there with understanding the "other mind." At the same time, we are also told to be suspicious of not only the other mind and it's at first hidden intents but also to be cautious about first impressions in general. But where or what is the threshold when we get beyond first impressions? People are complex and this seems a patent reality. So is it a matter of time and familiarity? What sort of familiarity? Personals ads notoriously suggests that people want to be "friends first," that is, before they become lovers. But in fact friendship takes much more time than does love. Love, if socially sanctioned and desireful, always comes before friend-ship in short term relationships, and it is a heady challenge to transmute the passion of the lover into the compassion of the friend. Many of us find we cannot make the long-term adjustment, and hence we move on.

But as far as reading the mind of the other goes, we might think we might as well start believing in séances; communicating with the minds of the dead. Things are not so dire as this. It is true that our knowledge of both the subjective and objective states of others is often severely limited (cf. Midge-ly, op. cit:145). Midgely immediately reminds us, as Natanson had done already, that if we did not know anything at all about these others' states of mind we would also know nothing about our own. This second point is as at least equally true as the first. It can be better framed by understanding that the person who is like me but not me understands herself both similarly and differently from me. Yes, we need to use our imagination here, but not as much as we might think at first glance. While "Within the compass of com-mon sense, the self is both a presence in and a concealment from the world," it is also true that "The Other is not outside the acts of consciousness which present him as loving or fierce but the very content of those acts" (Natanson 1970:3). We "confront" one another, if the term is taken loosely and not narrowly, only in the sense that we must take into account one another's presence as well as absence. The presence defies the sense that I am the only perspective within reach, and the absence defies the idea that once I can grasp the perspective of the other then I have the whole story that can be at hand. Neither can be had without the other, but we must also keep in mind that the other finds herself in the same predicament as I do. In our modern individuated social world, there is often no other option to this, and hence the idea that each social encounter is also a kind of "confrontation." What has created this sense also can be examined, for in older models of social organ-ization—now confined to non-Western populations or their diasporas; though the word "confined" must be taken advisedly as this still represents the vast majority of humanity—the much vaunted selfhood of autonomy and free will was almost non-existent: "The individual was much more subservient to the needs of the family unit and community networks. In some ways, the old mode offered more protection and benefits while in others it locked people into more set, hierarchical relationships" (Ben Mayor 1990:173). The sacred fetish of modernity, the liberated individual who is free to do and think as she pleases remain more of an ideal than a reality, even if it is also much more real than at any other time in human history. We have emphasized in this chapter that the self is only itself in the presence of others and that there can be no "island" upon which a single inhabitant recapitulates the entirety of human affairs. In doing so, we have passed from self-admiration and aggrandizement along to questioning the importance of the "I" to trying to understand basic sociality. Not to belabor any of these points, one must also come to terms with the general reality that one not only does, after all, have responsibilities to others—of varying degrees and pending the taking stock of many intervening variables—and at the same time one can expect certain obligations to be performed by at least some of these others on one's own behalf. We are not, as some intransigent and exclamatory attempts at ethics might have it, solely responsible for the state of the world, either historically or at present. All of us are responsible and mutually obligated. Responsibility, if it has a "quality" or a "virtue," constructs itself as virtuous and meritorious precisely because it entails human community and a shared ethic. No individual performs it alone. "Nor can an isolated individual perform any social 'role,' or 'social action.' Without a drama there can be no 'role,' or 'social action,' for a social role or a social action is possible only in the context of all the roles or actions of the play" (Sorokin 1939:46 in Sorokin 1956:214). This is so self-evident that we might not take its import as seriously as we must. Indeed, its sentiment, both rational and experiential, goes beyond the ken of selves and others to self as they are presented to one another on the public or private stages of social life. It also has an equally important facet that turns inward from these stages to pierce the veils that we place over ourselves when we do begin our social role performances and take "action" as agents in the world of norms. The individual is not isolated from the other, but he is also not performing this or that role or version of selfhood in isolation from the other aspect of human consciousness itself. The unconscious life is also always with us, and though it might be imagined to be less immensely social than agency defined in a dramaturgical manner, it is almost always more *intense*, and thus a more certain source of confrontation in the narrow sense than are routine role performances. Not that these two tandems are not analogous. Pleasure is almost always self-pleasure, though its general "onanistic" form is of course not at all limited to the sexual or even the sensual. Reality can be equated with social sanction and normativity, which in laboring societies tends to act against excessive introspective pleasure.

The fact that it also tends to limit self-examination in intellectual and ethical ways is often forgotten. Indeed, the limitation of pleasure in modern life would seem to act as a distraction itself, while pretending to distract us from joy or escapism, it actually distracts us from thought because we are too busy trying to make up the lost leisure and pleasure time. *We cannot dismiss the loss of thought as somehow secondary to that of joy* (cf. Midgely op. cit:68 for another take on substitutions of this kind). As well, we also cannot forget that individuals are only equal in the ambit of a species wide principle and never in reality: "The individuals happen to be not only rational but also nonrational and irrational, as human beings are; if they do not have equal access to information; if they do not always conform to accepted standards of conduct" (Sorokin 1956:134-5), etc. It is this inequality in practice that makes the other absent from us and also creates enough distances within ourselves for us to not feel "equal to" every social situation we may find ourselves in. The theory of universal human equality in fact bears no resemblance to specific human realties and any attempt to increase their identity relation ends in mass disaster or at best individuated murder. What we can do is seek universal human equity without the expectation of a *sensus communis*.

Since each of us takes some pride in constructing and then maintaining an identity that we call "our own," taking care of our own begins here. We, however, cannot be an end in ourselves, just as, somewhat paradoxically, we cannot not treat others as if they were not ultimately their own ends. In other words, to treat others only as means in the service of one's own aspirations is generally seen as highly unethical, though hardly unthinkable. This is manifestly not an epistemological question though it does touch on the reciprocity of perspectives or its absence, as well as the phenomenologically inclined social distribution of knowledge. Yet to treat others as their own ends without regard for the self is equally reprehensible, and so the sense that we revise the world famous and world historical Cartesian formula in some radically Levinasian manner is also out of the question. There must be both dialogue and dialectic in each human relationship. The first centers on the other as a means of self-understanding, the second recognizes in the self that we may resist a complete integration to another's desires and do so ethically. The dialectical aspect of any conversation contains a necessary critique: "What does the self-maintaining of the ego mean? Does the ego that vouches for itself in self-consciousness even exist? What is the source of the continuity of self-sameness?" (Gadamer 1996:11 [1972]). It seems awkward, even perhaps grotesque, to insert the predicating voice of the "I" somehow "inside" the consciousness that it has of itself. Even so, it is clear that our self-conception must include the construction of an identity to which we answer, and thus also answer for. Once again, the first states our position in the world; we take our place as a source of perspective, local, yet historical and also experienced. The second is a statement about us in that self-same world; that we have responsibility for our actions and thus *take* responsibility for them—we answer *for* ourselves as a unique ethical agent in the world. Indeed, we resent others impinging upon this self-responsibility, even if it sometimes seems like we enjoy pawning our work off on these others. This jealousy extends both inward and outward. Inward to the sense that I know myself better than anyone else can know me, and outward toward the sense that how I live and how I have lived is also somehow "mine". Yet the person is never alone in this exact way. There is nothing "primordial" about being a person, for it entails not only having a personality—something that has no meaning without others as it takes its place in the world of others and *identifies* us—nor is there anything original to a self that seeks to be recognized for what it is and what it is uniquely and "alone" in the midst of others. One establishes oneself in the presence of others. Their "full presence" is defined here not so much phenomenologically but only in so far as their absence does not sabotage the self's attempts at establishing itself as a force or "power." In the context of the reduction, the bracketing of the hyletic world is accomplished by imagining that we have these "originary" statuses, that the language of what is ontologically myself is a kind of auto-Ursprach, and that my experiences, unshared by others in the ultimate sense, recalled to mind only through the oddly miraculous act and fact of memory, are what forms the object about which social role and cultural identities orbit. This vision could only be one that emanated from a rapidly individuating society (cf. Heidegger 1999:70 [1988] for sentimental examples of how this occurs in the everyday). Nonetheless, the sense that at the heart of every subjectivity there rests an essential object that remains unassailed by the others and even by the generalized Other suggests that it itself is a kind of Other, uncanny and in league with the most occluded parts of the unconscious life. The "miracle" of memory springs from it but does not erode its competencies. The content of memory is of course immediately and immanently subject to the erosion of ongoingness, auto-history and the process and context of recollection. We may calculate a recollection in order to evidence an important point in a social tussle, or we may spontaneously and with some wonder recall something that we had not thought of in decades, simply because a friend has willingly divulged a secret to us: "In one sense we compose or *construct* our memories. From the moment we experience an event we use the meanings of our culture to make sense of it. Over time we *re*-member our experiences, as those public meanings change" (Thomson 1990:78, italics the text's). We also *dis*-member them, sometimes at will, without regard for either the going rate of public *exchange*, or the fact that times have moved on and we for this or that reason refuse to do the same. Memory is at first a tool for identity maintenance, but following closely behind this, a mask to distract others from gaining a too intimate portrait of that very identity. It is the prime source of the absence of the other in any social encounter, simply because we have not lived every moment with them and would not desire to do so. That "things happen" one way or another is, of course, inevitable. We may even lack the capabilities to accurately process experience in the first place, as when we are confronted by something that comes across as "uncanny" in some way. We might well ask of ourselves, "what was that?" in the same way another might ask of herself, "who was that?." Neumann refers to child psychology as "transpersonal" for this very reason: "What makes the real psychology of childhood so extraordinarily difficult to describe is the fact that there is no developed ego-complex capable of gaining experience, or at least of remembering its experience" (op. cit:330). Myth dwells at the epicenter of imagination and projection. The first is subjective in the sense that it frames what could have happened and that I am always at least a co-author of the potential. The second is more objective because it embodies shared experience that *becomes* cultural through its transposition into a narrative that all can recognize part of themselves within. The child, we are told, cannot fully distinguish reality and fantasy, and no doubt the media romances children and older persons as well are bombarded with does little to aid in the formation of nascent distinctions of this sort. But cultural narrative, whether of the allegorical and phantasmagorical variety or the more staid discourses of child psychology, for instance, underscore the fact that to become fully social is to fully embrace, not necessarily the homiletic of the story, but the fact that it is our own and that others feel the same way about it.

It is this assumption that drives the recreation of social reality on a daily basis: "There is a circle, then, in any attempt to analyze sociality: We are before I am" (Natanson, op. cit:47). And this "We" which is unlike the pure we of a strict phenomenological analysis continues to be placed before the "I" that is nonetheless so highly regarded, as we saw in the above. Perhaps this is yet another configuration of the social scene that seems to betray "us," as "I's" and not as group members. Discourse too, arising in its recognizably contemporary fashion only in the eighteenth century, has circumlocuted the "I," circumnavigated the self by coming up with the concept of the "subject." The subject is, somewhat ironically, to be considered more objective than are the other two ideas, even though in casual parlance we often substitute one for another at will. This subject that *we* are handicaps attempts at placing the self that *I* am in the center of things. It is more serious; it takes the form of an empiricity in the historical record and of an empirical object in the laboratory of the human sciences. It has a perceptual location and point of view that must be considered scientifically, at least since the late nineteenth century in physics and thence beyond. On top of all this, which is more a catalogue of results than a microcosmogonical analysis of sources, we are at once told that the subject is important and yet that we should also strive to avoid being the subject overmuch, lest the shared meaning of an objectifying discourse come to grief. Finally, and perhaps following from the confluence of all of these, the subject is not the source of self-understanding but what stands in the way of it: "From this interplay there has evolved, over several centuries, a knowledge of the subject; a knowledge not so much of his form, but of that which divides him, determines him perhaps, but above all causes him to be ignorant of himself" (Foucault, op. cit:70). This ignorance, "caused" in the sense that it is seen as an effect of other variables which combine to construct the concept of the subject and thence his subjectivity etc., is also causal and also produces effects of its own. One of these is surely the idea that we can be true to ourselves and yet piously loyal to certain structural variables, ethnicity, gender, creed or nation, and furthermore, that such variables as there may be that have come together to construct us as a self find themselves an authentic home in our subjectivity, which, once again, attains a curious objectivity only because we forsake the self for the subject so created. But modern social groups that have as their hallmarks large-scale life-chance variables of the kind just listed do not produce either selves or persons, let alone individuals, "true" or no, because they are simply just too large and amorphous to reach into identity at the level necessary for one's "subjectivity" to be one's own (cf. Neumann, op. cit:422). The "group," by contrast, is relatively permanent. Indeed, it can easily be taken for a fixture in the life of the person, and the selves which grow up in it and then continue to function in its service in a variety of forms and roles do so precisely because they are recognized to be part of its functioning, and not some additional statistic to a massive coagulation of citizens or protesters, music or sports fans, or television viewers or those who have been polled for politics or for the market. Here, the individual is adumbrated geometrically without regard for her person or set of selves she might otherwise occupy. One might strain the original sociological definition and suggest that "television viewer" is in fact a social role, but once again the very transience of the activity and the fact that it cannot be recognized as functioning in any other way than in its direct behavior vis-à-vis a contraption of purpose that serves not a group as a whole, but specific economic interests of a very few, continues to suggest otherwise. In a group, for example, individuals work to further shared goals that are usually decided upon within the bounds of persons with whom one has at least a passing acquaintance. A workplace might be a group of this sort, though a recent one, but a church is a more traditional example. The "intelligibility" of decisions that come to be made is something that the persons involved in the process can, and indeed, usually, must, agree upon. Not ahead of time, of course, but after the dust has settled. Yet this is also how discourse, including the apparently risky discourse of the "knowledge of the subject," as well as for that matter, the conceptions surrounding the perhaps equally risky "subjective knowledge," is also supposed to function in the same way: "The individual thinkers and their teachers refer to one another, 'surpass,' criticize, and struggle with one another, in such a way that the dialogue of the tradition is ordered by a logically intelligible context" (Gadamer 2001:104 [1999]). This describes a very formal "scholarly" or even academic kind of process, but it must reach, not so much a consensus about its results or its theories, but consensus on how to carry on its dialogue and thus carry on with a tradition that is both living and lived. Yet such a description applies equally well to everyday life, if we generalize its language just a little to include the mutually imbricated ideas of agreement and action. Regular social groups have to be more pragmatic than cultural elites, for a host of reasons, many of which are quite transparent. Elites tend to be served by the rest of us, and indeed, the "rest of us" sometimes includes a person such as myself, but often as not, it does not. Most of us, however vaunted our status position is relative to much larger numbers of working people who themselves might be said to be a "group," though a much alienated one, alternate or even float between the social roles of servant and served. If I am writing, for instance, I am both at once, for generally a book, no matter how erudite or perhaps pedantic, is intended as a public service. But in my role as a pedagogue, I am much more directly in touch with the public service, or I try to be, because that exchange is one of pure education, usually of younger persons, and is said to be the chief reason why I can claim a public salary. But if I write an obscure tome on a topic with little practical relevance to the world, I am much less of a servant of anyone except for possibly myself. These kinds of decisions run the gamut of "intelligibility" and may or may not have their own internal "logic." Pragmatism as a theory of practice has both, but as a philosophical disquisition it questions both. As a casual gloss for utility or practicality, it has little meaning whatsoever, and as a way of seeing the world, it might tend to the disinterested or even the dispassionate, calling into question the ethics of itself as, say, a philosophical undertaking. Generally, we know that persons in most walks of life do not make decisions that are kindred to small elite groups of thinkers and such-like, simply because regular people know that they will have to live with the outcomes of their decisions. This may seem to be a source of intense anxiety—the knowledge that one could make a mistake and then have to pay for it in a myriad of ways for an indefinite amount of time. But this is not how it works, after all: "The most harrowing choice in daily life, one which calls truly for individual decision, is made *within* the framework of an ongoing, intersubjectively valid world." (Natanson, op. cit:14, italics the text's). One may have to step *back* from the run of the mill to both get a sense of what any particular decision may be about and how it may effect things, but one never steps completely *outside* of any context. One is involved and remains involved, and perhaps more so at the time of decisions, routine or extraordinary, and the difference between being and remaining is simply the difference between feeling like you are, for the time being, at or near the center of things, and at some point in the not too distant future, you won't be. Even dictators run their course. The act of stepping away from a context announces the intent to make some sort of evaluation of it, and of oneself. It is an act of the self and not the subject. It recognizes that I am because they are, and that the "I" of fantasy and aggrandizement pales beside the I who must make a decision affecting the life of the group and thus also my own life. We humans are far from "total" beings, but as a species, and more specifically, in groups, we live as if everything is present. If it is not present immediately to us and us alone, then this is the way the world presents its own presence to us; making ourselves our own common denominator and then calling upon us to distinction.

Chapter Two

The Machine Messiah

Nevertheless, there is a lingering discomfort regarding our position in both the group as well as the world. The anomie of modernity produces an unease. The anonymity of our times generates anomie, subjective alienation, and this in turn has a tendency to make us imagine that we are not where we would ideally be. Not who we would rather be. Not our best self. We seek succor in the normative, for we know that while we might feel that a massive anonymity provokes *Ungeheuer* it also can soothe it on two fronts: one, that all others feel the same way so that we can suffer together, though mostly in silence, and two, that we can hide our feelings of existential homelessness in the midst of a throng that appears to be a community, appears to be in fact together in an authentic rather than merely an empirical manner. Riesman's "lonely crowd" contains of course the classic understanding of this phenomenon. "Other directedness" replaces "inner directedness" as the original concept of vocation moves out of its "monastic cells" and into the world of material forms, as Weber famously reported. To be part of an anonymous mass does not absolve us from "keeping up" with things; newsworthy events, the sporting life, commodities and their fashion, mores according to self-appointed sages, official state political lines and tones, and even the weather. To lose one's hold on these items, almost all of them trivial and/or mundane, is to feel oneself slipping back into the real absence of easy camaraderie, the anomie from which I sought to escape. Since we do not truly know many of the "rest of us," the vector by which we evaluate our place in society is by looking around; that is, seeing what others do and not hearing how they think. We take the actions of others as, if not a true expression of self and personhood, a reasonable facsimile of their desires. They are, as we are, a simulacrum of a self. It is this appearance, this imagery, which unites us in

83

the face of the radical absence of community or sometimes even functioning group.

In this chapter we will explore one of the main modes of other-directedness that has only been indirectly linked with anomie, and that is the technique and technology of the modern machine, both as a metaphor for mechanism in semi-conscious working states of affairs—the public life of our large and general social role as "one of the others" and one of the mass, producer and consumer—but also the machine as a physical enabler, a force in the material world wherein it alleviates suffering with a view to assuaging anomie. The machine houses and promotes a new set of norms. It is never normless, although often mindless. It cannot suffer itself. It does not feel the wind chill, and though it breaks down it does not die. It represents, in its obliviousness to sorrow and to ennui, an ideal form for modern humanity. We would be as it is. Functional, able to work and nothing else, turned on and off in an instant. No degrees of emotions, only degrees of power and output. The machine as a workhorse does not so much replace the human being but exhorts him to become as it already is. It is simply easier in every way to move through a dispassionate life ignoring the passions that have created us. Machines are at once a projection of our ingenuity and a reflection of our disingenuousness. They provide us with a soulless solace. No energy need be spent in self-examination. A diagnostic mode is all that is ever required; the checking of parts and functions, with form only being questioned according to external necessities like changes in commodity production or marketing. And even though we are rapidly approaching an event horizon passed which there can be no returning, the construction of the "thinking machine," or perhaps better, a machine that actually "is" something in a consciously ontological sense, the mindlessness of the current machine is not the machine's alone. Finally, a short critique puts out the fire of ardor that we have manufactured as an insulated gallery within which the machine might be shown and adored. Marx famously reminded us that "the more we put into god the less we put into ourselves," but surely that is now somewhat outdated. What "more" does exist supplicates the machine and in its turn, it messianically proselytizes the false hope that human beings can overcome their very humanity.

2.1 SOULLESS SOLACE

Yet the machine itself is also none of these things. It is neither friend nor foe, hero or villain. It is an object in the realm of objects, and only begins its dizzying ascent as the paragon of modern life when it becomes a surrogate worker. It works itself out, as it were, and then it is cast off, its castings perhaps salvaged for another of its class or a new generation of successors that will be even better at the tasks given to their forebears. Machines also "evolve," but they do so through the cultural selection driven by the social world. The reason the machine can never quite be "itself" alone is that it only functions within that world, and that world, as yet, is one of humanity and not the machine as a stand alone form of being or type of consciousness. No, the machine by itself is useless, but this fact absolves it of any crime. The "satanic mills" are human places that dehumanize, and their contents are merely an expression of a suite of human sensibilities—greed and lust, certainly, but also curiosity and a drive to overcome previous limits—and thus resemble in no direct way the manner in which the machine works itself out on our behalf. The real source of the "tremendous order of mechanized petrification" lies in us. It is we who design the blueprints from which machines are then built. It is we who reap both their benefits and are impacted by their negative effects. It is we who defend ourselves and offend others through the prosthetics of advanced weaponry, and it is we who cannot survive the ultimate ends of machines. By the mid-eighteenth century in certain specific regions, we noted with chagrin that we were being turned into machines, and it is not too much to say that we wanted company as well as a role model. In order to have both, we also realized that our new companions, without character and personality—but this is, after all, what we also were fast becoming—still had to be cared for. The machine must be kept "healthy," as is the worker, in the same sense that we hear, every flu season, about how many person-hours are lost to the workplace by inattention to inoculations, poor hygiene and the like. This is an example of "neo-Nazism" even as it pretends to be about concernful being on the part of the state or the employer. No healthy person enjoys being sick, but the choice between illness and work is not always decided in favor of the latter. The companionate model of the machine—it is good to "have around," it performs without rancor, one does not have to "pay" it in any direct way, and it only produces things and does not consumes them (although of course it consumes energies and other resources)—makes room as well for itself as a model of behavior. Machines are the ideal workers. They cannot be unionized and it is always we who decide on their longevity and upkeep. The group of people fashioned to care for machines and related technologies are the technicians. In many circles today this word has about the same degree of negative connotations as does "bureaucrat" or "politician." Technicians are seen to be kindred to the machines they construct and take care of. They are the human version of the machine, the most mechanistic, and hence "soulless" of humans. They are almost perceived as a hybrid. They are subject to the harshest of blandishments, and they are typecast as villains in many quarters. But are we not all technicians in an age of machinery and technology? How is anyone exempt from both interaction with, and thus at least a modicum of care for, the technology of everyday life? We live in a mechanized culture through and through, and our nature today is to include machines as part of the character of what it means to be human. Given that machines can liberate us to consider other options, what is the nature of the technician's offense? "The behavioral scientist who has elaborated techniques of conditioning in his laboratory brings these forward as the basis of his claim that freedom is an illusion" (Barrett 1979:xiv). In a sense, the claim that we respond as does any other animal to inputs by exhibiting certain outputs and that these can be predicted according to the kind of sensory inputs provided is saying no more than we are animals who can learn and adapt to new situations. Freedom of a sort is built in to such a scenario. If we were not free in this adaptational sense we could not respond to new inputs and learn how to "behave" in new contexts. But this is precisely what humans *are* able to do. The inputs of general learned behavior are culled from socialization or acculturation. In so far as behaviorism, even with all of the baggage of reduction, claims that human beings learn and respond to new adaptational contexts, or better, construct out of the bare sensory inputs of what is new or altered, an adaptational and hence a cultural context, then they have claimed nothing but a support for the idea of human freedom. Yet in spite of this, it is always the reductive facet of behavioral science that is targeted. In order to understand why this is, we need to cast a glance back to what we imagine our natures as humans to in fact be: "The theoretical attitude, and the science and practice in which it is elaborated, must be seen as a new, unnatural species of life." (Lingis 1989:20). Why on earth not? One might well argue the very opposite: that science represents the epitome of human nature. It is methodical, driven by both evolutionary and adaptational necessity as well as curiosity, and it seeks to respond to the pressing existential questions of a finite consciousness. Nothing about our lives is purely of "nature" anyway, so the idea of the "unnatural" seems to be a non sequitur. Now we are aware, of course, that the products of science do not always serve our best interests as a species, and any tool can be placed in the hands of the self-serving. But this is neither a characteristic of science or an effect emanating from it. It is also part of "human nature" to become, or have the potential to become, quite self-absorbed, as we saw in detail in chapter one. Science is merely another avenue by which one can walk the path to nothing if one chooses to do so. But it is this very ability to *choose* that once again underscores the ongoing and uninterrupted presence of human freedom.

So far, in two forms of the critique of technique, we have come up against quite reasonable objections to the deadpan idea that science, scientists, and the technologies and skills they produce and enhance, are somehow in league with either a kind of genteel barbarism or further, the devil of unfreedom. Of course, hubris, also a characteristic part of human consciousness in most cultures, might get the better of us and our "prosthetic godhead" might begin to indulge itself in the grandiose: "He prides himself on what he believes to be his self-control and the omnipotence of his will, and despises the man who lets himself be outwitted by mere nature" (Jung 1959:26 [1951]). Certainly culture and technology, language and symbolism set us apart in a radical way from the nature that we had in the past shared with all other known creatures. Indeed, it is old hat to claim that the combination of all of these wonderfully human traits can make us arrogant to the point of blindness. But once again, there is a contradiction of terms here. Whoever has an omnipotent will never need to exercise self-control. He can have anything he wishes. He also, because of his very omnipotence, never has to bear any consequences for the fulfillment of his desires. This may be a fantasy of the super-rich in today's world, and perhaps some of these persons approach a kind of finite reality that exhibits this culmination of human passion and lack of conscience. But precisely here is where the logic of the criticism of hubris breaks down. In fact, humans are not possessed of an omnipotent will. We have a voracious imagination, no doubt, but not only is the flesh ultimately weak, so is the will. And, when all is said and done, we are all defeated by "mere" nature, because it is a fundamental part of our nature to die. "The most toys" may be an advertisement for human arrogance, but even those who collect and flaunt such ensembles and accoutrements does so with the knowledge that this is but a passing fancy. Indeed, one might suggest that it is the very knowledge of our limits that drives the desire to show off in this way.

Not to be blithe, but there must be more to the argument that technique, technician, and even prideful arrogance are fatal to the idea of human free-dom. It must have more to do with certain combinations of these attitudes. The sense that we might adore or fetishize a machine is not even enough, because we generally are attracted to whatever eases our suffering either individual or collective, and in our society, especially the former. So what is so wrong with a little genuflection directed at the soulless object that per-forms and outperforms our abilities? Surely it does not stop there, say the critics, and perhaps in some very specific, but important cases, they may be correct. One setting where adoration may supersede itself and bend our intel-ligence to the path of nihilism is when we imagine our science to be better suited to human needs in general than the sciences or the forebears of sci-ence, were for our ancestors. This is a different order of fetish than simply praising the ease and programmed skills of technologies: "The reality is that the object of his science, and his efforts to deal with it in his cults and rituals were just as successful in controlling and manipulating the inner forces of the unconscious as are modern man's efforts to control and manipulate the forces of the physical world" (Neumann 1970:210 [1949]). Now this is a little more interesting. It not only suggests that our cultural predecessors knew what they were doing in some way—this alone is sometimes offensive to contem-porary attitudes about the past and about past cultures; much of our media and humor, and even the manner in which history is taught concentrates on

the perceived lack of ability or even the outright ignorance of our ancestors—but that it is we who have inverted the focus and object of our attentions from the internal to the external. Does this mean that we now, or at
some point more or less recent in time, have mastered the inner world? Can
all of our efforts now, finally, be directed towards cosmic mastery? I doubt it.
The prevalence of neuroses, addictions, depression and anomie in our contemporary social world argues strenuously against such a simple determination. New modes of life demand new skill sets. But these self-same modes
also create new problems and wrinkles in our "nature." *There is no one
human nature.* But it is true to say that modern science is "outer-directed." It
is the discourse that fills in Riesman's tabulation of human perceptual attitudes. If the vocational Protestant was "inner-directed"—in this he does not
depart from his ancient forefathers in terms of the intent of his ritual, all he
has done is further personalize it in a process that we saw begins at least with
Augustine in the Christian West—and his contemporary compatriot is "other-directed" in a manner that creates the mass, "one-dimensional" man, then
there must also be present that which is outer-directed and thus also that
which is self-directed. We saw a great deal of evidence apportioning the
space of discourse of the latter, but here we can concentrate on the discourse
that occupies the space of the former, that of "outer-direction." How does it
work? Is it all of what is external that comes into its focus? "It would appear
to me more correct, however, to say that science makes possible knowledge
directed to the power of making, a knowing mastery of nature. This is technology. And this is precisely what practice is not" (Gadamer 1996:6 [1972]).
Succinctly put, science allows for the projection of practice. It thus creates
not only a new *mode of* being in the world, that of the practitioner or technician, but also a new *model for* being in the world. It is technique that occupies the space of the second form. The first, as an existential qualifier, provides the sense that our wills can fashion more than those of our ancestors.
There is certainly a new potency to this sensibility, though it is obviously far
from "omnipotent." Yet this new aspect of our self-understanding does give
rise to the imaginary sensibility that we might, over the course of further ages
of similar development, approach a real kind of physical and indefinite godhead. We would become, in other words, our own prosthesis and have shed
the mortal consciousness that originally created it. Instead of constructing
ourselves through sometimes painful and painstaking socialization and the
learning of techniques, we will have created ourselves, not as did the gods,
but using the model of their "behavior" as a guide. At that hypothetical point,
the technique and the technology merge and become indistinguishable. "Human nature," as we have known it, is automatically moribund and presumably would soon be forgotten. This is an empirically documentable dream
even today, though as one would expect, those who pursue this kind of goal
are already highly privileged in our very much still mortal and unequal

world. Today, we are almost always still in the position of clarifying the relation of technology to technique and vice-versa, and the question of creation is moot. Yet the idea that this must be the case, or if not couched in moral terms, will more practically always be the case, is not supported by the logic of the position. Just because something is the case today and for the foreseeable future does not mean it will always be so. Not long ago, the idea of a heart transplant was considered an unattainable fantasy by most. Today we scoff, but are still intrigued, by the news of a potential head transplant. Creativity in the sense used by Barrett was no doubt a major part of the process through which past scientific and artistic achievements, especially radically original and untried ones came to be. The whole of human history, including our proto-human progenitors, is based on this process. Creativity and freedom are inextricably linked, and it seems that once again, science and its techniques, methods, and even its products, are much more of an aid in this fundamentally human quest and vision than they are a limitation upon it.

Even so, we also experience novel limits that seem to impinge upon our abilities to not only "feel free," but to in reality be free of practical or mundane concerns. By "mundane" I do not mean that we should ever consider ourselves unfree simply because we have to maintain basic hygiene, cook and eat sustenance, or monitor the state of our dwellings and our relationships alike. All these too, as Heraclitus reminded us at the beginning of Western thought, are intimately part of human consciousness and thus also human freedom. These "gods" do not limit themselves in their presence, and thus they continue to provide a model for human behavior in the world at large that speaks both directly of and to freedom in that world. Doing work in that world implies freedom and creativity, and may indeed, depending on the task at hand, require both. And all tasks require of us some skill and knowledge even if these are now to be considered routine. We have always to recall that we, sometimes as much younger persons, were once without the possession of this or that stock of knowledge at hand. Its "at-handedness" was the province, and thus also the privilege, of others than myself. I had to learn it, but in doing so, I also learned that everyone had to do the same as I did. Learning in the specific sense does more than imply that in the general; learning means being part of a process that is both specific and general at once. Reading a book means learning about the object of the book, but it is also a course in literacy. Acquiring experience of a skill means at the same time becoming more skilled. This may seem trite. It is actually the more profound part of education in all of its senses. Can the same be said of feeling freedom or unfreedom? I think it can. But here we must investigate more fully before being able to lend credit to this more puzzling and seemingly subjective phenomenon. It is also a much more recent event in historical consciousness that persons should feel an unfettered desire of any kind. This,

I think, is also the result of a burgeoning and gradually evolving technology and the methods and techniques that lie behind it and also maintain it. It is, in a word, the very technique of civilization as we know it today that prompts the will to believe in an ultimate human freedom, and not the other way round, where this apparatus works to extinguish such desires.

But if this is correct, what of the problem of technology that distracts us from thinking in general, pretends to do our learning for us, makes everything "too easy" and constructs fantasy worlds where nothing of real import can ever occur? What of the fetish of information for its own sake? What of knowledge framed only in a "need to know" basis? (cf. Midgely 2004:15). But would any information even *exist* if it did not, from the first, have at least some passing relevance to people's current beliefs and attitudes? The "value-freedom" of information, let alone knowledge or practice, lies in being historically conscious about those every attitudes, needs, beliefs and gaps that already *do* exist and hence call out for adjustment in some way. Information, and certainly not knowledge, cannot be thought of as stand-alone objects that can be "brought into play" or applied to an existing system within which there was an absence that somehow was made to suit such an application. If this were the case, such gaps would not exist and would have been filled, if even seen as gaps, during the original construction of any system, technological or symbolic. Each system of signs is self-sufficient from the start. Alteration must be pressed from the outside in, and for that to occur one must already presume competing systems of thought and action that see the world just a little differently than each other. To understand this dynamic otherwise does not seem to make historical sense. At the same time, it is clearly more correct to suggest that information that is left to gather dust on a shelf somewhere is more or less useless, or at least, becomes so. The dust it gathers is the sign of its absence of value. But this is a gradual affair, things or techniques, pieces of technology or even symbolic ideas—the idea of God is the most famous example that modernists are apt to cite in this context—become moribund and once again gradually are completely forgotten. Why would not something like human nature also be one of these ideas in the future? Ideas maintain their relevance, and hence their value in human affairs by in part their "fulfillment of needs" but also in part by a culture's collective loyalty to itself; that is, the way in which it "worships itself," to borrow Durkheim's famous phrase. One might claim that there is at heart a function to this as well, but if so, it must be of the most radiant and abstract type. "Society worshipping itself" occurs in more than the religious sphere, and though Durkheim was speaking most directly about social contract societies, his contemporary analogies of the collective conscience also sparked great interest during his own time. In point of fact, wherever there is taken public notice that there is a society to be worshipped, the adoration, supplication, and perhaps even sacrifice to it have already taken place. Memorial celebrations concerning historical conflicts are a case study in this phenomenon. However much state propaganda is involved, one is ultimately drawn to the idea that what we are as a group, and hence, by an easy extension, what one is as a person, hinges on our willingness to defend the forms and norms of what we take to be "our own." This is related, of course, to our previous discussion, but it takes it in a slightly different direction. What we believe we possess also possesses us, and it is this difference that provides both the notion of what kind of things are of value to us and when we should put these value-laden items into play in any cultural system.

It is also at this moment that we realize the difference between technology and technique. We can learn techniques and thus construct technologies from them, but for the most part, once constructed and programmed, the technologies newly present cannot of their own accord, learn new techniques let alone assign new meanings to them. Indeed, "meaningfulness" is still an affair solely of human consciousness. We may well be on the cusp of seeing a sea-change regarding this absence of value-addedness, but generally we are still in the position outlined by Sorokin some sixty years ago:

> As a matter of fact, the total operations of any machine are devoid of meaning whether it is scientific, or religious, or aesthetic, or even "absurd meaning." The machine's operations are just certain 'motions' of its various parts, prearranged and determined by human beings. These motions have meaning only insofar as it is imputed to them by man. (Sorokin 1956:204)

Yet does this last point not in part obviate those previous? Machines do help humans make meaningful statements about the universe, though not of their own volition. At this time in human history the machine is the preeminent way in which we do make meaning. And there is more to it even that this. Machines can become part of us in at least two other ways: on the one hand, prosthetic devices allow humans to lead more meaningful, that is, more diverse and hence richer, lives. More meanings are constructed the more experiences one has. Machines and kindred objects allow more humans to do just this, and more of it in our day than in any other. On the other hand, some interactions between machines and persons take on meta-prosthetic dynamic. This extension of the subject through the object calls to mind Marx's sense of the transformation of commodity relations in ideal communism, where, instead of a subjection to the object, we have rather a fulfillment of a person's abilities by the tailored use of machines and objects. There are many famous cases of this even in capital. Lance Armstrong without his bicycle, or Eddie Van Halen without his guitar appear to us as somehow incomplete. This is no mere prosthetic, but an extension of a highly focused and practiced mastery of the subject into the world by virtue of an object that is no longer solely a machine. These kinds of specialized objects and their human possessors have created a category of machine that is a much fuller participant in the making of meaningful experience. In capital, such a phenomenon is severely limited in a way that Marx claimed it would not be in hypothetical communism, but it is still widespread enough to be recognizably distant from the simple sense that a machine is absolutely nothing without its human operator. This said, we could also call to mind Isaac Stern's famous comment about his Stradivarius on the Ed Sullivan show around the same time as Sorokin's comments were published. When in the post-performance interview Sullivan suggested that the violin had a beautiful sound, Stern retorted gently that he "didn't hear anything."

Now machines are one kind of object. This category has proven a little more diverse than just that which contains the material focus of a fetish. It also, and perhaps this is the first salient thing in our kind of social organization, contains objects that hold value within them. We are told that some things "hold their value" better than others, down to details such as the color of a sports car versus some other shade. "Resale red" is one adaptation of what appears to be an empirical statement. This kind of thing is trivial, of course, but the fact that it exists should give us a sense that the machine is a highly nuanced catalyst for meaning, even though it does not yet make meaning "on its own." But when is a machine ever "on its own" in any ultimate sense. Perhaps the wreckage of disused machinery, shipwrecks that lie buried in sand or rest uneasily at the bottom of seas and oceans, might be examples of a kind of aloneness that regularly assails human beings, but these are no longer functioning artifacts. Even in their non-functional status qua machine they continue to make meaning, sometimes far more than they did while "alive" in the mechanical sense of the term. *RMS Titanic* is perhaps the most famous example of this resonance from beyond the mechanical grave, as it were. It continues to exert a "presence" on our culture, both in entertainment and in homiletic. And here, it was nothing about the machine *per se* that led to its demise. Human hubris created it, and human hubris destroyed it. Because of this relationship, objects like shipwrecks "hold their power" in the way that other kinds of commodity objects hold their value. Their corpse contains a corpus, their body as artifactual and historical, yes, but also as something that can be read, a work about work and its demise. Work, overwork, the sensuality of romance and the daydream of nostalgia, the ever-pressing question regarding what it must have been like to "be there," *RMS Titanic* among other objects of this sort remain the preeminent loci of false memory and fictive kinship. They give us an insight into what it might have been like to indeed be somewhere else, for instance, at the origin points of the great religions. This much more profound "moment" is shrouded in a greater mystery, partly contrived by those who routinized the new callings, but also partly obscured by the simple vicissitude of a lengthy history where, the further it recedes from the present, the less record of it we possess in the present. These histories too have a corpus and a corpse, but the first reanimates the second in a perennial fashion. Just as a landmark film might pretend to have been there, whether on a ship or with a prophet, human beings rekindle romance and sensuality in general with one another every time we couple. These couplings are experienced as kindred to the "extension of the subject through the object" that artists and musicians experience, for our love-partners are also desirable objects and we wish to invest ourselves in them in a specific manner. They also can "hold their value" over the long term, even though the intensity of the experience of their value to us may, ironically, be heightened due to the briefer chronology of our affairs with them. The body of the person, exegetical text, shipwreck or some other disused or destroyed machine or for that matter, buildings—Hitler's forward eastern front command post in the vine-covered woods of Poland remains disused but it is considered to be a historical site of some value; less valuable perhaps but still extant is the Panzer construction and proving grounds complex, also shrouded in forest at present, in Germany proper—hold a power over us and also thus apply a power to us. Note that these kinds of places or things also have an aura about them, which approaches that of sacred venues. So does the person with whom I am in love, both before and after sex. It is not only a case of desire and nostalgia, or even reanimation: "At issue, rather, is the type of power brought to bear on the body and sex. In point of fact, this power had neither the form of the law, nor the effects of the taboo. On the contrary, it acted by a multiplication of singular sensualities" (Foucault 1980:47 [1978]). This sometimes geometric adumbration of a specific experience suits well the capitalist penchant for consumption and unit sales. One might take in a film, but there are present, almost as a kind of phenomenological envelope, all of the other accessories associated with the main attraction. A concert might have its t-shirts and caps, a museum display of artifacts from *RMS Titanic* the same. There are duplicates of the media produced for private use. There are gifts galore to be given to the lover, including those that animate the body via prosthesis and thus heighten the experience of sensuality and indeed, make it diverse. Such commodity complexes do quite literally "go forth and multiply" and Foucault's language should be taken in this metaphoric vein as well.

It is not so much the presence of a machine, moribund, destroyed, fully functional and current, or slowly eroding or corroding in the backwoods of our imaginations, and not even its original purpose, that is key. Beyond both presence and purpose is the calling of the machine. Though we might have invested great time and thought into its construction, we now have the expectations that it will perform for us a feat that takes us not only beyond labor, but also beyond thought. The machine, increasingly, does our thinking for us, and it is *in* this way and this way alone that its existence begins to impinge on the freedom of our own.

If we replace the subjectivity of human thinking with the objectivity of that of a machine, we begin to understand the difference between imagination and creativity and control and possession. The first includes and necessitates a certain "freedom" to be found in human consciousness alone. The second seeks and constructs for itself the will to certainty, and the ability to be certain contains the truth of unfreedom and thus necessitates neither creativity nor imagination. On top of this, machine-thought inverts the relationship between essence and effect: "Control is a by-product, not the essence, of scientific verities. A by-product cannot be regarded as the necessary criterion of verity" (Sorokin, op. cit:44). For human thought to occur, freedom is essentially part of its source. Since science is a particularly adept version of human thought, whatever control it gives to us regarding the surrounding nature in which we live is an effect, and thus an effect of thought. But machine-thought in its essence is about control first, and necessitates the ultimate absence of freedom. Until we build "thinking machines"—and note how we only manage to define thought in our own terms; are there other forms of sentient intelligence even on this planet that we do not recognize because of this species-bias?—this will remain the case. There is no "ghost in the machine," after all: "The soul was still an accepted part of the model in Newton's day. But it has always been an unsatisfactory device." (Midgely 2004:50). Indeed, the machines that have "soul" are, ironically, those that have been either destroyed or memorialized in some other non-functional manner. As long as a machine is working, maintaining its original purpose as something that produces something else that is also of material value—and perhaps, inevitably, of some symbolic value in many case—it provides the solace of the absence of conscience, the flight from soul. Its function alters dramatically when it becomes disused, and the manner in which it itself was sidelined or sabotaged can also mean much to us and thus to its power of regenerating its murky presence. So there is a continuity of value in a machine without that value being held to a continuity of purpose. One could argue that the "purpose" of a fellow human is to fulfill their self-defined destinies. We decide the fate of a machine, though enacting these decisions may come as a surprise, or an unintended consequence of incompetence or arrogance, accidents and design flaws, warfare or other deliberate destruction. Note too that the line between destruction of this kind and desecration is difficult to discern. Just as science is the child of religion, the technologies constructed by scientific discourse are kindred to the sacred fetishes of worship. Modern discourse may bely or even be in outright denial of this relationship, but in spite of this, the history, the genealogy, the pedigree of this kinship is well known and cannot be overlooked in any simplistic or reductionist manner: "Within the atomistic idea of nature there lies a distortion of the natural picture of the world oriented toward the forms of things and living being and, along with this distortion, a *depletion of meaning from all events*"

(Gadamer 2001:97 [1999], italics the text's). In general, this process has been associated with the "objectification" of the world. The human, with her ambiguous being experiencing the world as a series of puzzling aporetic or even aleatory events, cannot be, it is claimed, fully objective. Along with the ability to objectify comes the ability to disenchant. Between La Mettrie and ourselves lies the giant analytics of Weber. But surely it is the presumed distance between subject and object that creates the loss of "magic" in the world. For forces and meanings were objectified long before the advent of a serious and systematic scientific discourse and the rise of its technological enterprise. Whether the effect of the gods or other sources incompletely known to humans, the world and its effects, its fates and utter dismissals of human faculties and projects, were not "subjective" in any meaningful manner. They stood, rather, as objects over against our desires and more often than not, thwarted our nascent scientific abilities. Indeed, they might be influenced and cajoled by the instrumental use of magic, since the language of magic was also their own language, but they could not be ultimately harnessed and controlled with any certitude. It is just this combination of control and certainty, as we just saw with the outcome of machine-thinking, that was absent from a pre-scientific symbolism and literacy. But this is only one form of objectivity, and a very recent one at that. Indeed, the ancient gods were not so much seen as being "in control" of their powers, only as possessing them and apparently whimsically dispensing them in the world, underscoring our human sense that in spite of Prometheus and like figures around the world, that human life was still fragile and always on the edge of something other to itself.

Hence prediction was placed at a premium. Those who claimed to know the future were exalted. Those who made the further and more detailed claim that they knew how everything was controlled and for what purpose, past, present, and future, became so valuable that their priestly "calumniations" gained them, after a fashion, a more or less permanent presence in history. The priest proper is not of great interest today, but soothsayers and fortune-tellers of other types remain with us, from the analyst to the economist, from the fashion critic to the Las Vegas odds-maker. Anything to get a better sense of what is going to happen. This desire to "be there" before the fact is the obverse of the desire to have been there after the fact. Whether imagining that we trod the decks of the ill-fated vessel or the floors of the ill-lit and shadowy bunker, to consort with the vanquished or to be vanquished, to witness the finish of the derby as in a vision, or perhaps, more daringly, to attempt to know the hour of our own demise, this projected "metaphysics of presence" has been an *objective* combination of anxiety and aspiration for likely most of the length of human history. I call it objective simply due to its shared meaningfulness in the social world and the distance that we feel as living subjects of our own time and no other—that is, we cannot in reality trade the present for either the past or the future—as well as the problem it presents to us as an historical object and element of discourse. "Prediction" is not the same as predictability. The former is both an act and an object, the latter a process and a desire. They contain both a subject and an object. To objectify in this area is to do something quite specific: "Increase in efficiency at the cost of depth and intensity is the hallmark of this process" (Neumann, op. cit:401). This is the better-recognized part of the relationship today. Critiques of such systems are in great abundance, though not at all necessarily heeded in any general way, and there is no need to adumbrate them at this moment. But the subjectivity of the relationship is often still obscure, mainly due to the fact of our participation in it as well as our desire to exert that very predictive certitude that is predicated upon some kind of control of the situation, whether it occurred in the primordial past or has yet to happen. In a Kantian vein, we find ourselves torn between rationality directed to external events and social forces and the ethics of demanding that oneself be treated as an end in itself: "In his relations with others, the rational one requires that he always be treated as an end; depravity in social dealings is not identified as hard-heartedness or lack of compassion but as servility" (Lingis 1989:51). Here we find the subject willing himself to be objectified in an entirely different way than we do the machine. I take myself as my own end—though I may be willing, pending the context and goal, to act as part of someone else's ends as well—as well as taking myself to be above, though not aloof to, the nature that surrounds me. The dignity of the rational subject contains the person and at the same time controls the self. The "self," in this sense, is the space of desire. The person the space of the public and of community in the sense of the generalized other. Of course we can also desire community in the intimate sense, but this is not what is being spoken of directly here. Self and person must be distanced from one another in a way mindful of the distinction between public and private. Here too, the machine has none of these boundaries. There is no "private machine," only privately owned mechanisms that are as such elements of the means of production and objects within the technical category of private property, and machines do not require "privacy" in any sense of the word. Machines are only private or public because they are either deemed owned or used in these senses and spaces. Finally, there is no sense that the machine differentiates itself, or is differentiated by us, for that matter, along the "Kantian" lines of public person and private self, or that desire and anxiety may both conflict or be allied to one another pending circumstances. The human self requires these distinctions lest it fall into the existential category that contains machines and other objects. If the self is too self-possessed, it collapses is conscience and thus these other ethical and rationally defined boundaries also collapse. Instead of desiring the ability to be more sure of things, historically and future-oriented alike, we desire certainty itself. That is, we desire to be the *source* of the certain, and not merely someone who is informed of it through other sources. These kinds of people have lost their person *per se* and have replaced it with a kind of one-dimensional personality: "Their ruthless energy is accordingly very great, because, in its one-track primitivity, it suffers from none of the differentiations that make men human" (Neumann, op. cit:391). Certainly single-mindedness allows one to focus one's energies and aptitudes to a very specific task at hand, with a view to an abstract, but still specific end-goal. In this, we humans are "aping our ideals" in the way Nietzsche cautioned us against. The "forms" or essential figures of Western idealism might be brought to earth, though not to ground, by our focus and energy if we direct it long and hard enough at their current position. This attempt at action at a distance implies a number of disconcerting things: it recapitulates the anxiety about historical happenstance and the inability to predict one's fate, either short term or long; it is mounted on the same horse of hubris that constructs grand artifacts and then might also destroy them; it collects to itself the ends of others and transforms them into its own ends; it ignores the reality of its own finitude and seeks to become immortal within its own material time, etc. Ultimately, it too finds the path to nothing so interesting—how could there be an existing way to something that does not exist?—that it resigns from the job of being human: "Even as it is carried out, however, the Platonic doctrine of ideas sees, as it were, no necessity to discuss how the things of nature in their individuality and multiplicity actually participate in the being of ideas" (Gadamer 2001:134 [1999]). This disconnect prompts the action to bring the ideas to earth, to make the forms incarnate. No doubt this sensibility played an important role in the idea of a God on earth, an incarnate version or corporeal doppelganger of an incorporeal deity, suddenly human, or akin to human being, and thus, on the ethical side of things rather than that ontological, somehow also able to represent all of humanity in this intensely focused being which is also and essentially Being.

This process can also be seen as a kind of *a priori* supplication or worship. One hopes to speak into being the forms while also suggesting that their presence constitutes a communion. Like the classical cults mentioned above, we humans believe that to access this other kind of being we must transcend our individuality—the corroborree or the orgiastic agape and a great number of other versions of collective conscience-raising—and our multiplicity because the forms or essences are said to partake in neither. But the error here is more or less obvious. To imagine that a category can represent itself in its essence is to dispose of the reality that the elements that have been so grouped together have relevance to the principle by which they are categorized. We imagine, in other words, an inductive procedure to be a deductive one. We have observed similarities in the world. Sometimes, and especially of late with mass and technically accurate manufacture of commodities, such objects may be basically the same thing. It is these things that appeal to our sense of order and the logic of sets. The principle, the terms of grouping, follow from the observations and connections we make in the world. No form can be imagined without some sense of material "incarnation" first. To invert this relationship is to exalt the form over the substance: "This would be an interpretation of a formal principle of explanation as an actual force, which does not become any more real because men believe in it [ ] Worship does not transform an idol into a god" (Lösch 1967:243 [1945]). Indeed, one could more plausibly argue that while substance is given form by artifice and manufacture, the formation of things in the world, not so different from the socialization of persons, at once there is also a gestalt quality that is created by the presence of the formed object. Some correlate to human conscious-ness, though inert and non-sentient, may be seen in the material object, just as we append to natural forms the moniker "nature" as a holistic set of forces tending to the same purpose over the long term. We see, for example, utility in this or that item in the object world. But these things are also items *of* that world, that is, they represent a class of things that are manifestly different from those who constructed them. Perhaps the ultimate goal of the incarnate god was to prove that the subject too could become as the object, or further, that the subject was also an object in its essence. Materialism as a "doctrine of ideas" might have had its ironic beginnings in a discourse that promoted its very opposite.

If this is the case, then we have another way of looking at the messianic machine. It too becomes a full participant in the history of incarnation, the transfiguration of subjectivity through objectification into something that is both objective—we trust and believe in the measurements of machines, though we also understand that they can break down or make mistakes—and objectifying—in that the world itself now becomes more objective and cer-tain because it has been measured by something that has no subjectivity to it. The machine, since it cannot become distracted by the world, does not see the world so much as it gazes right through it. It discerns something about the world that escapes us, but the value of this aspect of the social world made object is ambiguous, even objectionable. We might well ask what is it pro-ductive of? What more can we know concerning our self-understanding through this non-human incorporated gaze of the incorporeal made material? Surely what it lends to us is more on the order of another set of tools, akin to the ethics that a God on earth might bequeath to us, the "teachings" of the messiah. The machine version of the messiah leaves us its teachings—data, in the broadest sense—and, akin to the gibberish of the logos that spoke forth from the classical temples, it now falls once again to subjectivity incarnate to interpret it and give it some meaning. It is our job, and our job alone, to make both the messiah and the machine meaningful in the social world as it is. No doctrine of forms, Platonic or otherwise, can accomplish this on its own. What we bring to data is experience, something a machine cannot have, and something that a messiah is not deemed to need—he is, after all, the God made subjectively real, but he loses nothing of his omniscience in being made so. Experience, including experience of interpreting the data generated by a machine, is the crucial element in any process of interpretation. Modern exegetics has nothing to do with scripture. It is completely oriented to the scripts that machines produce for us—measurements, numbers, and such things that by themselves rest no differently than the pure logos spoken in tongues. The tongues of the machine, like the tongues of the dead, speak a language wholly different from living human beings. But any language can be interpreted, and our experience tells us that in the case of the machine, at least, we have some idea of what we are about given the transfer of these data of forms into the world of substance and its measurable "success" in that world.

Not that religious ideas have been an abysmal failure. There is more argument about them because we are less trusting, at least nowadays, of the vehicles by which they are said to appear among us. These vehicles, oracles, priestesses, sermonizers, and other sundry role players are human as well. We may be soon approaching the time when thinking machines will have to be distrusted in the same way that we are always and already aware that our fellow humans might have ulterior motives even if they are being honest with us. Indeed, the thought of machines will make the idea of the machine obsolete. These will be beings like ourselves, sentient and conscious, with the ability, we assume, to also possess a conscience. The moment there is a ghost in the machine the machine itself is transformed into something else. We seem to both desire this moment and fear it, given our entertainment fictions that serve us equal helpings of salvation and apocalypse to this regard. It is not enough to say that because persons of Jewish background produce most of these fictions that we are somehow being duped into believing them. No, such commodities are produced precisely because the anxieties and aspirations that make them recognizable and even entertaining are already widespread in the larger society, no matter what ethnicity is involved. Machines can save us, and hence save our souls, in the same way as could this or that messiah. But machines can also destroy us, as the vindictive godhead of the same traditions was said to have already planned. The millennial character of the machine must be recognized for what it is: easing suffering in the human world is tantamount to death, for it is only in death that all cares can be forsaken.

Of course, this too can be spun in a way that suggests that suffering is the true path to a more mature humanity. This is utter nonsense. What we are being cautioned against is rather the sense that one can alleviate the pain of being human and in this way humanity is saved. It is exactly the opposite of this. The way we are includes both sorrows and joys. Taking either away amounts to dehumanizing. Perhaps this is the ultimate goal, but we should recognize it for what it is. Like the diversion, pastime, or hobby, such energies that are given to it, supplications of their own sort and design, cannot be said to be entirely of no inherent merit. They may force the unimaginative to gain some sense of vision. They may improve the technique of a skill that had lain latent within one. They may enhance one's sociability and teach lessons in history. It is only when they duplicate writ small in nebulous and unconscious fashion the mode of production at large that they fail in their business of expanding the mind: "Under the prevailing conditions it would be absurd and foolish to expect or demand of people that they accomplish something productive in their free time; for it is precisely productivity, the ability to make something novel, that has been eradicated from them. What they then produce in their free time is at best hardly better than the ominous *hobby*" (Adorno 1998:172 [1969], italics the text's). Like the logos within the walls of the temple or held within the mouths of the oracles, a hobby by itself can have no meaning relevant to human life. This much and this far one can agree with Adorno. But a hobby enacted, as an interest in the world, can and often does depart from being another mere manner of replicating the more necessary commodity relations by which it is supplied with the goods and tools it needs to replenish its vitality and live on. Certainly, hobbies and interests do consume things. Almost any hobby has surrounding it a plenitude of things that one can or must purchase in order to "do" the hobby in the first place. Thus hobbies too do not take one into another world. They are minor means of keeping the usual productive-consumptive cycle going. At the same time, these pastimes can become serious threats to the integrity of the proletarian relation to the means of production. The worker, in his or her "free time," may in fact construct the "free labor" of the communist. The interest may become more important than work. The interpretation of self that follows from this might turn our heads in the direction of humanity proper, rather than economy, as we begin to realize that there is much more to life than the work life. That hobbies seem to mimic work and require time in a similar manner is misleading. Such interests that are *not* demanded of us make us more human.

They may begin as a response to the hue and cry of "finding oneself" or even the sentimental idea of vocation, but they can quickly depart from such models and idols and become serious, intense, artistic and even ethical. The idea of working on one's own at something that no one else may care about takes us some distance from both the ancient notion of collectivity as well as the modern sense that we should all become as famous as possible and seek as much recognition and reward from the world as we can get:

> Everything modern is recognizable in the fact that it artfully steals away from its own time and is capable of creating an "effect" only in this fashion. (Industry, propaganda, proselytizing, cliquish monopolies, intellectual racketeering).

[ ] But they are only the masked cries of *anxiety* in the face of philosophy. (Heidegger 1999:15 [1988], italics the text's)

The self-absorption of the hobby or interest contains a protest against the anxiety of the modern. It does not cry out as a plaintiff, it speaks its way into being a critique. It says to the wider world that there is not only time for oneself but that there is also energy left over from the apparatus of economy and politics for myself. The private interest that masks itself as individuated and perhaps even idiosyncratic consumption has the ulteriority of authenticity. Perhaps in our world this is the only way in which ontological authenticity may be had? We must work something out for ourselves. This demand is no different from those who petitioned the oracle for a response regarding the future, the past, or even a present trouble that persisted in the face of common sense and experience. Simply attending the temple is not enough. One must put oneself into a dialogue with what animates the place. Our modern temples are no different to that regard. They present the opportunity for dialogue, but they are, as we are, one thing and one being, and to interlocute with oneself is in fact that specialty of the private interest, including hobbies. Even here, the self is not alone, as history and technique, design and pedigree all come immediately into play. To affect a presence is not to be present and thus is to miss the opportunity to understand something new through an interaction that is itself novel: "Art styles become obsolete like the old models of cars. Art and the artist become assimilated to the production lines of the technical order" (Barrett, op. cit:240). This attitude is inevitable if we have forgotten the purpose of art. If the purpose of the car is utilitarian—no matter its technical qualities it is a point A to point B machine; its virtuosity of design no doubt has an aesthetic to it (a fine marque produces the feeling of superiority in its driver and finery for its owner)—the purpose of art has no such function. It is fair to assert that the car, amongst other commodities and mass manufactured objects, has ascended in the direction of artistry, if not art, while some works of art and their makers may have descended in the direction of mere manufacture. But this dual inclination towards one another is not a function of the lack of "Culture" in modern culture. In fact, no society in history can boast of a more educated and literate general public, sad as that may sound to some ears. There is even great interest in becoming educated about consumption itself. We are aware that we are being exploited as workers. We are becoming more aware that human beings are destroying the earth. We do not wish to annihilate ourselves and are soundly suspicious of politicians who seem blithely unaware of the dangers on this score. Perhaps all of this is a case of too little too late, but we also are more willing to heed this chastisement as well. No, the working of utilitarian objects into art and the less obvious decline of the elite idea of what art should be tell us that we care *more* about our work in the world than ever we did before. The artist wants to be relevant to everyday concerns; the car manufacturer desires to improve the quality, and qualities, of his product. It is another error of judgment to think that art and function must be forever separated and, more critically, that the former can never stoop to the level of commodity while the latter can never overcome that same level.

Clearly even within the envelope of ratiocination—the unbounded rationalism of the forms set loose in the world of rationalized institutions and personal rationales—there remains room for human expression that is at once both humane and also has the potential to speak of inhumanity. It is both critical and ethical, in other words, and the space reserved for it is merely the ground zero of its always-immanent explosion onto the wider scene. The thinker who embodies both critique and ethic is responsible for the question of form in the world. Our response has not been a resounding affirmation that it continues to be so, but rather, a cautious but persistent murmur that says yes to the possible but not always yes to the actual, and never yes to the inevitable. We must work, in other words, to attain the space of the possible in all things human that seek their own humanity, joys and sorrows alike. It often seems that the latter are forced upon us, and that we would never do so choose them ourselves. But this is another error, this time in ethics and not aesthetics. This error—to see in sorrow only evil but at the same time to also see only insight in suffering—rests within a genealogy that contains the idea that we must make known both our sorrows and joys to others in order for them to be evaluated as being human or on the way to becoming humane.[1] Back to the hobby for a moment: these kinds of private spaces where it may well be that no one else cares about what we intensely work upon are the epicenters of a seismic existentiality that in turn can shake all mantles of discourse and rationality alike. Restoring antique automobiles or art lends itself to this quaking, this unsettling of the ground beneath us, that which we have assumed will always hold us upright and catch us if we fall. Here, in the space of the vision of the individuated interest, we move ourselves to fall harder than ever before. There are no witnesses. We must pick ourselves up. There is no doctrine of forms or soteriological manual, we must give ourselves incarnation, and we must save ourselves. These interests are introspective in the sense that we must work on them on our own, but they are not fundamentally divorced from the world or from history, because their material comes from both of these sources at once. The solace that is provided us is no mere opiate. It may begin without soul—it is only "possible," in the sense that Nietzsche was interested in descrying—but its intensity and focus creates a new soul, or the sub-text of soul is brought to light, or the occluded soul within the being is renewed in some other way. The details of such a process are not important, in the same way as this or that ritual of the diverse cultures of our shared human heritage worked to the same purpose by different means. That joy is possible suggests that its plausibility remains in doubt without action on our parts. It will not simply happen to us; in the same way that Sapir famously critiques the idea that culture could simply occur to us while we were at rest within the very confines of the absence of soul that Adorno and Barrett rail against. There is no culture machine. Even a messiah must have disciples. There is no progression of maturity or emotion, experience of joy or sorrow without the fullest agency and focus of human beings. And it is this combination of action and interest that is precisely, in our own time of rationalization, found to a great extant within the private interest or "hobby." It's real ominousness lies in its departure from the norms and forms of the expected everydayness of decaffeinated decorum. For in general technology provokes an emotional, even guttural response from us, especially since 1945 (cf. Gadamer 1996:24 [1972]). To make everything more certain is, as we have already stated, one of the chief motives for and effects of the presence of machines. Just as the old messiahs told us that such and such was the revealed truth of things, and all we needed to do was convert to this new framework and work for its worldview in this world, the machine takes this very world and works it into its own framework. We can all the more easily follow its workings, and need much less of the faith that was called on us to hold within our breasts by the messianic machines' human predecessors. All the same, we are hardly the naïve and docile sheep that are extolled as one of the ancient metaphors for the faithful. In pursuing or opposing rationalization, in focusing our "free" time in private interests or hobbies, in our political apathy we make concrete this-worldly choices to follow along and live within the new frameworks just as did our ancestors with those more traditional worldviews that somehow linger on in the face of the age of technology. Something sells because a desire for it exists. Now, it is true to say that modern advertising in large measure helps to create and maintain such desires for commodities, and their proliferation and diversity that have little to do with authentic or empirical human needs. But did human beings ever need the latest religion? In an epoch where material goods were, for the vast majority of those alive, basic and necessary, symbolic goods performed a function that in our own time they have lost. That is, they constructed the desire for the other-world where material limits and needs, ranging from hunger to death, were permanently overcome. Now that in "developed" regions of this world such material necessities are often met, the draw of the symbolism of another world that has nothing more to offer on that score at least has waned. We have seen, of course, that human finitude remains a limit to our desires, collective and individual, but the end-game of the presence of the messianic machine is the thinking mechanical consciousness, a form of being that places itself on the evolutionary stage as the next step in human maturity. Its ultimate card is its sense of dignity; not even organic death and decay can assail it, and it can thus move on to the stars.

It is human dignity that is appealed to by, and is also the appeal of, both religious and technological suasion alike. The first, as we have seen, promotes the overcoming of death, that most grievous insult to our sense of self. The second promotes the overcoming of labor and suffering whilst alive, which is certainly attractive as well. In the longer term, machines must scale the most daunting wall of organic ends in order to impart the same order of desire upon us as did the religions. But we are getting closer. The extremities of anxiety when confronted by technology or becoming its unthinking acolyte will both be answered by the thinking and evolving machine or self-repairing and replicating cyber-organism. That such an apparently outlandish goal even exists suggests that for humans, "their sense of dignity and the importance of preserving it even in extreme circumstances was not any the less vital to them. [ ] Imagination and fantasy are not on trial" (Bravo, et al 1990:103). Perhaps not, as the messianic promise of indefinite life while remaining in this world appeals so directly to both. Indeed, both imagination and at least the phantasm of rational projection into the future are required by such plans and goals. Those who shun technology "affectively" are content to believe that such worlds are only fantasy, while those who embrace technology no less emotionally are apt to entertain possible future ventures of this sort as part of the same category that includes what one might do for one's next summer vacation. Either way, we are not seeing ourselves, let alone the imagined otherness of machine being, in a very clear and rational light. The solace of escaping the burdensome soul of humanity acts like a light that draws the moth. Perhaps, after a certain large number had been burned, their Icarus-winged flights ended in ashen falls from grace, the weight and remains of their collected carcasses will put out the candle itself, and we will descend into the darkness of the nocturnal vigil once again.

In the meanwhile, the cult of technology fetishists continues unabated, while a rival group decries its existence. The presence of these two extremities, as Gadamer suggestively labels them, containing both proselytes and prosthetics, is hardly limited to concrete technological mechanisms, but pervades all of discursive and even social life. The interest in statistics and related programs of data collection and analysis arose around 1900, but it really took the stage after the Second World War: "The cult of 'social physics' and 'physicalist psychology' as a science of processes different from the physiology of the nervous system, has been growing indeed among modern sociologists and psychologists, and there is no clear sign, as yet, of its recession" (Sorokin 1956:187). Today such research paradigms dominate the social science scene. This to the extent that "humanistic" work is seen, sometimes good-naturedly as part of the academic division of labor, and sometimes with a sneer, as being part of someone else's duties, such as history perhaps or even philosophy. Even qualitative research within the human sciences occupies a scarce minority share of funding and activity. Why has this become the case? Simply put, the messiness of the human endeavor does not lend itself to finely discriminating analytics. In order to keep the idea of "the study of man" alive, those involved have had to adopt methods and developed faith in outcomes that resemble more and more their much more materially successful disciplinary cousins, the applied sciences. Most people are aware that natural science research has some relationship to applications therefrom, like chemistry and medicine or physics and engineering. All of us use the outcomes of this research dynamic every day of our lives. We rely on them in the same way as we rely on the machine. No social science can compete with either their presence in our world—not to mention the way in which they have, along with the machine, utterly transformed it—or their influence over it. At best the odd economist is seen on the news, and the perhaps even odder psychologist gains a cult following in entertainment media. Very little else from either the human sciences or the humanities and arts is ever so placed. Well, it is much more difficult to make the connections between these other forms of thought and research and daily life, and indeed, often enough there is no such connection to be made. At most, such conceptions that are traditionally part of historical and philosophical inquiries lie hidden at the bottom of our more mundane arguments, never brought to light because they are either taken as givens by everyone involved, or assumed to have become moribund and thus irrelevant. The harshly sardonic but commonly used phrase "its academic" speaks to this sensibility of thinking aloud being quite extraneous to anything of practical human import. But cases do arise where historically influential conceptions come to light, such as when we are trying to evaluate the presence of machine consciousness or technological prosthesis in our lives. But when they do, we are unsure of what to think about them or how they apply: "We need some conception of human nature that we think they ought to fit as a criterion for judging them. We are always developing and updating that notion, but we never try to do without it" (Midgely 2004:107). Here, Midgely is speaking about institutions in general, but the point holds all the more so for developments that in fact will alter the conception of "human nature" in a permanent fashion. The whole idea may have to be discarded, and it is this that requires the enlistment of all human beings in the action of philosophical work. For the ultimate irony in all of this would be if, in working so hard to overcome our own humanity and its limits, that we give over the final judgment on the presence of our work to that which is patently non-human, and thus has no real responsibility to carry such humanity along with it into its brave new world.

2.2 THE MINDLESS

If our conceptions of this possible world have not merely shuffled off mortal coils but also those immortal, what of intelligence and also, more important-ly, thinking and thought? Must thought always frame itself "non-affectively" to be a serious contestant in the contestation of ideas concerning the human future? The sense that thinking is done in this way and no other is certainly one of the errors that many persons live by, especially those responsible for technological development that emanates from scientific research. The cult that is centered around such a device is sometimes aptly called "scientism" (cf. Midgely's comments on "scientistic imperialism", op. cit:22-3). If nature is everywhere one and the same thing, why could not the study of nature mimic more closely its reality by becoming a singular framework? That science is the child of religion should not mean that it couldn't assume the same proportions as its parents if in fact the reality of its object dictates it. But is it really nature that is driving this conception? Heidegger asks where the definition of the idea of rationality comes from. How has it become deified? And, further, and more profoundly, what if rationality really were completely different from any aspect of religion or even the "irrational"? "If it turned out that the basic employment of the term 'rational' was limited to something utterly empty of subject matter, what could this rationality ever achieve?" (op. cit:34).[2] The term "subject" here must be taken in at least a dual sense. Not merely as the lack of an object to be studied, but as the absence of the subject as well as the subjective. This idea of rationality is said to be empty of the "matter of the subject." Hence it could never grace itself with any achievement whatsoever, for it has entirely forsaken the human equation and the idea that all knowledge, based on human experience, ad-dresses human concerns. These concerns may of course not be entirely ra-tional, perhaps they rarely are. Nevertheless, if partially non-rational or even irrational humans are doing the work of scientific rationality, the methods of science are charged with a much greater task here at home, in their very laboratories, observatories, and perhaps most especially clinics and markets, than they would ever have to face in the cosmos at large. The "desubjectifica-tion" of human interest encapsulates this task, and one can immediately see not only its daunting challenge but also its erroneous complicity. All credit to its boldness, certainly, as one of the first instances of its vision quest oc-curred at the very heart of human intimacy and communion: "Not only did it speak of sex and compel everyone to do so; it also set out to formulate the uniform truth of sex. As if it suspected sex of harboring a fundamental secret. As if it needed the production of truth. As if it was essential that sex be inscribed not only in an economy of pleasure but in an ordered system of knowledge" (Foucault 1980:69 [1978]). The secret was that of the non-ra-tional desire for communion with a deity, of placing the sanctity of the covenant as in between two human beings. The truth was that loving one another led to the love of the deity, that, more aptly, the non-rational could be produced out of the irrational and thus overcome the latter. The knowledge was to keep all of this close at hand and *not* let it become objectified. Discourse and science sought to overturn all of these complicities, indeed, saw them only as such by casting them as devoid of sacred content, of "subject matter," as it were. Jung states succinctly that the "imperialism" of this narrow conception of rationality lies at the new heart of material humanity and thus has positioned itself as the very first step towards machine-life as overcoming that very humanity: "Above all the rationalistic hybris which is tearing our consciousness from its transcendent roots and holding before it immanent goals" (op. cit:221). The most obvious incarnation of immanence in this new utilitarian and rationalized sense is the test and the measurement, to which all of us have been endlessly subject (cf. Sorokin, op. cit:62 on the ironic abnormalcy of such testing contexts). The mechanistic sense of rationality is "rootless," and Jung's language may be taken as a clear advisory of the conditions ahead. Like the path to nothing, such a road is emblazoned with both promise and honor. Like the path to hell, good intentions might even abound, though latent functions, and ulterior motives will also be found here. "Immanent" should suggest to us the presence of Being, or at the very least, a phenomenological sensibility regarding the object world or more intimately, the presence of another to whom I must respond in some way. But here it is being deliberately emasculated of its own "transcendent roots" in order to give the appearance that the here and now is all that can ever be of concern to us. A test, for instance, measures this here and now with some precision. The problem has always been to relate such scores to how people live in the ongoingness of authentic immanence. But if this is no longer seen as the issue at hand, then such tests can stand alone in the same way as does the existential moment in a thought experiment. The pedigree of the idea of the day to day is not something modern rationality has invented. Yet in all other historical and traditional cases this "second nature" was left to itself. It was not tested or measured to see how far it had either departed from normative reality or how closely it continued to resemble it. The "second nature" of a person's culture and heritage was not given a discourse, was not made into a discursive object, was not seen to hold threatening secrets, was not occasioned to summon the truth about itself, did not need to be compelled to provide an object of knowledge about itself.[3] One could somewhat blithely state that "it was what it was" and nothing more. Perhaps it is our modern conception that there must always be something more to this or that situation or even dream that is what is truly compelling?

If so, what is the source and nature of this "more"? No doubt we are well acquainted with its presence. We might even equate the presence of a material thing to be also the presence of its abstraction, the idea of its being-there, and the formation for the formula. Yes, in the specific sense that thought is portable and that one can read of another's genius and study the techniques developed by one's predecessors, and it is these items that are the more basic constituents of consciousness for human beings. The portability of human invention can give itself over to a kind of abstraction. So much so that it appears as a form of "second nature" to us in the same way that an abstraction is unquestioned and somehow therefore inaccessible to us, having been born into its norms and borne along by its forms: "The absence of an intelligent idea in the grasp of a problem cannot be redeemed by the elaborateness of the machinery one subsequently employs" (Barrett, op. cit:115). But if the intelligence of things appears only as an abstraction, never as an "immanence," how is it that we can become acquainted with the idea that we face a problem at all? If we are lost in the face of a specific challenge, to which we respond by magnifying the mousetrap of utility and convenience, we are doubly lost in the absence of intelligence as an aspect of consciousness, or even as a mode of being in the world as it is. To take on this or that issue in our society or our larger world is then to wade into a murky body of water with the belief that only the most raw trial and error of experience can provide some semblance of a solution: "The result is the mass-manufacture of doubly subjective products which are then thrown in great quantities on humanity's mental stock-exchange" (Sorokin, op. cit:298). And yet this procedure comes to be seen as the most rational, for it addresses the pragmatic sense of "immanence" head on, as it were. Not only are we not denying our subjective presence, we are using it in the most rational manner; as a hip-wader and a form of insulation to protect us from the irrational manifestations of a hitherto unknown object or force. Subjectivity "itself" has become a form of homegrown technological prosthesis. "Man as object" has indeed birthed "man and his doubles" in Foucault's famous sense. The doubling over of the one who encounters the discomfort of a foreign object, an alien landscape, even an indigestible dreamscape, is righted by the presence of one's subjectivity "after all." After all, this was only my experience. After all, I may have been irrational. After all, I saw only what I wanted to see, and such sundry rationalizations here in lieu of the authentic rationality of self-examination and potential self-understanding. The technologies of subjectitude provide for us the way in which we can charge the world with our desires without being charged by them (cf. Gadamer 1996:18 [1972]). The mindlessness of the machine impugns the use of our own mind. It seeks, though passively and in a non-conscious manner, to make each interface with the non-machine more akin to itself. It is commonplace to note that one feels more like a machine oneself when one is constantly using them. But machine-thought and other forms of mechanical presence in our lives are not limited to the interactions with actual mechanisms as working objects. Inasmuch as the machine messiah saves us time to potentially pursue things like thinking and thus critical freedom, it also has overtaken that very path through the Fordism of mass education techniques and the presence of other "objects of mechanism": "The elementary texts serve up this potpourri of informative odds and ends in a sketchy but well-chewed and even over-chewed form easy to swallow and digest without any mental effort on the part of students" (Sorokin, op. cit:314). This is also a well-known facet of the increasingly omnipresent mindlessness, the unthought of modern mass culture. At the same time, the "overview," the panorama of research and ideas that we have inherited does at least give us the impression that thinking once had a place, or had to be done in the past in order for us to take up our present positions. This has the power of contradicting the ability of any member of this or that society to live on in the shadow of thought but without acknowledging the genealogy of thinking as a living mode of ongoing being in the world. The "abstraction" of which Barrett spoke is representative of a complex and conflicting mixture of ideas and historical events. Once it is undertaken to delve into these kinds of archetypical social facts and suasions, they become quite diffuse, sometimes even vanishing before our eyes. Beyond this, however, we have today reached a phase of existence where one's standing apart cannot be recognized as being in good standing. Here, we are always tempted to become part of the space in which one is celebrated and can become the "bonhomie" of one's own good time and good timing. This situation is symptomatic of a social force that can hire at will due to its resplendent resources. Every critic and thinker desires to have his or her ideas put on the public table. Recognition may be hard to come by within the cliques of intellectuals themselves, simply because such thinkers are also already outside the norms and fashions, the publication catalogues and the networks, and risk further marginalization by continuing on the path of "free self-expression." This is the very opposite of the path to nothing, but it is also manifestly not the freeway to any metropolis of fame and fortune. Indeed, what seems like sage advice and even a chestnut way of ethical being forsakes certain instances of historical actuality. One easy example which in general is quite reasonable to take to heart in all such cases of both temptation, collusion, corruption and marginality to the point of being a pariah, runs "you are never as good as people say you are, but you are also never as bad as people say you are." Praise is cheap, and criticism also a cheap shot. But there are cases where the person does not fall into the center of things in the way the homiletic implies. Nietzsche received much praise from his small coterie of friends and his editor, Peter Gast, but he was actually far better than even they surmised or were able to recognize. Hitler was seen as a bad figure early on by his critics, but it was only after his death and the end of the war that the world found out just how bad he actually was. So we must also beware the consolatory epigrams of the hallmark world of the normative even when they appear to tell us that the judgments and thus the norms themselves by which the mechanism of the public realm runs are to be lightly regarded.

This sensibility, where we are reminded that mindlessness is both portable and transportable, it can be carried around by us even if we do not display any symptoms thereof, as well as it being able to carry itself around under a variety of guises, from the ironist's cage to the "sell out," from the position of the marginal thinker drunk with the opium of becoming the spokesperson for humanity to the hack who can "serve up" a textbook rendition of modernity for at least the captive student audience, is a form of our contemporary expectations of *techne*. This term today connotes technology and not know-how, as it used to be thought of by the Greeks (cf. Gadamer 2000:74 [1996]). Knowing how to construct something is not the same as the construction itself, but for us these two things have become indistinct. The results of any process are referred to as somehow part of the process. This is fine in terms of thinking about a result in the history of ideas, or as a way station on the way to self-understanding through the hermeneutics of suspicion and the like, but it loses its veracity when applied to the object realm proper. It is likely that one of the variables involved in the blurring of process and product is that, between real advances in applied research and planned obsolescence, we are made aware that what we have today is very much like what we know after all. This product, new and improved, really is something different, at least to a point, than the one that preceded it. There does not seem to be a moment where things stop being produced, which suggests that the idea of process as *techne* never itself comes to a halt. There is no final outcome; no "result" that results in the stoppage of the play of a technical process of know-how. So is it reasonable to suggest that there should be some discretion here? The single-minded fabric of technological tapestry is at once presenting itself as not only whole cloth, but also whole mind. But for any mind to encompass everything about itself but also itself as a whole, it must in effect, lose its mind. This is perhaps the more serious and saturated notion of "mindless" that we have been discussing here. To stand outside of oneself you must lose yourself. This is not entirely possible for human beings, but what if, since we have not yet given credit to the machine for either possessing a soul or a mind, machine-thought *does* in fact rest outside of its form as well as transcend its formal application and formula? The modern sense of *techne* suggests a unison of both unthought and the mechanism of programmable thought processes. It takes itself to be one thing and thereby imposes its single-minded will upon the world (cf. Barrett, op. cit 198). It should be noted that in one respect, this "great transformation" has made history much more relevant and authentic to itself, and that is within its dispensing with teleology. We now know that human history does not arc along a predestined path towards a specific goal. There is no world-historical object as in purpose or calculated outcome. We work our way into the future as it "is," that is, something that is not yet but could be or can be or might be. There is no ultimate *telos* to the run of events. It was perhaps Darwin who in the most astonishing manner altered the course of the *idea* of history. The most radical thing about organismic evolution was its ad hoc structure. No further goals, and especially, no goals outside of its own processes, could be imputed to it. And this is crucial for our more general understanding of what we are doing and where we might be going. Just as the product of natural selection, mutations, gene flow and so on could not be seen as "final" in any sense other than that generational, evolution "itself," having no goals outside of itself, let alone the specific goal of producing humanity from the proverbial soup of proteins, could no longer be summoned as a sage who expressed a faith in that very humanity as the scion of its own history. Nor could it be summoned as a disciple of the previous metaphysics. Darwinian evolution was a real-time real-world case of *techne's* self-involution and involvement and nothing more.

The most impressive part of the evolutionary mechanism, famously discovered in Darwin's lifetime but remaining unknown to him, was that it seems to function "by itself," lending it to the dreams of a *perpetuum mobile* or even an unmoved mover. This rekindled abstract ideas of both Aristotle and subsequent religions that were in appearance quite anti-Aristotelian. But we cannot be swayed by these appearances. Evolution does not contain reasons. It acts and effects, but does not reason things through. This is more what it means to say that something occurs "by itself." Even "by its own devices" does not really cover the sense that Darwin had of the forces at work both at the level of organism, and as we have extended his notions to cover and explain an indefinite spectrum of events, that cosmological as well. Reasoned outcomes imply the process of *techne*, which is both a conscious and a self-conscious mode of being. Just as the presence of a mechanism implies the being of the one who constructs it, the "doer for every evolutionary deed" resisted personification, although equally famously today, we understand that evolution does not in fact imply the complete or necessary absence of a creator being, either itself evolved through the same processes as everything else, or setting in motion the current version of the cyclical universe's evolutionary systems. All of this must be taken back to the beginning of Western thought, where concepts such as causality, reality and appearance were first formulated: "Thus genuine knowledge that gets behind sensory appearance certainly acknowledges that there are no accidents and that everything has it reasons; it just does not, however, acknowledge these reasons themselves" (Gadamer 2000:95 [1935]). By exposing the reasoning at the foundation of events, knowledge becomes a discourse of the abstract. It cannot know itself then, in the same sense that human consciousness cannot get "outside of itself," and implying the modern sensibility that evolution has no 'reasons' outside of itself and just as importantly and radically, no reasoning as part of its internal apparatus. What then does it accomplish? "Its achievement, rather, is only that the observation of appearances facilitates the tireless drive of the real science of causality that lies within it, the idea that everything happens as it should, that everything, governed by the same mechanical necessity, happens 'by itself.'" (ibid). But what is this 'itself' by which everything else is moved? Is there to be countenanced some kind of mover that is itself unmoved in the Aristotelian sense, and if so, how can we ourselves countenance such an idea, or, as we imagine our ancestors in fact were, be countenanced by it? Democritan worldviews aside for the moment, what is truly at stake by adopting a mechanistic model of the universe, a universe that increasingly over the modern period came to include ourselves in an indissoluble way? Excerpting ourselves from the processes and products of cosmic evolution is no longer a metaphysical option, and the limits put in place by recognizing that it was at first not a material or physical option pushed open another kind of door; to be carried over the threshold of this portal was to become ensconced in a world where "reason" itself was unreasoning and where the mind could "mature" into the mindless.

It is quite correct to say that abstract conceptions are constructed with only the barest references to the "science of causality" rather than the more evident abstraction concerning society or history adhering to some other kind of science, that of Weber or Dilthey or even Mill. "They are actually metaphysical sketches, ambitious maps of how all reality is supposed to work, guiding visions, systems of direction for the rest of our ideas" (Midgely, op. cit:119). In the same way as scientific facts intrude in our daily lives in either only an unacknowledged sense or in the most practical of venues—Newtonian physics is still an able descriptor of human-perceptual level events on earth, for instance, but it is no longer viewed as "causal" in any genuine manner—where the collision of vehicles, for example, is avoided by the combined guess-work of a number of drivers' experiences and skills. Lösch reminds us that "In any case, it is not necessarily the most skillful in any ordinary sense who gather together in an occupation" (op. cit:237, emphasis removed). In any context, there are present both a variety of skill levels—measured by their aptitude and results but *not* departing from the contemporary conception of *techne* where the process and the product are seen as part of the same thing—and amounts of experience. Insurance rates for vehicles, to continue our easy example, reflect the outcomes as well as the speculations regarding these possible contexts. Not everything can be predicted with the accuracy an insurance underwriter might idealize, but clearly, given the profits to be made in that particular service industry, predictions made usually come to pass. Is this because either "everything happens for a reason" or is it due to there being an abstract unreasoned unreasoning that lies behind and shapes every event but at a distance? If reason is itself defined *into* the context of events this is accomplished in almost all cases by the assumed presence of a mindless mechanism that "acts" as only a series of effects. That is, there is no cosmogony attributable to the car accident or the suicide that cannot itself be taken back yet a step further. Causality, opened up at both ends, necessitates an infinite regression of acts and outcomes that cannot be, after a certain point, calculated or even known about in the present. We set limits, and all limits thus set are arbitrary in the "causal" sense. The decision to "explain" a series of events by starting at a knowable and perhaps even observable point is an act, not of reason, but of utility. And the most convenient manner of doing so is through the mechanistic model of things and the world of things. It is, in its own somewhat tepid and practical-minded way, our version of magic. What it loses is both fate and agency. This is the same thing that was lost with Darwinian evolution. *No exteriority of goals, no interiority of intents.* This is why it sometimes appears to us that things "happen by themselves." We are not to take such a saying lightly, of course, but we also cannot take it literally.

Indeed, our modern legal systems provide their most severe penalties to those who are deemed to have actually participated *by reason* in the chain of mechanical or otherwise "causal" events. Those who calculate a crime, for instance, and then carry it to its fruition. Those who intend mischief or otherwise harm others because they are willingly working to this outcome. We are able to impugn individuals in this way precisely because the responsibility for being has shifted from the autonomous sphere of the other world as well as from the internal mechanism of things themselves to persons. The excuse that "the devil made me do it" is no longer acceptable in a court of law. At the same time, one can plead insanity. "Extenuating circumstances" is an acknowledgement of the infinite regression attached to all acts and events. How far one is willing to extend the circumstances in the direction of the defendant or in favor of the plaintiff is always a context of interpretation and thus is subject to many other threads of regression down to the level of each individual biographical actor involved. Jury selection acknowledges this issue when it limits who can serve. We are all placed as judges in our modern world. Not only with regard to our self-responsibility but as observers and defenders of norms in the world of actions and events. We evaluate others' performances with the knowledge that we are ourselves as well being evaluated. We *do* judge, and thus we *are* judged, and this in itself departs more or less fully from the older and perhaps idealistic ethics of "judge not." This is as important as Darwin's discovery and, in its much more intimate and human purview, serves to define consciousness as only self-consciousness and nothing more. The mindless then becomes part of the essence of both "fatality" and "destiny."

2.3 KILLJOY WAS HERE

Akin to the graffito on the bulkheads of the Liberty ships, the human factor marks mechanism with its unexpected and seemingly irrelevant remark. Contained within it is an implicit but nonetheless disquieting critique: all is not as it seems to be. It is an error to imagine that factoring out humanity constitutes a success of any kind. In a world of mechanism, the machine takes on the vaunted mantle of being culture, or being the center of what is cultured, and humanity, ironically, is forced into the margins of a nature that objectively and historically it can have nothing to do with: "Conscience is the voice of nature as it emerges in a being who has entered society and is endowed with language and hence reason" (Taylor 1989:359). If it is also true that "the idea of a recovery of contact with nature was seen more as an escape from calculating other-dependence" (ibid), then at the same moment, the idea of an overcoming of the limits of the nature of "man" gave forth a new definition of the other to which we could become dependent. We have already seen that one of the radical and unsettling threads of Darwinian evolution was that Man could no longer be seen as either a goal or a transcendence of any kind of nature, evolved or created or both. On top of this, however, was the growing sense that humanity was also neither a limit form of nature nor a special expression thereof. Man was not, in other words, to nature what machine is to us. Our relationship with technology—like language part of the expression of the being of reason and perhaps also of conscience—is perhaps the major mode of human evolution and the evolution of cultures. From the beginning of human differentiation from the nature that gave us our original and shared birthright, the "machine," stone and bone tools etc., are what set us apart. The subtlety and nuance of human language was presumably long in coming to fruition. The symbolic systems of humankind following from this, as well as the social contract and its hypostatization in religion, were also something that by themselves could not have separated our activities and agency from other animals. But there may have been a point of diminishing returns regarding the production of technology or, at the very least, a point at which that self-same technology presented itself first as our destroyer and then as our successor. We encountered the first threshold some seventy years ago, and it is highly likely that before the next seventy are up, the second threshold will have been crossed.

So the presence of technology in a human context was, right up until the marks of Kilroy—who, unbeknownst to himself, acted as a prescient prelude to the first threshold of the atom that was crossed just months after his anonymous activities apparently ceased—could be seen as a material expression of both reason and conscience. The inklings that it was not to taken indefinitely as such an expression were first heard in the enlightenment, and Taylor's synopsis of Rousseau's critique attests to this incipient doubt. Indeed, by our own time, reason in machine had been replaced with logic, and conscience is almost replaced by cognition. More than this, these replacement parts have doubled back on us. The human intellect is now of much greater interest than the human conscience. Consciousness has by far the greater discursive status than does conscientiousness—let alone the soaring prevalence of passion over compassion in entertainment commodities—and logic is still extolled as a focused tool of the more nebulous reason. If both reason and conscience were inherently unlimited—they encountered more or less severe limits only within the living and changing contexts of human existence, but at the same time they both were adaptable in an oddly authenticating Darwinian sense—the very fact of the objectificity of the machine or the object status adhering to technologies in general—from lithics to cybernetics, the second threshold of artificial consciousness has yet to be surpassed—produced inherent limits. That is, such limits were already and always present in the machine itself, and did not appear only when the machine encountered a certain context. No doubt these other kinds of ad hoc limits are also present, but this is not the crucial point. For these secondary limits are of the same kind that humans themselves encounter in living on, and they may be negotiated and even overcome through the local genius of people working together and thinking things through. Even our current situation where we face our collective destruction and yet have not sufficiently come together to collectively face it down, may be subject to overcoming. This moment in human history though is fraught with the anxiety that in order to overcome a catastrophic fate we may need to in fact overcome *ourselves*, that is, what we have been up to this point; fractious and parochial beings who have limited foresight and are too self-interested. But the limits inherent in the machine do not allow for it to think itself anew. The machine is "dead" before it begins to function, whereas human beings face their singular deaths as a limit on the extent to which we can renegotiate reality and thus also remake ourselves. The function of children today remains the same in this sense as it always has, even if other mode of production oriented functions—strength in numbers for agrarian labor pools and the like—have slipped away with technological and sometimes even attitudinal shifts.

The immediate and ad hoc utility of the presence of machines remains unquestionable. It is only when we ask "them" to do more than they were designed for that problems arise. Unlike humans, machines can only accomplish and fulfill expectations related to their original design specifications. The concept of what is useful itself, because it is now oriented to the self-limiting quality of technology, has migrated in a similar manner, as have the concepts of logic and cognition, doubling back into ourselves. Upon arrival, it immediately encounters the problem of being displaced and thence misplaced: "The real difficulty in all measurements of utility lies in the fact that we have no idea what 'utility' actually is. Often we surmise its meaning, to be sure, but frequently enough we decide upon two mutually exclusive courses, not because it seems preferable, or because it makes no difference to us, but because something or other must finally be done" (Lösch 1967:224-5 [1945]). This necessity for action in the face of either a challenge or a puzzle is ultimately one of the outstanding hallmarks of the human condition. It presents itself to us as both a threat and an opportunity. The "realist" takes it into his purview as both at once, and only the optimist or the pessimist, with their lenses equally diverging from reality, is either flustered or inspired in some unilaterally ascendant sense. The presence of reliable technologies that can be counted on to perform within the confines of the designed or specified contexts, other things always being equal, has given the concept of utility both a cachet but also a monumental quality. "Making oneself useful" now has a mechanical ring to it. Something or other must indeed "be done," and the most useful human being is the one who can either do it themselves— hence the prevalence of the DIY commodity fetish that Adorno railed against—or who can marshal and then command the forces needed to get the job done. At the same time as Kilroy's self-proclaiming slogan, the official exhortation "Give us the tools and we'll finish the job" appeared in posters. With its oddly gendered realities—here, men were speaking to women, women providing the technologies and men using them—the sense of utility might have reached its most soteriological heights. The requirement of the presence of munitions and hardware in a crisis situation was transparent. It was clear by this time that what was winning the war for the allies was strength in numbers and reliability and not the general quality or sophistication of the technologies at hand. The Russians had figured this out earlier than the Western allies, but these latter inevitably copied the winning formula. "Utility" had come home to a working definition. Through this victory, it was this particular definition of what was of greatest utility, the one thing most useful, was *numbers*. Hence in our post-war period the ascendency of rationalized production of all things, from food to university graduates. The more the merrier, the faster the better. What is good for the goose is good for the gander. Indeed, goose and gander, men and women, were increasingly expected not only to both be able to do the same thing—equality and equity in the women's movements rested in part on this new definition of utility— but to actually be the same kind of human being. Globalization promotes its own yet grander version of the utility of sameness, numbers, reliability and predictability. What began as the convenience of an M4 "Sherman" starting up each morning and getting itself to the battlefield, while the German Panzer crews often had to hold their breath during the same process, had become a mantra for an entire civilization. What has been ignored for the past seventy years or so is the reality of human diversity. The focus of a crisis is not, in fact, the way most people live or need to live, other things being equal. Like the controlled atmosphere of the science lab, with everyone involved working towards a common goal, a global crisis gives us the impression that overcoming it means "all in." The world crisis was the laboratory writ large.

It may be that we are approaching a moment when another global crisis, that of the ecology and biosphere, pushes us to put into play a somewhat reexamined notion of utility and the "all for one" approach. But in general, crisis is not the *leitmotif* of the human condition. In thinking that it is so, we risk turning ourselves into a more complete mimesis of the machines we have constructed to carry out ad hoc performances. We can function only as if there were an ongoing crisis. Certainly, media sells copy and thus advertising by manufacturing the aura—or better, perhaps the *glamour*—of crises, petty or profound. But we can see through this with a little help from our critical friends. What is more opaque is the idea that true utility can be found only in the savior, and saviors only announce their presence when they, or perhaps some others, perceive a crisis, whether it be purely moral or an external threat that reflects on our collective morality. This very narrow and improbable definition of utility acts to focus our remarks; it is the killjoy that wishes to place its mark on our day to day meanderings, but it is also a killjoy that says to the machine that a human being was here first, and what that means is that there are inherent limits to the idea of what is useful. Along with the sense that we "already" know the outcome of each social context and, like the machine's mindlessness, can simply cruise through each encounter with other human beings as well as the corollary encounter with our own humanity is shot through with both the hubris that we noted above, as well as the concept of narrow utility that represents the consummation of crucial but momentary convenience—the all or nothing instance of one for all and do or die—that is itself mostly unrepresentative of the very humanity that constructed it. These new confines present to us a situatedness of Dasein that makes existence a mere "ontic" faculty and that, like atomistic theses, does not query the reasons behind all that "occurs by itself." In turn, training in the inquisitive arts of the discourses and of the sciences also bends itself to the utility of the ad hoc and the momentarily convenient. Those who have the skills of a machine are the most highly valued: "We seem to be a generation of competent technicians rather than of great discoverers and creators" (Sorokin 1956:315). "Seemingly" so because this is always the outward appearance of a social organization that functions within the realm of competencies predefined by the inertia of the new confined situatedness of being. Of course creativity and curiosity remain. They may be muted or undersold, but their very presence is what nudges the technician more closely toward the center of things. And this in two seemingly contradictory ways: on the one hand, I may feel that in order to maintain my social status and market value, that I should shun the imagination of the creator and the adventurousness of the discoverer. But on the other hand I also might glean some crucial piece of an existing puzzle that has nagged the arena of competitive competencies from within, as it were, and thus make myself even more highly regarded by the center of things. The technician loses his sense of equilibrium both positively—curiosity acts as a killjoy to the smug convalescence of a confined consciousness—and also negatively (that is, in the eyes of the centered machine-thought values)—as he is pulled out of the center by the centrifugal force of the human imagination, which in its essential character, never rests contented with any current situation.

Even here, however, the sparks of imagination and the flights of curious fancy are indentured to the task at hand. They are expected to perform the role of toolmaker. New jobs require new tools, and there is a right tool for every task. Give them to us and we will finish or even finish off the problem that is as well always "at hand." It is this sense of at-handedness—based on but departing from Schutz's conception of the stock of knowledge that is knowledge of and not knowledge about—that all things that can be known must by definition be "at hand" in this narrow manner. As well, we can recall here that the concentric model of the social distribution of knowledge places the stock of knowledge at hand in between that of "about" and that of intimacy, and this belies the presence that behind all of this lies human reason and imagination proper to the general challenge of living on as a human being toward death. Our misrecognition that the inherent limits of human life—mimicked in a much more specific and limited manner in the design of machines—can be overcome by projects and rational action allows us to see our technology as not only messianic but as a permanent remark on itself, as if it had no history: "So long as we can negotiate the triumph of technology successfully, we are unconcerned to ask what the presuppositions of this technical world are and how they bind us to its framework" (Barrett, op. cit:223). Thus there exists a disconnect between the regularity of machine "life" and that of day-to-day human ongoingness. They appear to us to be the same thing, and in this it also appears that there is in fact no such disconnect. If the machine's powers are predicated on its function—what it can produce is by no means limited to products such as commodities and, by the same token, the commodity is itself also not limited by the sense that it can be purchased or sold; human beings also "have their price," as is said in shadowy and perhaps also romantic circles, but more to the point, it is human beings who enter in contractual and mechanistic relations with one another—then that very function of the machine lends itself to the task of whitewashing the disintegration of human contextualities. It helps us who seek control over the ambiguities of our existence, but in so doing removes us from the space of capability wherein the combination of reason and imagination confront the only task in which they must see each other in themselves:

> In the end, however, this integration does not come about through the methods of modern science and its mode of unwavering self-control. It accomplishes

itself in the praxis of social life itself. It must always take back into its own purview that which has been placed in the power of human beings, and it has to vindicate the limits that human reason has placed upon its own power and recklessness. (Gadamer 2001:125 [1999])

This "taking back" is certainly apt. It represents not something that has been lost, but something that has been misplaced. We must place it back within our own powers in a landscape that tends to envision power as something possessed and not only wielded, as something physical and not also symbolic, as something that "does something," in the manner in which Lösch referred. The idea of vindication also has a great aptitude but its strength and its sense of justice point to just how far we travelled down the path to nothing by way of the mechanistic morality of ad hoc technologies. Vindication suggests that we have something to justify, whereas in fact it is the ongoing treadmill of self-negotiating and apparently triumphant technology that must be vindicated, and is precisely something that cannot vindicate itself. So we are faced with the dual task of justifying the continued presence of human reason and imagination in a technical world—as well as the presence of the creators and discoverers in a world of technicians—and of finding at least a rationale for the continued use and usefulness of the now indispensable machine. Vindication, if accomplished, marks upon the process the killjoy of a reality check, but this time what it dispenses with is either the mock self-laudatory tones of the triumph of technology—*what*, after all, can technology by itself triumph over but its own inherent limitations, and we have seen that this is impossible without the human posing at least as an engineer—or the complacency of those who habitate within the center of technical life. Like the unity of science based on both common cause—here we see yet again the notion of the do or die crisis to which all must dedicate their unremitting practical strengths and moral fortitudes—or common end—for instance, that the idea that a "theory of everything" can not only be found but that it would be the most profound discovery (cf. Midgely 2004:19)—the narrow conception of utility, in relation to its more material cousin, that of modern *techne* is, as we have seen, a way in which human beings not only give themselves purpose but exalt their consciousness as Babel. The diaspora of the Logos, the diversity of human tongues, does not mean in any ultimate sense that we should not once again find a manner of communicating with one another and live as do the gods. We have staked the claim that science and its mathematically orderable basis *is* in fact that language, the Logos of nature and thus of humanity as well. So it is quite understandable that the unity of science should be not only a human goal but that it rests as an inherent function of the presence of science. Science is one thing because nature is one thing. It is only the killjoy of human diversity and logos—in both the plural sense of there being many tongues but also in the recent sense that advertising marques and slogans act, in a strangely authentic but also ironic manner, to unite us in the face of our empirical and stubbornly self-interested global diversity—that delays both the discovery of the "theory of everything" and the uncovering of scientific unity. But surely even if nature is cut from the whole cloth of evolutionary text and textile, our understanding of it must, because it remains a human understanding and that the evolution of consciousness does not appear to have anything to do with an identity relation with nature—of course, we may be wrong here, perhaps maturity can be measured by its contiguities with the cosmos; perhaps the cosmos itself has a consciousness of which we are yet unaware, and so on—we can fully rely on the differentiation of perspectives that both the subject of our humanity and the objects of the different discourses brings to the table:

> Discussion of the unity of the natural sciences and the human sciences is thus misleading as soon as it does not proceed from the fact that the functions of these two sciences are fundamentally different. [ ] In fact, the natural sciences themselves tell us that their concern is with achieving advances in knowledge and, with these advances, achieving control over nature and maybe even society. Culture, however, exists as a form of communication. (Gadamer 2000:31 [1998])

In the communications of cultures, both within and directed toward one another, the crucial factor is, as Gadamer suggests, that those who participate are members of cultures and not subjects of the discussion. They are not subjects cast as objects. We have seen that the machine presents itself fully as an object in the world. Its success as a both a source and a model of utility pushes us to try to act like it. In doing so, we objectify ourselves and pretend that we too can be as fully an object to the world, and thus accomplish more that is of the utmost, the utility of the task at hand. We can add the further convenience of treating each other as only objects—both in the sense of a self-interested goal or purpose and as a thing that can be commodified or contracted—in the Marxian sense of the double alienation of consciousness. The fact remains that due to culture and its diversity, the logos inspired by the Logos, beings directed toward Being, our subjectivity resists the mere subjectitude of objectification. *Subject* to the next circumstance is the name of the language game. We have seen that new experiences are negative in the hermeneutic sense. A machine cannot experience, as of yet, anything at all, so the idea of the new as presented to an object of this non-sentient sort is meaningless. It is through communication that humans negotiate their own triumphs, and at the same time, are called to recognize that in speaking to one another, the possibility of being wrong about the new is always present: "Communication is not only something external to the verity but, as a matter of fact, is associated with error no less frequently than with truth" (Sorokin, op. cit:45). It may well be that the error shows us the truth. It is at least correct to suggest that we can be shown the truth of our errors. The machine cannot learn from its mistakes, it can only be corrected in its functioning by the human designer and operator. The technician is, in fact, not at all bereft of imagination, though there are formulas and scripts for almost every occasion. This alone does not put out of court the specific abilities of the technician. We are all technicians with regard to the performance of social roles and public life. We may strive to act outside of what is expected from time to time, but this too is part of the libretto of what might be expected of us. The "idea person" or the "inside dopester" remain valuable commodities, and it is they who are charged, in a formulaic manner, with upsetting the status quo and engaging in thinking. That there is still a socially sanctioned space of thought in our technical society is perhaps as surprising as it should be inspiring. Like communication, however, thinking does not always lead to the best form of truth. Facts alone are no guarantor of utility or further creativity let alone ideas such as human freedom. We have thought into being the means of our own annihilation, and, without regard for any other form of life, it too. We can say that it is the comparative lack of communication or even its total absence that leads us to situations where the most potent expression of our imagination can be unleashed. Like the dreamless sleep, upon waking we experience both visions and hallucinations. The mind must continue its work while the brain is up and at it. The unconscious intrudes upon the conscious, and we are at a loss to know what is really there and what is merely apparent to us alone. There is an intimate connection between the world situation and what appears to ourselves as singular subjects of perceptual consciousness:

> The atomic situation is now at the end point of this process: the power to expose the whole population to death is the underside of the power to guarantee an individual's continued existence. The principle underlying the tactics of battle—that one has to be capable of killing to go on living—has become the principle that defines the strategies of states. (Foucault 1980:137 [1978])

The discourse of bio-power must control its own destiny in this manner. It intends no less than the granting of life or death, or both, to every one of us. What appears to us alone is the competing but juxtaposed vision of indefinite life under the auspices of mechanical and rationalized world systems and the hallucinatory nightmare of the death of that world and ourselves included. It is thus all the more understandable that we crouch behind the more hospitable aspects of living in nations and working within institutions. They insulate us from their own powers of destruction. We internalize, to an extent, this idea that not only conforming provides the safest space but that thought itself should also be monitored. After all, it was the human imagination that produced the means of our own annihilation. We must then ask, what is the nature of this self-understanding that now contains within it the knowledge of its own destruction? Is there a latent resentment against our originally Promethean situatedness of being? Along with the future, was there also presented in this moment of becoming fully human the sense that we should strive to know more precisely what had been taken from us? That our knowledge, in order to be considered complete, either as a form of introspective self-examination or as the more objective sensibility that we can characterize human consciousness as a historically enabled and weighted phenomena, should posses once again, but this time in a reflective and reasoned manner, the moment of our death. To possess *this*—and we do, more than metaphorically, possess this knowledge once again through the presence of nuclear weapons and the means to launch them rapidly and without further recourse to alternative options once launched—is to know *what we were*. It is to know our origins as proto-humans, in close proximity with other large mammals and indeed, as their competitors and their prey. Did not the narrative of Prometheus and that of Raven contain within it the caution that to once again retrieve the knowledge taken from us would result in our demise? Like the final option launch of nuclear weaponry, we have, in regaining a form of control over our own deaths, launched ourselves on a predetermined course of events that may not be able to be halted or derailed. In adopting a machine mentality, in adapting to a machine world, we become much more like machines than they become like us. This may, as we have stated, be about to change, but for now the situation is one of a human being faced with a new challenge regarding his humanity and one that is entirely of his own manufacture: the full presence of mechanism as a form of unthought within the ambit of consciousness. This is not merely new, but radical, as there is no historical precedent for it in the object realm alone. The closest aspect of human consciousness that may be said to exhibit a form of unthought and is thus swayed entirely by a deterministic insensibility would be ideology or dogma. Not so far behind these would be teleological argument. We have seen that these kinds of conceptualizations and their arguments often walk hand in hand, or at least may follow from one another. Before Darwin and Wallace nature was conceived as having a purpose or a direction, and statements concerning the nature of Nature were thus couched in a deterministic language that today we would find at best quaint: "The idea of the good, especially as it is presented in Plato's *Laws*, is the real essence of nature. Nature cannot be called blind necessity or coming together of things, but rather the very condition of having been directed toward the good: *psyche* and *techne* denote the same thing" (Gadamer 2001:113 [1964). Who's good? Directed by what or whom? How can mastery or animus suggest a manner of know-how? This last at least is suggestive to us: it is correct to say that someone who possesses *techne* can both ascend to the mastery of her subject, craft or art. She might also already be in such a position, the skills possessed only polished and refined to such an extent that they appear to us as outsiders to be effortless and part of her soul. In this, we can more easily understand Plato's conception of Nature possessing this kind of amalgam or even symbiosis of these related traits. It is the telos, the goal-directed sensibility that today, after Darwin, strikes us as fantasy. On top of this, the fact that we tend to think along the lines of "a watch is present, this implies a watchmaker" or what have you does not mean that human perception grasps the "essence" of things. Human analogies—the mechanism of the watch in no way is by itself suggestive of the mechanisms that drive evolution—have limitations that today we do not imagine nature herself has. It may be that because of the advent of high technology and mass manufacture, that we have shed some of our local human limits, such as when we can view the universe from our singular and relatively immobile vantage point through the prosthetics of telescope, satellite and space voyaging vehicle. In shedding these perceptual limits, we may now be more apt to understand nature as less limited. In doing so, we have of course to recognize the possibility that it is the culture and historical diversity of human perception that casts itself as the explanatory factor for the cosmos simply as a human projection. The problem of "perception as projection," or even the more delicate issue of the two of them being the same thing, is something of which we must always be aware. The fact that we are often astonished by what we perceive in the universe is a good sign, however, even if we then immediately attribute it to evolutionary principles in much the same way that Plato attributed the astonishing revitalization of nature to the principle of the good. Perhaps, given the challenge of deterministic unthought and the muted but still present desire for a teleology of human life—if not now so much life in general or even the presence of something rather than nothing—we should pay closer attention to the rise and distribution of modern discourses that tend to possess within their ambit veiled versions of ultimate statements and goals (cf. Foucault (op. cit: 84ff) for a detailed list of such attributes).

We should also not be dismissive of the thought of our forebears simply because it sometimes seems remote from either our interests or our sensibilities. We still like to believe in goods, if not necessary the Good in itself. Most of us strive to "be good" in some vague manner relating to either past religious dogmas or the "Laws." We still use vernacular oddities like "Platonic relationship" denoting one that is intimate but sexually chaste. We also are very aware that someone like Plato, in another famous text, seems to still be exactly correct about the character of human desire in the realm of the political: "The just life is most advantageous—even in the absence of success in the world of action and power. In fact, the truly wise, just, and thus happy—person is disinterested in the world of power" (Taylor 1989:120). We remain rightly suspicious of those who seek power, either of the wide political sort or between individuals in intimate relationships. The two texts, the *Republic* and the *Laws* are closely related. Is it only the case that when the ancients speak of human affairs that their truths resonate for us, and when they speak of the cosmos they are more or less out to lunch? There are many moments when the two worlds are densely imbricated. In the *Phaedo,* Socrates claims that honesty is the best policy. In our modern world, we know that there are many persons who cheat their way to success. But what kind of success, and at what other cost? As leverage for the argument concerning the immortality of the soul—and note once again that the soul is a pet project for many human cultures, a kind of metaphysical hobby if you will—Socrates suggests that even if the case cannot be proven with certainty, it is still better to lead an honest life (cf. Gadamer 2000:42-3ff). We still generally agree with this, atheists and theists alike. But why? Does being honest not determine our actions even if it does not dictate our thoughts? The goal of being honest acts itself as a kind of telos. Are being and acting then to be taken as the same thing? If our thoughts can harbor the dishonest, ulteriorities of occluded intents and desires, just because we then cast these adrift and decide to act honestly in spite of the apparent options, does this mean that we are in truth honest in our being?

This may all of a sudden appear to be a major departure from machines and mechanisms, but it not only serves to underscore the difference between humans and their tools but also points up the fact that machines do not have to ask these kinds of questions of themselves. They are "relieved of the trouble of being honest," to paraphrase Marx's sardonic comment concerning the lifeways of the wealthy, and of course can be equally said to be so relieved in the realm of dishonesty as well. No thought and unthought are related, but they are not the same thing. We cannot accuse the machine proper of unthought, because it does not, as of yet, think at all. It is *our* attitude in the presence of the machine that creates unthought, just as it did with ideology, dogma, and perhaps certain forms of teleology as well. And it is this that links the two topics quite closely indeed: honesty requires thought of a kind that opens up onto the world scene and requires others then to think as well. Dishonesty seeks to close off the aperture of vision into human affairs and sneaks around in the shadows where all is *assumed* to be functioning correctly. It, in other words, seeks the space of the machine bereft of its human operators, for even if one cannot fool this or that real machine, one never has to admit one's wrong to it. In the absence of human oversight, being caught by a machine means nothing. We can simply ignore it and move on, as if the photo radar camera existed by itself and carried no further implications, implications that involve the action of other human beings. Barring a society that Ray Bradbury envisioned where the machines continue to act without human oversight or operators—surely they would break down at some point, unless they were also self-repairing—we must recognize that unthought and mechanism are not only kindred, they need each other. The greatest error we commit in this realm today is believing that unthought is the most convenient guide to action and that mechanism is that same thing in the world of forms and objects. In the face of the messianic call of the thought-less machine, we can either respond with our own very human form of unthought that includes the intentions of the dishonest, or we can settle into a lengthy and critical dialogue with our own desires as projected onto and into the world.

Chapter Three

Wanted Dead or Alive: God

We are living in the time of the afterlife of God. As such, there is an odd surreality to our visions. We might think we should by now, after more than a century, be able to either shrug our shoulders at the "God is dead" declamation, respond with a "so what" of our own. And this not so we can keep the belief alive that God or the gods remain living in the same old way that they were once imagined doing, but so that we can either make a decision to move on without them—after all, they may have left us first—or that we can understand their presence with the same grace and hope we often give to our own. Why, if we continue to either have faith or hope or at the very least, a curiosity that even may be framed in a scientific manner, concerning the possibilities of our own afterlife, should we turn around and deny the same thing to God or the gods? No, this is clearly a form of resentment speaking in us. If we recognized the death of God and at first felt liberated because of it, we also gradually gained as well as sense of resentment about it. That is, we the living. God gets to die but I have to live on. And now, I might ask, with the death of God what am I living on for. Nietzsche is absolutely correct to state that with the death of god, the death of Man cannot be far behind. Perhaps by now this too has occurred and we are only beginning to recognize it. Maybe we as well are living in the time of the afterlife of man. Certainly we are, as mentioned in chapter two, on the cusp of altering our definition of what it means to be physiologically and even cognitively human. The old human may soon be dead, just as the "old god" of morality, or whatever it was that he was said to represent—and definitions no doubt vary considerably on this point, both historically and theologically—is already. This too may in part be a function of resentment, most especially that to the fact that I must die, even as a prosthetic god I cannot live on indefinitely. Or can't I? Between stem cells, cybernetics and other synthetic replacement parts, why can I not construct my own earthly afterlife; a life after the original and much more fragile human life has run its course? It is *this* idea—that we may gain all the mythical privileges of an afterlife and yet not have to die; that our "souls" can not only be made immortal in this life but that we can even allow ourselves to have a soul, though for this express purpose only and not necessarily as part of our ethics or conscience (who will be able to become immortal in our world of inequality and capital and who will not?)—that drives the astonishing feats of medicine, prostheses of genetic organism and cybernetics alike, and the personal engineering of devices that extend the senses in all directions. We want to live on without having to face the question of what occurs to life as it lives on. We desire mortal immortality.

Let us look at three different aspects of this recent error by which we desire to live. First, the concept of a God who is dead yet continues to exist or persist in some way. God is neither alive nor dead in our modern world, and this may be one of the reasons why "we have never (really) been modern," to borrow Latour's phrase. As well, if this is correct, then we also must face the possibility of the zombie god, that He is actually undead and walks amongst us unrecognized, in search of our dead souls. Finally, we may also want to begin to distinguish between our loyalties regarding these questions: are we fans or fanatics when it comes to holding onto this or that aspect of the premodern metaphysical systems that were created in and then dominated the agrarian civilizations for millennia? We might well be the first when we hope to some form of continuing consciousness after empirical and organic death, but the second if we adhere too literally to the imagined moralities of our ancestors and their systems of belief. The fact that we live in the here and now does not make every fanatic into a fan. The human imagination can find fulfillment in as much factual error as it needs. Indeed, what is the character of these "facts" to which this or that loyalty lends itself? We may find that, like God, the concept of the factual too now either rests in an uneasy repose just under our blithe gaits, or, more disconcertingly, walks with us, at our side, unseen and undead, but ready to topple our living selves and show them up as the hollow idols which they may be.

3.1 THE AFTERLIFE OF GOD

If God is dead but still exists, what is the character of his existence, and why do the vast majority of people around the world still at least pay public lip service to the idea that the gods remain with us in some kind of conscious form? "Still today, decades after the death of God for Western philosophy, myth lays claim to be a discourse that does not require to be demonstrated, counting on self-evidence, a last remnant of sacredness after a long eclipse of the sacred" (Passerini 1990:50). Perhaps it would be all the more apt to say *"remanant"* rather than mere remnant. It is something that haunts us, appearing in visitations rather than visits. The *subito* of the first, the unknowingness of the perceiver, the utter difference in its form, smacks of the uncanny. Visiting someone as another living being is a day-to-day routine affair. It has the character only of the mundane life. It is somewhat difficult for us today to imagine a culture where visitation was itself mundane, but such cultures existed all over the world until very recently. These were the societies of the social contract, and within this contractuality, nature and super-nature were also intimately involved. The world of spirits and the world of men were not only contiguous, sharing a spherical border with one another, the one enveloped in the other and also in a reciprocity with its mate—the soul here was passed back and forth between the two worlds without evaluation or even much delay—but could not exist without each other. Perhaps it was the advent of the concept of the afterlife as an extended period or even a permanent rustication that was the wedge that drove these worlds apart, ultimately resulting in the world of humans no longer able to believe in the existence of any other kind of world.

This is certainly much the case today. Visitation is considered an effect of a cognitive failure, even a derangement. The messiahs and prophets of other modes of production would be cast as lunatics by our own standards of conduct and right thinking. Vision is something one gets from the telescope. And in no way should we be seen as impugning such visions as we do get. They are equally wonderful—and perhaps all the more astonishing because we did not invent them—as were those religious in nature. But it is just *this* sentiment, the sense that there was something spiritual about nature itself, that there was the "religious in nature" that we have forsaken, or, that has forsaken us: "If religious faith were like some particular illusory belief, whose erroneous nature was only masked by a certain set of practices, then it would collapse with the passing of these and their supersession by others; as perhaps certain particular beliefs about magical connections have" (Taylor 1989:403). Though it is quite reasonable to say that it is in religious behavior that human beings make these connections, the "magic" of being part of a community is not, in fact, entirely lost on us, as anyone who has faced the challenge of living alone will tell you. We cannot then make the strict claim that ritual and action in the world are mere covers for the absence of authentic belief. "Works and faith" may go hand in hand, but their apparent *de facto* separation also works its way back into faith. We cannot continue to live in a community without giving something back to it. We do so in good faith, the faith that tells us that not only will our contributions be taken by others in equally good faith but that these others will respond to our actions in the world by continuing to welcome us as part of who they are, as one of the constituents of their self-definition. All of us must have at least this kind of faith, even if it is no longer directed up and away to some other force or figure that is patently non-human but retains some kind of human interest. Perhaps this continued notion of interest, as a projected self-interest is also a necessary part of contemporary faith. This is why the pure atheist can be imagined as the "ugliest man," for he dismisses the action of faith altogether: "The atheist is the one that reveres nothing; he will appear on Zarathustra's mountain as the ugliest man." (Lingis 1989:67). In his negation of the truth, he finds himself at once claiming to have discovered the truth of truths and yet no longer knowing why he believes in a truth at all, nor yet why he is able to believe. Just as atheism is a religion that includes within its beliefs the denial that it is a religion—as if religion and the idea of God were inextricable; any cursory examination of the history of ethnographic records will tell us otherwise, and if one persists in stating that atheism generalizes the persona of Godhead as a gloss for *any* force higher or larger than human beings, one would have to suggest that atheism rename itself as naturism or scientism since the faith in *these* higher forces remain cardinal to it—the atheist finds himself in the uncomfortable position of self-denial. He has discovered, if anything, that there is an anti-Cartesian position also at hand; "I don't think, therefore I am not."

But since the atheist remains stubbornly human—and perhaps it is here that we can reinsert the coming sense of non-human consciousness that may be at hand in the form of a cyber-organic sentient mechanism; these beings might become the first real atheists in the sense Marx was thinking of as someone to whom the very idea of God could not occur—he then must find a way to explain away this humanity to the rest of us who are trying to find a way to explain it. To do so takes him on a surreal journey where desire, anxiety, and general human feeling seem to be in the way, instead of things that are on the way, to becoming human: "Whenever we seriously judge something to be wrong, strong feeling necessarily accompanies the judgement. Someone who does not have such feelings [ ] has missed the point of morality altogether" (Midgely 2004:105). But perhaps the atheist also strives for, not immorality, because this is a function of what is said to be moral, but amorality or even a Nietzschean "non-morality," the concept he made famous in his 1871 essay on "truth and lie in the non-moral sense." Well, amorality is commonly associated with those who seem to lack a conscience. But this is an error of casual language. Only animals are amoral. Human beings who behave like animals are still immoral because they remain fundamentally human even if they have departed from most of the bonds that allow us to be human together and thus become more than our own individuated humanity could ever accomplish. It is the continued recognition of this kind of "more" that in its absence distinguishes the psychopathic criminal, perhaps, from even those lawbreakers who have developed codes of honor and duty of their own and are loyal to them, such as organized crime syndicates or terrorist organizations. The one who is closest to amorality would never understand the necessity for confession, say, or the idea that a truth can be told apart from one's desires or immediate perceptions: "Confession does not consist in making known—and thereby it teaches that teaching as the transmission of positive knowledge is not essential. The avowal does not belong in essence to the order of cognitive determination: it is quasi-apophatic in this regard" (Derrida 1995:39 [1993]). That is, it names and unnames itself at once. Its apophasis retains the order of morality and even thus anti-morality in order to remark upon it, put it under erasure—it lingers there, just as does God, in a remanant-like state, ready not to visit us but to "visitate"—so that any "knowledge" that could be said to have been divulged in this way cannot be pinned down as a truth or as something knowable in itself: it has at once masked itself under another guise, that of the confession of the confessional. So the *amoralist* is someone who has no knowledge of himself and thus cannot be held accountable for his actions. And indeed, with insanity as a category of para-being in modern legal statutes, we do not in fact hold such people accountable for their actions as moral vehicles. We only seek to protect ourselves from the possibility of their continued actions. Just as Gide's famous "immoralist" sought to defy or mock the established institutional order by simply acting against it whenever the opportunity arose, the moralist too knows her actions as a form of truth ahead of time, that is, knows why she is about to do something and also knows in part at least, if it is in the right or tending towards the wrong, pending local definition and actual outcome. The amoralist has no such knowledge, and thus all of his acts are a kind of confession of the absence of self-understanding.

What then of the non-moralist? Nietzsche's shadow is not ugly, but it is a little difficult to fully distinguish its features. Here, we must assume that the one who appears to be non-moral—or "extra-moral" as the incomplete and misleading English translation of the 1871 essay sometimes has it; not unlike the catchier but equally misleading "use and abuse of history," another famous essay of the following year—does so in order to institute, or at the very least, insinuate (incipit Zarathustra!) another in its place. The new gospel of the overman would be one such optional replacement. Like the one who traversed the wire, we other rope-dancers cannot be assured not only that we will not fall, but also that there would be anyone to witness our demise. When we do ultimately fall off the torus of living being and perhaps pass onward to some other form of consciousness, those who remain in our stead tend not to entirely hold onto either an immoral or a non-moral position: "Even in atheistic countries Christian or other religious practices are admitted alongside the otherwise political and secular ways of honouring the dead." (Gadamer 1996:66 [1983]). The witnessing of human finitude may make us wince, but we still present ourselves to it in a manner that has some certitude, unlike those who through happenstance alone gawk at the rope-dancer and then move on. And just as we might think we are honoring not only the dead—not of course as dead, per se, but as one who has lived as we yet live—but also various religious traditions that remain alive through their practitioners more than through their believers, we also honor the pedigree of religious thinking in general. Jung mentions that the Epiphany is actually an ancient Pagan festival, and the monstrous forms related in the book of Revelation hail from beliefs quite distant from the nascent Christianity and "cannot be explained in its terms" (cf. Jung 1959:104-5ff [1951]). The current states or even the statuses of our beliefs—traditional, customary, ritualistic, public but not private, external but not internal, or what have you—cannot be used to judge either their historical gravity or their ethical profundity in terms of the cultural evolution of the human species as a whole. We tend to see only the surfaces of things to this regard. Symbolic forms "function" at a variety of levels. They certainly appear as the glad-handedness of faith communities in terms of being able, as a member, to assume that your compatriots are heeding similar notions of what it means to do or be good in the world, or how one honors the recently dead or venerates in a different way the "majesty" of death. Yet they also are at work beneath the surfaces of these fascia, like the course of water that gets into everything and everyone. [1] The afterlife of God in this sense may be framed as the conscious state of affairs overtaking that unconscious. In this situation, we have ourselves to think things through and know that we are not only still reliant on such symbolism and mythic metaphor, but have also made it more real in that we can call it to the fully wide-awake consciousness of the everyday life, and not have to make pilgrimages to specifically sacred sites or geographic destinations where the abode of the gods exists. We have moved from a topography the sacred to a topology of the sacred.

Jung gives us a further and more famous example than the Epiphany, and one in which this process of existential motion from historic to the chthonic to then finally as a mnemonic is fully realized; "The fish symbol is thus the bridge between the historical Christ and the psychic nature of man, where the archetype of the Redeemer dwells. In this way Christ became an inner experience, the 'Christ within.'" (op. cit:183). What then is this form of memory but the knowing that what lies within us is immortal and redeemable. This kind of redemption can often seem alien to us today, especially when the word has migrated into contractual use within the realm of commodities. One can "redeem" coupons more ably than one's soul. Yet it was the rebel who called upon the socius to become a neighbor and to thus redeem himself in this way, through the acts of a good faith that lies open to the other. No authority figure that stood within what had been could have accomplished this motion. "The advocacy of the canon of values inherited from the fathers and enforced by education manifests itself in the psychic structure as 'conscience.'" (Neumann, op. cit:173). Not all forms of authority stand positioned in this way, however. Famously, Weber saw "charismatic" authority as the force that not only stood up against the tradition and the symbolic institutions thereof, but also because of the dialectic that originated in this questioning of traditional authority, initiated one of the great world-historical dynamics, a major trope both in literature and in myth. It may be that each new generation is possessed of the sense that *something* must be changed, no matter if such an alteration represents no real revolution but more an adjustment. Indeed, one might venture to say that this is both the safest and in general the most functional manner of changing society for the common benefit of all. However conservative this may sound to youth, it is clear that all successful changes to social orders come about because the old guard eventually is won over to a certain extent. They can see enough of themselves—whether as persons or persona, Neumann mentions that this is irrelevant (cf. ibid:174ff)—in the new picture to get behind it, no doubt after some haggling and complaining. It very much matters whether or not their successors exist in larger numbers than they themselves, as was the case of the "baby boom" in the mid-twentieth century in North America, and also whether or not, as youth age into positions of power and privilege, these new helmspersons are willing to chart a course not so dissimilar to the one's set by their parents. That they most often do so Weber called "routinization," and it is easy to see why this otherwise clunky English gloss was chosen to translate Weber's original term. But this concept can be used in an even more profound setting. It also describes one of the key differences between myth and thought. Mythic narratives are set in the routine language of the everyday. Though their content may be fabulous or phantasmagorical, their action, plots, characters and motives are quite familiar to the listener, and can be accessed through his own experience of daily life and his biographical datum. The conflicts amongst the gods or other forces, the fates and the afterlife, destiny and tragedy, all were larger than life analogies to the challenges human beings faced within their own local and mortal settings. Not so philosophy: "Myths, unlike history, were originally narratives trying to express all that and to do it in a pleasant form. More pleasant, according to Plato, than *logos*, the tool of philosophy" (Passerini, op. cit:49). To this day, people who read, read fiction. Stories are what capture the imagination of most, and simply because they are not exactly real in no way suggests that they bear only a fleeting resemblance to reality. What they do not force the reader to do unless she chooses to do so is *analyze* that reality and her place in it. The lonely textual alternatives of authors such as myself are no match for the enduring human interest in the narrative form. No matter how convivial philosophy might be made, thinking requires the reader to work, as if there is not enough of that in the world already! But this is also precisely what the messiahs and prophets imagined that we should be doing. Their formula was generally more successful, especially over the short term, than was philosophy's. The reason is simple; they portrayed the changes they wanted people to think about allegorically, by the construction of new narratives—that of the "good Samaritan" is one such famous one from Christianity—and the presentation of a new version of heroism—the "neighbor" as a mode of being and not as a socially sanctioned social role, for instance. In doing so, an entirely new world is opened up and redefined: "With this, everything becomes clear. The lone god, the new God, is what we call the universe. This is the only thing that exists. For the Greeks, 'god' is a predicate" (Gadamer 2000:91 [1998]). People could identify themselves in these new narratives, in spite of the differences in content that they presented when they, as they necessarily must have done, compared and contrasted them with the stories of their childhood and of their culture history. In the famous parable, where Jesus eventually exhorts his audience to "go and do likewise," the new neighbor figure stops and helps a very marginal character by the side of a road, someone whom others would not shake a stick at. On top of this, there is also a latent sense that being of the Samaritan ethnicity would make it unlikely that one could even be "good," in this way or others, hence the added qualifier to this new hero's identity. Today, even though the metaphysics and the explanatory territory of the then new religion have been overtaken by science and our ideas of consciousness have been disenchanted, we still refer to those who engage in helping others with no sense that they get much of anything out of it as "Samaritans," dropping even the qualifier "good." Whether or not there remain any actual Samaritans, living in Palestine or nearby, who can claim that they are the successors of those ancient ones, one of whom is described in the gospels, is entirely beside the point. Many later interpreters of the gospels lent them a sense that their contents were also to be taken seriously as an ethics. This is important, because ethics was defined as a department of philosophy, and it was Aristotle who made the first move to dissociate it from metaphysics as a separate project of thinking and a separate, though related, aspect of human consciousness. These interpreters, "were rational in their outlook, but they had a religious inflation instead of the rationalistic and political psychosis that is the affliction of our day" (Jung, op. cit:84). Such an editorial, if one may call it that, is not quite justified. The Gnostics and others were groups of thinkers, and thinkers in any day and age are not at all representative of the whole of their cultures. Indeed, in order to claim to be one, at least as a recognizably social role, no matter of how little general value and certainly almost no value to a market, ancient or modern, one had to set oneself apart from the going rate, "political" or rationalized as the case may be. So it is not the case that our ancestors were more generally amenable to starting philosophical conversations than are we. We sometimes might imagine this to be the case simply because history has bequeathed to us their records, the records of the literate and the privileged, and not the case studies of the billions of ordinary folk who back-dropped every cultural scene going back to the origins of agriculture. Thus we have a very small and poor sample of all that history actually could represent, all that *happened*. On top of this, we have only a partial sample of the elite thoughts of most ages, and this problem of representation only begins to become ameliorated in the West by the Renaissance and only in certain specific regions for some centuries beyond. This *partiality*—in both senses of the word; we have a fragment of the whole and we are also loyal to it due to its very presence amongst us, a keen-eyed well-spoken voice of the dead—sometimes betrays both our logic and good sense. Nevertheless, what we do know about our past is almost seen as sacred, which is why the destruction of archaeological sites is considered to be a war crime, on the order of a crime against the entire species, to whom these artifacts and sites rightfully belong.

This attitude toward the past, the more reverent the more distant from us, is also a variable that plays it's part in the enduring notion of the afterlife, whether or not one grants a god to have this characteristic as part of his or her nature. With the rise of irrigation monopolies in the Near East and their attendant and ascendant archaic empires, all of those people of whom there exists no record are said to have thought their leaders to be quite literally gods on earth, which is where the later religions like Christianity get their characterizations: "People spoke of him as 'God,' and this is not [ ] a 'fine phrase' merely, but a symbolic fact" (Neumann, op cit:149). This figure was also himself original in the sense that he was "uncreated," unevolved and came from no other place but his very own. This "ipssissimosity" combined the autochthony of the local sense of ground and thus also being grounded, as well as authenticity—there can be only one original (yet another mythical trope borrowed by modern advertising): "The first, true, one god does not move but rather rests in himself because he is none other than the universe and is the predicate that the universe deserves" (Gadamer, op. cit:92). One's very-ownness also is its own by virtue of owning the cosmos. The cosmos means order, but the One *is* order. The cosmos is ordered but the One *orders*. The most commonplace phrase in our contemporary service sector is either a direct mimicry of this sense of giving and taking or some kind of paraphrase of it: "May I take your order?" or even the more generic "May I help you" are ubiquitous today. Even here the Heraclitan admonishment might be said to appear. The Gods remain present in a consciously symbolic or rhetorical form. This is part of their afterlife. That we can be as gods not only prosthetically through object realm technology, as we saw, within certain crucial limits, in the previous chapter, is yet further extended by our reliance, most often commercial and contractual, upon other living fellow-humans like ourselves but with generally less good fortune. At the very least, their age-gradedness belies their possible social status in some temporary manner, as most service sector workers tend to be youthful, and indeed, specifically female youth is sought after to perform these roles and thus garner various remunerations, taxed and untaxed, for their appearance on this usually transient stage. Taking one's "order" then implies that we are able to mimic the place and power of the gods or God, the original power and creative act, for that speaks to us as the voice and source of all cosmogonical narratives. The beginning of a special night out, the ordering of a meal in a personalized context of the ritual of the communal feast—and even here, as with funeral rites the sumptuary character of the wedding banquet retains its cosmogonic apparatus, for after all, the ultimate act of that evening is the sexual union between the divine partners producing the offspring, the life of consciousness that will inhabit the young universe of the newlyweds—also "orders" what is to come, whether the number of courses or pending further events and interactions. The politeness, however rhetorical, of the one who serves is tantamount to supplication, even sacrifice, as we know that wait staff do not perform their roles lightly given that they are hoping for the best tips. All of this suggests that we are kings for a day. (cf. Neumann, op. cit:251). Of course, once the night is over and the new day begins, we might retain few of the honorifics that had been ours just hours before. This usually does not bother us, however, because we are now wrapped in the rapture of human affections, and these hold our rapt attention for the time being, and perhaps for a lifetime, though this too is now seen mostly for what it is, yet another myth.

Naming ceremonies are yet another context where the afterlife of the gods continues to preside. We look for or imagine personality traits that then can be denoted by personal names. We check the ancestry of one's family name to see if it suggests anything to us. We wince if we adopt someone with a name that somehow is aesthetically foreign to us, or has negative connotations or associations. Joshua, perhaps the most famous name in Western Christian history, means something to do with the fish, hence the cartouche like logo that Christians display in the most unlikely places, including the trunk lids of vehicles. But here too the afterlife of the gods represences itself. A convivial remanant is always in the offing for believers, and one need not feel haunted in any of the usual somewhat disconcerting senses by using the ancient logos in this or that mundane manner. Jung speaks of "Joshua ben Nun," a legendary Khidr figure that is the son of a fish (cf. op. cit:111).[2] What one may say of the naming ritual one may say of the interpretation of history. It is mythic "thought" that links them together and makes them complicit. Portelli suggests that "history can tailor the desirable to what is given," and in this sense the entire history of the one who is named to be a certain kind of figure—perhaps, the next god on earth, as Nietzsche exhorts to women, "may you be the mother of the overman"—is unfolded in the act of creation. So too, in subsistence societies with high infant mortality rates, the first real name is not given until the child is up to four years old and is thus much more likely to survive until adulthood where the names will change in an existential manner yet again. The very conception of history is shot through with the idea that it is *not* set in stone. Morality, yes, but not history. We even have developed the commonplace sense that what has happened may be judged as going awry and thus it should be set right. Further to this, it is just as obviously up to us to do just that: "While uchronia claims that history has gone wrong—and has been *made* to go wrong—the commonsense view of history amounts to claiming that history *cannot* go wrong—and implicitly, what is real is also good" (Portelli 1990:152, italics the text's). So in essence, what is being claimed here is that the wrongness found within a certain series of events has been placed there by forces external to the world-historical dynamic, whatever its nature, because the internal clockwork of the timepiece that records and speaks to us of history is itself inviolate. That is, it cannot sabotage itself. From this we get the sense that what the outcome of historical events is in the present is not only real but, if history has not been tampered with, also part of the good in the same way the we saw Plato understanding the good as the calculated direction driving natural forces. Such forces do not have a history as such; they merely have a development and a direction. Should history too then be thought of as a mode of being "supernature"?

This is hardly a new idea: "The idea that God designs things for the human good took the form of a belief in good order of *nature*. Providence was understood in general terms: it was reflected in the regular disposition of things" (Taylor 1989:272, italics the text's). Environmentalism of all kinds reclaims and maintains this idea. It is always human beings who are the saboteurs of nature, just as some of us take on the villain's role with regard to history. Uchronia at a biographical level certainly could be dismissed as neurotic wish fulfillment, but it includes more than this when viewed symbolically. It too is part of the afterlife of the gods, for it seeks to appeal to the supernature of the designer of history to adjust what some of us have interfered with. The ultimate challenge for all uchronic leanings is the confrontation with personal death. One may have already died a few times during one's lifetime and thus become "immortal" in the Nietzschean sense—we do realize as we age that who we once were was not always who we were and certainly not who we are at present, and that this too will change, giving us a sense that a lifetime contains a number of actual *lives*—but we still must face the fact of understanding that there is a finite limit to the process of rebirth. Hence the notion of the afterlife in which rebirth is merely the liminal moment of a cosmogony that announces itself through the shadowy visitation of death. It is a radical and perhaps even a little romantic announcement, much like an engagement or the emotions at weddings and funerals alike, but it holds its own history to itself with great persistence, and is breeched not even by our rational and technological surroundings and perhaps even discourses: "But if it is true that even this scientific Enlightenment, like that of the ancient world, finds its limit in the ungraspability of death, then it remains true that the horizon of questioning within which thought can approach the enigma of death at all is still circumscribed by doctrines of salvation" (Gadamer 1996:69 [1983]). And this soteriological intent works both ways, as it were. God's perfection, we are told, hinges on Man's ability to perfect himself through being the goal of creation (cf. Neumann, op. cit:119). For if the creation of God does not carry itself through to its fruition, then the creator himself has only himself to blame, though later on this idea was reinterpreted as being a function of the free will given to human consciousness by the creator. At the same time, the distance between humans and gods begins to grow right at this point. The advent of free will, even within a strictly theological context, was the beginning of the end of the living God. God's death throes begin here. The "scientific enlightenment" merely marked the funeral procession of a being already dead but, as we have argued, not yet gone.

But if this solemn and unknowing procession undertakes the death of creation and as well the idea of creation—the Romantic movement resurrected this idea with regard to both art and the artist, and this, in spite of its rather ridiculous quasi-religious overtones, continues to be the most commonly held view of what an artist's "purpose" is, yet another testament to the afterlife of God—it also ironically "created" something new: "The infinity and silence of this new universe beget anxiety because they bring with them the uneasy sense that mankind may be only a tiny and meaningless freak within nature." (Barrett 1979:122). This assuredly is one response to the individuated social reality that at once desires community and does not quite know how to perform it, all the while imagining that it was somehow better performed by our predecessors—an suggestion that has little evidence to support it—and at the same time desires the autonomy of free thought and will. The latter desire is assuaged through technology, as we have seen, the use of which produces certain freedoms such as that of mobility and various creature comforts. Could not the former also be assuaged, not by technology, but by the enduring if subaltern presence of the knowledge that the desire for human community is an authentic mode of being for us? That is, to have the sensibility that to live only as an individual is to live in the absence of part of our humanity is to also realize that we often experience this absence and that there should be means to assuage it. Barrett's malaise is only half the story here: "Rather than being pushed off into a realm of inaccessibility, transcendence reveals its proper status as a force *within* the human career, as forceful and as 'present' as the startling realization of intersubjectivity: the appresented reality of the Other as a being like me" (Natanson 1970:146, italics the text's). Out of the common sense that my desires may well be present to the consciousness of the other is produced a notion of the transcendental. This experience—I am interested in the welfare or the intents of another, I can respond as well as ignore her desires but I must *do* something in the face of not only her presence but also her will—does not replace the gods on earth, it continues in their absence, in their distance from us. It is, more than anything else, their legacy to us as well as their historically laden task left for us to work through. But we work through this task primarily with one another and not by ourselves. "Transcendence" begins at home. It seeks what is not at the moment present to us. Yet it also provides the means of making things present, and this includes the creative genius that constructs a technology that might not merely alienate us but also destroy us. Is it possible, that despite our differences and our anxieties regarding the presence of the other—I might well wish the world were more like me, and every writer who speaks to the other desires to at least open a conversation with otherness in this way—the technology we have invented to protect ourselves from him is also an expression of our desire for a world that is unlike the one we currently have? Even our most grotesque arsenals make this demand upon us—to change the world or die.

And this change is an example of transcendence. And since all forms of transcendence as a "force within us" are resonant with the full presence of the afterlife "within" this life, we are pulled to recognize the presence of something other to ourselves already and always calling us to immanence. One part of this story is alienation, but this is the passive aspect of modern humanity. The active part of our self-understanding, the part that reaches outward instead of merely dwelling inside our acknowledged limitations, is the part that seeks to transcend itself. It still has every reason to desire this, if not to be able to quite accomplish it in the fullest sense. Even so, it has the power to bracket out its ultimate limitation in order to accomplish the living task that life presents to us. The power of the presence of an afterlife *is* the future. It is something that is not known in the same way that the present or the past can be known. But its "existence" as a postulate based on experience is of the same character as the existence of an afterlife that has been posited by a tradition. Traditions are the human experience writ large. Persons have biographies, cultures have histories. There is as much or as little reification in both, given the play of mortal memory in the one and that of politics and fashion in the other. It is not even enough to suggest that what follows the living-present is like an afterlife because the idea behind this traditional concept is of something that occurs or follows what we now know as life and living-on. No, for us, the afterlife is the future in its most broad sense. That it cannot be empirically known before it occurs provides the analogy with the conception as viewed through the lenses of a society where God was not yet dead. But since God and the gods have already matriculated to the afterlife, our task is follow them in our own human way, our "transcendence" dictated by the reality of having to make a future together. Indeed, one might suggest that the afterlife only "occurs" as it were, once one passes into it, just as does the future. God, in dying and yet continuing to exist, now also has the capability of resonating through all that surrounds us. Just as we imagine that the soul has a presence that the body cannot duplicate, the living god—beholden as he was to his earthly life and to his heavenly abode alike—is not as portable and transfigurable to our modern consciousness as is the one who is dead. We tell ourselves that we return to nature, ashes to ashes and the like, precisely because our gods have already returned there and now speak to us from this diffuse vantage point. But their message is the same as it always was—save yourself and humanity from your own self-made menaces: "The infinite theater of nature now replaces the infinite gaze of God as the theater in which the being, the significance, and the worth of each life is maintained unrestrictedly" (Lingis, op. cit:172). Why is nature seen as infinite in the first place? It is because it bears the mark of creation for us. It quietly murmurs the message of consciousness, even though for the time being we understand that we are empirically alone and can only hear our own voices echoing back to us from vaster and vaster distances as we continue to reach out to the stars. But the very fact that we reach out is the ultimate attestation of the human desire for community and for self-understanding. To know the cosmos is to know ourselves. It is also to know what it means to be a being that can forget things and find replacements for them: "Once metaphysical ideas have lost their capacity to recall and evoke the original experience they have not only become useless but prove to be actual impediments on the road to wider development" (Jung 1959:34 [1951]). But such ideas do not lose these capacities on their own. We either continue to use them in our architecture of being—pediments rather than impediments—or we transform them into new materials. But the task remains the same. It is true that "One clings to possessions that have once meant wealth; and the more ineffective, incomprehensible and lifeless they become the more people cling to them" (ibid). But it is also true that just as often, and just as willingly, people slough off the impedimental dross of hollow idols—we often do so by recognizing that which is holding us back from maturing as persons first and foremost, and this realization gradually spreads to others and is spread back to us in turn—because we are aware, even in our clinginess, that we are dependent upon them in some negative manner. Even most addicts recognize that theirs is but half a life, living out its dangerous half-life with the warning that others should not come too close. The radiation of the negative is not lost on us. We may lose various ways of being; cultures and their gods come and go. What we do not lose is either the will to the future, forward-thinking, projects of action, phantasms and plans of all kind, as well as the knowledge that such may have unexpected outcomes, that the future is "not ours to see." It is life after life, but it almost always occurs in spite of its present impenetrability. The experience of the future becoming the present and then being consigned to something that had occurred, both empirically and existentially, is living proof that the afterlife remains a viable place of consciousness.

3.2 DEAD SOULS AGAIN

Wanting God or some equivalent being to be either dead or alive is one of our chief contemporary errors of unthought. It comes from the projected and misplaced analogy concerning how we view our own human life. But gods are not human. That was the whole point of imagining them in the first place, as a role model to direct us toward the "transcendence" that we have heard some thinkers speak about in the above. Knowing that we must live on in the face of death is one thing that presses in on us, but it also demands that we live out this life in an exalted fashion, because it really suggests to us that there is a great heroism and exaltation in so living, in having to live in this way, unlike all other creatures, including those that appear only in dreams and visions: "When the sages of the Enlightenment deposed God and demystified Mother Nature, they did not leave us without an object of reverence. The human soul, renamed as the individual—free, autonomous, creative—ascended to that post" (Midgely 2004:89). This is no mere semantic sleight of hand. The sense that there should be both a beginning to things and that these things should also have an essence to them—whether or not the essence is posited as portable beyond the existence—makes us creators in very much the same way as our larger than life analogues were imagined. We continue to be both creative and destructive, mimicking what we take to be the bookends of cosmic principles. That the sacredness of this new version of the essence of consciousness, the individual as both soulful and whole-souled in her passions and compassions, still parks the vehicle of essence squarely within the human range of sensibilities and sensitivities. The cosmos is still a human place, despite its vastness and strangeness, since it remains we who are able to reach into it and grasp something of ourselves. This fact confirms, for us, the connections between consciousness and cosmos, between what is ordered before and after us, and what perceives the order within and without: "It is after all scientifically justifiable to regard consciousness as one of life's experimental organs, more justifiable at any rate than to gloss over the fundamental fact of man's spiritual existence and explain it away with reflexes or behaviorism" (Neumann 1970:303 [1949]). If there is any concern about reduction, it is that we are made aware that though we can have a connection with the larger than life, we are ourselves not exactly the same as those other forms of life, perhaps many of them conscious, and many others intelligent and technical like ourselves. We cannot reduce the infinite for the sake of human finitude, but perhaps the continuation of the idea of the soul in the individual person who is self-possessed in this way allows for us to resurrect the dead in the present; their presence is what has allowed us the glimpse of the cosmic connections we daily make more real.

So much for the sense of essence. But what of origins? For the moment, if soul is still a useful conceptualization of an aspect of consciousness, organic or somehow in the relation of a gestalt of organicity—without any suggestion that it be reduced to actual physical elements, though, our age then immediately wonders what else could it be?—it compact nature should also be seen as already a reduction. "Soul," is after all, a definitive statement about the nature of humanity. It is not so much of interest today because somewhere along the line it was taken into the folds of gradually organizing and institutionalizing religious systems. These world systems, however, did not invent the soul. It is a reduction of the "original chaos" of creation into an incipient form of what would eventually become conscious of itself. It became, or thought itself to in fact be the very creation it was reduced from, and was associated with the "eternal" feminine very early on for obvious physiological reasons (cf. Lingis 1989:61ff). We can even speak of souls being "dead," our own, perhaps, or those that were once alive in the breasts of those we hate or disdain in some other manner. This suggests that the order of things, the social world, the ecology of the planet, or the cosmic order, has also regressed or at least retreated into a more primordial form, one again approaching the chaos of its origins. In a sense, something of this kind of retreat is inevitable, even necessary. Consider the problem of human history alone, where, as mentioned above, we can have no real knowledge of the vast majority of our predecessors, in spite of the fact that we had already granted them souls of their own: "They form a truly massive cemetery of the imagination in which the epitaph is simply—they were!" (Natanson 1970:50). Archaeology aside, there is little more to be said on their behalf. The invention and then the possession of the soul as human essence are quite understandable just along these lines even if there were no other arguments to be made in favor of its continued relevance. If what passes, passes like the wind, eventually carrying everything away with it, or, if one prefers continuity and not simple removal, a temporal river erodes its banks, exposes its historical stratigraphy and sentimental sediments, carrying these off as well, but continuing to be present as a connectedness with its own future and its past. The river metaphor is old hat, but this is because it so aptly describes, and perhaps even manifests, the way in which we feel our own biographies passing before us. We seek an anchor in the soul—though in our time it has more of the nautical character of "an anchor out to windward," meaning that one is hedging one's bets about it—and though we know it cannot permanently arrest our motion—that is certainly not its purpose in any case, for we must mature in order to understand our own finitude and cannot stay in one place, nor do we generally desire this kind of perennial stasis—it serves as both ballast and balance as we are carried along. The soul is also a compass, moral or existential, because it is a reflection of the society into which we have been thrown. Yet all this can be as apt a description of "personality" or perhaps yet more vaguely, "character." Whichever umbrella term we choose to hang our hats on, it must orient us not to the past—lest we join too soon those who lay underneath that all too concise epitaph—but push us to always look forward: "Although the far future cannot influence me in a strictly causal manner, my interpretive awareness of what will happen long after I die has an important reflexive meaning: I appropriate the future to the extent that my orientation toward it becomes part of my present reality" (ibid:52). Of course this too can be overdone. But unlike history, where the souls of the dead "were" once more than they are, or more fully present than they now can be, we cannot with any certainty say to any future version of humanity "they will be!." For our post-war age is shrouded in the new knowledge—and it is a knowledge in the epistemological sense before or rather more than it has been an aware-ness in any ethical sense, at least so far—that we can be the final generations of humans. We ourselves, in other words, can *be* the end. This might well hold some attraction to it. Not so much as a death wish, either personal or as part of the architecture of one version of the unconscious, but it undeniably has an aura to it. This is so because we have always been in awe of the beginning. The enormous powers that created the current universe as we know it are unimaginable and indescribable, apart from some mathematical formula that fail to make any serious impression upon us, since they involve quantities and numbers well beyond our ken. On top of this, not only are cosmic origins remote; note the aura and even glamor surrounding the gradu-al closure of our telescopic gap between our present cosmic coordinates and the big bang. We may well be able to "see" the creation of all things in a few years. Of course what we are seeing presently happened some fourteen bil-lion years ago or so. The paradoxes of cosmic vision befuddle us as much as they fascinate us. Nevertheless, a puzzle is a puzzle, something that has always been attractive in one way or another for we higher primates. We desire with a great passion as well as with a more sober curiosity to know where we have come from and how we got here. And this knowledge is of the utmost, equal in every way to our ability to steer straight into a blank future and, while we might well wince, to follow that path into the apparent void. Knowledge of the beginnings gives us the courage for the ends.

So we thus continue to approach the origin of all things where something can partially be seen, even as we inevitably continue to approach the next horizon over which nothing can be seen at all. All of this has an existential purpose that may be called part of the soul. This is so because it is not only abstracted from existence in a manner that is suggestive of essence—not forgetting that what is essential in the day to day is our duty to it, as Goethe said—but because the things of which it speaks to us are remote to not only our senses but to our generally quotidian sensibilities. We can, and have, taken this abstracted perspective and applied it to more local phenomena, such as economics, migration patterns, ice-core eco-geology and the like, but it has its limits. This criticism assuredly applies to the idea that an economic history, or even a materialism, has within it large vacancies of application.

But to suggest, as Midgely appears to do, that Marxian thought as a whole cannot inform us on these other questions is just as assuredly saying too much. At the same time, philosophical work that patently aims to be "moral" in our modern period also has its limits, and the practicality or utility of its claims could be seen as off-setting other problems, whether acting towards or aiming at makes little difference (cf. Taylor 1989:3). There is an immediate insinuation that the latter is somehow of a higher order than the former, but it need not necessarily be taken in kind. Utility too has an idea of the larger good, otherwise we could not come to any conclusions about what would be "good to do" even in the short term. A "good" action in the world serves to either maintain a present good mode of being or to redefine what it means to be good or to participate in the good. Such "goods" as defined in this way both predicate all kinds of acts—they may be normative and thus more often understood simply as "correct" than truly "good," or they may be taken more seriously as acts that are necessary to take in a crisis, where the concept of the "bad" has suddenly arisen, which in itself is not generally part of the routine of the day to day—and are also predicated on them. For if one stops acting in a "good" manner as predefined by social norms or cultural ideals— and we have already seen ample evidence that these ideals are still resonating with the imagination of both the "higher" and of the other world and its denizens—one also eventually stops *being* good as well: "All frameworks permit of, indeed, place us before an absolute question of this kind, framing the context in which we ask the relative questions about how near or far we are from the good" (ibid:45). Even if such definitions change and thence they themselves alter both the course of good actions and the goal of an existential goodness or the "good life," the process by which we imagine such qualities has not itself changed for some time. Modernity alters the course of the goods while redefining the good. It does not abandon the concepts, just as Midgely stated that we have not let go of a concept of human "nature." Just because "nature" as a term is a little confusing in the sense that what is natural to humans is not nature *per se* but culture, and just because notions like "the good" were, like the soul, attached and attended to by religions for millennia, does not mean that they lose their portability. Like Durkheim's concept of the sacred, there may be other concepts that represent aspects of human consciousness that can survive even the withering structural shifts of metaphysics—from transformational to transcendental and now within our own anti-transcendental systems—or those of modes of production—"subsistence" to pastoral to agrarian to industrial-technical and beyond—and thus demand that we examine them much more carefully than we have been doing. We have also suggested that certain concepts or even posited beings that our language only refers to, like God or the gods, may well be dead but in spite of this continue to exist. Life and existence for these ideas is not necessarily the same thing. The same goes for the soul. Here, we are dealing with another one of these portable conceptualizations of consciousness as well as "ultimately with the question concerning the immortality of the soul and the absolutely singular character of our own death. With this the soul is burdened with the strange distance from the body produced by that peculiar intimacy of one's inner life which does not seem to leave any space for 'thoughts belonging to the shared spirit'" (Gadamer 1996:151 [1986]). The problem of sharing much of anything is rampant for contemporary society. Is it plausible to suggest that some of these issues have arisen for us because we have generally lost the sensibility that what we are is part of something larger than our own individual lives? From history to culture, to even the polis or local communities and their state-sponsored or voluntaristic associations and institutions such as churches or school, participation as a public person has been on the wane for decades. We often feel that we do not owe anyone else anything. At the same time, the "self-reliance" that Emerson extolled was not, in the author's mind, a one-sided affair. Though it became the bestselling non-fiction book in the nineteenth century United States, his sibling volume presenting a devastating critique of religion was ignored. We clearly wanted to consume the cake of individual freedoms and lack of collective obligation while preserving the cake of more metaphysical doctrines. But social norms are like that. They recognize, rather pragmatically and without sarcasm, that if one has one's cake one can also eat it. Whatever conflicts might arise with such behaviors are problems for philosophers and culture critics only. Indeed, the perennial quality of persons doing what they need to do in spite of what discourses or other abstract models tell us provides long–term employment for such thinkers. The audience of myths of all kinds understand that the purpose of society is to provide useful fictions by which we can live with more or less little friction in the day to day. From kinship rituals and genealogies, to a nation-state's geographical boundaries, to concepts that have animated this chapter, we find in them the nexus of utility and morality: "Myth, in short, is not only a simple way to transmit history but also a selective two-sided process through the which the past is handed down—or obliterated" (Cabezali et al 1990:172).

Whatever referent may be imagined that our concepts stand in for, whether other forms of consciousness that are reflected in our own, or the essence of thinking and reasoning forms of life like ourselves, or at least, one of the species' self-idealizations, the conflicts between their theoretical models and how they are acted out in daily life are of interest in another way than providing mere fodder for philosophical dissertations. One can accept just about anything. To be able to do so is the "two-sided" real world variant of the character of myth and mythical thought. Adaptation to crises serves us in the short term and often saves our lives. Over the long term it simply kills us. If we continue with our example of the dead but still existing soul, we can partially agree with Simmel's opinion: "The problem proceeds from the (in my opinion) monstrous paradox that a soul which has once come to exist at a definite instant is now supposed to continue existing into eternity" (2010:88 [1918]). Thus stated, it is a bit of a puzzle how this could logically make sense. But I said that we can but partially agree on this point. This is because before agrarianism the soul was not seen in this light at all. The soul was already eternal and simply was passed from host to host as human beings died and were born. There was no being "born again" as a human, but the limited pool of souls reanimated without reincarnation the next generation of persons. This belief reflected the structure of both mechanical solidarity—everyone knew the same thing and there were no individuals—and satisfied the sensibility of the collective conscience—all like souls likened themselves to one another interchangeably. There was no intersubjectivity in these social groups, only interchangeability. Today, our definition of the soul has to adapt to our peculiar circumstances, without necessary recourse to perhaps any ideas including that of the apparently primordial reanimation, the later rein-carnation, and the one Simmel questions, the spontaneous creation by a high-er power of a thence immortal essence of consciousness: "Randomness in the emergence of a particular human life may not simply be rationalized away—as astrology certainly attempted when its horoscopes interwove the day and hour of birth into the context of the entire cosmos" (ibid). It is certainly correct to say that birth itself is happenstance given our contemporary exis-tential predilections. It is another expression of the desire to be an individual first and foremost. It is also the origin of the challenge to which self-reliance responds. We are "thrown projects" with softer or harder landings and we have no control, at first, over our trajectories or the communities, or lack thereof, into which we land. It is a key feature in the career of the heroic self that it take on these challenges and make of them what we may, "playing the hand one is dealt," as the famous popular song has it. That there is no specific dealer of this hand or of any hand in the game of life is also a feature because it permits the very randomness that is seen as the birthmark of modern heroism. Hence a new set of myths, Horatio Alger's children if you will, about the self-made person in the face of a world of obstacles. New immi-grants to the West have adopted much of this myth to tell their own odd stories, and also have wielded it against all of the natives of their new homes who, in spite of being born in lotus land, somehow have remained marginal. Their "spirit" is called into question and not merely their wit. It is this link that crucially reanimates the soul for many of us. Our character's relative weakness or fortitude rests upon that of our soul. It is the latest incarnation of the usual affair of doubling over the notion of the spirit and its physical manifestation. The allegorical seeding and planting we find in Near Eastern archaic civilizations with the embalming and preservation process of the form of the body manifested in the presence of the corpse clearly seeks to replicate what actually was the case for crops. One could preserve against decay certain foodstuffs that themselves were the source of continued life. Why could the same not be done for that actual life that was made of, fed on and given sustenance by, those preserved crops? (cf. ibid:232ff for the mythological figures associated with this understanding of "ascension").

The sense that one can preserve the life of what is dead is astonishingly portable in itself. Poe's "The Strange Case of M. Valdemar" fashionably illustrated this desire with the interesting if romantic idea of hypnotizing a person on his deathbed to see how far beyond the grave autosuggestion could evoke a response. Our own deaths may be singular, but they retain a relativistic context when juxtaposed with the concept of death "itself." But what is then the essence of death? If it only is made apparent to us through the specific instance of one's own death and that of others, and more thoroughly and consciously in the latter than seemingly in the former as one cannot "experience," in any customary sense of the term, one's own death, then does it even have a nature that lies beyond these manifestations? It does have such a nature, we think, because it is of the same category of concepts as are the soul and God, amongst others. Good and evil are also of this type. We just witnessed "liberal" philosophers attempting to define or at least suggest a concept of the good in itself, and now Jung can be seen making use of the essential sense of its very opposite: "It is quite within the bounds of possibility for a man to recognize the relative evil of his nature, but it is a rare and shattering experience for him to gaze into the face of absolute evil" (op. cit:10). The theogonical possibility that there exists in itself an evil that is formless and yet retains a unity of source and cause is difficult to imagine today. We do not see its presence in anything else but ourselves. Nature is neither good nor evil, *pace* Plato. The cosmos contains no morality. Just so, we also then begin to question the existence of essence, any essence, anywhere. Jung's counseling face comes to the fore just moments earlier when he states: "With a little self-criticism one can see through the shadow" (ibid). Perhaps more than a little is necessary for some cases, but in principle, the difference between the appearance of personal darkness and that of the vacant and anonymous void is surely a difference worth noting. But when and where does this other darkness, the archetypical shadow as Jung refers to it, manifest itself? Indeed, by definition, an essence can never "manifest" itself at all, for in doing so it becomes a mere appearance of itself, and not its authentic and holistic being. So the problem then becomes one of self-responsibility rather than one of only preservation. The sense that one must retain the notion of the *essential*—whether of the self, as we saw earlier, of that God must be alive to exist at all, or that death is a force beyond mortal human lifetimes, or that there is an objective good which everyone from any culture can recognize or agree on, or finally, that there is also a transcendental evil to which we must always succumb—is the same sense that seeks to preserve life and soul in the face of apparent death and loss. Our loyalty to the living is the origin of our will to life and not the other way round.

This said, the induction of the essential proceeds always in the same way no matter its perceived topic or the idea that a location cannot be known for it. It is the same when we confront the past, ours, or that of our culture: "What haunts us about the past, then, is that its transcendence is given to us by way of the familiar: we, in our present, sense the weight of what has gone through a balance of which is itself inevitably marked to follow suit" (Natanson, op. cit:108). The inertia of history, it's "dead hand" in fact continuing to live through us, (yet another example of existence after death), seems to place rather precise and narrow limits upon our thoughts and actions. It is well known that any hermeneutical discourse concerning history and "the tradition" locates the majority of agency at the structural rather than the personal level. Certainly throughout the life course we consistently and even continuously encounter sources of social action that are either difficult to control with regard to their effect in our own lives, or sometimes even impossible to respond to in with any semblance of a truly autonomous dignity. Yet at the same time, if the task of history is both not to repeat it but also to come to understand it as only the relative part of us—rather than say, another member of the list of essences whose apparitions furtively mask a greater, and more terrifying, truth about themselves—its gift to us is that we force, willy-nilly, our successor generations to do the same with the legacy of our actions: "We become the instrument, then, through which not only the transcendence of the past but our own future transcendence [ ] is intelligible and imaginable. At this point type gives way to symbol" (ibid). Here, common historical and cultural examples abound. Weber famously remarked upon the origins of new religions as the manifestations of the displaced intellectual classes' remaining desire for power and influence, once warrior and economic castes were in ascendance. This experience of incomplete marginalization gives rise to the sense that one can, after all, *preserve* oneself and one's ideas of the good etc. if only one has the wit and courage to do so. This may also be felt in personal life, where one's remaining privileges become sacralized in more private contexts. "Those who have ears will hear" is hardly a phrase coined by Nietzsche. The intellectual elites of the archaic empires may have been bounced from the executive, but they were neither pariahs nor slaves, nor would they ever become like these other forms of life that in those days were hardly to be considered human at all. No, the symbolic life was still wide open to them, and Weber notes that aside from mythical work, sexual theater of the most sophisticated kind arose in these quarters where time was no longer a luxury. No doubt it is the same amongst the wealthy and cultured elites of our own day. And this dynamic goes back much farther than the presence of irrigation empires. The secret societies of pre-agrarian cultures had much the same origins and destinies. When women became ascendant in horticultural subsistence patterns, "The males attempted by intellectual and religious-magical means to retrieve what they had lost in economic and social life" (Neumann, op. cit:430). More concisely, a new definition of what power was came out of these dealings. For us, inhabiting a state-sponsored culture of political power and central authority, our options to do the same seem much more limited. But to imagine that we have no means at our disposal for accruing to ourselves a redefinition of the stakes of the social game is an error. For there exists the history of the concept of power, or of the good, or of truth, and within every such history any genealogical analysis reveals that all the structures of manifestation of this category of conceptualizations are fragile indeed. They remain so because we are keen to retain the concept of the *essential*, importing to all other portable and key concepts this other characterization that is deemed both authentic and sacred. This is likely why Durkheim chose the sacred as his mascot concept for his theory of ideas. So now we can see that the essential, instead of limiting us, actually is the source of an absolute and enduring freedom against whatever political parables or fascist fashions of the day seek to set in their stone only.

The power of the present structure is derived from a redefinition, or at least, a reorientation, of the notion of essence. The current state of affairs seeks to possess its own essence, gladly forsaking historical consciousness: "Hence the importance that the theory of power gives to the problem of right and violence, law and illegality, freedom and will, and especially the state and sovereignty" (Foucault, op. cit:89). Clastres had already made this same point: our conception of power is based on our own societal model of it. But this is not the essence of power. As suggested above, power is the contemporary rendition of magic, something that can be wielded or brought into play, but not something that can be possessed. It can be used as a tool to operate on or manipulate things, but it itself cannot be manipulated. We will see below that almost the same situation applies to one of our other favorite concepts of the modern day, that of freedom. It is no coincidence that power and freedom are both associated with one another and ranged against one another. The one who "has" power has a certain form of freedom; the freedom to exercise his will. But the one who is free has her freedom over against such controls that the one "with" power desires. In either case, there is a belief that the essence of things informs our dealings with it. One the one side, this essentiality must be controlled so that it can be pressed into the service of our aims. On the other, the essence remains aloof to our claims upon it, manifesting itself in our interpretations of it but staking its claim to its essential freedom and thus allowing us to always come back to "its true needs" as a path to our own. Our example of the soul fully illustrates this relationship. It can be given a vastness or a locale: "For the Miletians, the soul was the exhalation of breath; for Heraclitus, on the other hand, the soul is the great mystery of the unfathomable limitlessness within which the thinking soul moves" (Gadamer 2001:17). At first glance, the first definition seems to be a random reduction, even though the second, in its obscurity, appears to be singularly unhelpful in its own way. Upon closer examination, we can understand the empirical bent of the Miletian school as noting that the breathing out is not only a sign of vital will and the movement of a conscious being that, in spite of its ability to reason, relies heavily on the non-reasoning and automatic aspect of his being. The first outward sign of this system of automata is the soul. With Heraclitus, we understand that it is Being into which having a soul places beings. It is the soul that not only animates the body in a physical sense, as the Miletians have identified, it animates *consciousness*—the "thinking soul"—and envelops it in a less empirically identifiable version of "breath." We must take care to maintain this vital connection, for it in its turn revitalizes us in the face of the vicissitudes of mortal life. Later on, this was interpreted as being our task in the light of the covenant a God had compacted with us: "Humans serve God's purposes in taking the appointed means to preserve themselves in being" (Taylor, op. cit:225). In our own time, we have retained this sensibility. We see our true freedom in enacting the cosmic drama at a local level. This constitutes existence, and though it may be in part the desire of a finite creature endowed with the means of overcoming his own finitude through the legacy of history, literacy, reason and science, reflection, inter-pretation and dialogue, it is also an empirically identifiable reality precisely because of the presence of the thinking soul that thinks within the over-soul of the cosmic envelope. We are co-participants in its ongoing exposition: "Man has been transformed from a spectator to an active participant in the drama of becoming. Room has been made for decision and choice, which had no place in the older scheme of things. What was formerly fate has become history" (Margenau, in Sorokin, op. cit:255). History is the textual manifesta-tion of the exhalation of breath. It is inherently made of possibility, and hence "limitless" in an originary way. It is also incompletely known as well as only partially played out in its possibility, and hence its "mysteriousness." Both the scientists and the philosophers of the Ancient Greek polyglot of city-states were after the same thing: the essence of what is, or consciousness and of cosmos. That their language speaks to us with a great deal of its fullness and to a great deal of our own sense of what it is to be, and continue to be, human, should not be so astonishing. Though their cultural construc-tion often seems alien to us, they were faced with the same day to day challenges of living on in the face of finitude and within the ambit of a tradition that, though it contained wisdom, was also of its own time and not their own. Our modern sense of individuation is perhaps not as new as we like to think. Nothing canny comes to us from the void of non-being. We are both the inheritors of history and the creators of history anew. To live within a specific time is the way of things in the world of norms, but to live as a temporal being is of the essence of things. It is the form of life that finite consciousness must take, no matter its cultural suasions and diversities. It is what makes us what we are in the most pressing and the most liberating sense, and to attempt to be more is to serve an injustice upon the very presence that we are at present: "Friend, let this be enough; if you wish to read beyond, Go and become yourself the writ and yourself the essence" (Silesius, in Derrida 1995:4 [1993]).

3.3 FANS OR FANATICS?

If it is the case that we not only are possessed of a suite of essences, but also possess the essence of forms within ourselves as the gestalt of organic con-sciousness—whether or not this form of life is infinite in itself, it clearly participates in the infinite through the means adumbrated in the previous section—what are the implications for human agency in the world of forms? We often are attracted to human causes, manufactured or spontaneously real. Our allegiance to them is an expression of seeking an essence and, perhaps, of pushing the politics of the either-or appearance of the One who must be dead or alive. This "One" is exemplified, so we think, in the cause at hand. Staffing the barricades or writing letters to the editor are two extremes of placing ourselves in the position of the One as if he were here with us on earth, possessed of a human interest and also, perhaps most surprisingly but also most revealingly, taking sides. When it becomes apparent that the es-sence of things does none of these other things, we begin to feel some resentment, perhaps even *ressentiment*—the malicious existential envy that desires not only the demise of the other but also specifically so that we can replace her—in that we now move from being a fan of a cause of the essence to being a fanatic thereof: "Fanatics are not just stern moralists, they are obsessive ones who forget all but one party of the moral scene." (Midgely 2004:155). The one so obsessed feels himself possessed of a kerygmatics of thought and action. He not only knows the truth of things, he must speak, preach it to whomever he encounters. Not only this, but his audience must fully understand and take up his cause as well. If they do not, they must be vanquished in some way, even unto death. There are many people who make a theater of this version of the mission, such as television evangelists. We might flatter ourselves that the epoch of the authentic fanaticism is long over, the reformation and the counter-reformation had enough of the purely politi-cal and cynical within them to discount even these horrors from being of the type we imagine the classical world experienced during its transformation into early Christendom, or with the Islamic conquest, or still later with the Crusades. The Columbian conquest had a material motive; the metaphysics was a whitewash that simply washed along in the wake of the conquistador's

genocidal actions. True fanaticism, we think, is one of those shadowy motives that can be consigned to the dustbin of ambiguous history. Is this really
the case?

Like the other concepts discussed in this chapter specifically but also
investigated in this book as a whole, the movement from being a fan to being
a fanatic involves a conversion to the cause of essence as imagined in a
particular time and place amongst peoples indigenous to both of these. Fanaticism might well be more aptly understood not then as an historically outdated outrage upon reasoning consciousness, but part of the unreason of Being.
Like God, the soul, the afterlife and others, fanaticism was certainly co-opted
and adapted to large-scale religious movements during the period of agriculture. But once again, it is not an invention of either these movements or this
particular historical period. Obsession and compulsion found a home in sha-
manic role-players in subsistence societies. Perhaps this is what led to their
characteristic traits being manifested in specifically religious contexts later
on, but we have no data on such an obscure and ancient point. It is at least
clear that without a cultural niche, such aspects of human unreason would
have destroyed their small-scale hosts cultures in short order. The shadowy
charisma these persons possessed and are possessed of has only short-term
in-crisis benefits. More importantly for us, this form of charismatic authority,
however muted in rational-legal world systems, appears in its most capable
form in our own societies and historical epoch. The great monomaniacs of
the modern period attest to the enduring presence of the *essence* of fanaticism. Whatever their self-doubts and neuroses—Hitler had plenty of both;
witness his never-ending private practice of his self-written speeches and
scripts, theatrical displays and dramatic equipage, or Stalin's anxieties that
everyone around him would at the least instance of the drop of his monstrous
garb, destroy and replace him—in the public stage where fans are turned into
fanatics, these persons captivated millions and led to the greatest short term
human catastrophes we have known. Fanaticism has many new and powerful
options to let itself take center stage in our time (cf. Neumann 1970:443
[1949]). But we should not let the apparatus of large-scale state institutions,
policies, and technologies—many developed precisely for this purpose, including television and film directing techniques—obscure the presence of
what actually makes the message. It is not the mere medium that contains the
entirety of its heart and soul. The "kerygmatic" content, the religious truth of
the content of the stage show is held within the kernel of our consciousness
that desires to be heard and to be part of something larger than life. It is well
known how persons both young and old behave quite differently in a crowd
than by themselves, with gradations of this transfigurative spectrum along
the way, from small groups of friends who get an idea in their head that each
would consider unwise or even reckless had they taken a moment of time by
themselves to think it over, to cults and cells of terrorists, to the mass rallies

of National Socialism. The essence of all of these behaviors lies in the positive aspiration to become something in the eyes of not others, but the Other as a community of souls and as a representative of the over-soul, and perhaps also negatively, in the anxiety, to avoid being outcast from such a group if and when it appears without us. So on the one hand, we seek to present ourselves as a fan of this idea, supporting it and acting on its behalf without lending it our whole-hearted belief and being—without, in other words, "selling our soul" to it—and often this theater of self-projection is enough. But if the ideal itself takes on the proportions of an obsession, than being a fan may not be enough for those who are driving the issue; we may need to throw ourselves bodily into the fray, taking with us our most heartfelt desires and converting them to the fuel necessary for such causes to spread, their wildfire consuming all in their path. It is here that the archetypes of mythic thought can lay hold of us, even if their current content is nonetheless a provincial expression of their essences: "For such constructed myths have an extraordinary power to rally, whether at the ballot box or on the battlefield. And in exercising that power, national myths and the sense of national history which they help to build must also raise the fundamental questions of just who belongs and who does not" (Samuel and Thompson, 1990:18). And this is where our anxiety takes the place of our reason. To not belong—as was the case in primordial times of the social contract—means death. No one wants to be the scapegoat, and the ability to join in the scapegoating of others reinforces our sense that we are all the more safe because we have done so, as well as reinforcing the new norms of communal action and correct behavior. But this, like the myths themselves presented, is an illusion. The one who scapegoats can always be the next victim, as such a social dynamic can never rest contented that it has expelled the final outsider from its midst. The Nazis started with the most marginal persons in their state, those whose demise would excite the smallest censure. If the genocide would have continued unlimited, there would no doubt be very few members of the in-group eventually left It is even imaginable, as with some cults—Jim Jones is called to mind—that by the end there would be no one left at all.

That we are still willing not merely to go along with these movements instead of even standing side—perhaps we know that this second action presents to us no viable long-term option, and indeed, we are correct—but to be adopted by them in the full presence of our attestation of being, swearing both our undying and our dying allegiances to them, speaks highly of human reason's ability to take the path of least resistance when it is confronted by a threat to its sovereign will. That we are swayed by myth is more a function of the structure of mythic thought being a child of reason in its own infancy, when unreason had at least an equal say in human affairs or, at the very least, was a necessary part of the human imagination that constructed the allegorical phantasmagorias that populated archaic myth and were to find a new abode in that modern. In the present day, even more convivial and seemingly more all-inclusive reifications can be used to rally human beings to this or that celebratory cause; conceptualizations such as the environment or the planet, the human spirit or our collective human future. There is no doubt that we need to attend to the details summarized by such abstractions far more than we need to adhere to the goings on associated with more archaic lists, including nations and people. But to make necessities into causes is always fraught with the risk of fanaticism. Far better to recognize the threat implied or actual by our own action in the world—the extremities of the forces of nature cannot yet be controlled with any certainty and so they must be negotiated as part of the ongoingness of a consciousness aware that its place is so far unique in the presence of other things, and thus it may impute to itself a unique responsibility for its own actions, and thus by extension, to the workings of nature—than to fetishize it either positively or negatively. "Just do it" or "get on with it" are casual phrases that come to mind here. Don't make a "big deal" about it. Pragmatism is perhaps one of our closest allies in the fight against fanaticism. It tends to downplay symbolisms of all kinds. It takes a sober look at what works and what does not, and it is born out of necessity and not the luxury of either indolence or incomplete marginalization (cf. Midgely's common sense view of the earth amongst the heavens to this regard, 2004:134). This practiced practicality can be applied, if that is the correct term, to any event or issue that consciousness can fathom. If the soul of its own being is not in fact as "unfathomable" as is the enveloping being in which the thinking soul resides and moves, then we should not be afraid to place ourselves in the midst of the questions we sometimes hesitate before. To do this is to provide an active agent against our ability to objectify and pretend that we are carrying something outside of ourselves around with us, worshipping and adoring it, serving it unto death, and sacrificing others to its honor and glory. Far older questions than that of the future ecology of the planet, for instance, may also be subjected to this dialectic of self, soul, and action: "Simply in the interest of his own freedom, the individual is compelled to put the religious question to himself—however he may answer it" (Barrett 1979:xxi). The key here is putting the question to oneself and oneself alone. It is not, in other words, to wed oneself to the cause of the question but to question the question by virtue of one's own experience and wit. At the same time, if our experience is shrouded with a series of events that tell us that to make up our own minds concerning such issues is the most dangerous thing we can be seen to be doing, we may think it quite rational and pragmatic to become a fanatic, whether Hitlerian, Stalinist, Maoist or whatever we might dare imagine for the near future. As James cautioned over a century ago, the absence of a God concept in religion is no guarantee of either pragmatism or freedom. Indeed, atheism, the godless religion, personal or institutional, is just as fanatical as the worst of the more traditionally defined religious world systems—that is "traditional" in the sense that we understand them to be representative of a specific epoch and similar transcultural contents, not necessarily "original" to the idea of religion itself—that did include gods in their beliefs. Midgely's comment regarding the relationship of atheism to science (op. cit. 17) has to do with the pronounced mispronunciation of science as the scion of religion as having killed its own parents and thus becoming "atheist" in some abstract manner. But science asks the same questions as does religion, and seeks the same ultimate response. Other concepts may be used, other terms derived and other forces may be given other sources—anonymity is still an author, like the proverbial poet—but we are now able to identify in much more detail how things occur and what they are made of. This is no doubt an advance, but it does not imply, nor necessitate, an atheism of any kind. It also does not justify in any ultimate manner the denial of an afterlife to the gods, as we have seen. At most, the correct position for any self-conscious modern to adopt is agnosticism. It remains an empirical question whether or not a God exists and how it might exist in our universe. And, after all, what is a God but another form of being, much more impressively advanced or evolved than ourselves, or yet perhaps something infinite that even knowing what it is will not help us to understand how it has become that way or what lies in its future. How much will be "revealed" to us over the course of human tenure is also by definition unknowable until the experience of it is had. Even then, what we are today as representatives of human consciousness will also change, and thus we would expect our experience of such questions of being and form to also change over time.

Hence the ability of myth to still engrosses us. It puts into cosmic perspective the comic, into history the histrionic, and into the human drama the idiosyncratic or personally melodramatic. The figures that populate these allegorical hypostatizations of our own frailties and maneuvers idealize our best qualities and also our conceits combined: "The hero has supernatural strength and is capable of great anger, but he is in full control, and only uses his strength to save his integrity and to rid himself of people who are irritating or nagging him" (Johanson 1990:134). Heroic in both wisdom and strength, the ethics of the mythic figure that represents humanity is often pitted against that of the *"athanatoi,"* or deathless ones. The immortals are the truly threatening irritants to the hypostasized human, as they chide him not merely for his sense of right and moral outrage at being the one who, in spite of his perspective and wisdom, remains mortal. Those who have ascended into divinity did not necessarily follow the path of the heroic ones, but if they did, then their chastisement of the hero is part of his or her testing along the way to their own ascension. From this, we get the misplaced essentializing of certain tropes as necessary to becoming either heroic or divine (cf. Gadamer 2000:54ff). But the truth of things for humans is in fact a pathless land, as Krishnamurti famously stated. If in myth the confrontation between the darkness and the light is accepted as a reification of both as well as their conflict, in the human realm such polar oppositions never truly occur. There is nothing that is essentially good or evil in the social world, for even the most heinous of crimes benefits someone. Robert Merton's dictum is everywhere applicable, if one is seeking the source of the maintenance of uncomfortable things in the world, from wars and genocides to unaffordable housing and the presence of the homeless, simply ask "who benefits?." For some, manifest evil is a relative good. Though no evil can be said to be a good in itself—that is, nothing bad can be seen as benefitting everyone equally or with respect to his or her relative needs—the fact that neither the essence of good nor evil rests as a capability amongst human beings in fact provokes discomfort among us. We would rather, it seems, place ourselves in the epic world of myth than face the ambiguities of our own existence. And this is where all those who seek power step right in, at our weakest and most needy point. Because the world often seems to thwart our desires and turn our self-styled destines down what we perceive to be the wrong path, we might well imagine that we live with oppositions whose very nature is polar and that we too, following from this, must take on the mantle of the hero who can only do good and never evil (cf. Jung, op. cit:124). Within the realm of the conscious then, we are not automatically immune to fanaticism. We must exercise reflection and then push it towards the reality of the social world in which we participate. That reality is essentially ambiguous, and in realizing this we also realize the essence of the essence, so to speak. Since it is portable across structural gulfs rebuilding the architecture of historical forms of human consciousness, it itself does not take on any specific form. It is formless form, and not even a form of formlessness. Now this sounds more like Heraclitus, and we must not pause here too long lest we feel that mythic language can suffice to translate mythic thoughts. What we can take from this metaphoric moment is that what is described as allegorical is also something true. The essences presented in myth are coagulates of forces that are not in opposition to one another if left to themselves. They overlap constantly, and cannot be polarized. The hero seeks what the villain already has, or vice-versa. The mortal seeks what the immortals possess, but the immortal is threatened by this search, because he knows that what he currently possesses can be stripped from him. Like magic, power, and the over-soul, the unconscious life of humanity is something that cannot be possessed by individual manifestations thereof or therein. History and culture too occupy this ambiguous place in our consciousness. We will see below, that love, home and freedom as well fill out this category of "essences" whose essence is to be formless and ambiguous. It is perhaps the greatest error by which we live to attempt to grasp onto any of these ideas and try to find a home within its imagined static form.

Now that the self as the sacred manifestation of the individual as form has taken over our imagination, we are all the more at risk of committing ourselves to this suite of errors. The fight against the institutions of a previous age has been taken as heroic and as giving us the privilege of exalting our own immodest ambitions as not only the going rate, but as the cause for which another expression of fanaticism is well-suited. Even here, the sacred individual is not immune from its own further essentializing: "Obsession with the churches has distracted attention from reduction employed against notions of human individuality, which is now a much more serious threat. It has also made moral problems look far simpler than they actually are" (Midgely, op. cit:40). The fanatic deals in the stock and trade of polar oppositions. The either/or sensibility is not merely unrealistic, as we have seen and will continue to investigate below, it sets up antagonisms based on that unreality where, as is the case with any anxiety to belong to a community, however contrived, or to feel oneself part of something larger than one's own life, and perhaps even something that can be claimed to be larger than life itself. The detail of world systems does indeed contain the devil: "For anyone who has a positive attitude toward Christianity the problem of the Antichrist is a hard nut to crack" (Jung, op. cit:42). Jung continues by reminding us that Satan only attains his role as the contradistinctive villain to Christ's heroic essence with the rise of Christianity, and even "as late as the Book of Job he was still one of God's sons and on familiar terms with Yahweh" (ibid). Mythic narratives actually do contain, if taken as textual tapestry over longer period of time, all of the contradictions and conflicts that real life in the mortal realm of humanity contains. These are often suppressed, just as oppositional thought is used by social norms to cover over ambiguities in actual social relations in the day to day or in ourselves. The evil of the Holocaust disproportionately affected poor Jews and others who were too marginal to escape its Juggernaut. This had the effects of "benefitting" all of us who did escape or who were not around to be victimized by it. All the death of the past means as well that those that lived on generally lived better as long as the world was and continued to be a place of structural inequality with a variety of bases—and not just those defined as "racial"—just as the aftermath of the Black Death saw the beginning of the Renaissance, as a lower population load with the same access to resources created a new culture that became aware of luxury in both things and time. No doubt it is disquieting to make note of the reality of historical fortune. And it is not always the case that crisis produces anti-crisis in the way that mythic thought had Christ producing Anti-Christ –or was it the other way round?—given counterexamples of the Columbian genocide and residential school systems. On the other hand, we have not seen the longer-term effects of these blights. Generally, it is a historical principle that "the fewer the higher." The Reformation brought about its own version of this principle by narrowing the scope of God's intercession to that of the individual, thereby raising his status not only in his own eyes but also potentially in the eyes of God. The presence of an intercessionary church was, for Luther and others, a priestly "calumniation" that could not be taken seriously in any authentic soteriology that was presumed to be authored only by God: "This whole theology could only be a presumptuous and blasphemous refusal to acknowledge the sole and entire contribution of God to our salvation. It was an arrogant attempt to fetter God's unlimited sovereignty" (Taylor, op. cit:216). This much more recent usurping of the divine space has its Babelian overtones. But there is a lengthy history to the idea that God needs our help to work in the world, since he is, by definition, not of this world even though he may be presumed to have created it. In order for a God to be thought of as standing apart from his creation he might well also be thought of as not having complete control over it given that there are other forms of consciousness dwelling within its realm. This is one logic, but not the only one, as it is also commonly held that the creator retains omniscient control over his creation and human works and even faith are relevant only to humanity's own salvation. But this logic came later. Thus the early Protestants could be seen to be in league with a kind of meta-history of the unconscious that in actual fact led to the non-history of beings of both the world and of spirit. To resuscitate the origins of their beliefs in this manner in turn led to the unending schisms and factionalisms that are the hallmark of Protestantism. Sectarianism of the Northern Europeans and their empires has something in common with the so-called Folk Catholicism of (rural) southern Europe and its attendant empires, but its call to specific and individuated arms can significantly differentiate it. For some sectarians, there is the only true path. They are, in a word, fanatics. Catholic fanaticism is always directed toward an external threat, including the reformers, but even more historically evident when contraposed with that of religious systems outside of the Christian ambit. But every perceived threat, whether internally defined or coming at one from the outside in prompts a reevaluation of one's own beliefs. Often, the outcome of this sometimes brief analysis is to more staunchly defend the principles which leap out at one and concern the apocalyptic aspects of faith; the end times which may be seen as approaching through the foreshadowing of schism in belief or yet further presence of the infidel, or even more catastrophically, the unbelief of modernity (cf. Neumann, op. cit:433ff for one of the most famous examples of this dynamic). One is forced to renounce anything that may bear the slightest resemblance to that which has now become defined as a threat. Disowning one's Jewish friends and neighbors are, of course, a recent example of this flight from the world into the space of insular fantasies and mythical contraptions, but it is based upon a more general, and sometimes more principled, letting go of what was seen as precisely what was holding one back from a more authentic participation in the being of Being: "Paradoxically, Christian renunciation is an affirmation of the goodness of what is renounced. [ ] In the Christian perspective, [ ] the loss is a breach in the integrity of the good" (Taylor, op. cit:219). The apparent paradox of pushing something that is part of the inherent good aside calls to mind the problem of ambiguity in the history of symbolic forms and metaphoric imagery. Jung provides the familiar example of the snake: "The snake is not just a nefarious, chthonic being; it is also [ ] a symbol of wisdom, and hence of light, goodness, and healing. Even in the New Testament it is simultaneously an allegory of Christ and of the devil, just as we have seen that the fish was" (op. cit:245). With this kind of realistic ambiguity, pragmatically reflecting the often conflicting and inner-conflicted human attitudes about others and to the world, there arose dualisms of various kinds that, the more they polarized, the further from reality they travelled. Their representation in one-sided exegetics of myths could only carry them back so far towards a human affinity. Our immediate reaction to a real snake is trepidation, sometimes outright fear, especially in regions where sectarian Protestantism has long held sway. But this is still a symbolics of real forms. The practical utility of alertness and caution in the encounter with snakes is that in certain regions they actually are quite dangerous and unpredictable. Teaching this to the inexperienced children of these regions involves similar, if much smaller scale, conversions from the "peace-loving person" to the fighter as mentioned above. We may well have to defend ourselves against physical dangers, but in the absence of the light of experience, symbolism and story provide the preparation for later alertness and awareness. To personify the actual animal is, of course, considered to be at best old-fashioned, but nevertheless, the pedagogic strength of such imageries is not lost on us even in our own time.

But if teaching through fictive kinship still works in certain cultural suasions, the principle that we are actually related to other forms of life has long been recognized and even provided the basis for overturning the entire metaphysical system that had previously, though not originally, been erected upon this notion of symbolic kinship. What was "misleading" about this new order was empirically at least, though not necessarily, as we just saw, pedagogically, was our projection of human traits onto other creatures and thus our misrecognition of both their "nature" and their "history." But this was still a kinship that in fact had removed any divisional fence or well-maintained boundary long before Darwin. What Darwin *did* do was state firmly and permanently that no real fence could be built between us and the rest of life. But this was precisely what the ancients did *not* do, though they probably did not always recognize its scientific impossibility. Their fence was always of the symbolic kind, propped up with the very notions that we have been exploring throughout this chapter. As with more traditional ambiguities, our modern narratives also hold within them things that are both unclear and even can be outright misleading in their own way. Perhaps it is a little more realistic, if not really any more clear, to think of our connections with the larger forces of life and its manifestation in other creatures in this way. In order to avoid both a fatalism or what could appear to be a cop out, one should immediately add a pragmatic take to this "mystery." Its very quality of being unknown allows us to orient ourselves to it, and this *is* one of the evolutionary traits that indeed *does* distinguish us from most other life-forms on our world, as well as underscoring Darwin's point about the relative character of our relatedness to specific groups and categories thereof. Symbolically, we may still feel a little affronted that our civilized and domesticated humanity survives by virtue of the same basic apparatus as does the dirty and smelly monkeys in the zoo and elsewhere, but this too can be assuaged by the perseverance and historical persistence of myth: "The ambivalent attitude towards the fish is an indication of its double nature. It is unclean and an emblem of hatred on the one hand, but on the other it is an object of veneration. It even seems to have been regarded as a symbol for the soul" (Jung, op. cit:121-2). If Jung's pairing of the male and female archetypes in the animus and anima double over into us as the "syzygy," this dual character of things in general is constantly and consistently pointed up and pointed to in myths both ancient and modern. Vernacular literatures of all kinds and hailing from all corners of the globe feature these dualisms, with their structure manifest in more than simply content. The style of texts and oral traditions also portrays this sensibility that the one requires the other. Ash speaks of an "antisyzygy" and refers to both "down to earth realism one the one hand, delight in the wild and fantastical on the other" (1990:93). There is a purpose to this seemingly conflicting loyalty to this world and to another world that speaks to us in its own enchanted tongue: "The accumulated workings of myth is not to diminish its content nor to constrict its telling, but to expand upon them. It is to unharness the implausible or fantastic and to project it into the world as an enactment of power" (Nassan 1990:120). This kind of power transfigures its surroundings, but in its contact with the earthly reality of the world of humans, it is also transformed. It becomes part of our ken, personified or at least, anthropomorphized and perhaps even taken into the stock of knowledge at hand in terms of our learning how to bend its larger forces to our local wills. Whatever the source of its origins, we humans become immediately interested in its effects, and the possibility of controlling them. The most famous, and indeed, perhaps the most important of these kinds of events and our eventual canny reaction to it must have been the observation of lightning over the primordial period of our proto-human ancestry. Once the control of fire was established, as in the Promethean category of myths worldwide, the whole universe, from our newly human perspective, must have opened up in a singular manner. For about one million years it is estimated, this new version of humanity has travelled far indeed.

This kind of control of an unearthly, or at least an inhuman power and then making it part of who we are is uniquely a human attribute. The primate curiosity that evolved it has also had a profound influence on the evolution of both culture and intelligence, including even the physiology of the brain. Control implies observation, care, attentiveness, and an ongoing comparison and contrasting with each new experience in light of those previous. This watchfulness is also reflected in mythic narratives and fittingly, its theme is human life and death:

> In such a context, the idea that one turns into the watcher who watches takes on the meaning that the fallen one, like the caretaker of the just, places all virtue and glory before the eyes of others. Perhaps even the Christian sounding phrase "over the living and the dead" has a genuine original sense here: these icons of bravery stand erected to the survivors, just as they do for all the dead upon whom fame attends. (Gadamer 2001:28-9 [1974])

And it is just here that the "arts" of subsistence and survival begin to turn into the arts as we have come to know them over the past ten millennia or so. Even before this, archaeology has revealed that our cousins the Neanderthals painted, sculpted, and memorialized their dead as well. For the one who watches is also obligated to take the time, to spend the time constructively and concernedly. We might well imagine that the ability to perform both ritual and to make more sophisticated technologies and tools begins with the ability to be in control of other things. Around the fire at night, or even by day, where no other predators for the first time dare approach, small bands of our most ancient predecessors gathered and were able to *be together* in a new way. What came out of this community we can only guess, but it is by myth that we have some clue to the astonishing ability of the new mode of being human together to produce both the eminently practical and the most wild of the fantastic.

This alone should exalt both our imagination and inspire us to attempt to do the same in our vast world of billions. It should not be impossibly diffi-cult, though our ancient ancestors would never have dreamed of such a task. It is an epic task that has been best suited to the epic arts of humankind, myth, religion, and the aesthetic creations of all times and places. And it is also a sacred task, not only because of what is at stake, but also in the way we must approach others in this same concernful mode of being that began with the one who was able to be still and focus without fear or threat of imminent death. This sensibility is very much still with us (cf. Taylor's description of the piety we extend to artists even in our own time, op. cit:422). Without needing to become fulsome, much less covetous or resentful, our perception of the artists still rings true along the lines of her being able to create some-thing new in the same way that the controlled campfire was both a brilliantly functional, but also seemingly ethereal and beautiful creation. One can easily become sentimental here, for all who have camped out in the wilderness and built a fire can appreciate fully both its charms and its utility. It still fascinates us, and perhaps this fascination has become part of our very being through a lengthy evolutionary dynamic. Those who cleaved close to the fire survived longer and reproduced more, we might imagine. But there is no gene, as far as we know, for the aesthetic appreciation of controlled fire, just as there appears to be no instinctual fear of that which is uncontrolled or even simply hot, as any parent of an infant or toddler will know. Even so, in principal, invention and use is clearly part of the hallmark of human culture, in all places and all times. This sense of creation and of the new brings forward both the living and the dead and, as the art work or the tool potentially last far longer than do we, it preserves metaphorically all that it has watched over for coming generations to come to understand in a new way (cf. Natanson, op. cit:122). The very appearance of the world to us ranges itself in this manner. Of course, it is we who make the connection, positively and negatively, concerning what, or for that matter and more importantly, who, will be our allies or enemies, but the scope of this world of forms, is *essentially* presented to us from the beginning. This is ultimately the case for all things, and this is why we perceive in their appearance also the outline of their essence. Not just because like objects and even like persons appear and reappear throughout our lives, but because the manner in which the world worlds, worlds them into these forms without many exceptions. Between the advent of highly structured social norms—this too is quite ancient and precedes the written word at least for a geological time period, so far as we can speculate—and the growing knowledge of the order of nature, the speaking of the language of myth and art took on a synthesis of the two: norm and form, what became for us both "normal" and more and more formal. We bring all these into what we are in order to breathe in a world that was not at all created for us or anything else in particular: "All things in their breathtaking otherness have nothing to do with us, but our deepest desire insists on bending us toward them, stripping us from ourselves, from language" (Lilburn 1999:49). This is as necessary as the inevitable return to human tongues and to language in general. Our ability to speak of the world and of our experiences thereof rest on this flight of longing. We must step out of what has been the case, and what has been the case has already been fully captured, dissected even, and desiccated by our language and its contextual usage. The risk of long-term lifelessness is prevented by our reaching into the mute world of anonymous forms and wild things and creatures to listen for a while without preconceptions or expectations. Then, after some time outside the controlled fire of the human intellect, we are forced to return. It is always a bittersweet affair, however necessary and regular, for language stands as the uniquely human ability to retain an understanding of the essence without throwing ourselves body and soul into the uncontrolled flames of fanaticism:

"This does not consist in the ability to signal one another, but in the ability to form a particular language community and thereby a common world" (Gadamer 1996:166 [1989]). Bringing the other world into our own is the express function of language in all its expressive forms and moments. Art and religion, science and myth, even the politics of the day and the mechanics of our tools prepare us for future encounters about which we can only speculate. It is of the essence to recognize the continuing presence of ideas concerning the essential and thus also our continued reliance upon them. We are something other than ourselves without their watchful presence. We are something less than humane without our ability to be guided by their concernfulness and their very existence is the one thing in the world that has very much everything to do with our continued presence in that self-same world.

Chapter Four

No Place Like Home

It seems that if there was one thing that could define us it would be our place of birth. This assumes that we came to know it throughout a good portion of our childhood, and in our transient and migratory age, this is not always the case. It also assumes that our time there, during our first set of formative years, was something at least tolerable, where nothing that would create an anathematic reaction took place. This too is also hardly always true. Yet in spite of these two caveats, most persons state that their home is where they, as children, came to know the world first and had their first series of encounters with others that affirmed rather than countered their earliest self-understandings. At the same time, our loyalties to our homes in this specific sense are always also partially mythic, fictional, and contrived later on for the purposes of staking a claim or placing oneself in a largely anonymous world. We rewrite our early histories, partly because we have to in the face of the loss of early childhood memories—this is quite normative and "normal," and in no way necessarily attests to trauma that may or may not have been actually present—but also due to the increasingly critical character of gradually maturing experience. The new light that is cast on us by our peer group shines differently than that of our families. The contrasts are often strained, even stark. The peer group, as Riesman classically maintained, is devoted to and constructed mainly from sources based in both the institutions youthful strangers find themselves thrown into without their consent, and the media of the popular culture of the day, ever-changing its content, never changing its structure or message. The period of divided loyalties, early adolescence, is when the concept of home first takes shape, though in an oddly negative manner. One begins to disdain what the home represents. The wider world has been glimpsed, and its apparent diversity and difference are both a clarion and a siren call that is interpreted as freedom. Pursuing this calling takes a few years, but most of us get out of not only our family homes rapidly enough, but many also take the further step of leaving our "birthplaces," sometimes never to return. This suggests that while "home" is originally associated with the largest portion of a lived childhood, it too is one of those portable concepts like the sacred—after all, we must have a home in this world even though the world itself has no personal concern for any of us— and can be found, if not just anywhere "we hang our hat," as the old song has it, then in many other places we might find ourselves inhabiting. The title of this chapter then should be taken in two ways. The feeling that we are home and can be at home is like no other. There is no other place like it. But we also discover that, whether or not we desire to return to our birthplaces or their surrogates that there is also no place quite like this home because all other places are not this home. They are different places and we, in abiding there for shorter or longer terms need also to be different to continue to live as if they were our new home. So in this double and contrary sense, there really is "no other place like home," and neither is home thus a specific place alone.

We will examine the errors associated with not recognizing the double character of the chestnut "home" and its implications by first reminding ourselves that our birthrights were random, with no apparent design or meaning. All of this must be constructed after the fact of birth. It is how we do this that constructs home itself, both as a conceptualization of where and who we are, but also as the physical reality in which we live and the demands that it makes upon us with relation to how others have found a way to live there. Another old song lyric informs the second section, but we in fact find that in all places, though not necessarily at all times, the view of both ourselves and our sense of coming home or being at home is occluded by the metaphoric stormy weather of the travails of life and the comings and goings of other people and their desires. Losing one's home through events that could have happened anywhere is an oddly disconcerting paradox that almost everyone has to come to grips with, and later come to terms with. Finally, if we ultimately find ourselves relying on yet another cliché to both adjust ourselves to the constantly changing circumstance of contemporary life as well as the ins and outs of the lives of others, is it really fair to claim that the heart always finds its home, always lands on its feet and is able to remake itself anew? The placement of the heart—still our metaphor for the space of human feeling and the emotional lover but also adjudicator of the instincts of the "gut"—is not to be taken as an assumption but rather as the beginning of a series of existential questions regarding how we make our place in the world of others as well as in the world of forms and objects. To do so is to imply that it is more important for the human heart to find a home that it is for our somewhat less metaphoric head. We may also question why this is the case. That the emotional character of the concept of home is always ascendant over its logical or rational aspects tells us that the concept itself is not rational, or not entirely so. It takes its place amongst the other errors by which we think we must live in large part because we associate it with its equally non-rational peers such as God and love, freedom and the self. The confluence of all of these might well take us to both the heart of the matter, and also thus to our ideal home.

4.1 RANDOM "BIRTHRIGHTS"

It takes some weeks or even months for the infant to clear its vision and be able to see the minute part of the world that presents itself to its young eyes. This is the first motion of the opening of being onto the world. Breathing and consuming, excreting and growing are also done in their own way inside the womb. But sight is of the world. There is not other place before or beyond life where seeing can occur and when it does, the incipience of humanity begins to take shape: "It is the focal point of origin of a perspective, a point from which there is a view, the source of lines of perspective and currents of efficacity that then go on to die on the horizon." (Lingis 1989:152). It does not, of course, mean very much at first. It is not only a beginning in the radical sense of there being nothing before it, an origin, but also in the sense that there-being itself did not really know how it existed and the implications of its existence until it could place itself, even a little, in the wider ambit of the world envelope: "The determining efficacity of an existence does not consist in its power to die but in its power to come to birth, to begin, to take on existence as something it initiates and bears." (ibid). Starting something in this way implies that one must follow through with it in some way other than the mere beginning. In the biographical reality of the individual, this too takes some years to gain an inertia of its own being-there. Presence of "mind" comes later than that of consciousness, as one grows into being more and more human. It is only our technology of birth that gives us the false impression that our babies are human. They are genetically and physiologically, but this is not what separates humanity from any other creature. The baby in fact represents best the Darwinian connections discussed above, and the more it grows the more it departs from these connections without of course ever losing them completely. If one error of human conceit is thinking that we do at some point transcend our animal nature, then the corresponding error is, as it were, that we are only these connections and not much else. No, the human infant is human in name only, and our ancestors, unequipped with the life-saving and life-preserving high technologies that occupy premature wards in hospitals and clinics knew more of the truth of the matter than do we. Indeed, we have ironically also been able to extend to a great degree the processes by which a child becomes a fully human being to about a full generation. If childhood itself is an invention of the nineteenth century, then the twentieth century's contribution to this new form of quasi-humanity would have to be adolescence. Boas' famous ethnographic request to his young student Margaret Mead can be taken as the first "moment" of the recognition that this had taken place, beginning in the 1920s. The malaise that appeared to be afflicting this new phase of life that had been rendered more or less useless through labor laws and school laws alike, now found itself in the unenviable position of playing the unadulterated consumer to the new systems of over-production. This is a role that it continues to occupy apace today.

Mead found that in Samoa, at least, youth were not alienated. Mainly due to the fact that they were not allowed to occupy a liminal and unproductive position in society for very long. Boas thought modern society needed to learn from these small social contract oriented groups, and one can easily understand why. Each phase of life has its shelf life. Over-determining this in any case might be risky to one's mental health and the sense that one's humanity is worth living at all. Teenage suicide is always a concern for our society. Adolescents have no serious place or function even now, and thus it is all the more difficult to take them seriously. They are Janus-like, one moment acting very much like any adult, the next like any child. We have constructed them, and in our dismay and our irresponsibility, now mainly simply put up with them because we have to. Shame on us, certainly, rather than on them, but at the same time they could provide us with an object lesson in the realities of human life precisely because they are in the process of still becoming human. If infants are human in the organismically strict Darwinian sense, adolescents are human in the sense of beginning to learn the unique sociality of their humanity. As this is a life-long process, we adults can learn from our youth about ourselves.

Learning that we are always beginning, and that living at home in the world is always a new experience: "Perhaps the true sense of 'beginning' is nothing more than this: that one knows the beginning of a thing means that one knows it in its youth—by this I mean that stage in the life of a human being in which concrete and definite developmental steps have not yet been taken." (Gadamer 2000:17). The "excitement" and "uncertainty" that Gadamer suggest are hallmarks of youthful vigor, anxiety and expectation are things that are muted in adult life, but not absent from it. That we strive to avoid them is a mark of adulthood in its social guises, but avoiding them at all costs is actually a sign of continuing insecurity and immaturity. We organize our lives around avoiding existential threats or even mere questions that demand that we respond with our sense of purposes, values, goals and even the means by which we may or think we may attain them. This rationalization, or even ratiocination, of living on is also the greatest threat to the querying and still wonder-kindled youth in all cultures: "Today this fundamental experience of being young is threatened by the excessive organization in our lives—so much so that, in the end, the young no longer know or scarcely know the feeling of launching into life, of the ongoing determination of their lives from out of their own lived experience." (ibid). This situation has occurred simply because of the nexus of youth being useless as a form of life within capital—beyond their raw acquisitive abilities fuelled by their parents' wage-labor and the fact that they can be manipulated more easily than can most adults—and that youth represent some fundamentally human things that adults have generally lost: wonder, vitality, the ability to question, and the skeptical character of curiosity and inexperience combined. So in our resentment against them—indeed, it smacks of *ressentiment,* as we would often like to replace them with ourselves—we have constructed complex cages of schooling and associated activities such as sports and the arts as well as the idea that one must compete against one's fellows for a place in the hierarchy of labor and market. Any excuse to keep their unfreedom close to home is good enough for we adults. We conveniently ignore that it was not their fault for being born. It was *our* decision to have them, and now we do not generally want them around, aside from the fact that in order for us to survive the way we imagine we should with regard to both life-chances on the serious side, and "quality of life" on the much less serious, we are often apart from our own children in any case. Schools provide the tax-funded public daycare systems, far beyond the age where that might be considered cognitively necessary. Indeed, like a circus ambulance that recklessly ploughs around in order to drum up its own business, our school system keeps youths dumber than they would be otherwise, with the excuse of filling their heads with mindless unthought and the language of parrots. The university is eventually even more hypocritical to this regard, as it claims to be both the space of thought and therefore also that of human freedom. No doubt there is some bad conscience about all of this on our parts, but we assuage it by thinking that we had to suffer through it as well and it does not last forever. What about its lasting effects?

To keep from ourselves the truth of leaving home is part of the motive for keeping youthful wonder at bay and constrained, intellectually, sexually, and even with regard to productive labor or creativity. The ambiguity of the concept of home rattles us, in the same way that we sometimes try to get a grip on where we live by "rattling" around the house. The full-presence of our selfhood never quite seems to come together in these meanderings. Aside from the better-acknowledged sense that we cannot "be all things to all people," there is the ontological undercurrent of never being able to become our fullest and widest potentialities. It is this that ultimately fosters the resentment we have against others' youth or even our peers' abiding or remaining youthfulness. We harbor an enduring "guilt" and sense of betrayal about the manner in which we had to finally come to terms with "growing up":

"The sense that my being in projecting itself into existence is responsible for nothingness is its guilt with regard to its own being." (ibid). A life that has "amounted to nothing" is, in this manner, a testament to the absence of both authenticity—we may have strived for someone else's goals or have been proselytized into a mission that is too objective to be possessed and made personal, or we may have been traumatized beyond repair, though this is much more rare—and efficacity—to have accomplished nothing of import, this being defined by the standards ironically set by a social system that acknowledges that most of what its adult members do has little merit. Producing and consuming goods and services is an excellent way to kill time, but it is more difficult to imagine what existential or even rational purposes it serves over the long run. These activities, in order even to be means, must be converted to serve some other set of ends that *do* address the existential questions of being at home in the world and finding a purpose for doing so. There must be constructed, in other words, some sort of differentiation between what one does for a living and what one does to live.

One way in which we do attempt to accomplish this experience of difference is by reminding ourselves that we have, after all, grown into something that we did not ourselves design and that we cannot find intimately personal fault with ourselves, just as we cannot fault our bratty teenager for her presence in our home. To begin to explore the character of being at home or having a home is to start with our own conception of what it is like to have a past, to have lived in the "what has been": "History is interested precisely in these *differences*. Only by starting from these differences can we understand that what happened, even in the minds and in the imaginary, was *not* necessary." (Passerini 1990:59, italics the text's). The opening up of the possible in our past reminds us that we do not set our future in the immutable stone of the "principal" for all times and places. We can also enlighten ourselves by the fact that the intervening years have given us a distance, and thus also a potential perspective on our earlier experiences. We may find, to our chagrin, that we have often repeated mistakes from childhood onwards, but we also find that we have not done so in all possible cases. These "differences" in the way we have managed to make decisions then may well be reflected in outcomes. Lest we travel too far down the path of a popular counseling manual, it is important to immediately make some abstract sense of these now partially recalled events and actions. Events might happen to us, or we might "cause" further events by our acts or our inactions, but we are never entirely passive in the face of a living history because we are in fact co-authors of much of it. To deny this is to deny history and how it is made. A classic example of the problem of culture memory and its susceptibility to its then current political conveniences: "We must shake off the prejudice of the patriarchal family situation. The original situation of the human group is prepatriarchal" (Neumann, op. cit:138). Today we have shaken off all of the assumptions about how our primordial predecessors arranged their affairs of kinship. Ethnographically, we find examples of every possible permutation, though over time, extended families are asserting their agrarian birthright and coming to dominate once exclusively bourgeois settings. We are able to make much more structural statements regarding modern family life, and the amounts and relations of hangers on, affines and consanguines, morganatic kin or simply "blended," as the recent diplomacy regarding one's household has it, are purely secondary almost the point of irrelevancy: "The family is the interchange of sexuality and alliance: it conveys the law and the juridicial dimension in the development of sexuality; and it conveys the economy of pleasure and intensity of sensations in the regime of alliance." (Foucault 1980:108 [1978]). Now it may be said that the presence of multiple others to whom sexual advances are frowned upon or even prohibited by law increases the intensity of desire while disallowing the "spending" of sensation in this model. One is thrown back upon one's own devices, as it were, and this economical practicality is another growing facet in the consumption of reproductive artifices and apparatuses at a time when developed nation-states' populations are in striking decline. We may have slain the archetypical father but this narrative has the narrow experiential focus of not only the male heir but also the bourgeois situatedness of masculinity and power. By far most family homes do not operate on such a principal, though there may be cross-cultural glosses in play. More realistically, and certainly this can be seen demographically, "the hero has *both* the First Parents against him and thus must overcome the masculine as well as the feminine part of the uroboros." (Neumann, op. cit:170, italics the text's). Of course this relates to the structural relations of archetypes and has nothing to do with one's personal parents (ibid:182ff). The tensions and distances between the generations, their proverbial "gap," recur with every demographic shift. They in themselves seem to serve little purpose other than to annoy the elders and frustrate the youth. But their shadow follows the successive generations and saps their vital energies that could have been charged with working within the political sphere as mature adults, always actively seeking change and questioning the parameters of the status quo. For adolescence to do so is a form of rebellion, but rebellion and revolution are as different as is the going rate from any departure from it. As with most of the other aspects of the new phase of existence referred to as adolescence, it is quite literally a "teenage wasteland." One seeks to advance from it as rapidly as possible, often without regard for either grace or dignity. Understandably so, the growing awareness of youth can only express its outrage at its systemic impotencies in all areas, including that sexual and economic within and without the household alliances. One of the consistently present undertones to this period of angst is the origination of an idea that childhood proper was a much better time of life: "The memory—real or exaggerated—of a 'golden childhood' can be seized and staked out by its 'owner,' rendered a preserve for recollections to live without fear of destruction" (Natanson, op. cit:91). This is as commonplace a fiction as we saw the narrative of the "self-made" person was. It has rather the same ultimate effect, as one can partake in an element of dubious faith regarding one's own experiences that later on, in the face of the often harsh semblances of reality modern rationalized routines lend us, might become a refuge. "At least" I had this, one might be tempted to say, when one's dreams about what one could become when "one grows up," another unpleasantly unnecessary error we foist on our young children that almost always is itself destroyed in the very manner we seek to protect our memories of the "golden ages" from. As such, these familial designs are instruments for the construction of both a fictional life and a fictional faith in one's ability to live: "Bad Faith amounts to the freezing of temporality, the denial of the openness and flexibility of the present as a basis for the reconstruction of the past no less than as a foundation for assessing and selecting lines for advance to the future." (ibid). "Living in the past," either at the individual level or that of the surrounding institutions of culture—the nation-state is the most egregious culprit here; the replacement of colonialism with neo-colonialism, the competition to the point of open war over resources and populations, the control of "bio-power," as Foucault has labeled it, all point up the nostalgic and archaic tendencies of a political system born centuries ago and having since outlived its usefulness in overthrowing both the church and the church-dominated feudal organs—means abdicating from one of the most pressing responsibilities of life; to live on in the face of the open character of linear existence. That one cannot go back, that one has now a history and not merely the seasons of the annual as if one were a kind of sentient form of vegetation—note how we even associate this word with those who appear to be doing little or nothing with their lives—accrues to it an admittedly daunting responsibility. But it is not one that is impossibly hard to bear. The archetypes that are said to be the hypostasized abodes of human feeling and character do not really live in the narratives through which they become known to us as literary and mythical figures. They percolate through mundane life, as we have seen, while remaining offset from the center of daily activities: "The ordinary person, however, moves within the mystical without being conscious of it. [ ] he is unaware of the ground of his ethical existence." (Barrett, op. cit:61). Routine use of habituated ethics, a contradiction in terms when examined more closely, may indeed serve us, as Barrett suggests, in many encounters with others. But it tends to fail when we have to confront ourselves in the world where we understand that we cannot rely on the mundane sphere to passively carry on and thus carry us with it. This mostly occurs through the problem of the self finding itself contradicted in some manner by its imagination of the other in abnormative circumstances: "The experience of being bereft of my own center of action, the loss of my freedom, reveals the subjectivity of the Other. I find myself in someone else's world." (Natanson, op. cit:43). "Abnormative," that is, because we mostly bump into one another in the shared world of public norms. To truly step into the world that appears to belong to "someone else" is to transgress both the other as an individual—of course, we might be invited in while still feeling alienated by the result—and the mundanity of the everyday world. The shock of intimacy, whether spoken in the *sotto voce* of confidences or enacted in the sensate of shared eros, has this effect upon us. Trespassing into the world of another has also opened up our world. We are indebted to this experience, no doubt, for it gives us a valuable perspective. And indeed, the origins of these kinds of encounters are to be found in adolescence, all the more furtive in almost all cultural contexts not because adults are concerned so much about misadventure, but that they are both jealous of youthful romance and sensual wonder as well as, more pragmatically, concerned about its possible implications regarding health and unwanted children. Though young people are generally able to avoid such issues, adults attribute the fact that they do so due to adult surveillance and control. But every study we have suggests that the more strict such control and surveillance is, the more negative outcomes there are. But such nascent perspectives of "other worlds" or the world of "another" who is enough unlike myself to warrant both inspection and subsequent astonishment, creates the kernel of a duty and debt that can only be sloughed off if we imagine ourselves to have remained unaffected by the encounter. This may be part of the fiction of the golden childhood or youth, where such shocks of otherness were romanced away in hallmark fashion, or declaimed by the autocratic "moralities" of guardian adults, or yet further simply *dumped*, in all senses of the word, in a way that duplicates the "original" and mythical fall of Man. However, "Debt is neither as sign nor the consequence of a fall, nor, moreover, of any such occurrence. It does not result from a contract, but directly places man in the status of a debtor. This status itself is made concrete and diversified in a series of duties or of partial debts" (Derrida, op. cit:137). Debt is here related as a mode of being, or, perhaps better, a mode of the para-being of being partial. Not only of being made aware that one is now made incomplete as a form of waking consciousness that is distracted by the duty of being a debtor, but also that one is concernedly aware of this "status"—is it simply a social role or is it the placement of a subject into the object realm of the "world of another"?—and thus remains "partial" to oneself as well as being the previous "of" oneself. Such a doubling over of partiality into the being able to be of oneself in the world of one's own subjectivity, the visitation of which begins to turn it to that of subjectitude—reminds one as well that one cannot be at home in the world of the other in this manner: "Now, who will ever show that this haunting memory of debt can or should ever cease to disturb the feeling of duty?" (ibid:133). We might well question the "should," the moralizing character of the ought, depending upon the nature of the debt. Some debts are judged to be both necessary and wise if the sphere be narrowed to the strictly economic. An easy example is that banks will be much more ready to lend if the use of the funds is to improve one's real estate or increase the value of secure assets in some other manner. Thus home renovation became fashionable not because people all of a sudden wanted to become do-it-yourself masters of the trades. Hardly; from the 1980s onward in North America this was the easiest way to get private or personal funding from financial institutions and continues to be so today, when the fiscal restraints on banks are much more strict themselves. Indeed, one can go so far to say that the "haunting" presence, or, given the sense that a "series of partial debts" gives one the impression of a "unceasing" presence, represencing debt as a manner of one's hopefully temporary mode of being in the world of perceived objects, is itself constructed by the order of what is deemed necessary in the structural sphere involved. Personal assets, especially real estates, admit to a relatively narrow contiguity of economic and familial landscapes. This is also one's home in the physically personal sense. Its politics is that of a centered authority of place and meaning. Compare Lösch's comment about the difference between an actual resource hinterland and a center of power; and the astonishing implications thereof: "The goals of economic landscapes and states are different. If those for states are arranged in a descending order as follows: continuance, power, *Kultur*, prosperity, this order must be exactly reversed for economic areas. Entirely different sides of human nature are expressed in the political and economic orders." (1967:199 [1945]). How so? Because if something fails to satisfy the direct and pragmatically defined needs of a resource extraction, production and consumption network it is either altered or abandoned completely, hence its lack of interest, relatively speaking, in pure continuation of any specific thing about itself. One might argue that, following Weber's definitive statement about the number one goal of any rationalized organization being its own self-reproduction, that the more bureaucratic the economic agency is, the more its continuity *in itself* will be of import, but this is more of a feeling that is ultimately derived from being able to be at home; here, the entirety of the way of life, its mode of subsistence and continuity are expressed as integral to home. The aspects of "human nature" then that are being expressed are these desires to know one place as one's own, to be from somewhere, yes, but to also be able to tell others that one is the master of one's abode. At the national level, this necessarily must remain mostly a fiction. Nevertheless, "although this 'nation' is an hypostasis, it is psychologically true and necessary to make such an hypostasis. For, as an effective whole, the nation is psychologically something more and other than its parts, and is always experienced as such by each part of the group." (Neumann 1970:275 [1949]). The being of its effectiveness places the value of continuance in the status of its debt to itself. Hall reminds us that the "homogenization process have been central in the history of nationaliza-tion," and that these "inevitably [ ] bring economic and political efficiency in its tail." (2005:11). This debt then can be projected inasmuch as it is in actuality transferred as a financial burden to the people who now call this or that country their home. But this entails a newly minted reciprocity with its newly defined citizenry: "The safeguarding of the power of the state in the long run demands that a state make its economic interests of the citizens its own." (Lösch, op. cit:201). We share the burden of the national debt—one's domestic economy and its financial practices, the single-family household as a census category, for example, is often compared in its frugality, short or far sightedness, or canniness to the national economy and its attendant financial dealings—and are the more a loyal citizen if we run our private household-er's economies in an air-tight manner. Generally, given the diverse commit-ments of government spending, the microcosm of the home is more of a role model for the macrocosm of the nation than the other way around.

None of this has any sense of the perduring mystery that the haunting presence of debt brings with it. We have public auditors and private financial planners, and though money and sex share some of their shyness—and even more so when they come into actual contact with one another—we can be opened up about monetary behavior more easily than we can about that sexual. The notion that a debt is a besmirchment of moral character is of course salient to the connection between the ghost in the home or in the finance department as well as the prudishness surrounding other aspects of being at home, such as sex or even the now negatively sanctioned archaic discipline of children. The key to all of these is the *lack of control* one has acted out regarding oneself. The spendthrift, the one who constantly desires, the one who has lost authority over the young all share this need to cover up what has been going on. So debt in this way brings home to us the necessity for vigilance in the same way that sexuality brings to the home some form of surveillance, but in either case it must also stop short of the outright exacting of punitive damages. The narratives that attend to both the action and the reaction to it are secretive, for after all one has to oneself hire the financial planner or consult the counselor or call the police, or what have you. But there is more to it than even this: "The story is kept secret, yet somehow the imagery is so powerful for the person who holds it that the rest of the family picks up that imagery and ends by re-enacting it. [ ] It looks as if the family ethos is being transferred through a mute unconscious." (Byng-Hall 1990:223). This kind of scenario is more to the point if we are to begin to take seriously the resonant factor of the idea of home producing necessarily a debt in our hearts; one that permits itself visitations, shadows us and indeed acts as a remanant as long as we also feel the reciprocal sense of obligation—mutated but also "mute" with regard to our relationship to the state, which is also "our" home and thus homeland—to keeping the idea of home alive.

Precisely, this "continuance" is by its nature the highest political value, as Lösch stated. Re-enacting family histories is transparently self-evident in spending habits and the creation of real financial debt. It is such a common story, and yet also very much part of the larger concern of being able to be a part of something greater than oneself. This wider concern is "a particularly poignant one in our day, of how this aspiration to connection can motivate some of the most bitter conflicts in human life. It is in fact a fundamental drive, with an immense potential impact in our lives." (Taylor 1989:45). This includes, of course, being able to find a home in history, both one's own biography and by extension, one's family history or the history of one's culture or ethnic group, language group or other such larger structural entity, but as well, the idea that one has a place or at least a function in the ongoing and present-day history of one's workplace or living community. History in this sense also represences a series of partial debts that give us the status of being "in debt" as well as being able to make ourselves a place in it while trying to get out of it at the same time. History itself, seen from this local absence of perspective, looks like it is one long seriation of getting into debts of the greatest variety and then getting out of some of them. Such mundane activities when told together in a familial setting might well take on the grandeur of something akin to myth. Or, they might be cast aside as something that only happens to persons more dimwitted than ourselves: "In any case, the stories of yesterday, in the telling and retelling, may be the legends of tomorrow." (Byng-Hall, op. cit:221). The secrecy that attends to the process of retelling the familial stories of home and its denizens keep us at home in a different way than we can be merely through our present tenure. It links us, so we imagine to those who have lived there before us, and this is especially the case if one grows up not just in the same region or city as one's ancestors, but in the very ancestral home or site. What occurred there, over the generations, cannot be known in experiential detail. There is no direct communication with those who have passed before us, as it were, and in spite of the tales told about Ouija boards and unearthly tenants, bumps in the night and once again, the visitation—perhaps we also imagine that we owe some irredeemable debt to our ancestors—all of these also contents of their batch of family stories becoming legends, but in spite of this real absence, there is retained a presence of place and sense of being at home that often overcomes historical distances in terms of how we in the present perceive the past. This itself is a secret that families do not share outside their kinship alliances, even with affines. It, like the sexuality and perhaps the crimes of the past, is considered in its own way to be sacred and thus, for this or that family and its home, participating in that which transcends one's respective places in time. Its magic is that it favors place over time, and in this it is also close kin with sexual intimacies and unions of all kinds: "It is an object of obsession and attraction, a dreadful secret and an indispensable pivot." (Foucault, op.

cit:109). Any real events that occurred outside the ken of the present disappear with the demise of mortal memory. This is a dangerous moment for cultures, but it can be a cleansing one for families and even individuals (cf. Samuel and Thompson, op. cit:17ff). For to be unable to speak of something that should by all other accounts have remained a secret that no one but the principals involved would have had any original knowledge of, is to repay the debt we found ourselves within as a mode of being indebted to those principals who, at some lost point in the history of our home, were betrayed and their experiences thus desacralized.

4.2 CLOUDY SKIES

There are a number of normative means by which one can avoid both the betrayal and the debt of being born by happenstance into a specific lineage and place. Taking up the fashionable call of all ways of life is one of these. Intellectual discourses, a sure-fire way to bury one's head in the sediments of moot monuments in any case, are certainly some of these. The products of such fashions establish the norms of unthought by which "even" thinkers commit errors by which they can live on with certain pedigrees and find a home in the bourgeois and otherwise bureaucratic systems of educational institutions: "Such literature dominates the industry—everyone sees and gauges the progress and vitality of academic disciplines with it." (Heidegger 1999:63 [1988]). Within the ambit of the problems discussed here, the issue of memory and memorialization is an ever-present one: "In the realm of philosophy, historicism has often produced the paradoxical result of misjudging the difference between immediacy and reconstructed immediacy." (Gadamer 2000:110 [1996]). What is "of the moment," or on "the cutting edge" of things is not so much transparently recycled from the historical record or from intellectual histories of ideas and the like, but rather misrecognized, sometimes deliberately, for what the original actually contained and how it thus could have spoken to us. Even if we are working in the same "natural" language, this error lying somewhere between commission and omission, can easily occur. "Immediacy" in the sense of experiential immanence, the immanentiality of which is a phenomenological item of some import and implies some form of transcendence or proximity to Being, cannot simply be remade at will in the present-day consciousness of those who are self-consciously seeking to place themselves within the home of Being, or where it is suspected of being. Reconstruction occurs because it must inevitably be the outcome of an arc that seeks to place itself in this way. It is only our imagination that allows—and disallows, if one understands the limits of specific human experiences whether in our own time or some other—us to think that we have captured something of either the past, a memory, or a record of a lifeway. In part, this sensitivity to the experiential promiscuousness of the historical record and its interpretations—ultimately stemming from the guardedness by which sacred texts are drawn into the fold of the once again reconstructed immediacy of a posited though routinized transcendental sphere—is opened up to us through the concern over scientism and the latest flavor of neo-positivism. This has always demanded experience that is value-free or objective, "free from standpoints," as Heidegger phrases it. More than this, however, "It cultivates a strange modesty and grants a general dispensation from critical questioning by means of the apparent self-evidence of what it demands." (op. cit:63). Through this imaginative reconstruction of the possible but implausible idea that to have "been there" was in fact to have been anointed by objectivity, "history repeats itself" in a version of the unconsciousness that a culture must confront but that a discourse has no excuse for mimicking (cf. Jung, op. cit:95). This repetition can be found just about anywhere one looks, and it would not be reasonable to point the sole finger at discourse. One does expect, however, that the thinkers involved would be more scrupulous about their research, but even in the brightest cases one cannot possibly know about all that had been accomplished before one set pen to paper. The deliberate misconstruction or misrecognition of ideas is, however, a culpable moment in the history of academic publication. At the same time, one can question the objectivity of any argued context that one has somehow "taken something out of." It does appear that arguments do have to be made and remade, interpretations built and then built up again, in order for the proverbial conversation of humankind to carry on. In this, perhaps Heidegger is too strident in his critiques of just about everything that was going on in the European theater in the early 1920s. At the very least, however, there is no ongoing or scandalous question of a contrivance that pushes interest outside the intellectual elites and seeks the mass market of fashionable phobias and decoy maneuvers the middle classes eagerly help themselves to, generally to cover up their own crimes and misdemeanors: "The press harries the child sex abusers too: until the experts discover too many of them in apparently ordinary families. Then the tabloids turn on the women social workers as child-snatchers, or as would be stepmothers. So old myths resurge to give new comfort to ordinary fearful parents." (Samuel and Thomson, op. cit:16). Yes and no. Part of what parents *fear* is that they themselves will be found out for what they are actually doing, as the first part of the citation attests. Adults regularly project their desires on their children as a rationalization for their criminal actions. It is well known that sexual abuse excuses itself through the charming proclivities of the youth. "Leading one on," an excuse also performed publicly at thousands of rape trials, is still seen as a cogent variable for the defense. We certainly see what we want to see in such cases, as media and market portrayals of youth give the impression that their overwhelming presence, their best feature, so to speak, is their not quite innocent sexual attractiveness. Children too learn very rapidly how to ape their elders in this way, and then, hypocritically, we adults take that to mean that they have cognitively and experientially matriculated to an adult sexuality: "The child's 'vice' was not so much an enemy as a support; it may have been designated as the evil to be eliminated, but the extraordinary effort that went into the task that was bound to fail leads one to suspect that what was demanded of it was to persevere" (Foucault, op. cit:42). Surely this is also a game of hypocritical hide and seek, played out beneath the bed linen of countless homes and generating its own saucerful of secretive secretions. Part of the recent script to this new but somewhat shadowy take on the bedroom farce is also the counselor who "knows" what is going on ahead of time, perhaps because he has participated in very similar fantasies, enacted or no. Either way, "it shows up the psychoanalyst's habit of making a spurious universal principle out of late personalistic phenomena." (Neumann 1970:184 [1949]). The "principle" in this case is that youthful sexuality is both uncontrolled and uncontrollable and that this is catching for adults, who then dive right in, so to speak, with either real-time abuse or out of time fantasies—mostly worked up and projected into media constructed situations and scenarios—and thus further to this, that sexuality is in principle uncontrollable so no series of defenses can ultimately defeat its desiring destinies or conquer its lascivious landscapes.

With the exception of the secret of the home itself. Here, as in no other place, there is a guided and misguided recognition that the sacrosanct nature of the home can and does stand in place of fantasy worlds such as Las Vegas, where "what happens" there must "stay there": "This is why in life stories hardly anyone admits to adultery or child neglect, to serious mistakes at work, or disloyal rivalry; to any of the socially reprehensible acts that we often commit, but which we delete from the official or public version of our personal history." (Peneff 1990:39). Though others are most often involved in these acts, either as victims of them co-conspirators, or even by-standers, we can at least push the historian—or the new lover, third spouse, or what have you—to investigate much further than is generally possible to find out just how much others really know about us. And then, if push comes to shove, we can always deny such acts outright. If they really were so private as those that we imagine Peneff is categorizing here, we should be able to bluff our way through more or less, and carry on. Perhaps we may do so with the awareness that what is reprehensible is itself a form of the Kantian morality where the Vegas of privacy is covered over by the maxims of the public citizen and socially upstanding moralist. At the same time, the quite regular and normative acts of the private life, most of them occurring in the home, have enough diversity of motive and effect that even good intentions may bring down the house. It sometimes takes a lot of energy to "keep up appearances," certainly, but what of the fatigue necessary to exist always upon the threshold of one's actions becoming too public too quickly, or, for that matter, remaining too clandestine when in fact they need to see the light of day in the same way as we sometimes need to leave home or at least get out of the house once in a while? "Fatigue is the inner sense of this weight of the effort, which has to overcome itself, overcome its own resistance to the launching of itself into position." (Lingis 1989:154). Perhaps much of the action we take that would have been better left untaken—to "undertake" in this sense means that we are also the authors of our own demise, whether in the long term that comes to all of us, or in shorter terms that herald the movement of dying "before" one's time, kindred with the self-sabotage of the addict or the perennially off-putting person who suffers from a class-based or otherwise sourced lack of sociality—is simply a reaction to the humdrum throbbing of living on in the face of inaction. We might rather let entropy set in and have done. Hence the presence and persistence of the habitual routines that "get us through the day": "This tendency to let something ossify into a fixed habit is clearly rooted in human nature. And yet in the scientific culture of modernity this natural proclivity has developed into what is now a way of life. The life of each individual has now come increasingly to be regulated in an automatic manner." (Gadamer 1996:112 [1991]). It may be difficult to distinguish between what equally clearly is a social pattern of such force that it envelopes any of us who at least attempt to remain normative. Everyone works in this way, we would think, and outside of the odd places where the norms shift just enough that one's usual guards can be let down—the most noticeable thing about places like Las Vegas (the actual resort area and not the city itself, of course), is that everyone appears to be in a good mood and complete strangers find one another at least tolerable if not downright interesting. Why? Because we do not have to participate in the usual defensive postures that keep the life of labor running on its cold steel tracks; it seems to be the only way "the public" can be maintained in modern mass society. That our behavior has become more and more constructed and "automatic" is not only to be expected but it is even welcomed, as this shifts the burden of the work involved to larger systems and more anonymous outlets.

This is ultimately reflected in the system that each of us works within, that of global capital. "Human resources" are still the subject understood as his labor power and his cost. Which one will defray the other is always of the moment. Such an irony allows us to continue to understand ourselves as agents, willing or unwilling, it does not matter, in a process whereby each of us is turned into not merely an object, but a representative sample of the social process of the public. We are commoditized in both Marxian but also symbolic interactionist terms. This may aid our sardonic muttering when we have to get up and go to work each Monday morning but it would seem to be of very little merit otherwise. It must be thought of, rather, as another part of both the "alienation from human potential"—that is usually assumed to stop where one has figured out the amount of sacrifices one has made to the skills left over in one that one can sell to the market as one's labor power; but this is not all that is lost—and as something that leads more intimately and more insidiously to "false consciousness," as Engels referred to it. Akin to the ethics of religious world systems as opposed to their institutions and rituals or even their metaphysics, the face-to-face aspect of Marx's work now appears more important to us than his structuralism. This is something that certain commentators have sometimes ignored.[1] The fact that the works of Marx and Engels then became Marxism and also then became the world-historical movements of socialism and "communism" with their generally disastrous consequences—that is, when dictatorships self-styled as communist took over the entirety of national affairs, and *not* to say when socialist ideas percolated through democracies and made them more livable for everyone—pushed many in our time to either completely commit to this set of loyalties or to completely oppose them. These now more or less jingoistic loyalties linger on long after the facts have either come out or the remaining socialist states are making the giant adjustments necessary to keep their nations relevant to the world picture. Generally, the martinet quality of loyalty to systems is well known. It appears in the small scale of attendance and ritual in voluntary organizations such as churches, to the extracurricular and lower-level staff oriented functions at workplaces, to the idea that one needs to come out and "experience" either the city parade, the city parks, or the dreadfully ambitious school plays one's child might find herself in. Each of these contains the world crisis writ rather small and unbecoming, but its resonance reminds us that these feelings of loyalty, the human group, and the sometimes authentic and sometimes shibboleth sense of "community" are also proclivities of human "nature": "What started as a total commitment, a response to ultimacy, may then change to a fierce loyalty and a continuing devotion but without the unique quality of absolute concern." (Natanson, op. cit:142). The effort to remain part of something that is even slightly larger than oneself is also, in its obverse but also its similitude, the effort to bring what is larger than life home with me, home to the others who are already with me, and thus finally, home to me in a way that it will remain within me and no longer be able to go astray and find itself wanting only the prodigality of yet another stilted homecoming. In order to accomplish this feat, I tend to develop as well at least the mock, if not bluff, arrogance that not only can it be done but that I am the one to do it, perhaps the only one. That this seldom lasts the longitude of the lifetime is fortunate. Trading one set of loyalties for another is a horizontal shift in unthought. The vertical dimension of reflection, which must stop the syntagmatic chain of deference we show to the deferred and itself deferential string of signifiers is nowhere in sight. The "illusory" potential of any aspect of a worldview is always present, lurking, if not ready to leap out at us, in the underbrush of the day, the fashionable fascisms of planned obsolescence, the planned parenthood of the new and improved, the planning of lives based on the means of others existence. If it were to pounce, like the hunting puma of the real forest that surrounds the hinterland of excesses we call our quality of life, we would then be torn from any illusion and be forced face to face with the shattered significance of warm-hearted hearth but homiletic home.

4.3 WHERE IS THE HEART?

Though we carry such doubts around with us in the private spaces of anxiety and even concernful being—in our culture, women are more likely to make this space public, men more likely to try to ignore it—the concept of home being the ultimate space of affirmation rather than doubt is ideally ascendant. In order to keep it so, we can resort to a sense of "pragmaticism," a faith in the facticality of everyday life, the enactment of enactmental complexes as the surplice of surplus, the finery attached to what is fine if it had been left to itself, including other persons. Not entirely practical because of the some-times-exorbitant efforts and extra cost of such decorations, more or less rococo, but as well not entirely aesthetic or ethical due to its enduring use value after the domestic crisis has passed. The wine may have been gone but the crystal remains for another day. We who are gathered here will submit that the moment is of the moment and the doubts are cleared to the side, as at any wedding: "Since under rational conditions all those who assemble who find their highest utility here it follows that there is good reason for the special attitude toward space that binds these persons together, such as love for a native place, a feeling for economic landscapes, or national pride." (Lösch 1967:247 [1945]). This feeling of a loyalty that cannot be displaced or dismissed as mere bigotry tends to need to keep itself on the small side. Only when there are "too many" persons involved, Lösch continues, does the good feeling and solidarity deteriorate into chauvinism. Smallness of size not only increases the intimacy of contact as well as its likelihood over the middle term, it also suggests that what is "special" about the feelings are that they can actually be shared and there is some direct evidence of this, instead of merely the rhetoric of the workplace "culture" or that of the nation, for that matter. Sorokin reminds us that the average lifespan of even larger organiza-tions is rather shallow, and smaller ones such as small businesses, arts and cultural groups and even families is also quite short in terms of consecutive operating or existing years: "Organized groups are started with an expecta-tion that they will develop and live a long life." (op. cit:261). This is the same flair by which marriages occur, but we know that in North America half of all vows collapse, many after a comparatively short time. So, along with the smallness of size for authentic home-oriented gatherings or social groups, we also have the sense that the more formal the relationships committed to, the older the persons should be, to increase their chances of longevity and other attendant successes such as those economic or filial. What Berger and Kellner called the "marriage conversation" occurs as well in other long-term relationships where the words of the other and his manners are trusted as if one could read telepathically his intents and see transparently all his possible motives. This in itself is the attitude of concernful being in the world. It is other-oriented without being other-directed, and it manifests the "homebody" of the person who does not let the world get him down overmuch. He does not go out into the world as either its martinet or its stoic supporter, nor as its saboteur, but rather as an extension of the care he brings to the hearth. His "heart" is in his gait rather than in his mouth or worn on his sleeve. He resists in so far as he can the routinization of human feeling that is to be found everywhere in the "ontic" spatiality of the public. He knows that "Care disappears in the habits, customs, and publicness of everydayness—and this does not mean it comes to an end, but rather that it does not show itself any longer, it is covered up. Being-concerned-about and going about dealings have the immediate aspect of *carefreeness*. The world being encountered appears as simply there in a straightforward manner." (Heidegger 1999:80 [1988], italics the text's). This last is the origin of the idea of the everyday world of wide-awakeness to be found later in Schutz and G.H. Mead. The "natural attitude" of Scheler is what we adopt in its continuity and its presentation to us. We duplicate, writ small, its *"Offentlichkeit,"* and can justifiably take pride in ourselves and our behavior in public and as part of the public if, at the end of each day, we have caused no strife from strafing its shared barricades or cast no stones into its collectively held pool of sympathies. It remains a conscious act to have been so pliant and maintained our "cool" just a the right moment, even though for perhaps the rest of the day no moment arose that called for any serious reflection at all along these, or any other, lines: "But this means not just that we happen to have such reactions or that we have decided in the light of present predicament of the human race that it is useful to have such reactions" (Taylor 1989:6). Perhaps not entirely, though the utility of having a public face is crucially well known to everyone who maintains a social conscience, in other words, for everyone who holds concernful being as the ethical outwardness of the lighted space of Being, and there are also many, if not most cultures around the world that do not at all share the European enlightenment official understandings regarding the universal sanctity of the person simply by her being a member of *Homo Sapiens*. Taylor is, however, expressing this ideal as if it could become the form of a global concernfulness, where the worlding of the world revolves around the ideal and not around the reality of most human relations to this day. In this, we might concur as Euro-American intellectuals or even as the "decent person in the street," though only on a good day, that we should be striving towards this ideal in the world and ultimately as the world. In this, we are making ourselves a valued member of something larger and thus also extending the conscience that we bring to the home as an effort to bring it home to others: "This being-well-known in the with-world is one which is average, thriving in everydayness and developing into its contentments. This familiarity is not simply a characteristic of comprehension, but rather a mode of the being-encountered of the beings-which-are-there themselves, being-'in.'" (Heidegger, op. cit:77). Here, with-beings who our with us as a form of socially constructed *Mitsein* different from what we put "into" the relationships within the home, our apprehension of them loses its originating quality of apprehensiveness. But perhaps this is saying too much, or something too one-sided, for we might desire also to imagine that an at least equal origin of the draw towards concern for the other as myself in the world—not as necessarily the "neighbor" but as an everyday occurrence and also the margins of social role rational action that has its goal of utility and "familiarity"—is to apprehend their quality of existence unto mine. That is, we note in the presence of the others an already always sense of the familiar simply because they are also putting on the public face of civility—for the most part, and docility. This assuages our own doubts regarding the inauthenticity of social relations outside the home and allows us to "put our hearts into" the scene in order for it to give everyone the impression that this is but an extension of good-heartedness and warm-heartedness of the already well lit spaces of Being-at-Home.

There is also the ever-present history of desire for the other that has both evolutionary inertia and the consciousness of history about it. The agora of desires was not at all always confined to the actual house or home, but the heart and its vehicular body were outwardly expressing their interest in creating beings-for by being-with. The sacred space of temples of all kinds expressed this desire to be in the world together: "And since the temple represented the whole world, all human activities were portrayed in it; and because most people are always thinking about sex anyway, the great majority of the temple sculptures were of an erotic nature." (Jung 1959:217 [1951]). The desire *for* the other is assumed to mirror the desire *of* the other. That this is not always the case person to person does not obviate the fact that it might well be the case in principle. Actual sex, rather than the discourses surrounding sexuality as an object, is something that binds communities together and thus also encourages the denial of labor and of competitive marketing; this last, at least, when the cards are on the table and one is committed. Taken too far, of course, one can develop the same kinds of bigotries that were seen as the enemy of authentic group membership, the "chauvinism" of the elect or equally of the mass. One should also be able to say, quite inconsequentially, that "its only sex" and leave it at that. If not, we risk placing ourselves within the very discourses that objectify and idealize it ad nauseum, and thereby circumscribe it, quite literally, "writing around" it from all places and directions, in dizzying sentiment. For example: "The bourgeoisie began by considering that its own sex was something important, a fragile treasure, a secret that had to be discovered at all costs." (Foucault, op. cit:120-1). The interest in intimacy as an aesthetic was not new, particularly in the East. But the fetish concerning it as both a commodity and a kind of self-adoration, a cult of the occult where what was already hidden must be at once brought to light and yet kept from almost everyone's comprehension, especially that of children and youth who had, in the previous centuries, been no strangers to any of it, was something entirely novel. Its very novelty seemed to stem from the rising structural fortunes of the new middle classes—its political victories, its burgeoning wealth, its staking of the claim to what was fashionable in the arts and in clothing—and from this confluence of social mobility and quality of life variables came the dual sense of having leisure time to fill as well as being aware that others were now looking to them to set the model for the good society. The bourgeois household, with its tiny drafty rooms, its myriad of fireplaces, its interior lavatories and kitchens, its spaces of schooling and disciplines, its boudoirs borrowed and simplified from the aristocracy, and its much smaller serving staff, was to be the place where the most important element of "pleasure and economy" took place. Sex could become the vital and revitalizing cog in the new system of production, rather than something that might have been its chief distraction. With all of its technical amenities and rationalized division of labor, it appeared to be paradise brought to earth. But this new model of the household and its householders was in fact a house of cards when it came to the serious project of constructing a meaningful culture: "*Naturally* there is art in this utopia since there is leisure—as if leisure by itself were a sufficient condition for the production of any kind of culture worth taking seriously." (Barrett, op. cit:340, italics the text's). The assumption of an inevitably productive connection that could be seen as the "nature" of the entire model, its ideal functioning on the ground as a real set of practices, was submitted to trenchant critique as soon as it had gotten off the ground. From Marx to Spencer to Nietzsche to Sapir to Adorno and well beyond, the bourgeois sensibility—aping what was higher in the desire to replace it while shunning what was lower for fear of falling back into it—was constantly looking over its collective shoulder while at the same time trying to keep pace with what was just in front of it. Its "nature" was not truly its own; part of it borrowed from the fading aristocracy and landed gentry and part of it inherited from its own mercantile and working class roots. This hybrid of compulsive labor laboring to become the leisured set could not survive over the long term. Today, we have seen two generations of the withering of the middle class, and political parties of all stripes vowing to "save it"—from what, one may ask, from itself?; unlikely, and one might

186 *The Bungle Book*

also ask, what is it about the middle class that would be worth saving?; it's moral panics, it's decoy behavior, it's self-righteousness, it's cultural pretensions and mediocre aesthetic, it's false worldliness based on the travel brochure or guide, yes, all of these and more, perhaps?—and on top of all of this, the appearance that it is, in spite of itself, still a healthy model to be emulated by workers and to be aided by the elites. Its "nature" is neither nature nor culture, and its consumptive brand of quality of life that began in rapid and reciprocal response to the over-production of the 1920s has taken both into its maelstrom: "In short, a spot in the heart of nature that was once suited to residence and the storing up of reserves of health is now so transformed as to waste them. If man is surrounded by bungled instead of few perfect things, if he does not keep the symmetry of nature constantly before his eyes, he will be destroyed himself in the end." (Lösch, op. cit:353). Such an early "environmental" sentiment here may be applauded, but more salient to this discussion the idea of the place of the heart as necessary to claim a nature for oneself, a nature of oneself that was inclusive of what one was, is of the utmost. All social groups make versions of this claim, telling themselves that they know where the heart is and must remain. Certainly, my own predilection is for the "heart of nature," but even here, one must admit to the reality that whatever dwelling one constructs abutting the wilderness is not a part of nature *per se*. One is *always* an interloper, and it is the lack of this awareness that leads to the destruction of both the ecosphere and life within it.

If this necessary sensibility is lacking, what we do know is that somehow we are placing the heart at the end of the "path to nothing" in order that there should in fact be something at its terminus. We do not know how long this path is, its meanderings giving it the air of sophistication when in fact it is mindless, as we saw mimicked in machine-life. And we also know, it is claimed, that in doing so we are forsaking our future, though this point is something that really ought to be demonstrated by ethnographic data which I suspect might very well be lacking the very sense that Midgely thinks is already present: "What we need to grasp in such cases is not the simple fact that people are acting against their best interests. We know that; it stands out a mile. We need to understand, beyond this, *what kind* of gratification they are getting from acting in this way." (op. cit:72, italics the text's). Being seen as clever when one is not, pulling the wool over the eyes of the other in unexpected ways and not generally being exposed for doing so, and most of all, living on as one chooses with little or no responsibility to the global others who die supporting one's choices are some of the instant and addicting gratifications that come to mind when one is discussing what the sense of home means to the middle classes of the developed nations. Is it a coincidence that the technical and managerial classes have arisen from the bourgeois? That the critical students have in the main come from either the elites or the margins? Why rock your own boat? But the most obvious reason for the absence of thought within the middle class is that it is self-absorbed and obsessed with its own doings; both those shadowy that while it perpetrates them it seeks to cover them up, and those outwardly inclined to show the rest of the world how neat and tidy their lives are and that we should emulate all that they represent. One must look away from oneself to gain any insight into the human condition; we must attempt a genuine understanding of the other both in ourselves and in the world at large. This is the case whether we are speaking in the rarified air of a critical philosophy, or more commonly and perhaps just as importantly, when we must gain some perspective on the day to day challenges each of us faces: "Even as the most independent adult, there are moments where I cannot clarify what I feel until I talk about it with certain special partner(s), who know me, or have wisdom or with whom I have an affinity." (ibid:36). Do the middle classes even have what Aristotle, for one, would have understood as an authentic friendship? Do their marriages offer more than economic convenience and the potential for status? Is there any "wisdom" of any kind to be found in their midst? Well, surely this is asking too much in both ways: on the one hand, with such numbers, there will be instances of authenticity and wisdom at the level of specific individuals who possess certain sets of experiences that are not directly derived from the coincidence of their class status, and, on the other, we should not expect this to be a goal for the rising classes whose main purpose is self-reproduction and closing the gap between them and the elites. The troubling issue that arises from the bourgeois sensibility is not even so much about its veneration of things for their own sake, the fetish of commodities and borrowing status from them, but how it views its own intimacies and communions: "It is that aspect of itself which troubled and preoccupied it more than any other, begged and obtained its attention, and which it cultivated with a mixture of fear, curiosity, delight and excitement." (Foucault, op. cit:123-4). The promise of community, well known and aspired to by the classical cults and by much older forms of social organizations as we have seen, is certainly of interest to the middle class home and its denizens. But with two income earners out of the house in order to keep up the expected standards of leisure, children also absent for a schooling that prepares them to do what their parents are simultaneously doing and that is extended to the nth degree precisely to keep adults in the work force endlessly producing and consuming, the middle class suburban home sits mostly empty of life. The odd insect, perhaps, enjoys some solitary endeavor, foraging amongst the scraps left by the younger children, ignored by the father as women's work, forsaken by the mother who is working her "second shift." If we were to gaze into the middle class home we not find any sort of heart at all, at least for most of the waking hours. Even when these consanguines collect there, they are busy with the surveillance mechanisms of their indentured servitudes, homework for children, take-home from the office or take-out dinners, and the extracurricular spaces of mindless activity arranged so that parents and children can avoid the very intimacy that the home is supposed to both nurture and give safe harbor.

This is the effect of affectation. The absence of effective affections, the presence of distractions—electronic media of all kinds; child "care" on the cheap; sex, having served its purpose of reproduction of the next demographic of producer-consumers is more or less abandoned or engaged in furtively as if one was yet again fourteen years old and living in one's own parents' house—and the mistaken sense that any encounter with intimacy or the other is a risky business, impinging on the soul. The real shock must indeed be the sudden realization that this person was next to me all this time, all these years, and I had either forgotten about her or had simply taken her close presence for granted. Aside from all of the usual suspects regarding divorce—unequal divisions of labor, especially after children are present, is a key feature here—one might venture to say that two persons, in their attempt to create a home for both, have missed the point that such a home must also then contain both of them at once. It must, in other words, be the synthesis of two separate ideals, or at the very least, the space of an ongoing and well-intentioned dialogue between them. Though Sorokin speaks of prison inmates and citizenry, surely it is much worse to have chosen an intimate partner and then find oneself in an "automatic" relationship with them; "And such 'automatic' and 'undesirable' memberships play a much more important role in the life of hundreds of millions than the voluntary or sought for memberships." (op. cit:239). The latter may quickly turn into the former if we are not always and already aware that *I am no longer alone.* This sense of being-present-to-another is not something that comes "by nature." It does not have its own heart at its origins, for this union and communion must not only be constructed but maintained. There is, no doubt, labor involved, even "work," and it is the perennial message of all relationship counselors and self-help manuals that "marriage" or its surrogates is always a work in progress and something akin to a garden. Gardens, rivers, trees, or anything else that either grows or flows aside for the moment, the kerygmatic kernel of human intimacy is at once not sex, and certainly not sexuality, as well as not being held by the desire for and the anxiety about being "soul-mates" for one another. It is, in a word, the being able to be-with, the being comfortable with letting go of the illusion of the self and its projections (cf. Jung, op. cit:9). That we so often imagine and then use the other to populate our own inner fictions in undeniable. Those who resist our encroachment are seen as those unwilling to urge us on, to encourage us to "develop" ourselves at the expense of others. But we do so in any case with the global structure of trade and commerce, and perhaps the exteriority of these kinds of anonymous and "unknown faces" reassures us that we do *need* the world even if we are not aware of its needs.

Such a world is ultimately given towards its own generalized conception of home. The *world* is where the heart is: "There will never be absolute safety in any region smaller than the earth itself." (Lösch, op. cit:203). The world is what the earth becomes when it is constructed as social through the presence of human beings seeking to make a home upon it. Hence the "life-world" or "worldview" of the phenomenologists. Understanding the presence of another as being either "next to me" or whom I will encounter next after myself, and in doing so, encounter myself anew, is to depart from the sole effect of reason and to venture forth with both the shadow and the soul as companions. To approach the other and to be invited into his home is to place oneself as worthy of his respect. To do so one must adopt the mode of being-with. This is the heart of the matter, but it remains weak: "If you want to discriminate more finely what it is about human beings that makes them worthy of respect, you have to call to mind what it is to feel the claim of human suffering, or what is repugnant about injustice, or the awe you feel at the fact of human life." (Taylor, op. cit:8). There are distractions aplenty from being able to "call to mind" any or all of these finer feelings. But the largest impasse that stands in the way of such experiences is the fact that they too are historically provincial and in large part, remain so. Migration and immigration have brought to the Rhodian shores of enlightenment-sourced cultures the other fact of otherness in the world. The other exposes us also for what we, in part, are. No commercial transaction can completely obviate the reality that most people do not care about the fates of most other people (cf. Lösch, op. cit:307ff). The "way of the world" does have the merit of bringing people together over shared business interests. We have seen that it is also the most convenient manner of making a home and family. To argue for something more than this might appear both vain and sentimental. It might also appear to be an unnecessary extension of the practical utility of having diverse cultures arrange themselves so to serve each other, equally and with equity, but also with a maintenance of distance and aloofness, disinterest in any final communion that demands of all of us to not only like the other, but to be like him. Perhaps one could care too much about such a world, as it too seeks to mimic the mythic paradise, the *garden* that we still feel somehow cast out from, thrown into the world and running along towards mutual death: "Caring is concerned about itself and attends to itself in that it meets up with itself in a worldly manner in the there it is encountering. Caring as such is precisely what originally has the world there and puts temporality in place in such a manner that the world is something being encountered in caring and for it." (Heidegger, op. cit:79). If each culture has within itself the ability to care for itself, the personality of our own *souci de soi* is not a necessary export. Its expatriate status should remind us that by itself, it could create no diaspora. The world as such worlds itself rather more in spite of us than because of our presence in this way. That is because it contains worlds of being that are foreign to us, and the self-care of every culture contained in such a compendium would not lend shelter to any sentiment that claimed it to be only its own. If we are made more aware that the time of this encounter is about the timing of it, the whole-hearted commitment to the moment of the meeting-with, and then the being-with, in the world which is now made other to both of us, this can be called home in the most immanent sense. We now walk forward together in a new world, knowing that the heart is no longer alone with its self-delusions and projections. But to do this is to participate as well in the poesis of desire and the ambiguity of anxiety. We do not leave either the shadow or the soul behind us, we simply bracket them, in an auto-phenomenological reduction, so that those of the other can be attended to and "cared" for. We are on a mission to attend to the otherness that is not yet our own, to the dwelling that awaits the dweller, the abode that is missing the ones who abide, that which is nostalgic in myth but pragmatic in reality; and all of this is the poetics of the heart's self-consciousness: "Poetry is consciousness dreaming of domicile at the core of the foreign world, the mind deeply homesick and scheming return, the tongue contorting itself toward uttering what such a return might be like. It is mind remembering the old world of the *Garden*." (Lilburn 1999:6, emphasis mine).

It is of abiding interest that we must feel that the heart has a *place*, or is in a place. It resides in the way human beings as a whole do. We are aware that to care for the health of one's heart involves both the physiological sensibility that we should avoid unhealthy diets and keep exercising regularly. It is a rhythmic structure that is unavoidable and it also keeps time—the metric of the living organism to which the soul is somehow apportioned and also finds its own "placement," however temporary or permanent—and thus we need to feel its presence through its beating metronome, the tempi it can express expressing the variety of emotions and tasks that humans face daily. The heart in this physical sense is also thus very much where "the heart is." To feel pain just there is to sense both the foreshadowing of one's own loss of consciousness, but also it is to have hurt feelings, not just feelings that happen to hurt. Making a pastime of avoiding this is, however, to engage in the projection Jung cautions us about. Concernful being, devoid of the errata of projection, takes into itself the encounter with its own otherness. It does so in the home of the heart of one's own being.

Chapter Five

Either In or Out of Love

Speaking of the heart, might one not also be inclined to say that we err when we imagine that it has but one place and for all time? Similar to the problem of God being either dead or alive, we often feel that we equally should be either in or out of love but not both at once or some other feeling that is an amalgam of the two polar sensitivities which in fact, are neither ever felt in any final and utter manner nor are they ever without one another. But this time it is not a question of employing a concept of the afterlife akin to afterglow. What follows is a series of discussions that seek to bring to light the ambiguity, the truly mixed feelings we have about one another in spite of, and perhaps also because of, the desires and virtues of the ideals expressed in the preceding chapter. "Because of," due to the strong loyalties we entertain regarding our desire for community, and "in spite of," due to the equally present obligations we imagine must attend the being who is first a self or at least, as we saw near the beginning of our journey, a series of related selves that must care for one another. With all of this concernfulness flying about, both in the direction of the self, the other and yet also the world, the amateur phenomenologist who is seeking to construct an ethics might well have empathy for Heidegger and others when faced with the division of the heart's labors. To find one's tempo in the flux of contemporary existence, to acknowledge one's contemporaries as one's peers but also as one's compatriots—*we live in the world together even when we are apart*, and *this* fact will be found to be a crucial element in the sense that one is in fact neither fully in love nor completely out of love—is to find oneself not in specific place or at rest, but to accept the movement of being as its singular form of contentment. To be at peace in this way is to know how one loves and the distinction love plays as a partner to concernfulness.

191

To understand the understated emotion of the heart's apparently perpetual but finite motion is to undertake the distinction between fantasy and phantasm. The one is in league with self-projection of the sort that envelops us and insulates us from the world, as Jung noted. The other is the imagination of rational action that projects the self into that self-same world and risks its self-knowledge in order to attain self-understanding. It comprehends only after it apprehends. The first cannot perform either function, and is also not rational. Its modus operandi is rationalization in the personalistic sense of providing rationales for something it cannot do, or is at least unwilling to do. It *excuses* itself in this way. This is why we casually use the term rationalization in the same way we use excuse, or even, more colloquially, weasel. Though rationalization is a technical term applied to bureaucratic organizations, very much stating the "nature" of their effect in the world as well as containing the character of their customary behavior, it is not such a stretch to imagine that such organizations have the same "personality," writ large, as the individual who is constantly making excuses for himself and accepts no responsibility for either his actions or even presence in the world. These persons, and perhaps all of us on a bad day, are wrapped up in the "red tape" of bureaucratic mentalities. For all of us commit acts that we would have rather not occurred. In order to find a way to move on from them, we seek to move away from them first, mimicking the process by which one attains the there from the here, for instance, or distances oneself from one's origins in order to "remake" the self. In doing so, we gain an inkling of what lies in store for us if we dare to unpack the devices of rationalization that orbit our gravity-conscious self-projections. We want to be at the center of things, with all other things in attendance upon us, waiting, serving, genuflecting, adoring. And this, we think, is what it means to be in love.

Being pushed out of the center means confronting a crisis. It is existential in "import" only because we have become far too comfortable with the comforts of another, forgetting that she too rests at the center of things and we are in her orbit. Perhaps it would be more apt to suggest that such a crisis in the life of the lover has an existential "implication," because its importance nonetheless fades over time and we do construct other centers of attention and, if we are learning, perhaps also of attentiveness. Because of the brevity of this process in our transient lives, it is fitting that this section is the most brief of all. We are almost immediately thrust into the space of coming to know that love is something that is shared only, and not possessed, this is supposedly its "magic," and however sentimental such a remark might appear, it has merit in the sense that it links love with other conceptualizations of being that we have already encountered, magic and power, being the nearest to it. The "wielding" of love may sound oddly inappropriate, even kinky, but love's power and magic come, for humans, from its ambiguous and mysterious presencing of the self with another and not it's being fully present. In a word, love's "being" is contained within a concernfulness that rests unconcerned about its abilities and its effects. It takes itself seriously only when it fails to be carefree and falls into carelessness.

5.1 FANTASY AND PHANTASM

What distinguishes our desires and our anxieties is not their efforts to plan and calculate. Both are present. In a very real sense, one is simply the negative aspect of the other. They are the obverses of the coin of sentiment, though they often project themselves as mere sentimentality. But in planning, in settling down to the rational business of making themselves heard in the noisome life of selves and others, they admit to themselves that they must join up with larger cultural ideals. They enlist them as if they were their masters, and this is the fantastic part of all projections, but they also must negotiate with them, and this places both desire and anxiety into the more realistic arena of phantasm: "Sentiment takes on moral relevance. For some it even becomes the key to the human good. Experiencing certain feelings now comes to be an important part of the good life. Among these is married love. But it is not the only one" (Taylor 1989:294). Indeed, even the most vanilla of lives is not deemed complete without the honeymoon desire of passionate embrace and enveloped penetrations, and if this is one of the hallmark instances of the "certain feelings" that we need to experience at least once—akin to the list of places to be visited that tourist agencies are constantly reminding us exist—and the ellipsis of which is always to be taken in the form of an ultimatum (this is the contrived anxiety of "before we die," also an advertising slogan), then we manage ourselves through phantasms whose goals are fantasies. This seems to be a necessary relationship for human consciousness and thus it cannot in itself be taken as an error. But we begin to misrecognize the elemental aspects of the relationship between fantasy and phantasm—not necessarily rational ideals and rational projections of action rehearsed as "daydreams," respectively—when we import too much of one into the other. This in itself is the illusory undressed rehearsal for our ability to imagine that we must either be in or out of love. We neglect the fact of fantasy and phantasm being connected to one another by sentiment, and not only the more commonplace sociological critique that such sentiments are themselves never our own and that we have been often duped by them, wearing their institutional or national badges on our sleeves. No, this often cited critique, though reasonable enough, misses the more important point that sentiment is itself the point of resistance to norms because it subsists only by way of the imagination, and this in turn participates in the historical consciousness of what is not only normative, but considered to be fulfilling. It is this sensibility that turns norms on their heads, as often as not, because we are also given to understand that what is good for others is not necessarily good for ourselves. In this, we become more or less individuated moralists. That there is an aesthetic dimension to morality speaks of Nietzsche, but it is Kant, according to Lingis, that initiates this reckoning, places the two great forces of the human imagination together and, without leaning too heavily on the third eye, that of metaphysics, states that a moral will should always be determined to will itself. This willing selfhood of self might act in the common interest as a public citizen of the polis, but should not, as we have already seen, place itself in the position where the wielding of power is judged a principle for its own sake. In this, of course, Kant and Nietzsche appear to depart from each other. But what they do share is a sense, livelier in Nietzsche no doubt in part because he succeeded Kant, that the moral imagination had its own notion of what love was and what it was for. It was something that approached an understanding that love, power, magic, the sacred etc. could not be sequestered at an individual level. Hence the related sense of the aesthetic, as it was already well established by this time in the West that the aesthetic object, a work of art, transcended both ownership and classification, though obviously both of these factors were nonetheless established; one by the patrons, the second by art scholars. The dual canons of market and discourse were also already well into their work, making art more like sex than love.

But the most salient thing about the presence of the imagination at the individuated level in the enlightenment scene was its objections to the inertia and the tradition of history. Poesis takes ultimate liberty with both the world of things and the world of time. Narratives, legend, myths and stories cannot be entirely trusted if one is only seeing empirical veridicity and bracketing their more worthy metaphoric contents: "All these stories are not about how history went, but how it could have gone: their realm is not reality, but possibility" (Portelli 1990:150). More than this, their realm is morality, because it is not even so much how things could have gone, but how they *should* have gone; this is the essence of the uchronic dream. Their aesthetic sense is also in full flower, for such a story must be better than the truth. That is, if history would itself have been morally correct in this rewriting of itself coming from the outside of itself, as it were, its "gentrification" is clear. We do not want to live in the tenements of history as they are. We prefer— sometimes infinitely prefer, and this is where the morality posited makes its way unto and into a metaphysics—the mansions of uchronia: "The representation is chosen for its beauty, and not for its truth." (Lingis, op. cit:60). Representation is quite literally Re-presentation, presenting something again and in doing so, revising it in the light of the experience of what actually is present. No one judges without already partaking of some part of the reality of living on in the face of a past that did not go one's way. We often do not give it much a chance to grow on us, as if we had already made up our minds that it was some potentially dangerous fungus that needed to be examined cautiously without physical contact, but we must have at least a sense that we would remake the series of events that led to this reality if only we could go back in time and do so. Since this is usually not an option—sometimes, as with famous revolutions of all kinds, there actually is a regression, a turning back to at least a portion of what reality had been before it itself was revised; it is well known, if disappointing to all "permanent revolutionaries," that sudden changes push the pendulum of culture back upon itself, and that this motion takes some time to even out and steady itself—we rely on our personal memory of the experience of what actually occurred in tandem with our moralizing imagination to revise the events we would rather not have lived through: "Memory is inherently revisionist, an exercise in selective amnesia. What is forgotten may be as important as what is remembered" (Samuel and Thompson 1990:7). Specifically, the import of what is preserved in memory rests on how it is recalled. This too changes over time, and not just because of the erosion of intervening years. We may well come to terms with our histories, both individuated and collective, allowing their fullest effect to be felt as a form of ongoing self-examination. Or, we may suppress even more of the unwanted occurrences than we did originally, if our lives continue to be so influenced by their trauma that no escape or even a trial egress ended up being possible. This horrifying fate generally is reserved for those who had experienced undeniable evil in their lives, especially at an age where memory and its neural apparatuses are already well-ensconced and not in fact subject to the physiological alterations of the still developing human child. It is somewhat ironic that adults have less of a chance to forget what may be necessary to shuffle off in order to live on as a human being. Surely it is one of the great challenges of mature being that it be able to let go of the awkward or even more so, the evil, in one's life through the power of forgetting. This is why memory is no greater than its absence in Nietzsche, for instance, who saw that culture was itself a vehicle for winnowing what was necessary from what was dross. This is why nothing culturally great could occur to the person of inaction, the person who waited for something to occur to him instead of going out and "making one's own history." This has the flavor of the mythic, and in this its morality takes on an aesthetic form. In acting one has a better chance of forgetting what is necessary to leave behind. Seemingly a far cry from the Nietzschean hero, but actually very much as heroic as any overman, is the situation of anyone who mourns, especially if the loss is one of love let alone the actual living presence of the loved one who still loved us. "Keeping busy" is the universal response to such a death, whether actual or metaphoric. In action we heal ourselves. Thought alone in these moments has the tendency to dwell both on and in itself. It has a brooding and contemplative aesthetic that might verge on melancholia. It desires the uchronia of absolute freedom to choose one's own past and experience it again and again. Things "should" have turned out this way, the jilted lover always says to himself or to anyone else willing to listen, for that matter. Or, at least, things "could" have worked out if only she had been more patient with me, or what have you. Rationalizations come later, but these too—"she sucked in bed" or "he had a small dick" are two gender-contrasted common-places amongst young people eager to be rid of some of the formative memories of intimacy and companionship—participate fully in revisionist biography as they are most likely to be at best only partially true and indeed, even this partial truth would have been seen as at least charming, worthy of further work and development, during the actual time of the relationship.

The height of uchronic meandering appears before us when, in the exalted efforts to dismantle our own experiences, we push ourselves over the threshold of both good manners and good taste and start enumerating impossibly arduous epithets in reference to our former lovers. Their inhumane or even less than human character has revealed itself in their rejection of us. They might even become members of the most derided category "life unworthy of life." The scapegoating of the ex-lover is part of the fantasy of how we ourselves would rather have loved. Perhaps at base, we did not take the love of self as seriously as we should have, and it may even be to an extent true that the vices of the other presented themselves to us because we lowered ourselves to be in their midst in the first place. We might, through revision, come to a certain apportioning of the "blame"—and there is always blame here, even when there is not—to ourselves as well as to the other. We can then scapegoat all the more easily because we imagine that in being rid of this other person, we have also overcome the very vice that led us to them: "The killing of the personification makes them feel that they have actually killed the vice" (Midgely 2004:166). The other is akin to the animal—Midgely's concerns can be transferred from actual to metaphoric animal life here, as indeed her commentary on scapegoating nature understands that very nature to be a symbol of something that it is manifestly not at all in reality (cf. ibid:151 for a declaration of the unscientific attitude of the metaphors of vice)—and as such is no longer worthy of our already duped attentions and compassions. The phase of mourning that includes revisionism of these kinds is akin to a form of madness. It does not seek the truth and jealously guards its own experiences of what actually occurred from others' examination. It desires no longer the other in herself, but some straw person to whom anything may be done with impunity. If the "moralizing" of this kind of work of mourning seems to be that of the fanatic, one might well call its results those of the "immoral imagination," since we often have no scruples in our love turned to hatred by rejection or betrayal. We replace the love we had for the other with a love of our own dark emotions, and may well, for a time become addicted to it. It is the opiate for our hurt feelings, even though no mere relationship break-up *by itself* could ever turn someone into an actual drug addict (cf. Gadamer 1996:170 [1989]). However long it takes for one to recover one's emotional equanimity—and we might well go through a number of other relationships and even fall in love again a few times before we come out the other end with some semblance of reality—we are generally unaware even in our subjectivity of the precise locations of these kinds of thresholds. Very often, addiction or no, the concepts are blended in the very way we have been arguing throughout this book. One is never completely within love and without at least resentment, for the slightest slight inside the affair of lovers might be overblown, taken to its nth degree and so very rapidly that all resistance is interpreted as betrayal. "Not tonight honey, I have a headache" might well be the death knell for the entire marriage, for instance, if one willingly takes this stratospherically romantic view of things. Somehow, love must forgive its own presence by forgetting what may be the signs of its demise. These too are enumerated ad nauseum by the jilted one after the fact, but it is not so much a list of wrongs that interests us, but the fact that we are engaged in the rationalization of how this specific love was shot through with betrayal and thus, in its naivety, ended up betraying itself: "Uchronia thus saves the precious awareness of the injustice of the existing world, but supplies the means of resignation and reconciliation" (Portelli, op. cit:157). A final irony to all of this may be ultimately added if we at length are able to vanquish the memory of the other's absence by placing him or her on a pedestal that is unreachable by ordinary mortals. For a time, we committed the extraordinary feat of the heroic lover and reached this paean of love through love itself, but others would be wise to keep away. The "high maintenance" woman or the lazy man are common examples of the more down to earth "podestalization," as it were, of former love-mates. Indeed, the hero within us discovered that the grail of love was not all it was made out to be—the commandments within the romantic ark had long turned to dust and were thus unreadable; the original covenant with the God of love could therefore not be reenacted—and it is *this* that marked us as in truth a hero: we had to confront and face the truth of things after all was said and done. Either way, as Barrett said of the Greeks, our gods of love for wisdom and reason, "We lose their reality for the dazzling image of them we would erect" (1979:267). We should immediately recall that the light of the other can blind us—as forsaken lovers, this is what "really" happened—as much as enlighten us. Both in fact occur during any love-relationship. The mutual admiration society it creates may give way to the more pragmatic and mature "marriage conversation," but if it does do, we find that the passion of immanent love and romance takes a necessary step to the side and remakes itself along more permanent lines.

In doing so, the two people involved park some of their lust for each other squarely in the realm of *Lustigeheit*, the ability to be merry and carefree in a more holistic manner that includes sexual adventures but is not at all exclu-

sive to them. This too smacks of the relationship manual, but its more profound point is that we have crossed a threshold between the jealousy and
resentment back-dropping the enactmental complex of fresh love and the
ability to recall what was just about our histories together. Indeed, this
threshold may be crossed even if the other has been long absent, and in this
case, represents a turning point in the history of our mourning for the our loss
of the other. The casual and seemingly fatalistic "it was what it was" may be
a step in this direction. It is also a step away from fantasy and toward the
remade ability to begin new phantasms, to project ourselves into the future
and think ahead, perhaps to new loves just over the horizon, but certainly
with the nascent sense that we should put ourselves in a position where these
new persons who encounter us should find us lovable and "ready." We might
well resent this motion for a time, and be tempted to turn away from the
future as having little condolence for us. We might retreat into the "madness"
of the divinity of the former lover, but this is also a way-station on the path to
nothing (cf. Taylor 1989:123). And what changes is, of course, not merely
the body of the lover as it ages or we grow accustomed to and perhaps yet
complacent with it, but the sense of being in love itself. Many relationships
break off at this point, captivated or even addicted as their constituents are
with the feeling of being in love—"we are more in love with love than the
beloved," as Nietzsche aptly cautioned us—and if the partnership evolves
into becoming more than romance—and this is where personals ads misrecognize human relationships in general, with the stock phrase "friends first"
appearing ubiquitously, implying that friendship is something more rapid and
less intimate and profound than romance when the exact opposite is the
case—this is taken to be a threat against the *feeling* of love. These persons
turn love into a fetish that is much more serious and focused than any mere
kink. The experience of being in love, like divine madness, takes no accounting of itself. It is simply *drunk*, just as it is drunk with itself. Like the
"bucket-lists" of shallow media commentaries, this experience is certainly
not to be missed, but it is also not to be taken for the whole of love. To our
contemporary tastes, no doubt many would prefer Juliette to Julie, myself
included. But the "nobler" aspects of being in love cannot be forsaken. At
most, they may be bracketed, set to one side momentarily, in order to consummate other forms of being-loving. These forms too cannot be simply
overreached as if they were only vulgar or debased versions of "truer" or
"higher" love. Indeed, the agape of the "love-feast" was such that there was
always struck a balance between eros and philia. The fetish of the either/or
approach to portable concepts participating in the sacred is in principle one
of the chief structures of error in our modern age. We have already seen that
it allows both unthought and unconcernful being to claim the floor and manipulate our attentions. It is a way to promulgate myth under the guise of
mythology, instead of knowledge subject to the scrutiny of epistemology.

Even demythologizers, moralists in their own staid manner, are apt to fall under the spell of "if something cannot be this, then it must be that": "Historians themselves, however rationalistic in their method, are by no means insulated from the appeal of myth, as can be seen by the symbolic categories they employ [ ] the grand theories we subscribe to and, not least, our own fetishistic faith in facts" (Samuel and Thompson 1990:4). Such facts as remain when one considers oneself "out" of love are prone to this kind of focused fanaticism. Being out of love actually tells the fanatic that he is *outside* of love entirely, and somehow, at any cost, must find a way to place himself back "in" love, that is, inside of its embrace in principal and as a moral principal, and so re-place himself and replace the lost love with someone else. Not for her own sake, mind you, but for the sake of love, which is regarded, like the religious fetish from which it ultimately stems, as an object of worship to which or about which real persons are merely vehicles. We use a series of others to fulfill our unquestioned assumptions regarding how we "should" feel as well as how we could or would feel if we were only "back" in love again, whether at first this dynamic stems and is thence directed back to the one who left us, or forward-looking in the direction of a new conquest or investment. Perhaps this fetish, the focused attentiveness of unconcernful being in the world of forms and not the social world of intimacies and negotiations, represents the height of the fantastic side of the coin of sentiment. It certainly consists of both the accumulated series of projections we have taken away from the love that was lost as well as those we hope to regain in the future. It is not a question of experiencing something new, but of replacing prior experience with a surrogate, or better, a "new and improved" version of the old love. In this it apes the wider commodity fetish and makes romance, if not love itself, into a commodity, the stock and trade of sentimental feelings of all sorts. It is this half-hearted and casual transformation that keeps us going to the theaters to take in the latest "romantic comedy" or perhaps even tragedy. These are the actual surrogates, in the stricter sense of exacting and exactable substitutes, and they serve to keep us going in the midst of the downturn in the value of our commodity fetish, the apparent art of being in love without the ability to be together with someone as an other. Just as certainly, we are not alone in this pursuit, but we are also not universally commended in taking this as our own vocation. Most others can see right through it, having been through it themselves: "No matter how obvious it may be to the neutral observer that it is a matter of projections, there is little hope that the subject will perceive this himself. He must be convinced that he throws a very long shadow before he is willing to withdraw his emotionally-toned projections from their object" (Jung 1959:9 [1951]). If this is the highly personalized version of a sentimental structure, insidiously burrowing itself into our conscience without our full consent, then we might be forgiven for hoping that we could yet overcome its hold upon us. But even though these sentiments can be individuated according to their biographical experience of them and within them, they hold to a fairly routine and narrow pattern. Such sentimentality is all around us. It plays on what is considered to be our "natural" lust for the other or our need for the presence of another to feel ourselves whole. But just because it is in our nature to heed and seek community does not mean that communion of the religious variety, the divine madness brought down to earth and in earthy tones no yet, is something that must be partaken of over and over again. It is clearly a fetish of a specific history and moment, adored more by a specific social location, and canonized by a specific discourse of objectification and yet, like the grail, something occlusive and to be guarded as well as guarded against: "This discourse on modern sexual repression holds up well, owing no doubt to how easy it is to uphold. A solemn historical and political guarantee protects it. [ ] it becomes an integral part of the bourgeois order" (Foucault, op. cit:5). Similarly, it takes charge of us at an early age, sentimentally dividing the majority sexes—there are, after all, clinically five different sexes, degrees of hermaphroditism, and an uncounted number of genders; it is stated, rather officiously, that "sex is biological but gender is cultural," but in fact sex is just as cultural as gender—into two opposing and opposable camps. It is astonishing how easily we go along with this division, pink in the eyes while blue in the face: "Without the disturbing influences from outside which foster the manifestation of sexual differences at an early date, *children would just be children*; and actively masculine features are in fact as common and effective in girls as are passively feminine ones in boys" (Neumann, op. cit:112, emphasis mine). This early division is a function of the fetish for oppositions that once again dominates our thinking and produces nothing but errors regarding reality. Because it can construct its own reality it has no need, it thinks, for either history or science. The specificity of oppositional thinking in itself, the critique of which in principle is no doubt old hat, also produces versions of the socially real that can be shared and thus mythologically reproduced over many generations. It is of interest to see that while we still regard children as sexually divided, we no longer are so beholden to the idea that gender and sex, let alone a gendered sexuality of presentation and appropriation, should be so fetishized. But this remains a regional and Western event. Across the globe, the offspring of agrarian empires continue to hold fast to the idea that men and women are polar opposites and can have little or nothing to do with one another.

Except, that is, sex. Sex is the nexus of the sexes. It may sometimes be the culmination of a battle, or the reconciliation after a lengthy war, but it is still the goal of the fetish of relationships and the means by which relationships maintain themselves as sentimental and "noble." We might imagine that this is the "secular claimant" to be the successor of agape (cf. Taylor, op. cit:516), but it rather has the tendency in real life to divide us and not bring us together in any larger numbers than a few at a time, or a few taken serially. What it could be seen as laying claim to is the bourgeois successor to medieval romantic love and search for the grail, but even by this time this object of adoration and adventurous pilgrimage, knights errant desiring the maidens who are ready and willing to err, had lost its metaphor of collective communion. A nascent competition had set in that was to become, over the centuries, a hotly contested market. Today, women in particular are pitted against one another due to the lack of "suitable" male mates. On the other hand, why take a long-term mate at all, if it were not for the problem of maintaining a comparatively lavish quality of life and having the sense that one has "arrived and made it." Less important, but probably still present, is that life is simply more interesting living on with another rather than alone, though some latter day pilgrims might take this as simply a bias of those who do not wish to face their fundamental existential lot. In saying this much, one would have to be committed to an anti-morality that places the empiricality of being singular—and we have already seen that this too is an error of our time—and not only this, that morality itself is something singular and this of a singular value, which also cannot be maintained in the face of historical and cultural diversity. But what can be argued is that morality is something that is "anti-nature," as Nietzsche famously proposed, because it cleaves to the fetish and favors the fanatic at the expense of the ambiguity of life, the waves that obliterate the Rhodian traces only to present a fresh palette to the human imagination: "If morality can only be powered negatively, where there can be no such thing as beneficence powered by an affirmation of the recipient as a being of value, then pity if destructive to the giver and degrading to the receiver, and the ethic of benevolence may indeed be indefensible" (Taylor, op. cit:516). This is indeed the "deepest challenge" to the received morality of Western thinking, but while seen from inside it is disconcerting, if one steps outside of this tradition as a thought experiment, Nietzsche's challenge is immediately diffused by the presence of ethics similar to, but also different enough from benevolence and pity in the Christian senses. Forbearance in Buddhism comes to mind, for instance. Tolerance as a stepping-stone to acceptance in secular modernity may also be a viable option. Compassion and empathy rather than pity, bad conscience rather than guilt, works and faith in them rather than faith in the transcendentality of the good rounds out a short list of successors to agape and to the self-seeking and self-adoring love of the romantic, medieval or modern. At the heart of such an issue is the problem of experiencing an absence of experience if one cannot immediately hang events one has lived through up on some metaphysical or at least existential hat. The essentiality of being-there is one such item that has been critiqued in the human sciences, especially in theoretical anthropology over the past few decades, but it is hardly the only one we use to secure and sequester our experiences. We have also seen that memory is a chief mode of being-present through re-presenting and even re-presencing the lived and unlived past. Like a kind of singularly willed fate, we project our image of the fetish from our viewpoint, provincial though it is, in order to hold onto at all costs what in fact has passed before us and even been lost for good. It may be as well that this is so, because something that is lost and not merely temporarily absent through being misplaced is something that can be then permanently mis-placed in our imaginations. This is not so much a challenge to received moralities but an adducement of them to our longing for the "being-within." If this at length has its source in the agape of community, it has travelled so far down the path to nothing that it no longer has any resemblance to the festival of ambiguities and the celebration of the moment that we also imagine occurred primordially precisely because it reflected the reality of human consciousness in the world: "Here, we are dealing with an allusion to the fact that human beings are practically emptied by their experiences between being and non-being. This is an allusion to the transitoriness and futility of all things" (Gadamer 2000:120-1). That things for us, as finite beings who know in general about their own finitude and thus must come to terms with it without of course being able to know its details, are always in flux, that change is the only constant, implies that all projects must end. In this they are "futile." Even so, it is not futile to begin things and set them in motion because this is how we must, nonetheless and in spite of the fact of the end and of endings, live on. So the fact that something must come to an end, that "all things must pass" is not an "intrinsic objection" to their being things or to one creating things, including participating in human relationships. It is in fact also rational, as well as based in our sense of being who we are at an emotional level, to begin projects and see them through as long as we can sense that they still contain a recognizable rationality. I once was party to a conversation where the talking point was whether it was better, that is, in this case, more rational and practical, to not engage in or try to start up any close relationships or intimacies simply because one was likely to see their end and thus be hurt by it as well as the more grandiose but still always possible event of the beloved's death while still in love. Aside from the romantic claim of it always being better to have loved and lost, which I think almost everyone would agree with if only because one does eventually move on from even the most intense of erotic relationships, there was a more interesting and rational suggestion that in avoiding intimacy we carry ourselves in the world more ethically. This was claimed because we would not become biased towards a single individual, a lover or spouse, and perhaps also our own children, if we stayed out of such relationships in the first place. We would, the claim ran, then be able to treat others in the world around us much more equally because we would not have any "master status" loyalties to the one or the few. What are the emotional elements of such an argument, and are there any intrinsic objections to it? It does seem that we would treat others more equally if we did not favor a specific set of individuals. Indeed, it has also been stated that if we felt the pain and the deaths of those afar in the same way as we felt those who are closest to us—an ethical but perhaps impossible ideal—then there would be a more or less automatic end to all human suffering in the world. This is one way into such a position: that it states an ideal that is not currently a reality in human affairs, and never has been one. The language of such statements has, traditionally, always been not rational argument, but myth. In pursuing our ideals, no matter how far-fetched, we immediately come upon this other language: "We discover a psychic dimension which recognizes the power of myth and unconscious desire as forces, not only in history, but in shaping our lives" (Samuel and Thompson, op. cit:5). Do we actually desire such a feeling, the ability to mourn equally? What would that do to the process of mourning itself, or as it stands in a culturally diverse world? The same for loving and intimacy; how does one love all equally when the constituents that make up this "all," all of humanity, are often quite different in how they would love or be able to recognize our love? What is the nature of an "unconscious desire" that is said to drive such ambitions or emotions? (cf. Neumann, op. cit:285). That is, it is our rational and waking self-consciousness that seeks to limit how far our unconscious and emotional aspects of selfhood influence our rationally cal-culated actions. We *feel* that if we suppress the element of feeling that also guides our arguments, that they in turn will not only be more acceptable to others, but as well to ourselves seem more plausible, even sane. We defend then against the sense that maturity and "improvement" of the human condi-tion also hinges on understanding our emotions, desire and love, fear and hatred, and this leads us into the error that only a strict rationality and practi-cal-mindedness can "get things done" in a world where people are inherently objectionable precisely due to the overbearing presence of emotions. This is a way of shunning human reality, the "principle" of which is ambiguity in our decision-making and in our projections of selfhood. It is a way of deny-ing the spontaneous dialogue of both love and philosophy—they are both creative, imaginative, actively thinking as well as emotional, and above all, they are both interested in the intimacy of one another's thoughts and feel-ings—and the further activities and interests that may well flow from such engagements. Nietzsche, whom the artist Otto Dix referred to as "the only real philosopher" was always on about this point, citing academic philosophy as the main culprit in ignoring the reality of what constituted human feeling and human reason: "They devote themselves to what most people think of as philosophical activity—geometric speculation of otherworldly abstraction or butcher-like analysis or political theory or righteousness—but that is in fact a way to strangle the convulsive erotic energy of philosophy" (Lilburn 1999:89). Well, philosophy as a discourse, and all the more so as a job, must have also its technical labors. Being in love also means keeping a household, feeding oneself and the beloved, and sharing the chores of daily life if one's relationship has so far progressed. In this, "academic" philosophizing has a role to play in the tapestry of human affairs. But thought as a form of love is of course different from all of these things, and may be compared directly to the thoughts we have of the beloved that are centered not so much on being in love as an abstraction that we were cautioned against earlier, but on the other herself as one who is worthy and, like all of us, needful of being loved and who is capable and can be created again as capable of being-with in the world that includes both feeling and reason. There are reasons, in other words, for being in love that are just as rational as those that seem to argue for staying out of it, which carries us back to the original point of this small arc. Arguments of all kinds participate in the anima of eros and the animus of logos, as Jung artfully suggests, though we would not wish to carry too far the sense that in women the first is completed more fully than in men, and for men it is the very opposite (cf. Jung, op. cit:14 for his tempering statements to this regard). So at most one could say that it is a reasonable choice either way. On the one hand, we do not experience the depth of feeling of being centered on the one or the few if we eschew close friendships and falling in love with specific people. On the other hand we may be more apt to generalize our interest in our fellow humans more broadly if we do not. The case for the first would have to include the idea that we, in missing the depths of feeling, have very much *less* to share with any other human that we come into contact with, no matter how shallow the acquaintance, and the case for the second would be that such depths bias us because we tend to associate them with only one or a small series of people and thus may come to believe that they cannot or could not have been shared with most others if the occasion arose. This is certainly an error; one can fall in love with almost anyone and it is part of our modern bourgeois interpretation of mythic apparatus that there is such a thing as a "soul mate" or only a select group of potential mates of this kind. Experience tells us differently, which is why only young people are sentimental about being in love in this way. Indeed, though having been married for over a decade, I am still approached by those who think that they can supplant my spouse because they are in truth my "soul mate" and have only just found me, after all these years. These persons are always young and idealistic, and while they are honoring me they are also dishonoring the reality of both a specific love and the nature of human love in general, which includes both loyalty and a sense of justice. Due to lack of experience—but also due to the competition amongst women for supposedly "suitable men"; a definition which includes the very unemotional and even cold calculations of who has power and resources at his fingertips and is thus to be considered a "good catch"—such women have a weak perception of what being in love is and what it takes to maintain such a relationship over the long term. This is another error by which we live through a phase of the human life cycle: "This weak perception prevailed not because of its truth but because of its anthropomorphic value: it was a sensibility that was needed in order that the species survive" (Lingis, op. cit:92). In that it too is a calculation that is at once rational as well as being a need that is felt emotionally makes it true to human life and history. We are not "duped" by it as by other kinds of errors that hamper our ability to live on in the face of death, loss, absence and mourning or the sheer lack of love in the daily routines of rationalized organizations and social norms. What distinguishes such errors is, as we have seen, their ability to act as the collective role model to which we harness our cultural energies and socialize future generations. The question we must ask of them is along the lines of, is this manner of living necessary to life? We are able to pose such a question because we have already been able to ask ourselves, with experience, is this manner of loving necessary for love? Do we need to love the few intently and intensely in order to feel anything at all for the whole? Do we need to have a concept of the whole in order to love the one fully or with dignity? The answer to both of these questions is, I believe, a wholehearted affirmative. Yes, it is a situation that contains irony. But what human aspect of the world does not have at least some of this timbre, given that it is part of the larger ambiguity that we share as beings of finite reflection? Indeed, we have developed other forms of role-playing to compensate and even put the presence of the general irony of the human condition to work for us in order to ease conflicts and get along with one another so that the mundane work of living on is accomplished: "The technique of this fine irony is to agree and act the fool and then continue to what ever was intended in the first place [ ] All claims of positive recognition by the superiors are sacrificed, although it is better if they are left in a state of suspicious confusion than treated with absolute contempt" (Johanson 1990:136). This is almost a universally commonplace technique. It occurs in all forms of social organization that have hierarchical human relations as part of their character. It speaks not only to our sense of justice—we know that those who wield power are not always worthy of doing so in the first place, on top of the fact that access to power tends to corrupt those who have it, noted most famously by Acton in the late nineteenth century—but also to our sense of humor and our understanding of the absurd. If there is absurdity in the fact of social hierarchy, we can also turn it on its head, all the more so if those who lack relative power are nonetheless more clever than those who happen, by virtue not so much of their own wits and skills but by some nepotism of other more structural means, to occupy more powerful positions than do we. But most importantly, the ability to appear to think and say one thing and do absolutely another is part of the language of the reality of love. No long-term relationship of this kind can function without acknowledging the absurdity of being in love—in our interlocution above, the argument that takes it too far is the one that tells us never to engage in it—absurd simply because in spite of our feeling and desire for it and in it, it will nevertheless come to an end. Equally, such a relationship could not last without there being in it moments where the one or the other is in control of the situation and their mate needs to accept a decision and follow along. This wielding of power is seen as it is in reality, transitory, ambiguated, perhaps ironic, but necessary all the more because it seeks not to provide errors by which it itself can live on but practical options for those who wish to stay in love and live on together.

5.2 CRISIS IN THE LIFE OF A LOVER

This indirect form of negotiations that avoids the showdown quality of confrontation is an error only from the strictly rationalistic outlook that claims all human relations must be taken at face value or else they are inherently dishonest and thus unjust. Once again, a too narrow conception of what constitutes reality, a *reduction* of the real to only one of its simultaneously occurring elements, produces errors of perception and thinking. At the same time, even with the safety-valves of other friends in whom one can confide one's doubts about being in love or the beloved that once in a while appear before us, or the shared activities that unite lovers without having to be actually making love all the time, there still occur crises from time to time where one or both of the persons involved may think that this represents the beginning of the end. The idea that one's love could live on after this or that perceived crisis challenges our imagination and of course almost all relationships of younger persons do in fact end because of some issue that cannot be resolved by any means or experience known to them, at least at that time in their lives. This simply has to be accepted, and over time, it almost always is. But what is the nature of love in that it can even admit crisis in the first place? Our ideals of it are of course always straining in the opposite direction: no cloud could or should or would ever cover over the bright sunlight of our love, we say to ourselves and to each other. Even so, we do practice the communication of our ideals of love to our lovers because we also know that being in love is not something that "just happens" over any amount of time. It has to be practiced, like any other human endeavor. We thus appeal to the perspective of the other because we know it cannot be entirely the same as our own, and this appeal is conscious, calculated and argued at the same time as it is emotional and desiring, needful and generous in its compliments, perhaps over-generous if a dose of "fine irony" is also deemed necessary. Such appeals are ultimately moral, because we wish to include not only the sense that we are playing fair in approaching the other in this way, but that we are speaking about what is good for "us" and also what is of the good in itself: "My perspective is defined by the moral intuitions I have, by what I am morally moved by. If I abstract from this, I become incapable of understanding moral argument at all" (Taylor 1989:73). We argue our case both within the ambit of the love relationship but also within the circumference of the previously agreed upon goods that have made our relationship "work" thus far. Taking the appeal outside of either of these environments of shared experience would obviate it and suggest to the other that one cared more for an ideal than what we actually have; that is, one would begin to suggest that our relationship is not what I wanted and that there are better versions thereof to be had and finally, that these other versions would approach my ideal for which I am actually arguing. This, if realized, would indeed provoke just the sort of crisis that we intended to avoid. We must convince the other that this is not, in fact, our intent even though we are asking to improve *something* in the relationship: "You will only convince me by changing my reading of my moral experience, and in particular my reading of my life story, of the transitions I have lived through—or perhaps have refused to live through" (ibid). It is the ambiguity concerning whether or not the beloved will accept our version of things and listen to us that drives both the reasoned and emotional tenor of our appeal. Whether it is an external threat to the cohesion and the viability of the relationship—these are often internalized and taken for something that they originally were not; that is, recast as problems about the people involved and not the world around them—or a previously unrecognized character flaw that hurts the feelings of the other in a consistent way, we must overcome both resentment and perhaps even anguish that the other has felt and expressed in our direction. No love relationship is without both resentment and anguish, and the trick is to stop them from becoming *ressentiment* and agony respectively. It is not merely a case of reassuring each other that, in Foucault's sardonic voice, "Tomorrow sex will be good again" (op. cit:7), or more seriously but also too seriously, that "we must love one another or die" (cf. Auden in Taylor, op. cit:483). Rather than either of these, there needs to be included in our appeal the common-sense sense that what has been has been good, and we would be better off if we continued in that vein. The idea of being committed is crucial, for one cannot even begin to argue the case for continuing any relationship if one or the other is not themselves salutary to the idea of continuing to love life together in this specifically intimate manner. Loyalty to the idea of the relationship does not mean transforming it into an ideal that it has not yet demonstrated, or only approaches in certain intense contexts such as sexual union or the sharing of sentiments. The facts of what has been in the case of lovers has to be marshaled in lieu of the next intensity of future experience if there is to be a future at all: "This is why commitment to ascertain the facts remains central in their stories, and why there is a certain tension between the spirit of the story and the conscience of the witness, the former being the life of the account, the latter the sentinel" (Bravo, et al 1990:98). One is always and already at risk of being manipulated by the one to whom one is so loyal. We have retold the story of the other, no doubt both in ignorance of some of the facts—we tend to not like to hear about past relationships, for instance, for fear of either being compared to them or that we will eventually suffer the same fate—and also through the convenient suppression of some of the others to which we have been privy. We tend, in light of both of these lacunae, the one being a subject of the objective absence of factuality, the other being an object of our subjective desires to see the beloved in a certain way and in that way if not only, at least primarily, to concentrate on shared experiences, the more recent the better suited for our purposes. This functions as not only a salve against dissension but as evidence that our union is the closer the longer it lasts. We even get to the point where we begin to claim "the same" experiences for each other, as if we were living the life of the other as well as our own, and at the same time. But this is also a contrivance that cannot really do what it claims (cf. Natanson, op. cit:29). Indeed, to understand the essence of what is self-same by working through the appearance of what is called forth as the way in which such an essence manifests itself leaves us not only curious, but puzzled and even downright aporetic. To suggest that the face-to-face intimacies of the love relationship have a structure to them is tantamount to saying that their patterns are not of our own making. Indeed, this is what much of human sciences suggest, and there is plenty of evidence for this as in any other social relationship. But this is something that we believe to be a *challenge* to our love and not a vehicle for it. "Making one's life one's own" would, by definition, include all experiences that have their more objective and shared meanings ironically more subjective. Intimate relationships present themselves as already being there when they might not be. Romances are highly scripted, and indeed, if we cast a brief glance around the non-Western world where the idea of individuality is still in its nascence, we are apt, from our perspective, to think that no experience in these other cultures can rightfully be "owned" by the person herself or himself. Everything is formal and structured to the nth degree. It would be oppressive for most of us to be set down in these cultures and have to find a way to live in them. Perhaps this is part of the anxiety we feel when we are forced to confront the extremities of reactionary movements emanating from these regions of otherness; they appear to tell the truth about the soul of their culture and for us, such a truth is very ugly indeed: complete control of all ways and walks of life through shame, taboo, scapegoating and execution. We also imagine that no human being would live like this unless forced to, and increasingly we are correct. But we are so only because of the forces that globalize our worldview and sell it, sometimes as shameless shill and Barnumesque burlesque, to these others for the price of their own cultural backgrounds and meaningfulness. What oppresses us today, we also have to remind ourselves, is also something that our ancestors lived with for thousands of years. No matter, because our sense of who we are projects not only across space but also across time as well. All of this hinges upon the threshold lying between a feeling of oppression or suppression, the repression of which we feel gives way to neurosis, and the liberating quality of simply being responsible for oneself in the day to day and for the most part. Through this latter, we feel able to join with another and live life "together," shared experiences aside for the moment, but from the former we get the sense that this *must* be done in order to preserve the dignity of our own individuality. This tension is magnified whenever we find ourselves "within" the envelope of intimacy. We are not responsible not only for our own feelings, but share a responsibility for the other. This does not go so far as to allow them to abdicate their responsibility, but like all things in long-term intimacies, such experiences are shared without being the same. The demons that were our own also become shared, and we can easily "drag each other down" towards them. The fact that this is a common response when we are asked why this or that relationship did not in the end, work out, tells us in no uncertain terms that we are very aware of the challenges involved in sharing anything at all. At first, of course, the so-called "honeymoon phase" of such relationships suppresses the sharing of the shadows. It is interesting that intimacy can be "measured" in a vague manner by the amount of dirty laundry that gets aired, and perhaps even cleaned to be worn afresh, over time in such relationships. To be able to state that "I know everything about her" is a badge of honor, an accomplishment that echoes through the years of the union. But we can never state this unequivocally. What we know is all that the other has shared with us. This has to be "good enough" for us given that we too most likely have a private reserve of secrets, but also trivial things that we have felt were too insignificant to be shared, that remain unshared and will remain so. That the honeymoon cliché also takes place in other relationships, most especially the work life, also tells us that we desire to either bring out the best in the other at first so that we can take the worst if we have to later on—the credit versus debit metaphor is a strangely and strongly attractive one for us in modern capitalist societies—and thus feel that we have been given enough credit ourselves by this new person in our lives to be worthy of sharing secrets with. Indeed, we are aware that things *must* be shared in order for one to move on "normally" and with some sense of grace. That we are willing to wait, perhaps with less confidence as time goes by, is testament to the credit the significant other has gained with us. We trust, hope, and have faith that she will be "back to normal" given the passing of other, mostly external circumstances. Indeed, we are always on the look out for ways in which to help make this passage a brief one, even to the extent that we might come to believe that suffering is inherently an evil that can and should be avoided at all costs. This is taking things too far, for human consciousness is what it is precisely because of both joy and sorrow and their odd combination in human affairs. The positive and the negative, the light and the darkness, come together as ambiguities in all things we do and share. This is why the shadow that accompanies us, the penumbra of personhood that we carry around within us, its outward expressions manifesting themselves in emotion and rationalities alike—the "cold" personality is often, we think, too rational; the hothead is always asking too violently to be taken seriously—is in reality more representative of how things actually are in the social world. These blends of opposites give us the sense that we can identify risky or dangerous extremes if we have to, because these poles, if suddenly breaking into the half-lit routines of normative affairs with either their blinding glare or their impenetrable black cloak are so obviously not "normal" that we flee from them. We can even construct a model of such affairs. The ubiquitous cross-cousin marriage found all over the world is one such model wherein the alliances constructed work against any possible extremities of behavior that might be exhibited by those party to them (cf. Jung, op. cit:229). These idealized and oppositional poles are in fact never pure in human action. This is one of the chief reasons why myth and romance get along so well. The ideal love occurs in the narrative of the heroic and not in our own biographies. At best, with time and experience, we are able to say with some candor that what we have experienced and whom we have loved were viable for a time and gave us what they could. But we do not let go of the myth, just the same. Its "pedagogic" function is, if you will, to provide a template of the abstraction of feeling, just as say, cross cousin marriage performs this same function at the level of the method—that is, how to construct a union out of the available parts—and this model for expected feelings has a script and a narrative that if performed well, or as well as could be expected by usually youthful human beings, we can expect the rewards of a fulfilling relationship for however long it can be maintained through the use of gradually individuating mythic scripts. The shock of the polar extremes found in myth of course push us to figure out how we can learn from their results without being able, or desiring in most cases, to exactly mimic the ways in which things happen in the mythic realm. The idea that "The incest produces a transformation of personality which alone makes the hero a hero, that is, a higher and ideal representative of mankind" (Neumann, op. cit:154), is not likely to inspire us to perform in the same way, nor do we generally have the opportunity to "demonstrate" the myth as reality in our own social world. Indeed, this is precisely the point: mythic or archetypical relationships cannot occur on the ground of finite human interactions, nor should they be able to, for that would obviate their essence as the formal synthesis of human desire and anxiety. The pure positives and negatives are, even in myth, mixed up with each other in the subjectivity of the hero: "Incest with the mother is in itself desirable, but it is made terrible by this fear of the father. The mother is supposed to be a positive object of desire, and the father the real obstacle" (ibid:155). In other words, there is nothing about the object per se that is prohibitive to us, in the same way, from the male perspective, any woman is inherently a potential mate, and anything that takes away from this pure potentiality is an external distraction, including the fact that she may already be in some other sexual union or multiple ones. The aforementioned competition amongst women for "suitable" men also has this same effect, though from the female perspective. Its "Electraic" quality harkens to its own mythic archetype, and the casual piety given by those daughters who adore their fathers, "daddy's girls," as the vernacular has it, attests to the flirtatious character of all cross-gender appointments, whether in the workplace or the home. Needless to say, just as with the much vaunted "Oedipal" complex, these myths are hardly ever enacted, and if they are, subject to the most severe social sanction. It is not merely the case that we learn to ultimately disdain and avoid such incestuous unions—our supposed "abhorrence" of them is mostly play-acting and has been shown to be hardly a cultural universal that the structural anthropologists once imagined it was; furthermore, it is the filial and not the sibling relationship which is feared and supposedly also tinged with an anxious desire, for there are many documented cases, both in journals and on dubious web-sites, of brother-sister sexual unions and these in turn produce no lasting deficits of either character or ability to mate with unrelated persons later on—it is also the case that we doubt any theory that bases itself on the myths that give light to the human desire for holistic intimacy and community that is played out in normative and socially sanctioned fashion in most families.

So the extremities of outcome that occur to the heroic figures that attempt to engage in these passions demonstrate the idea that we may or may not love another in a complete manner. Their tragic ends, their ultimate fates, and their sorrows during life all testify to the sense we mortals have that the prize is not worth the effort. Besides this, there are others aplenty from which to choose who may provide surrogates for our originally incestuous desires, if any of this is to be believed at all, and there are other forms of duplicity that occur during the life-cycle that can be acted within and without in the gray-scale performances of mythic tropes. Violent passions are fine for the artist because he or she has a stage or a medium through which such emotions can be expressed. Otherwise, they tend to be avoided by the rest of us, and their outburst is always accompanied by both a sense of limitation and the frowning reaction of those around us. We have, in fact, let others down by giving free reign to our passions, and we have insulted them because they have, at least in this or that specific social context, been able, heroically perhaps, to keep theirs in check. For our modern sensibilities, the control of passion, desire, and equally, anxiety and fear, is of the utmost. We help each other attain and maintain these controls, and seek to "rehabilitate" those who consistently do not seem to be able to engage such controls over themselves or for themselves. We also have the unequivocal mindset that such control is both rational and reasonable, and is thus also reasonably expected from all members of our society at all times public, and in most times private unless sexual or other forms of intimacy require that we "let loose" passions. Even here, however, their stage is fairly rigorously controlled through the scripts of both socialization and the narrative of the "marriage conversation." Thus control is both a reaction to the essence of things, and has become in our rationalized world, itself part of the essence of things anew. To have mastered this is to be as close to the mythic hero as a finite person can be. If the human version of the hero is to make good on his debts to humanity, he must demonstrate that he has the power of control over all things human. Cutting a heroic figure tells the audience that we have not only attained mastery once, but can consistently apply it when the relevant cases arise. This is no different than any set of skills we learn and thence possess, whether these be of the "trade" variety or that "artistic," or those much more ambiguous "people skills" that employers supposedly are enamored with. At the same time, the Cartesian machine, like any mechanism either held within or created by consciousness, breaks down from time to time and must somehow be fixed. The problem is actually greater than this, as we saw in the preceding chapter on machine thought in general, but for present purposes we may limit our discussion to the sense that we cannot in all circumstances and with all people be counted on to maintain the consistent mastery demonstrated by the mythic hero. As we age, certain skill sets, both artistic and athletic, deteriorate. There is a well-noted peak to our performance based on the activity we are working within, and indeed, athletics for the most part peaks very early on. But there is more to it than a simple relationship to the body and to motor-control. We can be worn down by a too present crisis, or an ongoing and percolating suffering that apparently cannot be assuaged, or worse, the experience of something that appears to have been fixed but in fact it has not, returning to haunt us perhaps years later with its almost uncanny ability to demonstrate that it lies beyond our powers to right it for good. Addictions are probably the most common form of this dark remanant-like specter, but certain behaviors found in intimate relationships have this quality as well. What is implied, then is that, once again unlike the hero of myth, we actually lack the ability to control anything at all, and the times when we feel in control are simply happy coincidences where variables external to us have come together in our favor: "Taken seriously, this hypothesis in the form of a question would be enough to give one vertigo. It would make one tremble, it could also paralyze one at the edge of an abyss, there where you would be all alone or already caught up in the struggle with the other" (Derrida 1995:8 [1993]). This is obviously why the casual phrase "losing control" is shot through with such anxiety. It can also, somewhat ironically, be used as a patent and normative excuse for deeds untoward or, equally casually spoken, "out of character." But what does it really mean to lose control over things? How can something be said to be lost if we do not truly ever possess it in the first place? This is yet another crucial error by which we live: the ability to believe in the idea that mastery can exude itself from finitude, that humans are capable of extra-human feats. The belief in this, sometimes constituted in popular essays as the "faith in oneself," has certainly had its full share of effects salutary to human evolution and maturity, but it has, like all things human, also been the architect of terrifying disasters. No "evil" person ever accomplished anything without this self-same faith, and it is this historical fact that makes us tremble, shying away from the abyssal plain where plain meanings are lost in the depths that defy perspective. It was Nietzsche that first noted this problem and suggested that faith itself and in general adheres to necessary illusions, or, better, self-misrecognitions. This is as true for the common person as it is even truer for the cultural elites (cf. Lingis, op. cit:62). The "value-neutrality" of the things we hold most dear also threatens to expose our loves for what they are: a play of meanings resting atop the thin sediments of the faith in shared sentiment, *not* the sharing of experience in the sense of it being the same or even being edifying or aspiring in the attested to sameness of the direction of love and loyalty. This threat is not so much existential as it is personal. Natanson suggests that it is precisely through our role-playing, including that of the lover and friend, that we are so threatened: "In command, I am yet in danger of becoming an officer of cognition, a bureaucrat of mundanity" (op. cit:45). "Sincerity" and "authenticity" are merely self-misrecognized sentiments of this sort, playing their part in the dissimulation of love or marriage or friendship, or yet further, claiming to support more abstract and essential elements of these social relationships, things like loyalty, truth and above all, themselves, the ability to be sincere or come across as a genuine person. But we are always genuine persons by virtue of being persons in the first place. That we can act disingenuously is actually not a limit to our honesty or a convenient bracketing thereof, but an authenticating exposition of the ability to be honest. It is, in other words, equal in its force of being to what is taken for honesty. We are as honestly dishonest as we are straightforward, and we put the same amount of effort of character or skill into the action. Our "mastery" is, in a word always available to the highest bidder, depending on the circumstance. It acquits itself only through its performances, and the content of these is in no way to be taken as a comment on the authenticity of its form, only on the effect of its strength of control over the situation and others that may be found within it.

If we are still "trembling" about this we need not be. All of it is as normative as it is possible to imagine. The letdown is based on our sense that we can perform the extra-human and extramundane feats of the mythic hero in real life. We certainly simulate them—and then participate fully in our own self-dissimulation to make them stick—but to carry on believing in them is in fact part of this self-same dissimulation and can be taken only as such. "All of us" are both subject to and privy to this theatre, the "aping of our own ideals," as Nietzsche refers to it, and thus we have no need to face the abyss of sincere meaningfulness in any way alone. We are not "alone" at the edge of this abyss, at least, for we can count on the other with whom we are engaged to hold up his end of the theatrical bargain lest he too fall over the edge into the void. What is being assiduously avoided here is not the lack of sincerity or authenticity, but the lack of meaningfulness itself. Since meaning is both the outcome of interpretation and the process by which further versions of itself are inferred and used, it not only cannot be avoided it is a must for human consciousness to retain its utility and its duplicity. In this way, society remains viable because sociality is enacted in the plain sight of the abyss of meaning; *this* vision, constantly attended to in our myths, serves as the stark reminder of the outcome if we do *not* endlessly participate in the attempt—by whatever means, Nietzsche tells us it does not really matter—to make meaningful the contexts into which we find ourselves placed. The abstractions of these attempts—the list of roles mentioned in the above citation—tend to make larger than life statements about meaning-construction in an effort to lend authority and authoritative credence to our more mundane and pedestrian day-to-day efforts. This edifying set of discourses provides us with both the tension and the resolution of the perceived problem of dishonesty or mistrust that dogs our every effort to simulate the heroic and understand nature and world: "Thus the one exponent of being-interpreted (philosophy) stands in opposition to the other (historical consciousness) and claims to overcome it. This disagreement is the public problem within today's being-interpreted. 'All of us'" (Heidegger, op. cit:34). The temptation, if that is the correct term to use, for today's person is to imagine that she can overcome this tension between meaning and meaningfulness by acting out a "total" reaction to their presence and form. This might consist in the over-acting of a role—the lover who brings flowers etc. each week, or speaks her heart through Shakespeare or, if the class status is different, through Hallmark—or she may find herself "at ransom" on a regular basis in order to demonstrate her commitment to the relationship. We hear of those who claim to be "all or nothing" in these ways, expecting that in return the other will also give everything over to them and thus consummate meaning within the embrace of human passions, as if this alone could overcome the test of both time and our awareness of its passage—part of "historical consciousness"—or our sober second thought about what we have done or accomplished by doing so—reflection, part of "philosophy." Such totality, real or imagined, also represents an effort to bring myth to the ground of human affairs as they are. We also think that prehistoric social organization was able to effect this reaction as part and parcel of its collective conscience. However this may be, our ability today to work in this manner is almost certainly a romance, which is why it is considered so "romantic" whenever one attests to the other in this "unconditional" manner. Likewise, we shun the total effects of such a reaction as they may have been felt by our primordial ancestors, for this is a sure way to lose both the control over and the mastery of any social situation, and thus in fact betrays the essential intent of our attempting to react in this way in the first place. The demonstration of the feat of the hero masks its truth. The feat is taken for the goal where in fact it is the courage to attempt the feat that is most heroic, that most duplicates the mythical in the historical. We are closest to our ideals, in other words, when we, in the process of attempting something, portray the human version of the passion and intellect shown by the hero who was also in the process of acting the act out. The romanticism that we brocade the outcome with distracts us from the experience of courage. "Following through" with a bold intent or maneuver suggests that we do at some point recognize the importance of this courage, but this recognition which this time is precisely *not* self-misrecognition, is but momentary in light of the desired result. The stakes are so high that we forsake the heroism of action for the imagined eternity of a place or intimacy where action ceases. To erase the need to act is seen as paradise because of the timeless quality of mythic action. Yet the action of myth appears this way because it is endlessly repeated. The stories are always the same; the hero has a "thousand faces."

So the best we can do is mimic the endless or timeless aspect of our ideals in the non-place of inaction, because all human action that is taken seriously in the context of love and intimacy cannot afford to accrue the same routine quality that is the hallmark of repetitive labor in the social world. We speak of the "death of love" precisely because the action of both the other and ourselves has fallen into the otiose and the expected. "Spontaneity" has disappeared; the "spark" is gone. There are so many clichés regarding this eventuality that it is clearly a patently recognized villain in the life of the lover, a true crisis: "The death of love, then is a phenomenon of sociality rather than an egological event. With its despair goes as well the loss of those features of potential development which otherwise would lead to the fulfillment of the symbolic self." (Natanson, op. cit:136).

5.3 NOT YOURS, NOT MINE

When this kind of departure occurs, it is almost always felt as radical, akin to an actual, physical death. The mourning process is, as we have already seen, much the same in both the case of the death of love and the death of a person. If we truly are more interested in being in love than in the other being, we will feel the loss nonetheless and perhaps for a time personify it in the absence of the specific person with whom we claimed to be in love. We will also, after some time has passed, begin to question how we were treated in a more balanced manner, by including within these broodings how we treated the other and if, through our treatment that may have included mistreatment, this was a factor in their departure. In principal, and especially if we are "in love," we are supposed to treat the other well and not badly. There is generally a fairly clear threshold between the right and wrong way to treat another given each social context. That we do not always observe these norms is also equally clear, but when we do not, everyone knows it. Unless we are somehow cognitively deficient in our ability to be socialized in the normative manner in this or that culture, we are aware, no matter how superior or arrogant, tempestuous or ill tempered, that we have transgressed what is expected by civil behavior in public or the relatively private settings of lovers. But behind the norms lies a more profound space where an ethics is understood to be in ascendance: "Clearly what is demanded is that we treat someone in the 'right way.' Does this mean that we fulfill a norm or follow a rule? In my opinion it means, rather, that we address the other person in the right way, that we do not force ourselves on them or compel them to accept anything against their will, be it an external measure or a regulation" (Gadamer 1996:109 [1991]). This can be taken as a general principle, applying to any context. Gadamer continues by stating that treatment itself always involves the "granting of freedom." Perhaps the acceptance of another's fundamental existence as a freedom extant and fully present to us in the other, an elemental feature of otherness is another implication of this line of thinking. It is precisely this challenge of the freedom of the other that comes under much closer scrutiny in the love relationship, to the point of it being put at risk for amalgamation with my own. We may well think that because we feel so much for the other and that they are worthy of that feeling on our part, that they also make themselves available to us in their worthiness through the limitations they put on their own self-conception of freedom. This is the error that I wish to speak of in this final section.

The subjectivity of a shared love is still something that lacks perspective. In its ability to be shared between or amongst persons, our understanding of love does not automatically confer an insight about itself. In order to comprehend the scope and depth of the experience, we must somehow be distanced from it. That this distance is almost always forced upon one or the other person involved by the sudden change in the dynamics of intimacy, to the point of the loss of love entirely, at least with respect to this specific person or persons, is also of little immediate value when it comes to understanding the precise nature of the relationship as it had been and now as it is at present: "The person who is still a participant in the We-relationship does not experience it in its pure form, namely, as an awareness *that* the other person is there. Instead, he simply lives within the We-relationship in the fullness of its concrete content" (Schutz 1967:168 [1932], italics the text's). The entirety of the social context that surrounds the lovers must be taken into account if either one of them aspires to gain the perspective that "grants freedom" to the other. Otherwise, living only within this adjudicated Mitsein, we are at a loss to explain the actions and feelings of the other to ourselves as objects. We can only accept them as the genuflection rendered unto us because we believe ourselves worthy of their love. This belief hangs its hat on a conceit that our love is of such interest to them that they should automatically and in turn respond with everything they are. Indeed, we feel a betrayal if this "fullness" is not forthcoming or that it has, from time to time, been withheld from our grasp. The freedom of being in love then, seems to be perched on a fragile peak of odds and ends, crumbs and rusks left over from the times when intimacy itself reached its various peaks. In residing there, akin to some "saint" who removes himself from society in order to ponder his own existence, its solitude masquerading as its entirety, we are unable to admit to ourselves that what we have promoted through loving is not so much the controlling of the other but her assimilation. Indeed, "…he is being removed from *his* perspectival centrality and dragged off into mine. His loss of freedom is not so much a lack of power as a loss of subjectivity" (Natanson 1970:42, italics the text's). The "object" of our love, a common enough casual phrase, betrays its true import through the use of the word. It is not merely a case of objectifying the other as we might do for sexual purposes specifically, decorating them or adorning ourselves in order to mimic a fashionable script of desire or some kind of theatre of the passions in which we can play a seductive role. This use of the object is well-known and either shunned or celebrated depending on the whether or not the context is deemed appropriate, There is burlesque in every intimate relationship and this is no way takes away from the freedom of the other. No, it is my sense that I adore a person who has become a thing in herself that is the problem. I have reduced her humanity to the one thing that I adore; the fact that she adores me in the "same" way. My construction of her objectificity as an enactmental complex in the lifeworld includes of course all of the other actions and perceived intents that I am privy to with regard to her being-present. What it does not include is the feeling that beyond my feelings for her she exists in another world, in a word, her own. Because of the depth and strength of my feelings, I cannot imagine her in any other world but the one that we share, or perhaps even closer to the truth, the one that she shares with me. We are certainly overcompensating for our ardor in these cases, and thus putting ourselves at risk for both dependency and autocracy (cf. Barrett 1979:270). This overfullness of being in love is part of its intoxicating draught. We let it slide at first because we are aware that the other is doing the same in her world and we have been taken into that world in a complete enough manner as to ignore the implications of our being objectified. But if love is to be more than mutual objectification and the ensuing action of absorbing the object into ourselves as part of us, then we must step back from this heady mixture of simultaneously being liberated from the usual social norms of mutual respect and distanciation and the loss of freedom that is entailed by becoming someone else's favorite play-thing. The "overassertiveness" that is the common response to falling in love and playing it out participates in "the dramatic, mythological way of thinking and speaking" (cf. Jung, op. cit:13), and in doing so, it relieves itself from having to continue to live in the wider world of normative social reality. In this way, we imagine that love of another absolves itself of loving the world.

This gap in our understanding is thought to be compensated by our being in love *in* the world, rather than directly being its wider and more public lover. And for a short while, the world takes no notice of our newfound intimacy and joy, because it can do without our care for a while. The implications of this are clear: when the fires of passion begin to settle into a more routine expression of themselves, when sexual unions or other intimacies and sincerities become, not scripted, but placed in specific kinds of contexts and occur in specific times which may be less "spontaneous" and more calculated, the world reasserts itself and indeed has already reasserted itself. We begin to realize, perhaps through something akin to resentment and cynicism, fatalism and "acquiescence," that our love must be placed back into the world from which it had been torn away in order to create its own. This is the beginning of the more sincere understanding of the other as lover and as person, an active being who has her own perspective and has also returned to her own world. This also sincerely dismays us, because we wonder if, in replacing ourselves back into the worlds from which we had emerged and encountered one another as the pure "We," we may be experiencing the beginning of the end of that world for all time; the other and myself do not coincide (cf. Lingis 1989:135). This is the first shudder of the seismic tone of "othered" recognition. If our love can survive this *éclaircissement*, then it may well last a long time. Who we think the other is to us is not what she actually is. This is the first principle of the "granting of freedom" that is entailed by treating someone else the right way, treating them well instead of treating them as someone whose only merit is how she is able to treat me: "Beyond all I have observed and understood of him, beyond all that I have comprised in my representation of him, the other presents himself. He presents his otherness in the assent he gives to my interpretation, in the contestation he makes of it, in the silence to which he returns" (ibid). We find for the first time that we are in love with an actual other. This in itself is an extraordinary thing. We are stunned that it could even occur, that I, as a being within the world of passion, could transcend my own autochthony and reach across the existential gulf into another's life and origins, changing and changing all that she had known. This is a head-spinning event, but it is also quite commonplace. Indeed, it is this similitude of the common and the transcendental that astonishes us. On top of this, the other has invited me into her world, even if at first only as an object and thus subject to her desires. I am a willing object because the lavishness of these desires washes over me like the love of a warm ocean, its ravishing caresses carrying me into the womb of all origins. There is a "pressing" quality to the invitation of the lover that at once does not oppress. We feel its presence and its touch. Its firmness is, however, not controlling but reassuring. It lets us know that it is there without us needing to check on it, but it also lets us go our own way and does not compel us to follow its circumlocution; it is not a directive. In its warmth is contained all of these nuances, and perhaps that is what we are referring to when we say that someone is a "warm person." They are not compulsive but nevertheless compelling. We desire to be with them because of the confidence they exude in our presence: "But the invitation must be pressing, not indifferent. It should never imply: you are free not to come and if you don't come, never mind, it doesn't matter. Without the pressure of some desire [ ] the invitation immediately withdraws and becomes unwelcoming" (Derrida, op. cit:14). And yet this kind of pressure does not put pressure on us in the usual sense. There is no deadline or even appointment; it does not "book" us in. It hopes for our presence as one hopes for an audience with someone great. The beloved has attained this stature because of our desire for her, of course, and also because she is now "warm" in this oddly secure sense, the sense that we are safe with her and that the world is made a safer place for both of us to wander in together. We share our hopes and dreams, and imagine that we have overcome that dual nature of human hope that includes all that we do not wish to experience. Gadamer comments on "Fragment 18" of Heraclitus as expressing the alteration in stature that occurs within the hopeful; they can expect also things that are unhoped for: "When one does not hope, neither will one find the unhoped for" (2001:66 [1990]). The Pandoran hope was, for the Greeks, an even-handed and realistic mode of expectation that in the post-Christian age we might find a little pessimistic. Hope could even be considered an evil, because it betrayed human beings as much as it fulfilled, perhaps more so. Our lingering sense that we must be "careful in what we wish for" resonates with this classical conception of human expectation and aspiration. Because we cannot know the future even when we are in love, the stakes of hope gain an elevated status and stature for us. We hope that love will "find a way" and that it will overcome anything that is unhoped for, placed in "its way." In our consummation, our union which is sexual, sentimental, existential and hopeful, we have broken the classical connection with what is truly transcendental of human affairs and brought it down to earth, sequestering within our passionate action and forceful longings. "Virginity," literal or metaphoric, is not of interest because of its inexperience and state of hopeful wonder, but because of its sacredness as a gift. Its sacredness is based upon its "psychic openness to God" (cf. Neumann, op. cit133), and, in taking this virginity to be our own, and in giving it to the other as her possession and something to be possessed, we are negating its elevation of stature. Our horizontal longings flatten it out; make it level with the ground of being human and being human together. This one-dimensionality suits our hopes, as we can only project ourselves from one point in time and space and thus can only perceive of one kind of hopefulness. The union that brings the sacredness of the once inviolate into our purview has the effect, for a moment, of widening the horizon of hope to include the alien desires and will of an other to self who is invited, as well as pressed, to experience the same thing. Over time, of course, we must respond to this call of the other, and "answer" to her for our apparent violations. She too, if she is not to remain a mere object, must answer to us for the same act of remaking the sacred in our own image. In doing so, we take on the existential longings, hopes but also anxieties of the other and only through this can we come to know her as a subject and as her own center of a complex set of subjectivities and subjectitudes (cf. Lingis, op. cit:146). We do not replace the other, however, in answering for them and to them. We *do*, do more than acknowledge their ongoing presence. But we do not substitute our answers for their own. We take up their answers and support them in a *solidarity* that transforms the passion of love into the compassion of friendship. It makes what is certainly beautiful but nonetheless human into something that is humane, something that closes the desacralized gap between ourselves and our desires and hopes and the transcendental space of reflection and thought; the space where the sacred sources itself in our myths concerning the origins of love. Experiencing this as a human experience means also bringing it into the ambit of reason:

> In philosophical reflection, friendship is a term for solidarity. Solidarity, however, is a form of world experience and social reality that one cannot plan for by forced objectification or produce through artificial institutions. For, on the contrary, solidarity precedes all possible concerns and effects of institutions, economic systems, judicial systems, and social mores, sustains them, and makes them possible. (Gadamer 2001:123 [1978])

Because of its principled self-understanding, it both apprehends and comprehends the world of forms and the social world of norms and puts it in its relative place, just as it had placed us, through the human experience of the sacred as union and communion, together in a way that no norm could have instructed and no form adjudicated. What we have found is something that is our own. In maturing to this degree, the love relationship transcends itself.

In doing so, I and the beloved, she and myself as the newly subjective other, willingly retreat from the bonds of passion and temper them with the ties of solidarity. What is "solid" within solidarity is not so much what binds us—this has the overtone of the tyrant and the slave, as above—but what brings us together consistently and willingly, pressing without oppressing, feeling the weight of the ability and duty to answer to and for another without feeling suppressed by the gravity of the obligation. Rather, it allows us to locate ourselves in a new way: "At a turning point in the life of my friend, *I* find myself confronting him with the core of my own being at issue" (Natanson, op. cit:65, italics the text's). This is the sheer implication of solidarity and the mature being of love. We are no longer only "in love" with the other but we have taken them on as a life of their own; not a shadow nor a shotgun, nothing riding beside us or following us around wherever we go. No, none of these is the correct way to notice the presence of the other as something that we cannot do without. Rather, whatever changes she undergoes are changes that I myself have to confront as being part of the world I also live within. I am no longer simply "in" the world that changes around me without my consent or with a shrug of my shoulders. In answering to and for the other, I participate fully in her changes and these alterations cannot but change me as well. It is often characterized as being in a "conversation" or dialogue, but it is one that occurs through the invitation of otherness. "And, of course, we cannot be said to actually possess this singular conversational substance [ ] We are therefore in a state that precedes conversation [ ] precedes even perhaps pre-conversation; we may be left simply desiring to desire these states" (Lilburn 2010:14). We can distinguish here between state and status, as the first implies something that holds us, the second something we hold. For the alterations of existence occur often without not merely our conscious consent or even the calculated acknowledgement that our efforts to in fact bring about such changes have finally taken hold, or that there is now evidence that may be taking hold over us, and in this we are without the human conversation. We have not been able to pin it down to the point where we can speak lucidly about it, and, perhaps, as Lilburn suggests the lucidity that follows from the explications of dialogue are also not yet in our minds as intents or projects of action.

But it is not merely the other who alters herself and thus as well myself in the face of such an alteration The world, in the meanwhile, precedes our conversation and alters itself while we speak and while we state the desire to speak but have not yet been able to. The implication that overwhelms us is that we must recover our ability to speaking into being the care of the self that so benchmarked this new relationship of solidarity. The other's burden, our answer to it and for the other, answers as well the call to conversation that is within the being of otherness and her being-present. This is the state of "desiring" another state: "For we must all learn to treat ourselves properly." (Gadamer 1996:100 [1990]). Treating others, granting their freedom as a given, is the primary mode on the way to the being-free of the self we inhabit when we approach the other as she is in the world. It is, in a word, the shortest route that returns us to the path to something. It is certainly the case that "Mutual dependence is central to all human life" (Midgely 2004:92) and to dismiss this, in Midgely's words, is to "distort morality by a lop-sided melodrama." To recognize this is to already answer to the other and allow the state of desire for conversation to become an active desire for one's fuller humanity. The love-relationship that cannot be possessed is emblematic of the conversation that is actuated but not held in any state or granted by a particular status or authority. That we give over the self-absorbed perspective of complete freedom without the world of others is merely to say that we have recognized that freedom, as we shall see below, can be had by finite consciousness through the presence of others that extend our sensibilities in ways that we could never do by ourselves. Given this, the granting of freedom through the solidarity of mature love is to participate in the morality of the one who is obligated and who has recognized the other as different from one's perception of them. The implication tells us that "you should never use others merely as means but should always recognize them as ends in themselves" (Gadamer 1996:122 [1983]). That this conflicts with our "instinct" to self-love is clear enough. "It requires respect for the other to enable us to meet this demand. But what is respect? Respect is a highly dialectical effort. It involves the recognition of the superiority, or at least the independent significance of the other, but reluctantly!" (ibid:122-3). We need not retreat into a Hegelian vision of the "magical power" of the dialectic to participate in its conversation (cf. Lingis 1989:78ff). This auto-critical dialogue places us in the desired state of being able to answer to the other and also be the recipient of the other's answers to our burdens and ourselves. "Superiority" implies a mastery over something or someone, but this is not quite what is meant here. It merely implies that we give over to the other their own being, place it back in their care but without letting go of our concernfulness for it and about it. It manifests its superiority in the sense that it cannot be overtaken by me, only taken on and carried along. That the other does the same for me lessens the load of letting go of a kind of self-care that works alone. We affirm then, without conditions, the fact that the other now has a place within me but nevertheless remains in her own place as herself. This ability to grant the freedom of the other gives her the necessary superiority to move unfettered within my consciousness and concernfulness. The dialectic of such a conversation is the tenor of the mutual negotiation and renegotiation of this new form of being-with. Over time, we can affirm all of this without feeling that we are limiting our own freedoms and concerns. This is the most recent formulation of the humane conversation of love, according to the post-romantic vision of eternal change and thus the constant alteration of things. The dialectical quality of the contemporary conversation concerning being and of the concernful being admits to affirmation only through acknowledging that it does not state a status nor does it desire one different from this flux. This vision is associated with Nietzsche: "He is seeking a mind that can affirm unconditionally..." (Lingis, op. cit:79). This absence of service to another disarms any sense of mastery over the other that the superiority of being free seems to imply. Freedom is here taken as form of love, while we will see that the obverse can also be argued cogently. They do imply one another, because they are clearly implicated in one another. One's freedom is at "issue" in another's presence, as Natanson noted. Changes in the other call to the fore my own being to answer to these changes, and to answer for the one who changes. Even though we desire that "nothing changes" between us, this is a nod to the imagined essence of the relationship that is not possessed and thus is not subject to the same kinds of alterations as is the world or people such as ourselves. Relationships are constantly changing, and we are never in or out of them in any complete manner. For even when they end, the ability to love remains, perhaps dormant for a time, but fully attainable in another context where it will appear also altered to the circumstances at hand. The memory of the once beloved and the mate of our "soul" demands of us that we continue to answer to the other and her now past presence in the history of our freedom. The fire remains alive and well within us, and seeks conversation renewed, solidarity anew, ever curious in its burning quest for its own humanity: "Love is but a fire to be transmitted. Fire is but a love whose secret is to be detected" (Bachelard 1964:24 [1938]).

Chapter Six

"Freedom of Thought," Thought Freedom

We have now come to the moment where we must face our own freedom. Thinking it into being, presenting itself with our desire, we take as an act of love. Momentous without succumbing to the monumental, granting our own freedom means more than the self-care that grudgingly admits the other to its conversation with itself. It passes by its own memorial, nodding in recognition but also acknowledging that this is not even a way-station on the way to being or a benchmark to which all future forms of being-with must pause and pay their respects. No, the problem of human freedom, though a historical one and one that we today in particular are partial to, cannot be bracketed as set apart from the world of all cares and the being of all concerns. The errors that are immediate and desirable in this case are the ones that either follow a specific path that is said to lead to freedom, or this or that way of being free—and this is the more recognizably transparent mistake that most of us are willing to admit to with experience—or the one that thinks that no extant path, tradition, custom, norm, thought or myth, has anything to do with freedom at all. This second error will inform the bulk of this chapter's discussions, but we cannot entirely ignore the first.

Krishnamurti's famous epigram "truth is a pathless land" might easily be seen to apply equally to the idea of freedom. This may be appealing in principle as our sensibilities concerning being free or ultimate freedom may be constrained or offended by the notion that a path laid down by others contains or could contain our own individuated freedom. And this is so, in so far as it goes. The equally famous Frost line concerning the "path less chosen" making all the difference must, however, be weighted against the starkness of the pathless land. For on this more obscure trail we find that we must pick our way through the world and in so doing, construct our own freedom regarding it and others in it. The challenge of clearing a path and discovering that others have also done so are mutually engaging when it comes to understanding human freedom in the light of finite and reasoning consciousness. In a word, freedom has its own history, and we are, in our quest for it, coming to terms with something that is new to us but is also already there, already present in the discourses, arts, ideas and discoveries of others. So while the experience of the truth of our being can be momentary and pathless, a sentience wrapped around by the torus of the essential condition of nature, freedom presents to us a complex and sophisticated network of meandering ways and means, some much more well-trodden, and thus perhaps even worn out, than others. Though our sense of being free is unique to our unquiet modernity, we imagine that the use of language, tools, kinship and myth, the hypostatization of the religious life, and the control of fire are also, as we have seen above, crucial elements to our shared human consciousness of freedom, and thus cannot be simply dismissed as "only culture."

And it is at first that we experience our ability to know something of freedom through our bodies and senses. This "corporeal consciousness" is of the world and part of the world, but it comes to know the world in its own specifically individual manner. Not only due to the life course of a person's biography, but even thanks to its particular growth and development and its relations with the others that its random birthright has placed in its path. Coupled with the evolution of an ethics—the sense of how one can and then must treat others according to the contexts given us; as we have also seen, such a "treatment" implies within its demand a "granting of freedom" which is essential to experiencing the "right" way of things and people—consciousness begins to feel that it is not alone. Indeed, given our conception of the soul and of feelings and sentiments more broadly, this "incorporeal conscience" reveals itself as the partner to reason and thought. It too reflects upon matters at hand, but its goal is not necessarily rationally defined nor might it always be able to be calculated ahead of time. Though we no longer possess the "collective conscience" of our earlier ancestors, we still have a relatively, though often inconsistent, strong sense of community and obligation to others—all the stronger the closer to home, which is likely the greatest problem we face as a species living in a global world—and this sense of the larger than self produces a conscience in principle or at least in theory unlimited by a self-interest that is centered by consciousness alone.

Finally, we also need to discuss the challenge of identifying the occasions for exercising our shared human freedoms. We are often deluded into thinking that we are free, only to experience the "pirouette of liberty," a volte-face that turns the back of the ideal upon us and forces us to reconsider the paths by which we attained this moment, got this far along. In so doing, we will once again encounter the same structure that human consciousness passes through along the way to a new experience; the history of the ideas or events at hand, reflection upon these ideas, and the taking of action by a being who has begun to come to grips with the challenges faced by others like ourselves, but different enough to provide perspectives that we could not alone begin to fathom.

6.1 CORPOREAL CONSCIOUSNESS

At first all of us experience what looks very much like the antithesis to all freedoms. As culture seeks primarily to reproduce itself, it pays no heed to the aspirations of youth to distinguish itself from what has passed before it. Each generation foists the hypocrisies and convenient untruths on its successors, and roundly criticizes them when they fail to conform to the going rate. It is not merely the present being of culture that must reproduce itself. The ways and means of attaining the culture that we have must be taught as well. One does not simply inherit a culture out of whole cloth and ready-made. The labor involved is ongoing and it is these processes that, when passed from generation to generation, create the problematic tensions characteristic of modern education and schooling no matter its form or degree. We are taught that self-consciousness is secondary to that which adheres to normative values and methods, and to be self-aware must be enthralled to the forms of production and reproduction through which the self itself is generated. But we have already seen that this self-concept in its singularity is a gross error of modernity and flies in the face of its own experience of itself. Just so, to hold to the centered idea of self is to become self-centered, which is also something that receives a mixture of messages from one's elders in today's society. Instead, we might begin to free ourselves from this conception and its ability to reproduce itself in many social contexts in spite of the evidence contrary to its continuity by thinking ourselves back into the very language that gave us human form: "With the *logos*, precisely that upon which the inner self-forgetfulness of speech is essentially drawn is pushed into view— the world itself, which is evoked by speech, lifted into presence, and brought into articulation and communicative participation" (Gadamer 2001:125 [1978]). It is language that both shows us the truths that human freedom has produced over the ages and the manner in which new truths and new freedoms that are forthcoming from them may occur. Needless to say, the more limited and technical the language is, the less opportunity for the creativity necessary to bring about truly new "hermeneutic" experiences there will be. In each "natural" language there exists, however, ample means to discover and rediscover the history of this or that idea or expression. When we follow these sometimes exiguous paths, we are brought into contact along the way and sometimes also in the very shadows and margins of our peripheral vision, with the freedoms of others, still glowing like embers in the otherwise darkened corridors of history: "In the same vein we might ask ourselves to what end life has gone through aeons of laborious evolution in order to produce intelligence if this intelligence is not itself to intervene in the process of life. The question is—and this is the real danger—whether it will intervene intelligently" (Barrett 1979:233). One can only be more sure of this relative to our intervention in the past. "Learning from history," another cliché and also a famous partially recalled quote—partial recollection is, as we have seen, a hallmark of convenience, and not only that political—is something that each generation also must do in the face of a new life and of the unknown future. The pattern and force of human reason presents itself as a timeworn tool of the trade of calculating life-chances both for ourselves and for humanity as a whole. But this tool is attuned to what passes for the great majority of human actions and behaviors, and thus alone cannot be entirely trusted or even utilized to seek the new. A certain amount of daring or sense of adventure is also necessary. Yet much of what we do is not at all original to us. This is a hard saying indeed, given that our much-vaunted human reason is usually seen, or is desired to be seen, always on the vanguard of things and events. But we must admit to ourselves first and foremost that simply due to the reproductive imperative by which all cultures must define themselves, all facets of human consciousness, and especially those unique to it and shared by no other animal species in so far as we currently can tell, will be also, almost by definition, primarily habituated and girded against the challenge of reproduction and adaptation, all the more so since the biological or organismic evolutionary paths to humanity have run themselves almost completely out and have been overtaken by those cultural for some hundreds of millennia at least.

This being the case, reason, reflection, phantasm, interpretation, communication and dialogue are by themselves not paths to freedom. Their combination along with the fundamental primate curiosity, may point us in the direction of various human freedoms, but not before they have "paid their dues" to the locale of history and culture that brought them into their current form of being in the first place. Today, we have a very specific manner of payment of discursive and historical dues: "There is a fundamental difference between modern science and the premodern aggregate of knowledge, which under the name 'philosophy' comprehended all human knowledge. This difference is precisely that what we know from 'science' is incomplete and therefore, cannot be called a 'doctrine.'" (Gadamer 1996:4 [1972]). There are two directions in which freedom finds itself called. On the one hand, the fact that the "current state of research" now constitutes knowledge and this, by definition, is ever and always open to new possibilities that accord themselves with the freedom of not only discovery but of thought applied to these areas, suggests that we are more open to freedom itself than we might have been historically. On the other hand, science does not claim to encompass or even represent all human knowledge, and so its borders are in fact more limited than those of the pre-scientific ages in spite of the presence of "doctrines." In this second light, freedom would seem to be present or "allowed" only if harnessed to a specific set of tasks. Before the advent and rise of science, the idea that "knowledge is opinion accompanied by *logos*. It is rationally established opinion" (Gadamer 2000:62), would have been quite acceptable to philosophical disquisition and political discourse alike. The model of our rationally established arguments based on the experience and measurement of empirical sense data, now mostly collected and analyzed by machines, is seen to be germinating within the idea of the human logos.[1] To be sure, our classical Western ancestors and their Eastern and Near-Eastern peers were not fools. They were not led on or deluded by the idea that anyone's "opinion" of anything at all constituted knowledge, an idea sometimes current amongst contemporary university students. At the same time, models of thinking were not so arranged in tandem with the facts at hand to provide a systematic and rationally defined order of nature that could only be explored from one angle; that of scientific method. So much so is this the case today that what was formerly taken as the entirety of human knowledge often apes this new method, thereby limiting itself and its still viable historical freedoms (cf. Barrett, op. cit:27). This "game", as Barrett puts it, has the real effect of delimiting the freedom of thought and reflection accorded to a set of open-ended methods that do not necessarily rely on, primarily or even secondarily, the physical realities of a wider nature or the rationalities of mathematical logic, assumed to be the human version of the language of that self-same nature. It is quite appropriate to have one or two aspects of modern philosophy occupied with these kinds of issues, logic, epistemology, philosophy of sciences and cognitive philosophy, for instance, but what we have seen is that these niches have taken over almost the entire space of what is currently called "philosophy" and made "academic" philosophy into the center and the monopoly of what used to be something open to everyone who was literate. This did not occur yesterday, but it is something that occurred with the rise of science itself and especially became the case in the cultures where science was of the essence to imperial and industrial aspirations. Gradually, these aspirations and their "real world" accomplishments so impressed the remainder of the cultures that they too could afford to linger no longer in premodern definitions of thought. Heidegger, writing at the time when this was becoming sedimented in German consciousness, is much more forceful than Barrett in his condemnation thereof:

> *Today*: The situation of academic disciplines and the university has become even more questionable. What happens? Nothing. Everyone writes "brochures" on the crisis of academic disciplines, on the academic calling. The one says to the other: everyone's saying—as everyone's heard—academic disci-

plines have had it. Today there is already a specialized body of literature on the
question of how matters should be. Nothing else happens. (op. cit:27)

This could well have been written last year, let alone some ninety-five years
ago, though perhaps the subject matter would have shifted from the "crisis of
European philosophy" to the general irrelevancy of all academic discourses
to the practical and the political lives of the vast majority of human beings.
However this may be, it is clear that the narrowing of the scope of both the
presentation of problems and the ways in which they can be questioned
presents certain definable limits to human freedom and the curiosity that in
part drives it. We have bracketed prematurely both the outcome and the
source of humankind's "edge" if you will, over what is natural and even what
is cosmic. Not that we can excerpt ourselves from these wider conditions of
what exists, but the existentiality of human existence is specifically adapted
and attuned to be quite different from its base layers: "In truth, it is a characteristic feature of the human being, indeed, even the sign of its superiority.
For it is humanity's mark of distinction to raise problems and to open up the
dimension of diverse possibilities" (Gadamer 2000:107). No instinct driven
creature has need of freedom. There is no truth or falsehood in its existence.
There is no desire other than that predefined by the organismic needs of its
life-functions. There is no goal other than to live long enough and healthily
enough to reproduce. Now it is this last that should ring a bell for us. For did
we not just suggest that it was the primary goal of culture to reproduce itself
akin to nature?

The reduction of the life of human culture to reproduction through the
production of what it has been is a dehumanization of our collective psyche
and its accomplishments. But on closer view, cultures never simply reproduce themselves in the manner as does nature. In order to assure their poste-
rity over the course of demographic and other shifts, innovation plays just as
much a role in reproduction as does mimicry. It is just the case that the
mimicry seems to have a monopoly on things as they are presented to youth,
and hence the disquiet amongst each generation's youthful being, because
one needs to learn the basis of what has passed for one's culture—and now,
increasingly, the world culture of the global geopolitical situatedness of
someone who counts themselves "knowledgeable" in this way—before moving on to be able to extrapolate from it or improvise within it. It is an error,
mainly but not solely of youth, to imagine that reproduction is the opposite of
innovation, or that mimicry has within it no sense of creativity or curiosity.
"Sincere flattery" aside, mimicry is also a patent way of learning the dynamic
of corporeal consciousness; a way to learn how others have learned and have
had to learn. This in itself should provoke the most intrigued and eager
opportunities for both critique and therefore subsequent innovation amongst
learners and teachers alike. And what emanates from such a dialogue and

such a situation is the realization that diverse options are always better, at least to begin with and perhaps also to continue with over the long term, than is the "one best way." The idea that there could be one way to do things in a changing world is at best naïve, and at worst, a form of fascism. To recognize change is itself a change in our patterns of self-recognition: "The deeper reason for the change is, however, that *we now have a much more realistic conception of what explanation itself involves.*" (Midgely 2004:50, italics the text's). What is this "real world" that is justifiably said to be so complex, and why is it only recently that we have "begun" to recognize it for what it is? The Aristotelian schemata that divided peoples has assuredly been overtaken in one sense, that ethnographic and the realization that has come along with this recognizance is that peoples and cultures are historically relative and equally sophisticated according to their symbolic aspirations especially, but as well their population loads and modes of production. But what has not quite been overcome is our sense that because it was we ourselves as a Western culture that recognized this—indeed, no other culture by itself has ever done so—and that we recognized this precisely through the advent of science, that we in turn can preserve our notions of cultural superiority as an *inherent* device for the explanation of culture history and cosmology. It is one thing to repeat to ourselves, "The world is neither tidy nor tedious; there is no excuse for stuffing its mouth with the mush of obedience" (Natanson, op. cit:154-5), and quite another to state openly that due to the history of a singular culture that all cultures must now obey our directives given that they are those designed to open all of us to the most diverse possibilities of human freedom. Surely there is more than an irony here?

It so happens that the reality of the "real world" is more symbolic than real in the basic or brute physical sense. This is the case both within our arguments for its reality and the complexity thereof and therein, and in the diversity that prohibits our arguments from attaining the mantle of singularity. We are not the sole source of light in the world, for what light there currently is has both the limits of its own illuminescence and the fact that much of it is controlled by specific cultural and institutional switches that could turn it on for us to continue to explore this world or turn it off to defend against our inquiries. The "light" is also a problematic conception inherited from religious traditions that almost always proclaimed that there was one path and one path alone to human freedom: "Nevertheless, we should keep the image of light; only it is not an electric bulb flashing in our head when truth happens, but some portion of the world that has become illuminated." (Barrett, op. cit:158). The phenomenological conception of the "lighted space of being" is yet a better image than even the reality of illuminating part of the world at large. It reminds us that what we are actually about is increasing our ability to understand ourselves in that world, and not so much the world itself. It is natural science that illuminates the world alone. This histor-

ical fact, and the authority and authoritativeness that emanates from it, remind us in turn that there remains an ample space for philosophy in the most
general sense of the term to continue to light the paths of human freedom and
of consciousness in general. The philosophy of the modern world need never
fear its own doctrines will become either transfixed on ancient ideas or made
immobile by stasis in the world. First of all, we already have seen that change
is the only constant in this our world, and that change occurs in a multitude
of ways. That the psyche too is a source of knowledge—its "Gnostic" recognition has informed much of contemporary human science, according to Jung
(cf. op. cit:174ff)—is in itself a "revelation" about the world and our place in
it. For we as both experiencers and observers of that world have not only
made our own in astonishing feats of *both* material and symbolic construction; architectures of both space and the inner space of consciousness, but we
have also managed to contrive an existence that no longer solely predicates
itself on survival and reproduction at *either* the species or the cultural levels.
In a word, human beings have learned how to evolve themselves, taking
control of almost all of what in all other circumstances was the sole purview
of nature. The implications of this cannot be worked out in a trice; no doctrine or dogma can encompass them. Indeed, our revolt against traditional
world systems of religion and custom has blemished one of the important
meanings to these terms: "The word 'dogma' has even acquired a somewhat
unpleasant sound and frequently serves merely to emphasize the rigidity of a
prejudice. For most people living in the West, it has lost its meaning as a
symbol for a virtually unknowable and yet 'actual'" (Jung, op. cit:175). That
dogma may once have pointed to the openness of an abstraction transcendent
of human aperture is one thing to note, but the use of such a term to denote
the enemies of freedom mask something else about our contemporary prejudices. We take what we know as a way to characterize human consciousness
before we question the way in which we know it. But the essential focus of
freedom within consciousness is to never let it rest content with how it is in
the moment. Today I am one thing and think one way, we might imagine, but
even this only summarizes a specific and perhaps habitual set of tendencies,
and does not replicate the pejorative state that has accrued to "dogma" or
"doxa" or doctrine of any kind. We are, rather, in a perpetual dynamic of
protodoxa and protest against it's becoming too rigid. There exists an infinity
of chances that we confront at a cosmic level, its vast panorama extending
only to the furthest horizon of our prosthetic senses. What lies beyond is the
truly infinite because it, like the nuance of dogma Jung reminds us about, is
truly "unknowable" and yet also "actual." It inability to be known is not a
function of its own existence, for our human horizons have been ever extended since our primordial ancestors first migrated from what is now Eastern Africa to Southern Africa. As long as we survive our own adolescence,
itself extended in a much more negative manner, this will continue to ever be

the case. In a word, infinity is the replacement for godhead in a scientific culture: "The idea of infinity will have this decisive role in Western cognitive life because it is not another concept which can be judged as to its truth; it is the decisive constituent of the philosophical idea of truth" (Lingis 1989:13). Note that this idea of truth is expressly stated to be *philosophical*; that is, not scientific. Science explores and catalogues the infinity of the cosmos both external and internal to us, but what it does not do is apprehend the psyche or the symbolic cosmos of ideas that led to its development in the first place and thence also to its growth. Indeed, in comprehending infinity as a staunchly non-empirical conception, we are retrieving the precise meaning of dogma that had been lost in mechanism and the sense that the infinite could only be opened up through the prosthetic of specific technologies adapted to that purpose. No doubt the discoveries of this angle of exploration have been both astonishing and liberating. They too point us in the direction of freedom. The mere fact that we now know of thousands of other planets, many with the same dimensions and likely climates as earth, and that by extrapolation we are rewarded with the prescient sense that our galaxy alone must then contain billions of similar worlds is a patent essay in human freedom of thought based in consciousness of the infinite. But this is not "knowledge" in the same sense that what is "knowable" is not dogmatic precisely because it contains no apparent speculation. The freedom associated with coming to know the facts of the local universe have more to do with our realization that we are the more provincial for our newly absent ignorance concerning this realm. Freedom of consciousness by itself then, contains an irony that is itself illuminating: "This comes from the retrieval of the lived experience or creative activity underlying our awareness of the world, which had been occluded or denatured by the regnant mechanistic construal. The retrieval is felt as a liberation" (Taylor 1989:460). We have been reminded of something that some of us may well have been suspicious of existing, but had not come to the wider awareness provided in this case by scientifically oriented tech-nologies and analyses. But along with width there must also be depth, and this second aspect of human self-discovery and self-understanding cannot be measured in the light years or parsecs that distance us physically from all of these other worlds and indeed, much more importantly, the sentient and even intelligent life forms that one would think would accompany many of them. The panoramic view still places us at its epicenter. But what consciousness of the depths can do is displace our surface centeredness and plunge thought into itself. Indeed, even historically it may be the case that consciousness that projects itself first before introspection is something that has developed along with the techniques and technologies of the scientific endeavor: "The con-scious state is the late and uncommon phenomenon, and its complete attain-ment is far more of a rarity than modern man so flatteringly pretends" (Neu-mann, op. cit:271).

One of the most common entry points into the depths is the dream world. Nocturnal imagery participates more fully in the mythical and archetypical than does the conscious projection of phantasm, even though we need both working in tandem in order to remain fully conscious of the reality of the wider world: "When we plunge back into the world of dreams, our ego and our consciousness, being late products of human development, are broken down again. In our dreams we inhabit an interior world without being aware that we do so" (ibid:276). This is not entirely true. A certain percentage of dreams and their associated scenarios are so transparently faulty or surreal that we, even asleep and unconscious in the basic and usual observable sense realize that we are dreaming, and sometimes can even manipulate the action and narratives the dreams are attempting to convey and through which their messages are conveyed. Aside from the "public service announcements" that also form a significant percentage of dreamscapes—finding oneself under a waterfall and waking suddenly needing to use the washroom—the fact that there exist dreams where we are an active agent instead of a passive observer and at the same time are fully aware that we are dreaming, though much less common, testifies to the mutual embrace the unconscious and the conscious have with one another. The ability to consciously act within the realm of the unconscious may well be an evolutionary mechanism. That there are limits to our actions when dreaming is also clear, however, and though I have myself attempted to do things that would be considered scandalous in the waking world when I have realized that I was in the midst of a dream, I have sometimes been prevented, by actions of the "others" inhabiting the dream-scape, from fulfilling my desires. This suggests that the morality of the sphere of the ego and of the generalized other is fully active even in the wholly "interior" world of dreams. This too may be evolutionary—though not inheritable *per se* in terms of specific cultural content—but this time the evolution at play is strictly cultural. The upshot of all of this is that we are not at all entirely free either to dream what we wish, or, in realizing that we are participating consciously in the life of the unconscious, to do as we choose (cf. Midgely's criticism of this, op. cit:142). Now one would be ashamed of the sometimes shamelessness of the dream-state even if one does not seek to add one's conscious version of cultural or egocentric desires to the mix, but this kind of interpretation has been shown to be of a rather surface variety. The action of dreams is not to be taken seriously in this way. But it is of more interest regarding the assumed corporeality of freedom—that it must be made up of conscious choices in the waking world only—that our respect for the freedom of others comes into play. Even though we know things are not real, we may be forced to play the narratives of the dream out as if they were taking place in the real world of actual others and waking states of consciousness. This in itself is an odd phenomenon, and speaks directly to the influence, not of the unconscious, but of consciously learned behavior on the unconscious, though we also often tell ourselves that what is learned in primary socialization occurs at a semi-conscious level and then descends into the "interior" yet further, only to be rediscovered as being quite present to us in and through our dreams.

Dreams thus are constitutive of reality in an unexpected way. They do not merely present themselves as set pieces. They are always after sending some kind of message to the conscious form of being, that is, to living consciousness. Whether the kernel of these communications is mundane though useful—one does not, as an adult, wish to wet one's bed, though this kind of dream as well may have a moral dimension at some level—or much more profound and thus also somehow mysterious—the dreams that purport to show us the "other world" or the afterlife, at least in our imagination, visiting with dead parents or other persons, including historical figures that we could not possibly have ever met—the act of communication "constitutes" more than an editorial comment on the world at large. Living and dying in that world are also at stake in the world of dreams, and thus what we had taken for the metaphysical structure of consciousness must then include an autochthony at the individuated level which is also part of the unexpected character of the unconscious life. It seems like a long step from Darwin to Heidegger, but we can understand Lingis when he suggests that the latter is the thinker who had to come to terms with the sense that what life was, in its essence, rested in its ability not merely to evolve in its own way but to also be able to die its own death. (cf. Lingis on Heidegger's conception, op. cit:28). Living its own life, the being-able-to-be the vehicle of a consciousness that knows of the unconscious mode of being-conscious predicates itself on a kind of regular rehearsal of the death of what is conscious of itself. For when we are asleep, the care of the world does not depart from us. In this sense, we are never "lost to the world" as we sometimes say of the dreamer—indeed, we sometimes make this remark also of the one who dreams while still awake—for that self-same world repeats its symbologies and mythic narratives, amongst other more utilitarian themes, as we have seen, through the dream-states and the dream-language. Now it remains true that the language of the communication emanating from the unconscious world of dreams—though we must again remind ourselves that it is not a wholly unconscious construction nor does it "intend" to rest within itself; it may be the interiority of the world but it is not an inner world in and of itself—cannot be taken in a straightforward manner, as Heidegger says of the space of carefreeness. We are not free, while dreaming, to understand the language of the dream in any way we imagine. We compare its works with those of our conscious state in the real world of others, the world that presents itself as something that we must attend to and thus care for: "In the leveled-off there of this carefreeness which concernfully attends to the world, a world encountered in this carefreeness as something self-evident, care is asleep" (Heidegger, op. cit:80).

This apparent analogy is no mere convenient comparison, but in fact a direct reflection of the transformation of care one encounters in the world of dreams, where being carefree is but one option, to be used accordingly with reference to the ultimate point of this or that unconscious communication back into the more conscious workings of the mind and its further activities. Carefreeness then, the freedom from caring, is *not* free of care. It is dormant in the way that the fully conscious "wide-awake" reality is dormant. In spite of this, it remains aware of itself as either the art of a prognosis made by the dream language itself, or as something to be enlisted by that language during the course of its unconscious narrative: "On account of this, the possibility ever remains that distress will suddenly break forth in the world. The world can be encountered as something distressing only insofar as it is a world which is of significance to us" (ibid). And what more pressing a feeling do we get when dreaming of something that appears to us to be of the utmost? The nightmare is of this distressing variety of being-cared-for precisely because its message is that we are *not* attending to the world in the way we should be. This also includes the internal world of our psyche, and perhaps especially we are moved to concern, when we awake in a cold sweat, perhaps, or shivering due to the momentary "experience" of our own deaths—the dream-language is notoriously melodramatic at times—that we must immediately change something about our self-care in order to right the error that is being foisted upon us by our own carefreeness. That dreaming allows us the freedom to do so is remarkable in itself. And it is through the use of language once again that human consciousness, even in its partially aware state of being asleep to the world but very much waking in its anti-dogmatic slumbers—or, given the problem of the modern connotation of dogma, perhaps we could equally say that dreams present to us a dogma that opens itself up to what is "unknowable" by day alone—and just as active in its own way as we are when awake: "Consequently, the essential openness of the language that we have to use for the purposes of life means that the world should lie open to us is the real and concrete meaning of freedom to which we aspire" (Barrett. op. cit:84). We are thus apparently always engaged in the navigation of the perceived routes to freedom, even when we are asleep. Perhaps especially so, given what we have suggested regarding the distressing character of certain dreams. Our very existence may be at stake—not always so much in physical terms, but, once again, in those moral; dreaming is ironically more of a space of the moral than the immoral let alone the "non-moral" of philosophical interrogations—and we must, as concernful beings in the world, respond to this in any way we can. Such responses rest now additionally armed by the "experience" of being "in" a dream, though our ordinary language strains at describing the odd veracity of our dreaming states, their surreal opacities and their occluded, but not excluded, middles of their altered logic. The work of the unconscious just this previous night might well inform us something about which we had only the vaguest conscious notion. So freedom adjusts its requirements of us according to the scope and nature of our self-understanding, but it never lets us abandon the effort. Given that our efforts to this regard, especially in our modern life, have a history to them and that we can, partially through dreaming and subsequent interpretation—most of which as well takes place while we are not conscious—use our knowledge of this history as an aid in the present, suggests that we are not alone even if we are by ourselves working on our individuated quests. (cf. Lingis, op. cit:148). This past is hardly "our own" in the strictly biographical sense of an "I" having lived by itself and actively constructed the entire world for itself. It is "autobiographical" only in the sense that it experiences the world through its own being-there. Being "thrown back" is not a simple inversion of the thrownness of projected being into the world and thence running along. Casting oneself back upon one's own experience is a daily necessity of the present and not of the past *per se*. But being thrown back is to engage in the conversation of humanity, which, as we saw above, is not at all limited to what we have experienced in our own lives as individual beings. History is almost entirely not of our own making, and yet we are thrown both back upon it and into it as a matter of course. There are opportunities for "making a difference," both in the sense of the care or love of the world and for others in it, but also, and equally importantly, in our "confrontation with tradition," as Gadamer has famously put it. It is here that the abstract notions of what a dream is, a vision, or the attainment of human freedom, takes its place in the world of forms, even though it is usually ideas and discourse that are first at stake. Midgely mentions that both Nietzsche and Sartre were not only persons of great integrity but were innovators in the sphere of *values*, a rather difficult thing to be given the inertia of custom and norm in all cultures and times and places (cf. op. cit:97). But it is precisely this sphere that freedom both speaks of and departs from. It is the source of our current ideas of freedom and the source of the resistance to all future freedoms. But it is the very nature of human freedom to be discontent with what passes for the present understanding of being free. In this, it is rather more like a concernfulness that is oriented to what is absent, even though we cannot directly point to the form of either the missing object or tell each other the way in which it is missing or it is missed. Yet one cannot retreat into the ethereal insensibility that because something is experienced that suggests to us an absence of an additional experience of some import—and this "addition" includes its own sense of self-importance, because there will always and everyday be other experiences that we eschew and do not therefore "miss" in the same way, perhaps because we know that the sights and sources of these other potential experiences are not themselves missing; it is only we who have "missed out" on them for the time being—that it automatically must reside in some other world to which all mortal access is inherently forbidden. The historical enactmentality of thinkers such as Nietzsche and Sartre and many others strongly evidence against this interpretation. In the order of their respective days, they also saw a chaos that threatened not only their own individual humanity, but that of the culture or even the species in general. Surely we are all the more so sitting amidst this version of chaos within the social order today, given our technical abilities and our still-competitive geopolitics. If chaos is traditionally understood as the inversion of cosmos, the back of God or the like, we can gain little by pursuing it: "But there is another kind of chaos, which is really nothing but order in disguise" (Lösch, op. cit:220). This would include all of the proliferating life around us, life that appears at first glance to be but its own proliferative energy endlessly and recklessly expended in all directions. How could this be the space of any value that would be recognizable to an aspiring culture of freedom? "We need to get rid of the notion that all natural things are valueless in themselves, merely pretty extras, expendable, either secondary to human purposes or actually pernicious" (Midgely, op. cit:174). This arc of the pendulum that begins with the sense that culture is so arranged to not only be the opposite of nature but to be, in its very being, in active *opposition* to it, is as well known to us as part of the liberation of humans from their natural origins, "moving steadily in a direction fixed from the very beginning: toward the emancipation of man from nature and consciousness from unconsciousness" (Neumann, op. cit:382). Freedom so defined loses the source of its own movement. In placing itself as against something it has lost the very freedom it so espouses as a necessity, for it remains always and already in orbit of that which it so despises. In this case, certain versions and visions of nature as inexorable and deterministic, parasitic or at best, as Midgely states, peripheral. Orbiting the parent, the hero will never "be free" of this orientation. The source must not be so much overcome as "forgotten" in the manner in which the butterfly "forgets" the cocoon. Surely this is plausible given that much of our early childhood memories are lost to us. We do not hold the experience of infancy as part of the experience of childhood, nor do we hold this next phase of life-experience too closely as an adult. Nor should we, for in becoming, developing, maturing into other forms, our very human life cycle is an expression of its own corporeal freedom.

What are much more of a distraction to the aspect of freedom that occupies the rational and reflective consciousness are the fruit and the detritus of our projection into the world of forms. It is not necessarily even norms, then, as we will see in the following section, but forms "themselves" that tend to get in our way. The "extension" of the sphere of values accomplished by radical thinkers extant within our collective cultural history does not always adjust our attitude toward the things we make and use in daily life. In being drawn towards them, in the overcare of our concernfulness about them and their "welfare," we once again attain only a shallow orbit, all the while maintaining a faith that their presence is an aid to freedom (cf. Barrett, op. cit:244). The distinction between what we can see with the naked eye and what our prosthetic vision presents to us on plates should be noted. But aside from this, we must take seriously the expense of our efforts in the direction of the most obvious aspects of corporeal freedom—that of movement, for instance, or the contrived consumer choices with which we are faced in daily life, or even what to do with "pests," whether human or otherwise—and ask of ourselves, "Is this the direction our existential effort and our concernfulness of being must expend itself?." What do those objects and institutions do for us in response to our care and concern for them? Do they in turn point us in the direction of human freedom? It is possible that they, when they resist our care, point us in a number of directions at once, but that some of those do concern our freedom. For when we encounter resistance to not merely our basic aims and needs, but to our desires and the outcomes of our projects of action that have not quite taken hold in the world, we are also simultaneously shown another threshold that leads into the unknown and the unexpected. We cast around in the ensuing darkness of indecision in the face of these new options, but we do not do so purposelessly. Gadamer reminds us that what we do for ourselves in these situations comes entirely out of ourselves and without the assistance of that which has already shown to be nothing but a resistance to our intents. In this we are "thrown back" upon our own histories. These histories include both dreams and deeds, intents and actions, thoughts and experiences, waking and sleeping, living and ultimately dying. Perhaps the earliest recognition of this dynamic of living within our form of life occurs in Fragment 26 of Heraclitus, which reads: "A man strikes a light for himself in the night, when his sight is quenched. Living, he touches the dead in his sleep; waking, he touches the sleeper" (in Gadamer 2001:31 [1974]). Living, we are touched by those who have lived before us. Sleeping we are touched by what has occurred to us in this life alone.

6.2 INCORPOREAL CONSCIENCE

The enactmentality of human freedom does not occur within the ambit of rational and this-world oriented consciousness alone. It also must include the often non-rational and imprecisely reasoned ethics of conscience. This aspect of our entire consciousness is usually thought of as somehow less "material," less corporeal than its reasoning counterpart. Because it tends to deal with the forms of ideals, abstractions that are sometimes attached to visions of other worlds and even other beings, it has been placed in a setting that is hence regarded as more noble or at least more aloof to worldly concerns. This is an error. Just as we saw with dreams, the ethics that have their source in the conscience, whether this is characterized as moral, social, collective or individual, directly have to do with the social world. We have already seen in some detail how the narratives and tropes of myth and art play an important role in defining this world. Ultimately, however, it is we the living who must not only pursue the ends of our own freedom but also parse these ends in a world of means and ends that cannot be accounted for by the enduring presence of mythic forms alone. In a word, the morality that structures the human conscience is not fully portable across either world cultures or expressly individual situations and social contexts. Morality cannot rest upon its mythic representation of itself and also retain any relevance for human beings living, sleeping, waking and dying in the world as it is.

It is our lot, then, to initiate and reinitiate an ethics. To do this, we are pressed to engage consistently and regularly in some kind of reflection concerning the way things are currently held to be done as well as the way things are actually done in our shared world. This is not only an option for us in our individuated modernity, it is a necessity. This should not be as remarkable as it sounds. The state of the world is, after all, what provoked discussion of its relative flaws and merits in the first place, as well as of course our state within the world. So mundanity, in spite of its routine quality of being both predictable and the home of unthought and the "carefreedom" of neither caring nor being free, is in actual fact also the source and nourishment of all thoughts that attempt to depart from it. This situation provides us with another example of why we cannot remain in orbit of an opposing force and so define ourselves through this opposition. We must rather "forget" the fact that it is a source; in the same way that we discover that mundane reality allows us to "break through" it at regular intervals. All airy flights of fancy begin firmly rooted to the ground. They also always have half an eye on their return, even if it means that both are transformed in the meantime: "Contemplation's vector is transcendental yet it bends as well into the world. There its subject is individualities, thisnesses. Contemplation knows the world as a spectacle of difference in which each thing is nothing other than its inscrutable self" (Lilburn 1999:28). Originating in the scrutability of the world at hand, our understanding of what we have been according to its rules and its ways gradually makes the way in which we know such things inscrutable. The processes by which we have become who and what we are then are lost to us. In some respects, this too is a necessary forgetting, as we do not rest within the static form of being present. Our "who" is our ability to overcome our "what." In taking stock of the stock of knowledge at hand in the world we place ourselves in contemplation thereof. It does not orbit this center of gravity, however, but rather floats alongside it, following its movements but not echoing them. It is no longer fully ensconced or enthralled to the motions of this our world, which in turn gives it a flavor that it is actually beginning to participate in some other world, some other form of being, hence its "transcendentality." But akin to the crises the world will inevitably bring about for us and within us, contemplation can ultimately result in no transcendental perspective, though it appears to promote the salutary nature of having one if we could. What is opened up, is that same understanding that mundanity is not entirely what it seems to be. At every moment there lies open a portal to the other aspect of the world, its ipsissimous transcendentality and self-overcoming. This might well be experienced as a crisis in itself, since we are so used to looking upon the world as the space of nothing other than its appearance. But this too is an error following hard upon the previous one: "The encounter with anxiety and death opens up no heavenly perspective for the self. It discovers in that encounter only its own nothingness. [ ] The fundamental human freedom is our freedom toward death" (Barrett, op. cit:154). This may take us unawares in the sense that such knowing has an "untoward" quality about it. It is almost uncanny, if the uncanny as a category of experience can be sourced in some version of the self. But the general character of that which takes us unawares is that which renders part of our everyday language momentarily meaningless, our tongues speechless, in its face. And we can also understand how the arc of contemplation also promotes a speechlessness in the face of the new knowledge that the world harbors within it the other world already and before us: "Contemplation grows out of the wreckage of other forms of knowing, other forms of being, is, in part, their wreckage. Language breaks up in it, identity breaks up, consolation is disassembled. The contemplative pulls away from what is untoward, what is implausibly certain in this knowing to bring it to light" (Lilburn, op. cit:12). There is a purpose to all of this apparent disorder and absence of method. Things falling apart right and left, before us and especially behind us. The past no longer a compass, the future no longer simply a blank slate but a disheveled mass of equally implausible possibilities. What can our human being be before this vision that contemplating things as they once were does to them once the process has begun?

What is untoward is our newly refined ignorance of things. But the arc of contemplation bends also towards the freedom that this "nothingness" of knowing the unknown nature of things as they are and beings that exist. It does not leave us "hung up" in its ether. Being aware in this way is an accomplishment not of the senses but of the sensitivities. It can easily be seen as a kind of existential "success": "Those who do succeed can hardly fail to be impressed by all that the ego does not know and never has known" (Jung, op. cit:19) But there is a price to be paid for bending ourselves to the arc of contemplation, either toward the interior of the world or that of ourselves: "This increase in self-knowledge is still very rare nowadays and is usually paid for in advance with a neurosis, if not with something worse" (ibid:19-20). We have already seen that the "death" of the self by its own living on is something both normal and necessary. It is "untoward" only in the sense of being disconcerting to the idea of the self, itself necessary to maintain a

consistent identity in the meanwhile but no mature self-understanding understands itself without the knowledge that what it has become it has become
out of another that no longer exists, either for itself or for others. When we
sometimes say to ourselves, in the wake of a loss, that this person will
maintain a belated existence in our memories or even more metaphorically in
our "hearts," we are speaking towards the unspeakably "disassembled" constructions of everyday language and its constituent supporters. Outside of
contemplating or engaging in some other form of reflection that is at least
originarily activated and calculated to begin itself, whatever passes for its
paths later on, the mundane cognition of all that there appears to be as the
world and in it allows us to keep radical transformations of being at bay. In
this sense, the world is an "escape from freedom," as it allows us to keep
ourselves from engaging in it. Thus our "freedom toward death" is, as Barrett
puts it, emblematic of human freedom in its most vivid extent, for it pushes
us to contemplate our forced renunciation of the world and of others before
the event itself occurs. We begin to sense its approach with aging, but dying
is an altogether different experience from mere aging. This is so because
"dying is also taking leave of the world. Beyond the death toward which I
advance resolutely and take hold of in advance, there is the death that comes
of itself, to take me" (Lingis, op. cit:6). This can be characterized as the
"other" death because its sudden irruption into the flow of what had just been
living and thus also alive to the world, at least in part, is representative of the
uncanny Otherness to which we must heed and about which we can know
little beforehand. It has "itself" in the same mysterious way that we, as living
beings, have ourselves. Whether or not we speak of these experiences in
terms of their relationship to a proposed essence is not of the essence. The
Otherness that death is seen to present as well as represent has its own
contemplative stance towards the world and those in it. This is not to personify. We are not imagining the shadowy agrarian figure, perhaps leaning on
his scythe before advancing to meet our advance. Surely, even in this dated
characterization, there would be some small flutter of the irresolute when we
finally got close enough to recognize what it is that is also intent on meeting
us. Our "resolution" in this life-project case is borne in a large part on not
being aware of the advance of the other and the Otherness of its advance
upon us. Whether we imagine death as something that accompanies us, a
focus of time in general, perhaps, or something that rather stalks us—though
this image is too personal given the sheer numbers of human beings walking
the earth in the same way today—we also must come to terms with it. This
means "owning" it in the manner that we also are expected to own our own
lives. As our death is inimitably part of our life, even though it brings it to a
close, we can be said to own it, or confront the ownership of it, as a necessary
piece of the thrown project that originally set us on its course. In coming to
know the ownership of life first, as it were, we become aware of the "itself"

that moves us to be in the world, and brings us back to that world after this or that flight of fancy or pause of contemplation: "The self-igniting of fire, the self-moving of the living, the coming to itself of the waking one, and the self-thinking of thinking, are all manifestations of the one *logos* that always is" (Gadamer 2001:79 [1990]). Like the social distribution of knowledge, however, the "itself" of the one who lives, thinks, awakes and falls asleep, as well as the one who dies, which is all of us, does not seem to be "distributed" in exactly the same way in every case of humanity. Whitman famously characterizes the human being as the one who must sleep and dream, amongst other activities, reminding us that the child and the criminal sleep, the soldier and the lover. But in more precise terms, we are not aware in ourselves of someone else's "itself" in the same way that they must be aware of it for themselves. This too is a clue to the elemental human freedom that does not bind us to the other in any ultimate way while we are living. We note the expression of this "essence" in others through their works, and in our modern period, Taylor suggests that we have taken perhaps too seriously the idea that originally seems to be found, equally famously, in the *Phaedrus*, where "mania" is the state of the artist—as well as the lover—that allows him or her to "see farther than the rest of us" (cf. Taylor, op. cit:22ff). Perhaps those so endowed with this version of the "itself" of Heraclitus have some foreknowledge of their own deaths. In this our own period as well, we have attempted to generalize the mania of the artist and rationalize it—as well as find rationalizations for it; everything from genetics to habituation to social class to the presence of artists already in the previous generations of family life, etc.— because the one true gift the artist has for the rest of us is not his insight *per se*, but that his works survive their author's death. It is *this* ability that we would wish to harness for ourselves: "That death is so carefully evaded is linked less to a new anxiety which makes death unbearable for our societies than to the fact that the procedures of power have not ceased to turn away from death" (Foucault, op. cit:138). Institutional discourses and the "spirals of power and desire" have combined to render death as something we must expect. To be able to face it existentially is quite a different thing than to have it called down upon us, watching over us and thus demanding that we watch over it in some systematic manner. For the idea is precisely if we can survey death, have always its approach on our personal radar, a radar that is supplied to us by the individuated knots of the net of power relations, we will be "ready" for it and thus also have the ability to do what we can to have our worldly accomplishments survive its effect upon us. For after all, it is only we who die, and not what we have done, we imagine. For some, this may be correct. Both the aesthetic sense and the rationalized sensibility take note of the same factical experience, that is: "In his typicality, common-sense man cannot make sense of the existential, but as a symbolic self, the individual is able *to become* the person capable of confronting the transcendent at the same time he remains himself in the world" (Natanson, op. cit:127, italics the text's). But while the aesthetic sense is immediately and automatically part of the symbolic world that in turn enjoins us to join with it in transcending the limits of the mundane, the rationalized sensibility demands that we construct a new symbolism of the self that is part of a larger group, institutional or political, that will survive *for us* our own deaths. Has culture not always made this claim? Perhaps, at least since the regional mode of agrarian production that understands the afterlife to be something that continues on into eternity and hence there is no return for the "soul" to another earthly life. *Perhaps this is also the origin of contemplation itself.* At least, the kind by which I transcend but also am called to transcend even when I am also called to "bend" back toward the living and the ways of the world. We certainly can imagine our most primordial ancestors pausing and thinking a specific problem out for themselves, no doubt over and over again. But such mulling is more like that found in the sciences, where a practical alternative or explanation must be found to replace something quite real that has either gone suddenly awry or is simply no longer viable given other changes which, for our early forebears, were most of the time related to the environment. But contemplation comes upon us because we at one time began to believe that the "itself" of which we were the living essence and breathing vehicle somehow continued without these earthly overtones. The undertone of such a shift in thinking about what one is surely could not have remained unnoticed on the ground, as it were. For now the ground took on a new set of symbolic apertures: at once it was the place of rest but also the process of transport. One's corporeal consciousness would be worn away to free the conscience, incorporeal and thus fully portable. To undertake one's own death is not to commit suicide in any contemporary sense, but to understand that the ground of being works the way it does because it is also the basis upon which a specific form of non-being occurs to itself, and for the first time. *Approaching this form of non-being during waking life can be called contemplation.*

This form of being-for-oneself with the world but not entirely immersed in its "publicness" or its ways or its carefreeness is, as we have seen, the more recent extension and sophistication of the primordial problem-solving mode. Not that we can ever do without the latter, we need it the more so now than ever. But we also and equally need the form that reflects upon itself as an ongoing set of tasks and not just on the problem of the day (cf. Gadamer 1996:53 [1964]). Such "tasks" have an almost infinite variety. But they include those that are solely directed toward our being in the world, and not to the world nor to the transcendence of it, nor to a specific problem or technical issue. The presence of what we are in the very moment of accomplishing something, "tasks" us with not only the work at hand and the skills and experience brought "into play" by it, but with being fully present to it. In a sense, this form of reflection is the very opposite of contemplation, for it immerses us in the dialogue extant between the task and ourselves. This is not "public," nor is it transcendent. It is neither because of its attentiveness to its own history. I cannot move on to the next step without being sure of myself that the previous one is accomplished "well enough." The task "before" me is such in this other way as well; it lies "before" me in that it has a history to which it must be loyal and from which it can issue its demands. I must then be attentive, concernful, and caring about what is "before" me in this way: "For this it is necessary to disclose the history of the covering up of the subject matter" (Heidegger, op. cit:59). Though Heidegger refers to this genealogy as a "regression," he states that it puts philosophical thought once again "before" the essential problems. So we too are "before" the task at hand in this way. It is this third sense of being before something else that opens itself up on, and up upon, the presence of the other. She stands before me—that is, she is already herself before our encounter—and she is before me in the observational sense as well. Upon the commencement of some sort of dialogue, no matter how utilitarian, steps are accomplished before other steps are taken. The trinity of "beforehands" suggests that there is also a stock of knowledge beforehand rather than simply at hand, or within such at-handedness there must be the understanding of history of what it all has meant to those who have also come before us.

But there is an even deeper issue at stake here, one that pushes its way into the primordial recesses of thought:

> It is above all necessary to understand the significance of *what is*, which in the earliest thinkers had merely been presupposed. These thinkers simply *tell* how existing things combine, how they arise, how they connect with one another. They *depict* all of this as a process, whereas the problem consists primarily in comprehending the meaning of being. (Gadamer 2000:64, italics the text's)

At once we are struck by two things: perhaps the essential meaningfulness of all things lies precisely in their process of becoming and their significance is a matter of relative context. Things may have meaning but remain insignificant. Things judged as being significant may have no "more" or "less" meaning than other things, events, people or processes. If there is a more essential kind of truth to all things, it would have to be somehow beyond or "before" these more familiar forms of meaning and significance: "The deepest truth in all things is numinous, the apophatic writers said, beyond reason, beyond language" (Lilburn, op. cit:30). Such a truth could not be considered either contextual or utilitarian, unless there is also a deeper purpose to the cosmos as a whole in which the essence of things serves in the same manner as a tool serves to bring its user before a task and thence help him complete it. This is at least possible, though all we know currently about the universe suggests that what one sees is what one gets. Once again, since Darwinian evolution is

our standard rubric in such a case, the non-teleological sensibility continues
to be our overarching guide. One might almost be tempted to call it itself a
kind of "goal." This might be ironic, but it too has the air of a morality about
it that, just because it cannot be placed in the usual sense does not mean that
it does not conceal a "deeper truth" of its own. Alienation aside, modern
humanity must build its own purposes, none of which tend to the transcendental as previously understood. What exists for us might be projected into
cosmic existence in a way no different than the metaphysics of transcendentalism was. For that matter, we are assured ethnographically that the metaphysical world system that came before that transcendental, that of transformation, did exactly the same thing.

Projections of this kind are an assertion of human freedom at the level of
conscience. But they do create a problem for self-understanding that casts its
meager light over too wide a space to begin to discern the differences between the cosmic and the human: "This self-concealing kind of philosophy is
also thereby parasitic" (Taylor, op. cit:339). Whether it is the utilitarianism
that Taylor has immediately in mind, or other rationalities of the "radical
enlightenment," the languages that posit that they are somehow beyond morality actually tend to rest on its "earlier formulations." Hence the "genealogy
of morals" is always a handy tool of making things more clear and of uncovering, not necessarily the "deepest truth," but one that lies "before" what is
being said. It is simply an ability to "ask a question" which today is always in
doubt: "The possibility of literature, the legitimation a society gives it, the
allaying of suspicion or terror with regard to it, all that goes together—
politically—with the unlimited right to ask any question, to suspect all dog-
matism, to analyze every presupposition, even those of the ethics or the
politics of responsibility" (Derrida, op. cit:28). Perhaps it is especially those
last kinds of questions that need to be asked, given the presence of "causes"
to which all can seemingly automatically pledge their undying allegiance.
Derrida rapidly moves on to say that such an uncovering of what has been
covered up—or even simply neglected by something that is by nature "parasitic"—is a "task" that comes before any future society and its future good
(cf. ibid:29ff). We must then decide what tools and skills are at hand to begin
such a task. Genealogy is certainly one of these, but so is contemplation. In
the case of concealed moralities, both are necessary. But another realm finds
itself involved in very much a friendly alliance with these two forms of
critical consciousness, and that is the world of the unconscious which itself
has a unique access to conscience and thus to the largely unconscious space
of morality: "Only unconsciousness makes no difference between good and
evil. Inside the psychological realm one honestly does not know which of
them predominates in the world. We hope, merely, that good does—i.e.,
what seems suitable to us. No one could possibly say what the general good
might be" (Jung, op. cit:53). This is the human condition in all of its impro-

visatory nakedness. One might wonder if Nietzsche himself was "twisted with the pain and fear of his own sickness," as Jung immediately suggests those who deem themselves "beyond good and evil" are, but however that might be, we are inevitably placed in a similar sphere of action: decisions must be made in the face of the unknowing and, for the moment, unknowable outcome of *any* decision. We are all of us not so much "beyond" good and evil as once again *before* it. Once action has been taken and the outcome experienced, then we may well be beyond it, at least for this specific series of events. History then in principle lies beyond morality although it too comes before it in a slightly different sense. This is true both in principle and in the daily sense of things occurring and passing before us. The incorporeality of all of these processes does not make them unreal. But their "irreality" is not lost on us. This phenomenological aspect suggests that not only are they present to us more of a structural appearance than one on the surface, but that they are also somehow askew of the general waking reality to which they bend themselves. This "bending" is not dissimilar to that we saw in action in the arc of contemplation. Consciousness can think about itself, but so can unconscious processes. The nature of their version of the contemplative to us seems chaotic and even recklessly bold, ridiculously overcompensatory and sometimes even sardonic. Anything at all to get the task of self-misrepresentation righted, we imagine. But the more serene contemplation that pushes us away from the world of norms and into the structures of what might form them is also a bold maneuver, not lacking in its look of askance, and hardly timid. The very first Fragment of Heraclitus speaks to us in a way that reminds us to link such things together that seem at first to have little to do with one another: "What human beings do while awake remains concealed from them, just as they forget what they do while asleep" (in Gadamer 2001:52 [1990]). Nietzsche's own famous, if sardonic epigram echoing this sentiment is also well taken here. Heraclitus, given our contemporary sense of the function of the unconscious, might seem to suggest that we ultimately cannot remember anything about what we do, as the world of dreams etc. helps to order and clarify what we miss in waking life, only to be forgotten again upon awakening the next morning! But this is too literal a comment on the ancient fragment. Instead, we know that the unconscious can store its own "memory" of things accomplished by the conscious life. The two of them come together in our conscience, and its "incorporeal" character is made in this way: on the one hand the unconscious is something irreal, and the contents of what had been experienced in reality are now transformed by unconscious processes such as dreaming before they are deposited as both an archive and a set of tools for the conscience to avail itself of in its being tasked with the reality of the morrow. Through this process we might be said to have the freedom of prediction within us; that is, we are able to forecast in broad terms not only what is likely to occur to us but more importantly, how we will react to it if it does (cf. Neumann, op. cit:356). It is no accident that mythology appresents the partnership as "wisdom." This metaphor contains both the apprehension of something that cannot quite be comprehended consciously, as well as the apprehensiveness that without it we would indeed be lost, and not just to the worldly forces but all the more fatally to our own passions. "Sophia," and our "philos" of her, always take precedence over their earthier versions, perhaps "Sofia and our phallus for her," if you will, because human compassion is more wise than is human passion. So "philosophy" in this more sentimental but still authenticating sense presents to us both the task before us—that of thinking oneself into being able to be in the world and then what it has meant to do so—and the task that lays before us—making decisions without the specific experience of morality to guide us; that is, as we have already stated, such acts take place before good and evil and their outcomes place the character of the acts taken beyond good and evil.

Although this language appears to take us into a "non-moral" sense of things, it is actually the deeper truth of what is inevitable and thus commonplace: "Moral insights are not explosions, interrupting all previous thought. However startling they may be, they always arise from a community, and they always aspire to go on and influence a community" (Midgely, op. cit:96). Similarly, just as philosophical reflection cannot abandon the commonplace and the quotidian lest its insights become increasingly irrelevant to the human lot which is its ultimate object if not entirely its subject, scientific reflection also must retain its implicit and sometimes explicit connection with the lives of humans in the world as it is (cf. Gadamer 1996:29 [1972]). The so-called "natural" attitude that presents us as having little more than the templates of moral suasion and normative adherence at their heart are nonetheless the iceberg tip of a cosmos of self-understanding that begins with every individual's life experience. It is the task of the human sciences to "work this up" in a way that differentiates it from the unconscious processes by which such experiences are ordered and catalogued. Both are equally necessary for the development and maintenance of human consciousness, and both are elemental pieces of the puzzling experience of human freedom. Along with imagination, rationality, contemplation, and the unconscious form the quartet of essentiality when we are placed before our own collective future. It is certainly more the case that when we move through our daily lives that we are not asked to utilize these four aspects of consciousness and thus access the deeper truths that in combination they have created. Nevertheless, daily life is shot through with the immanence of both wonder and crisis, and perhaps the two of them are not completely different from one another as we experience them. Wonder sparks the imagination and crisis calls it to arms: "Human freedom may be unique in the ways it becomes manifest, but it does have its roots in nature, and we have to able to imagine the cosmos in a fashion that is congruent with that freedom" (Barrett, op. cit:366). These "roots" originate the vista of possibility for human "nature" to bend itself towards, but they do not delineate in any narrow manner. The genius of the human species lies precisely in its ability to overcome and overtake its own nature, though in usually a halting and step-wise fashion. It is an astonishing achievement, even given the extended geological time period of our evolution and growth, because all around us we see in all other creatures that we know something about, an apparent stasis. Certainly we see the physiological evolution in the fossil record, just as we see our own. But what is missing is that "superorganic" element, as Kroeber called it, that cultural and symbolic and meaning-making apparatus that, however much dissension it also causes in the social world, nevertheless allows us to transcend in a Darwinian vision of contemplation, most of the sources of our collective nature: "The development of the human being is not fixed and is not dependent on the whole of the naturally given conditions it is subject to. The human being has the ability to think, to raise himself above these conditions, and to entertain a multitude of possibilities" (Gadamer 2000:99). Some of these arc towards an abstraction that makes their relevance questionable with regard to our daily conditions. This much we know from having to sort through the symbolic literatures and scientific discourses of every epoch to which we have some historical or archaeological access. But the imagination must ascend to these ionospheric realms simply to balance the tasks that are always before it and for which we *do* have much already at hand. It is likely, given our modern predilections, that "possibility" is indeed all we have access to, and that there are no deeper truths about the human condition beyond our ability to not only imagine but also act to overcome what we are today in lieu of the knowledge of the future. This is itself a wondrous experience, though it might not claim to utter a truth beyond its own self-understanding. But such a truth itself partakes in the abstract accomplishments of that self-same arcing imagination that sometimes promotes the dubiously relevant as the ultimately profound, and insofar as such truths help us speak into being who we are in relationship to a cosmos that must be understood as "congruent" with our freedom, they are not at all irrelevant but highly significant and meaningful. This is something we may say of all human thought, but especially that which finds itself being played out in the world, relevant or not: "The urgent need that there is, in studying social change, to understand what other people think they are doing—to grasp the advantage that they see in what they do" (Midgely, op. cit:71), places a task before us that is doubly interesting because it consists of other people's tasks that they are already working on and thinking about. There is nothing of the transcendental to be found. But neither is the sense that humans are experiencing their lives in the mundane world as fraught with challenge to be dismissed as only part of a quotidian life meriting no further comment. If we do this, we are no better

than the technician whose only skill is routinized competence and whose
imagination has been limited by his professional training: "Against them
philosophy must prove itself the most advanced consciousness—permeated
with the potential of what could be different—but also a match for the power
of regression, which it can transcend only after having incorporated and
comprehended it" (Adorno 1998:16 [1969]). Here we see all of the elements
that we have deemed necessary for the arts of being human to continue
without the nullity of the "last men" taking over in a more or less permanent
fashion. The "possibility of what could be different" is the key to any ad-
vancement of consciousness, that holism containing both the unconscious,
the conscious and its synthetic conscience, now increasingly something that
we must construct on our own as the task *within* us. We also note the appearance of both reflective thought in philosophy and the contemplative form of
reflection found to "transcend" what currently is the case. Note too that we
are not expected to overcome "what is," in the sense that Gadamer was
speaking of with regard to the first thinkers simply nodding in its direction
and calling instead to mind processes of becoming. No, such processes that
are experienced and many of which that can also be observed by ourselves
and others alike, are now to be considered as at the very least the majority
part of what is essential, for it is also pragmatically essential that they be
questioned, played out, worked upon, and given as a task to others who will
follow hard upon us. Not that we wish to delimit the future freedom of our
children. But we must impress upon them nevertheless that such freedom that
is humanly possible is only possible through imagining something that is not
the case. We have seen, most especially in the history of science, the wonder
at discovering that what was thought not even to be possible at all in fact
becomes not only possible but also real. This in itself should provide enough
evidence that the human imagination is the essence of "what is," and that
these processes are mostly something that is worked on, and works upon us,
within the soul of the intellect.

6.3 LIBERTY'S PIROUETTE

Now in spite of the reassurances we may feel at this point regarding the
"natural" human ability not only to be within freedom but also to create it,
there are some important questions remaining. First of all, one would like to
be able to do more than speculate about the character of freedom and the
experience of being free; what if both, depending on the context, are part of a
wider delusion that, though not taking us backward in the direction of some
kind of metaphysical determinism, nevertheless shred our sense of the future
by reminding us of the dead weight of human history. We must begin this
section by asking: "Are our philosophies, then, merely the inevitable out-

come of the body of fate and personal circumstance that is thrust upon each of us?" (Barrett 1979:4). Yes, but perhaps not quite in the manner Barrett imagines it doing so. First, our circumstances, fated or no, place us in the environment where certain tasks appear before us, as we saw above. The efforts put forth to negotiate and grapple with such situations is an exercise in human freedom, and there is nothing beyond the task itself that dictates our response to it. Unless we buy back completely a graven determinism in which each of our actions and even our thoughts is predestined without our knowing it, we can dismiss the first part of Barrett's question as a kind of pseudo-problem. They are an outcome, but not an inevitable one. The inevitability of the weight of circumstance, which is our contemporary definition of fate in any case, provides the starting point for human becoming, not its end point. If we are to be regarded as being able to freely think things through, then the whole matter of what thought consists of and why is up for grabs. "Beliefs" actually tend to be something that are inherited, so their effect on the "self-creating" responses of each individual may be fairly constraining. In saying so, we are to some extent reversing Barrett's language. It is not belief *per se* that allows for freedom directly. It rather tends to range itself against creative becoming and the freedom associated with it as an experience of moving away from one's starting beliefs and cultural imperatives. Taylor reminds us that the "free-thinker" was originally the definition of the "libertine" a term that for the last century or so has suggested someone who is morally reprehensible in some way (cf. op. cit:335). No doubt the two of these definitions are related, for one must strike free of morality in order to think. If some of the actions proceeding from such newly freed thoughts have to do with forms of licentiousness, this remains only one department of improvisation, and hardly a very important one at that. So overcoming one's morality does not necessarily mean that one's morals are "loosened up" to any criminal extent. It likely means that the person in question does not take as formally or as seriously some of the limitations certain moral strictures might demand, but it is more than likely that the person given to free thinking is also thinking about his ability to continue to do so. Imprisonment or other negative social sanction would seem to hamper this ability.

So much for this first assay. Circumstance is just as much an occasion for freedom as it is a proscription of it. If we go much further back, to the beginnings of Western thinking, when first the idea of thought must have arisen precisely against the mythic sensibility where we imagine things were much more "set in stone," we find Heraclitus telling us that we indeed cannot and do not rely on the divine to make decisions as human beings. This is at once liberating but also makes us prone to error: "Heraclitus sees the power of illusions that each of us has about ourselves—just as he correctly sees that human fate is not stamped upon us by the divine guidance of a 'daimon' but rather by the proper guidance of life ('ethos')" (Gadamer 2001:78 [1990]).

Life presents itself as an open book. We are fated to live and die; the book-ends of life are not ours to choose. But in the meanwhile, be it lengthy or brief, the long and short of it is that we must make decisions based on the perception and experience we have of what lives, including ourselves. To conclude this before we embark is of course impossible. It is something that occurs to us gradually, gaining ground with each time we invent or alter the circumstances given around us, sometimes also altering others lives in ways that they might not have expected, and then expecting some of this being presented back to us in return. Over time, the conclusion concerning the fundamental possibility of freedom takes hold over us and we become, if not less prone to illusion *per se*, at least more willing to take the chance that thinking accords us. This "essence" cannot be seen as the host of all that is culturally determined and then somehow made immutable by its archiving in the vehicle of conscience, real or imaginary. We do not know how to think and act in every situation ahead of time. Only the most basic social scripts are acted out in this way, their auto-pilot giving us the leeway to not only be content with observing our own action as if in a semi-conscious state but also providing a more general contentment that befalls us when we are not re-quired to take any working or effectively historically conscious action. "We" includes our "soul" psyche, anima and animus, etc. We do not operate separ-ately from it, or if we do, if we act without conscience in the world, we no longer are considered by others to be fully human, and rightly so, given the actions that follow from those whose conscience has deserted them, or vice-versa. Now this is not to be able to say of what a "proper" and well-directed conscience consists, we can only compare our actions and intents with the locale of our cultural upbringing and the "average" run of things within it. Like keeping up with traffic, we are likely immune from being "inoculated" by a police patrol simply because everyone is driving the same speed. That this average can be significantly above posted limits and still "safe," at least in the legal sense of the word, is an accepted norm to which even the police have had to accept for most of each month of surveillance. So far more than official norms that are inherited by us, it is the actions of the majority of others—in the case of speeding, freely choosing to do so with the rationale of "keeping up"—that provide the template for how much improvisation will be tolerated in each ensuing context. This is a sociological chestnut, and would not be worth dwelling on except for the lingering sense that we sometimes have that freedom must be also beyond these normative actions, must be so radical as to break free of all previous human action. This, aside from being nonsense, is also not possible for a human being who, like her peers, has constructed herself, after being constructed, around the norms and forms of the local lifeworld. What is a much graver threat to the possibility of freedom is not so much social norms, paid heed to more or less by others and by ourselves when and if current circumstances warrant—and note here, we did *not* say, when and if morality warrants or history, for that matter—but by the rationalization process of modernity. It is reasonable, if a bit old hat, to reiterate here that our interest in freedom, growing worldwide every day, is such that it attempts to match the equally rapid growth of rationalized models of conduct and production. This demand presented and then often enforced by the overwhelming presence of technique, and perhaps also the overween-ing and coinciding presence of the technician, we have already met in detail in a previous chapter. Here, we must go beyond the critique of mechanism to see just how far this very mechanism has influenced our notions of freedom: "This represents a fundamental alteration in our life. It is the more remark-able in so far as it is a question of scientific-technical progress as such than of resolute rationality in the application of science, which overcomes with a new uninhibitedness the durability of custom as well as the restraints present within 'world view.'" (Gadamer 1996:9 [1972]). It is one thing to note with appreciation that a hydroelectric project functions in China as well as it does in Canada, without respect to linguistic boundaries or "worldviews." This in itself appears to be mundane, but what it represents, as Gadamer is keen to help us understand, is something utterly new in the history of humankind. A language that overcomes the problem of Babel is one that makes the world the same for all of us. This language is that of the mathematical sciences, and in its application, the rationality of its logic and the practicality of its sensibil-ity become our rationality and our sensibility. But if there is a bright side to this event—we can share practices and a larger worldview that includes what we can know of the cosmos as a collective enterprise of human perception—there is also another side that continues to be bathed in shadows. And these shadows are not merely those it casts on the external world of culture. The recesses of individuality and "privacy" are also made subject to its tech-niques and technologies: "But let us ponder all the ruses that were employed for centuries to make us love sex" (Foucault, op. cit:159). The same kinds of forces of discourse that create resource based power and transform the world into a safer and healthier place are the same that have turned sex into sexual-ity and created a world, through the application of the theories of genius to the tools of self-centeredness and fear based on the worst aspect of every human worldview such scientific languages were supposedly overcoming, a much more dangerous place. So dangerous that fundamental human freedom is threatened with extinction both before and after any potential apocalypse. Such discourses developed a measure for anything, so we thought, and we have all lived through an age of measurement; of our faculties and perhaps even of our moralities. The critiques of these discourses are largely unnoticed or considered, ironically, the space of intellect untested and untried and thus unreliable or at least suspicious: "As soon as the intelligence tests are really tested, they turn into a set of paper-pen operations hardly testing, and still less measuring, either intelligence or other mental properties of human beings" (Sorokin, op. cit:80). Morality and sociality, the two things that tests of these kind seek to either expunge from their evaluations or further, to make normative according to a singular and technical "worldview" that is hardly deserving of that title—the middle-class managerial view constructed over the course of the twentieth century, a refinement of the nascent bourgeois ideals of that previous, where schooling and education is considered a good in itself and the Protestant Ethic predominates in the workplace; where democracy hinges only on voting and self-interest and protest is considered at the very least in bad taste; and most importantly here, where conformity in all things public and hypocrisy in all things private delineate how one can "be free"—and ignores any philosophical interest in any of these topics and many others to be merely a distraction or yet subversive. But we nevertheless ask "what about Kant's assertion that freedom is a necessary condition for a human being to be a moral and social person?" (Gadamer 2000:27). Indeed, in a world where randomness is presented as a kind of "freedom," the indeterminacy of certain aspects of the fundamental cosmic construction, because they escape the precision required by a neo-positivist scientific discourse, are somehow free of rationality and can be considered thus the sub-atomic equivalents of the insane. Gadamer reminds us that Kant's, and for that matter, many other thinkers' definitions of human freedom departs from such "non-determinacy of phenomena" (ibid). Yet at the same time we are forced to a new awareness regarding the stance and scope of freedom that was not part of the conversation in earlier epochs, and which Kant and his fellow enlightenment thinkers had only the first tastes thereof historically. The discourses of control and proliferation of norms are one thing with which we must contend. But what of the real sense that our quality of life continues to gradually improve? Who wants to build and staff the barricades of rebellion in the face of the comforting notion that life is all the *more* easier the more one conforms to the going rate and indeed, follows this view wherever it goes, matching its rate of progression? What price is worth so much more than that of peace of mind? It is precisely how we define both peace and mind that are at stake. At present, a few have the first and even fewer the second, if one considers the world picture instead of the "worldview," and if one considers that to have a mind in today's public world is first and foremost to have an audience, a market, an agent, a network. If there is a "mind" behind all of that apparatus then that is a happy coincidence, and not at all an impossible one. But what of all the "other minds" extant? Such a phrase now carries within it far more than even Husserl saw as a challenge for us. We must ever recall that "freedom means *freedom* for the false also, so planning includes power to do the senseless" (Lösch, op. cit:353, italics the text's). And thus our planning must also plan for the senseless to occur, as we will see in the conclusion. We also must plan ahead in a manner that does not assume the truth will appear before us as part of the task at hand or even as a definitional part of our freedom. But it is equally true that untruth and un-thought are also imbricated within the ambit of human freedom and cannot be dissuaded to leave its harbor: "We must be free for the truth; and con-versely, to be able to be open toward the truth may be our deepest freedom as human creatures. [ ] Truth harbors within itself, the tragic possibilities for untruth because of its intrinsic connection with freedom" (Barrett, op. cit:165). In the most basic manner we are asked as children to distinguish what "really happened" from our evasive fictions or wonder-filled fantasies. This distinction is difficult for young people, and not only because we have not been completely saturated with the socialization of normative and disci-plinary discourses. We, at a more fundamental level, have not had enough experience to understand that categories of human experience not only over-lap but that it takes perceptual work to contrast them and reflect upon them. Children cannot "contemplate" their actions, especially before they take them. They also have difficulty knowing that freedom is always couched in the moral language of obligation, simply because their experience of freedom is one of non-responsibility and thus carries within it no real knowledge of otherness. It is the responsibility to an other, as we have seen, that most clearly delineates the scope and limits of freedom. The problem here is not that children will never know this, but that those of us who continue to know it incompletely as adults have the tendency to gravitate towards those profes-sions that are purely technical. The less "sociality and morality" that is present within us, the more comfort we take in the technical spheres. Here, where there really are correct and incorrect responses to every situation, human freedom loses its meaning. As well, responsibility to human others is occluded in our labor to "keep things running." The power generated by technical discourses carries within it its own version of authority, but to link them too exclusively would be a serious error. For authority is never only power, just as freedom does not occur solely in opposition to authority: "Genuine freedom, on the other hand, is the capacity to criticize, and this capacity to criticize includes and is a precondition both of our own recogni-tion of the superior authority of others and of others' recognition of our own authority" (Gadamer 1996:123 [1983]). *Freedom is thus the dialectic of di-alogue.* It is the edge over which ideas must be run. It tells us where our guts are in that it spills the life-blood of our ideas onto the table of values at hand, which itself becomes stained with the living entrails and viscous vitals of human experience, such that it cannot pretend to be mere stone. Freedom seen in this more guttural and experiential light itself cannot then be used as either a dogmatic call to arms in the face of generalized and vague "author-ity" or as an ideological banner to uphold it. It should be understood, rather as the ability to retain what is open and imaginative about childhood without the dross of inexperience or naivety: "Creativity means an unforeseen, mas-terly realization of a new discovery, hitherto unknown and unpredicted. It is always a miracle, unexpected and often undreamed of by any except the creator. Sometimes it is a surprise even for the creator himself" (Sorokin, op. cit:258). This is not to say the exact opposite of Midgely when she stated, as above, that discoveries are not as "explosive" as they are sometimes deemed. This too is true. Nevertheless, the factor of wonder associated with the results of "free-thinking" or the so-called "pure" research is not to be underestimated. They, more than any other adult activity, take us back to the world of the child, where everything is wondrous and undreamed of and unexplored. That others have explored it historically is also no blockade put up against our new experience of them. The first time we hear what is actually a famous piece of music, gaze upon a well-known art work, or read a canonical novel is a discovery, for us as individuals, equal to the discovery of the unforeseen. This is where power and authority are actually in their closest proximity. And not because we necessarily know ahead of time that this is how we *should* feel about it. The canon has already dictated our feelings, or that the mere name of the composer carries all before it. No, we come to the new as new ourselves. We do not know whether or not these freedoms extend the historical reality in which we find ourselves, but that such a question is able to be asked in the light of freedom is itself a sign that freedom is nonetheless present in both our individual and collective history (cf. Gadamer 1996:51 [1964]). Perhaps the openness of this limit-situation is both an appearance and a reality at the same time, pending always the outcome of our ruminations or our wonder. We are sometimes carried beyond the normative limits of thinking in the same way as we may imagine ourselves transported to another culture or time period, perhaps to that of the author, painter, composer, thinker, or chronicler. Or it may be that we find within ourselves an opening "hitherto unforeseen and unexpected," where we ourselves leap over the limits that have either been imposed upon us by the local definitions of proper thought and conduct, or at least equally, those we have imposed upon ourselves.

In doing so, we create a new meaning for ourselves and have an ongoing opportunity to review this meaning in the light of yet further experiences, not all of which must be ethereal or intense. Life lived to its fullest includes the otiose as much as it includes the wondrous, and it is another error of our times to believe that the most fulfilled life is the one that has the highest octane. It is rather, and more simply and democratically, the one that has the highest amount of meaning *per capita*, and human meaning may be made in a multitude of ways. What it does require, however, is an ability to compare experience across the most broad spectrum possible, so this in itself obviates any sense that one needs to "live to the maximum" every moment of the day, or live as if there were no tomorrow. People who do this in fact tend to run reckless across the ability of others to live the next day: "The freedom of any individual life is thus inseparably bound with the presence or absence of some sense of meaning in that life." (Barrett, op. cit:86). For human consciousness, the ability to reflect both rationally and contemplatively, about the problem at hand or about the most esoteric abstraction is the key to making meaning. This is not something that is inherited from nature *per se*, but it is a definitional component of what we refer to as "human nature," though we should not then suppose that this phrase connotes any singularity or doxic prescription as to either the best or the uniquely solitary: "Freedom is not a fact of nature but rather [ ] a fact of reason, something we must think, because without thinking of ourselves as free we cannot understand ourselves at all. Freedom is the fact of reason" (Gadamer 2001:123 [1978]). It is also the fact that reason exists, or is at least, recognized as part of our thinking consciousness that we cannot do without, whether at the moment we consider ourselves to "be" or "feel" free or not. We do not, in fact always place first the act and art of thinking ourselves free in any conscious manner. But in thinking itself, we enact freedom in the clearest possible manner. This is why all fascisms of thought and action seek not to expunge freedom itself, but to negate the power of thinking, to expunge *thought*. For freedom automatically follows thought in the same way as slavery follows unthought. All thinking is revolutionary to all forms of fascism, and the "dogmaticism" of the fascist only holds in so far as he is able to clear our minds of anything but the focused drone of his own drama. This focus itself takes away the meaning of dogma that we saw originally also held within it the openness to the unknown or unknowable. It was the presumption that something was inherently unknowable that gave "dogma" its dogmatic visage. Today, the dogma of fascism promotes the idea that things are unknowable because the art of knowing itself should not be exercised.

To think then foments revolution, and not merely in the political sense (cf. Taylor, op. cit:364 for the apparent radicality of the influence of modern thought). Its power does not rest in its capacity for uttering the speech of world-historical events, such as political or intellectual changes. It consists, rather, by marshaling at its core the forces of an existential realization. Though it is of the utmost utility to believe in freedom as the mode of being corresponding to thought, it is hardly sufficient to simply suggest that thinking produces evidence of itself through its act alone. No, thinking produces freedom in as much as freedom is extant, is nascent, when we take up a problem for reflection. Though it is true to say that "Thus it is to our practical advantage to believe that we are free beings, and our subjective decision in the matter does have objective consequences in our life" (Barrett, op. cit:282), this is to merely cast the relationship between freedom and thought in the mode of the "Thomas Theorem," where "if one believes something is real it is real in its consequences." The more so that "Faith in freedom produces future facts that confirm it" (ibid), the more "real" such consequences of our faith becomes. But this is to say no more about freedom than can be said about every human affair, culture and norms most especially. And just like our faith in norms leveraging the dogma and sometimes even the fascism of the belief in their metaphysical foundation where none can be demonstrated, faith in freedom suggests to us that it is a fact of nature. This irony actually has the ultimate effect of impinging upon freedom, because we are led to believe that there is a specific architecture that is the hallmark of its structure, that it is designed to be used in a certain manner. The very context-based and improvisatory "definition" of human freedom ranges itself against this idea. At the same time, faith in the "existence" of freedom may as well suggest a lack of responsibility or concernfulness on our parts, since freedom is "there" anyway and available for our use at any time. We can never "lose" our freedom and, from another related perspective, are thus famously "condemned to freedom." This too is a limiting understatement of the meaning of human freedom. Instead, we can think of freedom as not having to do with faith *per se*, but rather work, and this term is not to be taken in any utilitarian or productive sense. It is a human ability and not a human actuality unless and until it actually occurs in the world. The immediacy of what we think we want lies ensconced in the norms of the day. It is not thought, but response to "the want" of the now and of the present only. Thinking takes time, and needs to give itself the time to think. The want, or for many, the actual need, sabotages this ability and leaves its actuation unfulfilled. In this, any human ability might not as well exist at all, so to "have faith" in one or the other of our faculties is at best a *post hoc* addendum that may help us get the job done *once it is started*, but not before: "The ability to behave theoretically is in itself part of the practice of humankind. It is clear without further ado that it was the 'theoretical' gift of humanity which made it possible for human beings to establish distance from the immediate aims of their desires" (Gadamer 1996:5 [1972]). Exercising the capacity for thought means "putting off" the action of the now, whatever its demands on us may be present. This is another patent trick of all forms of fascism: keep people busy so that they do not have time to think. The automated surveillance of schoolroom, homework, the so-called "extra-curricular" activities which in fact are as very much part of the official curricula as is any classroom experience, make sure that young people do not exercise either freedom or thought, much less begin to relate the two of them together. Though it may not "up to the philosopher [ ] to prove that freedom exists; he simply notes, describes, and analyzes the ways in which it does occur" (Barrett, op. cit:293), it does tend to be very much up to the thinker to engage in thinking. The tragedy here is that she is forced to engage in it on behalf of others who are, by their own native wit, as fully capable of it as she. But like anything human, practicing an activity is what makes it the more real. *Work*, not faith, produces the "real consequences" of the events of thought and the experience of projecting an intent into the world. Just as "Not every time needs to have a grand philosophical system" (Heidegger, op. cit59), not every moment of a human life needs to have a grand purpose, philosophical or otherwise. It is equally "real," and also of great consequence, to recognize that the effort of work is indeed an effort, and one that does not either go on forever in principle or that we must continue to produce the effects of these efforts in a shared social reality without regard for others or, for that matter, imagining that we do so without their aid. Though it is correct to say that opportunity to engage in thought is sorely lacking in our current society or rationalized discourses and techniques, even the practical utility of these base techniques required some thought to both produce and sometimes even maintain. We do not need, then, to imagine that it is because we think that the world stops for us and thinks as well, nor—and this may be more likely given the focus of the thinker and his corresponding and ironic parochiality precisely due to his necessary focus— that the world cannot think without us. To realize this is to recognize our efforts without the vanity of pretending that we *must* make such an effort only because others cannot: "This is not singlemindedness, but feeling the weight of all that has happened at one's back, the uninterest, the incapacity for, negotiation of this weight" (Lilburn 1999:64). The proverbial "weight of the world" may be "at the back" of the thinker, but this provocatory conceit is more like the conceit of faith itself, in that we use it as an *aide-memoire* to get us where we want to go. It is akin to the desire of the now, for it presents itself as the living presence of the present. We feel the weight because we *want* to feel it or because, more egotistically, we take ourselves to be the self-styled artist who *can* feel the weight in this way and indeed, we might become so habituated to it that we eventually can feel it in no other way. All of this is predicated on the romantic idea that thought is rare. But in fact the rarity of thinking is an empirical affair; one that can be demonstrated in the world of forms and one that has about it an objectifying language of argument and interpretation, dialogue and dialectic. It is not rare in the manner of being rarified, or subject to rarefaction. That a fraction of us engage in it is no evidence for its aesthetic purity, its elite status. Indeed, the cultural elites of our society have taken it upon themselves to preserve thought as an object of their self-veneration, rather than open it onto the world. This is not only an error, but because it is often calculated in order to sell thought as a commodity to those who apparently cannot think for themselves, or at least do not have the time to write books about it—and who is the majority audience of actual readers, and not consumers, for such books if not other members of the cultural elite?—it is a scandal. For "Our freedom is the way in which we are able to let the world open before us and ourselves stand open within it" (Barrett, op. cit:262). To sequester the act of freedom as well as the act that produces freedom, is its source, is to close off both the world and ourselves to one another, and to close these off to others who have not had the opportunity to practice it themselves. The fact that neither freedom nor thought in themselves are at all remarkable for human consciousness is thus lost (cf. Natanson, op. cit:63). Part of this "appearance" that we are often so concerned with making is that ability to give the appearance that we have thought things through. We have not, in other words, simply "appeared" and thus have the expectation that others either do our thinking for us or that there is no thinking to be done. Instead, making an appearance constitutes the occasion for thinking. We have presented ourselves within the living-presence of possibilities and we are thus to be accounted for, apprehended, and comprehended within its range of potentialities (cf. Lingis, op. cit:124). There is a strong, if unexpected element of mimicry involved in this process. Others have demonstrated both their own freedom and the possibility and potential of ours. What they have accomplished "endures" in this manner more so than in the manner of an object. We quite literally can copy their action, if not attain their results. But in this mimicry there is more than flattery or the hope that I too can become as they are or were already. For I realize that these others, historic or obscure, are not at all "this" way unless they have themselves first done the same thing I do, and then practiced it as I am doing. The pedagogic force of this realization is profound: it cannot be that I either must master thought or that it remains the master of me; I engage in it and it engages me. History too functions most "effectively" and "consciously" in this manner: it does not survey my petty triumphs with disdain, but encourages by its ongoing presence in the currency of the lifeworld me to work further and think things through in as detailed manner as possible given my own experiences and access to resources, including those more strictly defined as historical. But ultimately, I must turn to myself for the source of myself: "Reflection, the free process of turning in on oneself, *appears* as the highest form of freedom that exists at all. Here the mind is properly in its own element in so far as it relates solely to its own content. It is undeniable that this freedom in relation to oneself, this original distance, does characterize an essential feature of being human" (Gadamer 1996:50-1 [1964], emphasis mine). We turn to ourselves, and not on ourselves. Thinking as either rational reflection or aesthetic contemplation or yet the work of conscience, does not assail the mind for it is its soul of source and content. It does not mind a puzzle, it does not become offended with its own confusion or pedantry of logic. It minds itself in the way that we sometimes feel that someone has given "soul" to the object of art, the art work, or even the social scene. Thus it can be said that "aesthetics and ethics are one and the same" not with any reference to their internal logic or their lack of availability as useful signifiers with a polyglot of functions, but because they participate in the act of turning in on oneself, as does the sleeper with a view to working out the conscious contents of the day. We thus dream while awake; these phantasms are also the work of the mind, but within range of all that has consciously presented itself. It may sometimes attain greater insights than the unconscious, and sometimes it just as assuredly will fall short of what can be accomplished by the sleeper who awakes refreshed precisely because the mind has continued to work in the absence of full consciousness. The freedom of thought is echoed and foreshadowed by the freedom of the dreamer. We say, somewhat pejoratively, that the one who only dreams does not accomplish much; hence the conscious one who is a "dreamer" is perhaps not a "doer" and incurs our puzzled dismay. But given the "heritage of potentialities," even the daydreamer has her place, for she views the world from a free point unassailed by either self-recrimination or the sense that she must limit herself to the plausible and the actual: *"Here the view is free.* It may be the nobility of the soul when a philosopher is silent; it may have be love when he contradicts himself; and he who has knowledge may be polite enough to lie" (Nietzsche 1954:551 [1888], italics the text's). That dreams, whether by day or night, *work* out the experience of the consciously held and the semiconsciously accepted tells us that even when we are most engrossed in the technical or the utilitarian, the mundane or the routine, other aspects of human consciousness are still at work and exercising their freedom to be so. This work, the act of what is *faithless* in itself and yet never unfaithful, is the calling card of humanity as well as the stepping stone on the way to becoming a humane being in a world of humanity. We may desire the immediacy of a "definite end," as Lösch states, but we also live in a world that makes no distinction between means and ends. "Here the view is free," but most especially free of the problem of self-recognition that desires itself to be recognized for what it does in lieu of what it imagines others not being able to do. *There*, the view is ultimately unfree because it concerns itself about the absence of thought and the presence of unthought: "It is otherwise when we live everything instead of separating means and ends; when we rejoice in the game, surrender ourselves completely—only those can do so who are free of desire and filled with love. There are two worlds, and we are wanderers between them" (Lösch, op. cit:184). These two worlds, one Apollonian, rational, focused, and *ad hoc*, and the other Dionysian, exuberant, spontaneous, unfettered by what is at hand, are equally necessary to human freedom. One is the freedom of the other, so that both can be free from themselves.

Conclusion

Non-Sense: Making Sense of Nonsense

In any demythology of modernity we are faced with the problem of incompleteness. We do not know what will yet occur in an age we can continue to call our own. The "post-modern" can be said to merely be the realization that we are indeed, modern, in the same way that the "death of god" was only noted long after it actually occurred. We must ask, why these myths, and how do they make sense together? There are undoubtedly some other lists, but the suspects of self, machine and god, joined by the senses of home, love and freedom, seem to present a powerful suite of suasions for any person living in contemporary society. They have an intuitively present sense about them. They wear this sensibility on their sleeves, and yet it still retains a touch of the uncanniness, like an aura, that hovers about them. They have also preserved some of their jewels of their past glories, and in some cases glory not quite past. These gems preside over their own presence, reminding us that we cannot take them entirely lightly even today. Certainly they do not all "get along" with one another, but like any family with more than one sibling, their squabbles and divided loyalties stem from the fact that they share the same parents; the mythic and the practical, two persona that would hardly seem to be the soul mates that were proclaimed as being meant for one another at the very origins of primordial human consciousness. This first marriage, long before that of any garden, set in motion the evolution of all cultures in all places and like the background radiation of the big bang, we sense this motion still.

It remains for us then to examine the ways in which the siblings produced by this union have presented themselves to their hosts as both being sensible and able to make sense. We will find that in these two senses there is also conflict, and indeed we will suggest that in order to maintain our senses about them—a cautious but respectful distance, perhaps, and a suspicious and healthy skepticism—we may have to sometimes abandon the idea that they should always be harnessed as sense-making narratives and conceptualizations. In some cases of modern life, we may simply have to stop making sense in order to start being sensible. With this in mind, these final but lengthy two sections will serve to open up a new vista of dialogue and dialectic regarding what we might be able to expect from our continued reliance on these six salient sibling ideas, and how to avoid some of the errors associated with their use; errors by which we continue to live and die.

STOP MAKING SENSE

First of all, though we have selected arguably the six most likely suspects according to their predominance in our Western cultural consciousness over the past couple of centuries, their very presence in history is not an accident. They themselves do not refer to specific things in the object realm, nor do they occupy any particular space in the world. They are, in a word, concepts used to "make sense" of the combined effects of all the accidents of history, all the efforts of consciousness, and all the outcomes of the junctures of the two. They are abstractions because they do not appear before us as singular entities. Even if we continue to believe the mythical self as one thing, there are still a multitudes of selves represented by other persons. There is no one machine, no one god or if so, God does not occur to us in any one form or manifestation of himself. There is no one home for all, no one love that lasts a lifetime, and no specific moment or place where freedom reigns unadulterated and thus can never occur to us or anyone else in any other way. None of these connotations of such concepts can exist, even if we hold to all of them clearly and dearly, or whether, with full realization that they are error ridden and make us prone to error, we try to cast them aside. Either way, we are transfixed by them at first. The one adoring and desiring to be more intimate with "them," the other equally focused on getting rid of them. No, they are but renditions of *typical* experiences for human beings, even though this term cannot be taken to refer always to the otiose and the routine: "Typification, as we have tried to present it, is not reductionistic; it is an accomplishment of cognition and a victory of affective intelligence" (Natanson 1970:119). Our categories are very important to us. Cross-culturally, the schism of self-recognition that is usually cut from whole cloth when we encounter both specific others as well as the abstraction of the generalized other within our own society is all the more felt as something radical because the categories of thinking and doing have been altered. The "Ministry of Small Ball Games" in Beijing is barely recognizable in the West. It calls for a parallax of perspective to comprehend what is going on. What balls are included? When does a small ball become a mid-size ball? Table tennis, golf, racquetball, tennis and perhaps others are part of the same category here. And indeed, when we step outside of our usual schemes, we can see how some other culture might group such trivial activities together. Such an example does not present a very serious affront to our own cherished way of thinking about the world, but there are many much more profound threats abounding in the world of cultural diversity, including genital mutilation, beheadings concerning religious preferences, the wanton destruction of world heritage sites and the like. Whose heritage? Whose daughters? Whose Gods? Now these kinds of recategorizations *are* truly disturbing to us. No one really worries about whether or not the Chinese public funding of sport follows these rails or those. But of the moment, many other concerns leap to the fore of any list of typifications that are present in our shared world. They have the cumulative effect of demanding of us the questions, "Just how shared is this world you say is ours"?

Their very presence seems to obviate any easy responses to such questions. Even if the best use of typification avoids reductionism, a very common use of it seeks it. In doing so, it allows the errors of categories to be magnified far beyond what they need to be to live, and especially, to live together. At the same time, Western categories, though they have spread around the globe, carry with them their own parochial rationality, as well as a conceit that states that they can replace all other forms as well as improve upon existing forms of thought (cf. Gadamer 1996:21 [1972]). The very expression of what we see today as threats not only to our society but to our imagined general moral principles—cultures have destroyed the efforts of other cultures throughout history and we retain, through our high technology, the "right" to destroy all cultures within a day or so; perhaps what has changed is that most of us consider this to be a present evil, whereas in the past there appears to have been no such scruple—come out of the outrage that others feel about those very conceits and delusions. The negotiation and dialogue amongst diverse cultures may not bring anyone infinite joy, but it does tend to keep things rolling along without as much sorrow. To ignore this option, also always just as present and useable as our weapons of destruction, primed and ready, is to commit oneself too closely to the categories of one's own background and to allow their "radiation" to needlessly permeate the world picture. The half-life of such radiation is not only unknown, it has the ability, as if it were an organic agency, to mutate in the meanwhile, making future versions of it potentially unrecognizable to us. We might be able to contain it from time to time, as it comes within our technical purview, but as Lösch suggests of the already "dismal science," "it would degenerate into a contemptible or even destructive science if it were to consider tolerable and degenerate mass phenomena in the same way simply because both are common and actual" (1967:363-4 [1945]). This is a serious question for us: what can we tolerate about the world as it is and what must we, in spite of our best efforts at rational cultural relativism, maintain as degenerate? Clearly there are things that we will not put up with in theory—though we continue put up with them in a pinch, that is, when we feel too much of the pinch of the reality of going out and having to stop them—and then there are things that we might very well possess ourselves in our own home-made versions. We might be more apt to ignore these flaws and foibles in others if we recognize ourselves as participating in them, though there also seem to be few limits on our potential hypocrisies regarding these issues. But it is at least likely that we might very well believe in these flaws, and hence are gratified when they do show up in people we thought were so different from us. Whether masses or elites, such "dogmas" have "infected us with their ease of convivial convenience" (cf. Sorokin 1956:304). If we attempt to justify our categories at all, it is through some rather cynical politics of being able to both technically and economically push our way into the regions of another's consciousness and set up shop. We do not see it as a communal home, or even a shared domicile. Our typification of the world by definition extends into the hearts and hearths of the other, and we can rationalize this world historical dynamic by stating both our moral categories and our way of life as being universally the one best way.

At the same time, we have seen so many critiques concerning the problem of globalization we must push ourselves into these arguments and try to understand what favor they carry with them, what kind of rationality they employ against rationality. The only other so discussed aspect of the West, and indeed one that other cultures find either degenerate or even intolerable, is our ongoing auto-fetishism concerning sexuality. It extends itself cross-culturally and intrudes on everything, rightly or wrongly—hence the dismay over cultural practices which delimit it in any way—and it continues to occupy us at the expense of the actual populations of Western countries, all of which are falling, sometimes precipitously: "We conceal from ourselves the blinding evidence, and that what is essential always eludes us, so that we must always start out once again in search of it" (Foucault 1980:33 [1978]). There are plenty of unwanted children in the world, so this is manifestly not a question of finding ways, through the manipulation of "bio-power" to raise the birthrates of our chosen peoples. But what is of interest here is, in continuing to speak about sex in every possible way, we avoid actually doing it in the most basic way. This is the result of the error of typification that, in order to stay as far away from reductionism as possible, it arcs off in the other direction; towards unending and seemingly seamless discourse of every possible detail, with no attempt to order or generalize beyond the cases at hand. Sex is one example internecine to our culture, but culture itself is the wider and more pressing example that transports itself across the world of cultures.

In constructing and maintaining, producing and reproducing discourses of *principle*—thou shalt not limit sexuality; thou shalt not regress culture, etc.— we are unwittingly returning to the very thing we had hoped to avoid: the reduction of the real through our categories of it. This carries another set of implications which are equally unrealistic and increasingly, in the face of the resistance other cultures are now presently offering us, impractical as well. These implications include "that history is simply a translation of an original mythical archetype, memory a mere reminiscence of primordial ideas, imagi- nation *a priori* for all epochs" (Passerini 1990:57). Even the rhetoric of these images fails to make sense on all counts. How can one have a memory of what is deemed primordial? How is the imagination of each cultural epoch structured so that it never tests its inherent limits? Is anything altered or lost in the translation of myth into history? Certainly both Herodotus and Thucy- dides asked these questions, and through them produced a new kind of think- ing as well as a new kind of discourse. Myth "itself" was a gloss of real-time occurrences, if not exactly "events" in the newly historical sense. New cate- gories meant new events, new objects, and new analyses. But the "transla- tion" effect of having a memory based in other kinds of things, happenings, people and persona, half-human perceptions qualified radically by the ima- gined recollection of the times when human beings were not wholly con- scious of their own condition, is something that today is almost entirely forgotten. We are quite used to not only "having" a history but also living "in" history, which is itself an odd way of putting it. How does one possess the past? What does it mean to "be" historical as opposed to simply being human? The fact that history "itself" is also a category of thought, and one that the West has also given enormous concern to and has taken great care about—both in manipulating it politically and in critiquing these forms of propaganda—should tell us that in order to make sense of ourselves in the world we must resort to ideas that are larger than life. But there is of course a danger here as well, one that was well understood by the very mind that remade the concept of human history in as radical an original manner as did Herodotus: "Darwin understood that large ideas do indeed become dangerous if they are inflated beyond their proper use: dangerous to honesty, to intelli- gibility, to all proper purposes of thought" (Midgely, op. cit:62). Whatever may be called "proper"—and this is itself a slightly disingenuous term, an "odd-job" word that can never hold down a job, perhaps—the point that an abstraction, once allowed traction, can carry all before it simply because it is both novel—it presents a way in which younger intellectuals can make their careers—and also more profoundly, it appears to produce something from nothing. Before Wallace and Darwin, no one had apparently noticed much less understood the real relationships that united all living organisms. There was, in a sense, nothing to go on, nothing before the senses until these minds, and other diverse examples are historically abundant, cleaved to the reality that was appresented but not presented. That is, we assume that nature "understood" itself before humans understood it. This manner of making sense of the world is also recent, and it is likely not entirely coincidence that evolution as a concept of reality came about not long after the idea that nature was itself anonymous and detached from its former author and authority. Exit God, enter Darwin. Even the most trenchant critics of this our modern situation—evangelicals of all agrarian faiths—recognize the connection and find evolution still fascinatingly threatening in this way. In looking a little more closely at our categorizations of historical events, we begin to see that the boundaries between them, "levels theories" or no, are quite porous, their demarcations "flimsy," a term by which James famously described the discretions we imagine existing between aspects of human consciousness "proper." Indeed, the very separation of them might provoke unnecessary contradictions: "Human beings have the characteristic of getting into contradictions without noticing it because they conceive of what is absent as a non-being, and the delusion of becoming occurs because of it. That something could be produced from nothing is simply not acceptable for human reason" (Gadamer 2000:115). It is likely that, because of our inability to experience our own deaths, and the corresponding inability to imagine what it would be like to actually "be nothing" at all—this is the most radical contradiction in human consciousness, a contradiction in terms and in essence, for how can one "be" nothing, "be" something that has no being, no ability to be?—that we balk at imagining any creation *ex nihilo*, and by extension and of late, any kind of simple creation at all. But behind all of this dance of avoidance, providing the rhythm of its heated self-distanciation, is the serious problem of making sense of what in fact being actually is for us, in its being able to be. Here, as in each of our above examples, "The *ersatz* product represses the real question into the unconscious and destroys the continuity of historical tradition which is the hallmark of civilization. The result is bewilderment and confusion" (Jung 1959:109 [1951]). Aside from the obviously bewildering quality, the sense of something civil suddenly gone wild, of a loss of control and a disorientation that not only the idea but the coming reality of nothingness presents to the living, there is the less abstract presence that not all within our grasp makes sense in the same way. That is, we do not know how it works in the sense of being able to point to a specific form of technical knowledge that adheres to it as does a discourse to an object that it itself has constructed. Nothingness and death, as we have already seen, not only present limit situations to human consciousness, they also appear to limit our imagination, our "being able to be," no less than our becoming. There is no "how to" manual for being dead. There is nothing to do or make once one is dead (cf. Gadamer on the definition of techne, 1996:32 [1967]). Barrett reminds us that the Greeks did not have a word that specifically meant "true" and that this apparent absence of a key conceptualization gave their form of thinking an advantage over our contemporary form (cf. 1979:161ff). We tend to think about disclosure and exposition, in the very root of the term, something that has been exposed for what it is, as we would do so following along with a detective romance or in our own lives if someone is suspected of being manipulative. But for the Greeks, the closest term carries within it a sense of something being absent and not so much present or presented, a sense, as Barrett suggests, of "deprivation," or "the wrenching, or tearing something out of hiddenness; and in such a way that the hidden mystery persists in and through what is disclosed" (ibid:170). This is so of both mundane and profound truth. This sense of disclosure rather than exposure allows us to understand its comparative advantage, because in making something known we are not freeing it from its own mysterious existence. Indeed, we have in fact heightened the puzzle of its presence because we have come to know it as it is. In its presence, it maintains its aloofness to us as human beings, who can know it only by what it represents as before us. We do not know, for instance, either its own history or even the part of its history where we interacted with it in its previous hiddenness. We do not know if our knowledge of it will change in the future, or whether it might simply become something moribund, something that no one need have any further care about. If we depart from this idea of what knowing is, not so much a "truth" of things but their openness and their revealing, their presence and their absence caught in the similitude of our desire to comprehend them, then we ourselves must cover up part of their truth; the part that stands before us and does not lose its ability to "bewilder and confuse." A current example is the so-called "dark matter," which is said to make up a great proportion of all cosmic matter. It cannot be seen, but it affects light and has weight. It does not react to electromagnetism or gravity in the usual way of regular matter, however, and our knowing about it has in many ways increased the mystery surrounding its being and its presence. We do not, in a word, know exactly what it is, only rather more about what it is not. This definition by negation, the pulling towards reality by the demarcation of other known factors and thence factoring them out as explanations for the new, is part and parcel of our modern way of thinking about what is "true." For us, something that is true has to *make sense*. This was often not the case for our various ancestral traditions. Our version of truth, however, in occluding the bewildering part of presence, including our own oddly unique existence and the existence of a reflective consciousness, must hide something about itself. *It must cover up its own motives for seeking the truth.* Such theories of being "are caught in a strange pragmatic contradiction, whereby the very goods which move them push them to deny or denature all such goods. They are constitutionally incapable of coming clean about the deeper sources of their own thinking" (Taylor 1989:88). One of most common examples of this form of thought would have to be positivism and its entire historical offspring, especially the neopositivism of the Vienna Circle that denied any metaphysical suasion or backdrop. In the century following its advent and ascendance in the sciences and social sciences alike, it has been reiterated many times that it of course *does* in fact have its own metaphysical architecture—every theory concerning itself with truth and being does so, they are all ontologies in this sense—and thus it utters no specific advantage in principle over other theories of being or knowledge. But it is more difficult to pin down the structure of our ethical theories, something that Taylor in these passages is discussing, than our epistemologies or ontologies. This is because there is much more at stake in believing them to have a hold on what is considered to be the truth of things. In a word, this is so because the "things" at stake are human beings and their actions: "They utterly mystify the priority of the moral by identifying it not with substance but with a form of reasoning, around which they draw a firm boundary" (ibid:89). In part this is a necessary move. Ethical actions or the theories surrounding them, or the explanations of the connections between intent and action, result and interpretation, are not things of "substance" at all. Their effects may be substantial in another sense, but their thing-hood cannot be reduced to the usual material of which objects we call things in casual language are generally made. I say "generally," because our very example appears to be a thing and not at all a substance in the usual way; "dark matter," which some astronomers have suggested would be better called invisible matter, is clearly something present while having all the hallmarks of something that is absent. A fanciful interpretation that might find a place in a science fiction book would suggest that it consist of the souls of the dead, hanging in their place in the heavens as the material bodies upon which they had animated living existence moved along in their stellar and planetary courses. No astrophysicist would credit such a thing as an explanation, but imagination regarding what is occlusive knows no bounds. The fictions it creatively constructs are no doubt of interest, and may even serve to point us in the direction of what we take to be the ultimate truth of things, but we also know that truth is often "stranger" than fiction. The cliché points up an astonishing reality: for all our knowledge of exposition, *things still disclose themselves in their own way*. This was something that the Greeks knew in spite of, or because of, their lack of a specific word for "true."

In our own time, we obviate this fact, cover it up. This is why Nietzsche, Foucault, and others are quick to demand of us that we undertake a "genealogy" of concepts, moral, clinical, epistemological or sexual or otherwise. We can get a better sense of how we think by subjecting the categories of thought itself to our own ontological analyses. In this, we can also avoid that other pitfall of modern self-expression, the discourses of the everyday where nothing is not so much said, but spoken into a form of para-being that elevates it into a thing in itself; "Nothing," as in the same kind of non-thing that we have spoken of as being on the path to. There are a number of ways of analyzing this kind of communicative non-communication. Its sociological purpose is well-known as the source of the grease that keeps the quotidian world moving along and reassures each of his present role and that others are duly performing theirs. In so far as this is its own measure, it is a necessary aspect of social life. Its "existential" merit may of course be debated, but it is not generally thought to have this other more abstract role. To give it more than its due is also something that leads to error, and indeed, to critique it because it does not aspire to the more serious task of auto-genealogy much less the construction of a morality that is transparent and "true" to itself is asking too much of it in the first place. It is like setting up a straw person and then asking it to be made of steel. It is sometimes the case that both psycho-analysis (cf. Sorokin 1956:94) and existentialism have committed this very error regarding the everyday, and Heidegger, who seeks to overcome its debilitating flattening out of things, also seems to be somewhat tilting at windmills. It simply does not cleave to these purposes, and has a reason for not doing so. Its apparent "absence" is, like the lack of a word for "true" in Classical Greek, an actual advantage. For the routine of the day to day is *not* the place for us moderns to engage in the stuff of existential import. We are too pragmatic for this. Not because we are insensitive to it or simply insensible about it, but precisely because such dialogue is profound, even sacred for us, especially since the advent of the individual and the corresponding public/private distinction. To engage the other in a serious way in the day to day is to take her out of the context where things can be made true in a trice. It often serves more as a distraction than allowing for the traction that gives us a more profound sensibility regarding our presence in the world. Of course any thinker might wince at this a little, but to give proper care and due attention to serious topics, they need to find their own space in our society, and not simply pop up at any time. We imagine the Greeks were always ready to stop what they were doing at any hour of the day and engage immediately and seriously in affairs of ontology. This, I think, is a romance. No culture mixes and matches ontologies and verities at will and with no prompting other than a sudden "let's talk about life." No, the real issue lies in there not being such a space in modernity, or at least, hardly any space where the vast majority of us can speak up and speak out about the challenges of being human in the world today. There is no "forum" or "agora" where we can come together on a regular basis—the university classroom is at best a contrived and very transitory space where such discussions potentially, and not at all always and in actuality, can arise—and part of the reason for this is not so much the prevalence of the "everyday talk" that Heidegger and others object to, but that our laboring life is so all-consuming. We do not grasp the essence behind the appearance in the way the Greeks are also said to have been able to do (cf. Gadamer 2001:94ff [1935]), because our day to day existence is so much the same. Part of this does have to do with how we speak about it, but in general, the utterances of the mundane spheres serve to make those spheres *more* human and *more* humane, not less so. In so far as this allows us no further insight into ourselves science or for that matter, the oracles of ancient times did (cf. Sorokin, op. cit:265), so be it. We are not in need of such insights from these sources. Indeed, much serious "talk" on the form of scientific or objectifying discourses provides no serious insights of this kind either. These "paper doctrines," as Midgely refers to them, are not things by which "anyone could actually live" (2004:69). They result in "what is called 'truth': "There is an art, then, which is mendacious and which is shown to have been required in order that the species man prevail" (Lingis, op. cit:72). This is an apt description of the famous Nietzschean phrase reminding us of the "errors by which we live," and which of course gave this book its sub-title. But how could it be otherwise? We can, as we have attempted to do in the above, provide a closer and perhaps more sincere analysis of such concepts, myths and categories by which we try to get along in a puzzling and bewildering world, by which we try to find meaning for ourselves in an infinite and anonymous cosmos, and by which we try to learn to understand ourselves and others alike. This is the human condition, as Nietzsche reminds us, and to do otherwise would perhaps spark a kind of "collective neurosis," though by denying the reality of the sense that we masquerade our values under the banner of truths, we are liable for something worse than even that: "Loss of roots and lack of tradition neuroticize the masses and prepare them for collective hysteria." (Jung, op. cit:181). This "lunacy," about which there is as much undiagnosed as transparent, occurs not because we have literally lost our minds. But the idea of absence, like the *horror vacui*, presses in on us with its nothingness. Though we read on the backs of our vehicles the message that "he who dies with the most toys, still dies," reassuring us that part of our self-understanding is still present in a materialistic age, we have to counter the angst of life with the anxiety of death.

Filling up the vacuum of life with things is, however, just one side of the picture. Part of our interest in objects is quite rational rather than merely rationalized. Quite apart from the idea that many of these items improve the quality of human life in labor-saving ways, healthier states can develop out of them just as often as can those unhealthy, which Jung concentrates on. Why so? Simply because we have not forgotten that we are finite beings. Thus quality of life is of the utmost. Why should it not be, given that we must still face the same kind of death as all humans have previously faced? Its ultimate character has not changed, even though dying is just as certainly culturally construed and constructed and has been altered radically over the ages. But the shadowy passage into the unknown, the loss of one's senses, the experience of being alone and distanciated from one's loved ones, and the feelings of helplessness at the last, the acceptance of being closed off forever to this world, the only world we have yet known, must be the same for all of us. All of this might promote the scathing critique that Jung proposes, but it must be tempered with the equal experience of the good life, and for us, today, a significant part of that experience has to do with the "goods" of life or the goods in life. Through them we allow ourselves to relax the interpretive bond that connects us to the world. But with them we are able to face the vicissitudes of living on with a more stolid conscientiousness, a greater confidence than had any of our ancestors. For technology, used in the service of life, can make sense to us through its sheer sensibility. We can, though this requires reflective work and indeed, we must agree with the critics of modernity that this work is often lacking, dissuaded, distracted and decoyed away from its task by materialist desires, ourselves become more sensible, as we will see below, through the apt use of both technique and technology. But all of this in its own turn requires that we keep up our end of the interpretive bargain. We have to maintain our connection with the world, and not let our "toys," whatever they may consist of, get in the way: "What we have called 'choice' may now be made clear. It is the engagement of the individual in the interpretation of reality" (Natanson 1970:103). This process allow us to make choices, rational or no, in the world of both forms and ideas. The world of things is brought before us through such a process, though the narrower choice amongst competing brands does not so much itself partake in it. But about the process itself there is no choice: "The nature of our language and the fundamental dependence of our thought on language makes interlocution in the one or other of these forms inescapable for us" (Taylor, op. cit:38). It is through language that the connection with the world is made and maintained. It has a present and it is present. Its past is not so much past as something that has passed by us. Without the connection, history passes us by without our involvement. No order of forms and no set of ideas impresses itself upon us in the way of an invitation. We must always take the first step toward it. Occluded by material things, we are hampered in this movement, like someone trying to negotiate an attic room filled with the detritus of previous generations. One could, in a Nietzschean maneuver, climb out a window and onto the roof. But there are other, less radical options. One could begin by cataloguing the attic and cleaning it up. Selling parts of it off in garage sales or, with more antique and collectible items, perhaps on-line. One might argue that in order to get a view of the whole before engaging in this kind of ordering, we need to stand on the rooftops of our historical houses and peer back into them with the full brilliance of the noonday at our backs. This may indeed be the best case. But at the same time, most of us carry enough light with us, technological or otherwise, to at least begin such a necessary task. The things of today can help us pierce the veils that cover over the things of yesterday.

No matter how we go about "cleaning house," it is through language that we can negotiate the meaning of doing so, as well as communicating the relative import of each of the tasks involved to others. They may dispute the value of this or that historical object, this or that antique. And of course, in an old family home, the house of our culture, many an item that has little commercial or historical value will be uncovered that has great sentimental value. It lacks factuality, but our opinion of it nevertheless remains high. Given this, we must also keep in mind that "Facts and opinions do not exist as free-standing objects, but are produced through grammar and broader conventions of discourse, which in turn are interpreted by hearer or reader in order to register as such. Meanings exist because people mean and others believe they understand what was meant" (Tonkin 1990:27). Because it carries within it all human meaning, and indeed, because all meaningfulness in the world is, as far as we know today, exclusively constructed by humans, such languages as exist in this way are never purely technical, and can range from that didactically instructional and stilted to the ethereality and mysticism of poetry. Meaning, in a word, "occurs" for us and by us and never in some objectively external state, only "to" us. We ourselves carry meanings around with us as well. The idea of the sentimental object is a case in point. No other may be able to see what we see in it, especially if it has been long-lost to present consciousness and then rediscovered in the attic of our dreams. Its being brought into the light of the present represences its meaning to us in a bold manner. We suddenly can recall, through its mnemonic, the reason why it holds such meanings for us. Like a famous marque of automobile, such objects "hold" their value, and in this we find part of our own truth in being with them and even in their possession. For the possession is, in these cases a mutual affair. It is correct to say that we transpose what are in fact values into truths, as Nietzsche famously reminded us. But it is no less the case that constructing truth in this human way has great value. This is so because we, as humans, are not objects and neither are we generally going to object to the fact that though objects, like those antiques in the historical attics of our cultural homes, last longer than do human beings, that we are the ones who can make meaning, and not the objects "by themselves." This is evidenced every time we come across a strange inheritance held within its submarine or earthen tomb, and raised into our present light by the efforts of archaeology or, perhaps more dubiously, by wreck-hunters. We do not necessarily know what it "is," and thus begin the process of making meaning for it anew. We also must do this for ourselves on a regular basis because the meanings that we find fulfilling in various ways change over time. This is enormously true of our relationship to history in general, but it is also partially correct to view our own histories in this way as well. It may be offensive to us, or at least surprising, that we, who have actually lived the years and through the experiences which are not in principle "countless" and about which we pride ourselves in knowing much, are nevertheless also historians and archaeologists of ourselves. If we know much, we also have forgotten much. If we can recover some of this, there yet remains other aspects of our own life which cannot be so recovered. Witness the efforts at recovery ongoing with many today; hypnosis, depth therapies of other kinds, yet more marginal efforts to extend our memories beyond even our own births, through the so-called "past-life" regression—Sagan's comments on this phenomena are worth encapsulating in a brief nod to the possibility of it actually being true for some few people, though it suggests to the Western mind a kind of culturally alien sense of reincarnation—whatever the case may be concerning the aptitude of the method proposed, or the degree of "truth" or untruth in its individualized outcome, we must admit to the fact that we are almost obsessively interested in trying to lay grasp on what has occurred to us as we have lived on. Very often, in the carefreeness of childhood, but also in its attentive wonder, such experiences flash through us, never to be glimpsed let alone held within us again. This may feel like a kind of betrayal, as when a nascent love or friendship is suddenly washed out to sea by the tide of changing human feeling. The whimsical nature of this aspect of human life may also be offensive to us even though we are just as likely to engage its services when it is convenient for us to do so. Since the language of these encounters and trials and errors is with us always, it is easier to think of the meanings that are accrued to it, such as those in myth "as a 'second semiological system,' functioning through the distortion of the meanings of the signs which it appropriates" (Basso 1990:68). Basso quotes Barthes well-known suggestion that myth borrows and returns words but during the interim alters their meaning. We may not, at first glance, notice that anything has changed. In the same way, a person who is intimate with us may travel afar and return to us not at all the same person she once was. Many relationships end in this way, or, it may be even more true to say that they were about to end and the travel was a way in which one or the other partner could find his or her new bearings and then present themselves to one another as proof of the sea-change that has only just now appeared to take them away from all previous intimacies. The meaning departed from us and was returned transformed. Ultimately, and perhaps also historically, the archetype for this sense of things originates in the idea that our "souls" depart from us in death, only to return to the earth in another host, another human being, or, speaking of reincarnation, later on in a more recent historical epoch, as another creature entirely. Whether or not we view the soul "itself" as having been transformed through its otherworldly junket, the idea that it is replaced in some other vehicle that is not ourselves ends up transforming it in this world in any case. It is the case with all forms of meaning that they continue to work on us and in us, whether the recollection of them is but partial, abstracted and vague, as with a dream one has been gradually awakened from, or more detailed.

Though we seek to know the meaning of all things and even desire to see meaning within the things "themselves," we must also keep present the fact that we the interpreters are part of the meaning no matter how distant its sources seem to us: "Comprehending the objectives, the inner structure, and the context of a work is not in itself sufficient to clear away all our prejudices that arise from the fact that we ourselves stand within a tradition" (Gadamer 2000:24). What we can comprehend without as much ado is the principle that there is a *dialogue*, a quite literal instance of "throwing words across" the gulf of time and the absence of mortal and even culturally collective memory. We do receive some communication in return. This, akin to myth in Barthes understanding, alters our intended meanings but it does not do so beyond human recognition. We do not need to seek the deepest structures of our cultural evolution, nor even see them as specific stages which the species has passed through as a whole in order to understand the order of meanings held within what is antique or what is merely vintage. Our vantage point may sabotage the feelings or expressions of humanity that once were, but, given what we know of material history, there are no doubt many of these experiences that we would rather not repeat in any case. Human life, though cultured and literate, was still most often woefully brief in terms we would take any comfort in today. This is also not to forget that in some regions of our present world life expectancies are similar to those of our ancient forebears, and in this we do find the represencing, nay, even a kind of reincarnation of the history of the species right before our eyes. The difference is two-edged, however; on the one hand we can do something about it whereas our ancestors could not, but on the other hand, our inability to forge the political and ethical will to do so makes us *lower* than those who lived and died to create world history for us to live today and makes us more than culpable to them.

The lingering presence of myth speaks to the ongoing presence of mortality in our world in a way we can understand, despite the primordiality of its original sources. We do, in other words, recreate like sources in our own world and it perhaps the symbiosis of myth and reality that keeps recreating them in a kind of self-fulfilling prophecy. One backs the other. Reality continues to be unnecessarily harsh for many, so myth appears rejuvenated on the human stage. Myth speaks to us and utters its own transformed reality and we might seek to manifest our response in the world. But we cannot pause to place blame on the language and meanings of mythic thought just because we lack the ethical will to think of our contemporaries in a better light, or that they are deserving of the same dignities as we might possess. If we engage in this error, the presence of myth in the world is no different than the presence of material items; it decoys us away from the problem at hand. Its making sense of the world prevents us from engaging sensibly with the world.

Another kindred misrecognition has to with our "idealization of objects" that are much more abstract even than those mythic, and certainly those material (cf. Lingis, op. cit:162ff). This process, partakes in both "centroversion" and reification alike. Imagining that rational consciousness is the only thing that can "make sense" of the world and of ourselves as beings within its envelope is to annul the impressive skills of that very imagination. For creativity and wisdom both require of our consciousness that it be balanced and aware of its holism. Similarly, to dwell within the world of myth alone—in today's rendition, the juvenile fantasies of entertainment fictions that purport to represent architectonic myths for modern, mainly youthful, audiences—is to abandon the equally necessary rationality that emanates from our conscious mind in favor of the path that travels on the verge to nothing. Even if it sometimes appears that human life is cut up into a variety of pieces, phases, stages, or roles, we travel through all of them together as a complex whole of selves, a community of selfhood. This is so for "the fundamental essence of life is precisely that internally unified function, [ ] which immediately actualizes as *one* life what is then split—by feelings, destinies, and conceptualizations—into the dualism of continuous life and individually closed form" (Simmel 2010:13 [1918], italics the text's; cf. Foucault op. cit:18 for an example of how this unity is split from itself in modernity). If it is sometimes difficult to "live with oneself," as in the manner of reproach or yet mourning, and perhaps one is a form of the other after all, it is because of this "internally unified function" that here we have termed not transcendence but conscience. It is this synthesis of conscious and unconscious states of being that pervades us with either joy or sorrow, or most often, some degree of both. And we must live with this unity as our human reality both as a subject and as a species, due to collective effects of the contentment or the suffering of many that are placed before us either through global connections—a conflict in one area is brought home to us in various ways—or through the telekinetics of media. If much of this appears to make no sense, it is because we have not yet been able to order its sensibility with our conscience. Only either our unconscious or our conscious rationality has been exclusively involved, and this is not enough: "To suffer is to experience an antisense of the moral kind. A lack of esthetic value can be construed as a zero ('trash'). But suffering cannot, though some optimistic writers have tried" (Champigny 1986:19). Oppositional thinking is, as we have seen throughout this book, an attempt to evade the reality of the human condition, part of which entails a deep sorrowful suffering in almost every life. What we know as the whole of living cannot be recast as one of "life's ideals." It presents itself, it is at hand, it lays before us in its whole cloth of humanity, and, increasingly, in a powerfully additional form that takes shape as the earth rather than only the world. We should no longer be astonished that one of the penultimate effects of our humanity in the world has been to call into question the continuance of the very viability of this our planet. We might call this a patent example of human evil, but in fact it is merely, though still seriously, a manifestation and implication of all kinds of human action in the world, both "good and evil." To call upon patent labels for the reality of how we live is also an error, a decoy maneuver that insulates us against coming to terms with our shared reality as beings of conscience: "We must not overlook the fact that opposites acquire their moral accentuation only within the sphere of human endeavor and action, and that we are unable to give a definition of good and evil that could be considered universally valid." (Jung, op. cit:267). Today, we would doubt the separate existence of such "essences" in an anonymous cosmos, separate, that is, from our consciousness "of" them in our own world and as part of our own stock and trade. But moralizing in this way serves only to elevate the matter at hand out of reach. This is perhaps its primary objective. The apparent non-responsibility we have regarding cosmic forces is only the latest and broadest interpretation of the ancient idea that fate and the destiny of mythic narratives was always and already out of our control. This is another reason why we cannot dwell in the fictions of myth. Equally so, the idea that all is within our rational control is an act of hubris. To "accommodate" sources of cross-cultural and cross-temporal wisdom into our own device is both necessary and also risky (cf. Gadamer 2001:38ff [1990], due to the chance of a faulty interpretation bent on admitting itself to the politics or the fashionable discourses of the day. Given our growing sense of ecological catastrophe, it is all the more easy to "discover" proto-environmentalism in ancient texts, or to take the pre-Socratic discussion of the whole in this one way and no other. This is a guise of mythic thought, where the destiny of our species is known so far in advance to obviate any rationality of the present in its face. This kind of fictive thinking produces the error of non-responsibility in the face of the historical—but *not* mythical—task at hand. In like fashion, the over-rationalization of contemporary events sabotages any search for wisdom that our ancestors may well have regarding our current predicaments. This is the "overvaluation" of the conscious mind in full force and it has exactly the opposite, but equally mistaken, effect of allowing us to think that no matter the task or challenge, that we can not only control it but resolve it without much effort (cf. Foucault, op. cit:43ff, for an example of this discursive overvaluation of rational form). Either way, and in both ways, we are guilty of making too much sense of things as they are, or the world as it is. How can it be that "too much sense" is a bad thing? How can one have "too much" of something like sense?

It is because sense gravitates around polar entities. The orbit of what "makes sense" is pulled in by the fugal centrifugality of the One. Akin to forms of fascism, its sense-making operation admits ultimately of no error, no matter how many have been made during the interim processes of attaining or falling into such orbits. It is a flight from reality, the majority of which occupies the space under a quasi-Gaussian curvature of the social world. Most people most of the time live in *this* way, and not at the extremities of life. To imagine that wisdom lies only at the extremes of either myth or science, non-rational thought or rationality, is to imagine that people, our fellow humans, are somehow straw persons who only act *as if* they are complex and mutable. This realization of the fictional character of this assumption alone should put the whole apparatus out of court. Instead of this all too easy formulation, we must recover our sensibilities that we live as others do, in a world of change and ambiguity. The ongoing dialectical relationship the our conscience gathers together in temporary sheaves exposes the individual elements of its harvest when it meets the light of the wider world. It is only through this encounter that human beings can imagine difference and thus act creatively to enact it. The starting point for the "widening" of consciousness is always near the center of the spectrum of human history and action. It is under the center of the curve, a median point, if not also the modal point that contains within it the most common activities and thoughts of humanity. We have seen, from a number of sources, that sex would be one of these, both in thought and action, but even this expression of the human desire for community and security is but one of many similarly important venues and engagements to which we find ourselves consistently drawn. Our ability to rewrite our own experiences, in spite of various memories, is in part a noble, and sometimes, a vulgar testament to the shared need for both the new and for the familiar at once. To "make sense" of something like this we would have to artificially separate such needs and say rather pedantically, that one cannot have what is both new and old at the same time in the same way. But the fact remains that we indeed not only can, but do so, through the convenient forgetting, or even the actual misrecognition of previous experiences: "Thus, for example, the great mystery of forgetting. The computer is something impoverished because it cannot forget and therefore is not creative. Creativity depends on the choices made by our reason and our capacity to think" (Gadamer 2000:69). However mysterious not being able to recall something may be—and perhaps it is simpler to say that in the face of the loss of memory one must be continually creative, to the point of entering in one's mind other dimensions of "dementia" etc.—it is reasonable to suggest that "sense" in general is something that is not only socially constructed in a majority manner, similar to the being able to be taken for a person who is simply sane and not untoward in any cognitive sense, but also something that it makes sense *to* remember given one's experience of a series of social contexts (cf. Barrett's variant of this viz. pedagogy, op. cit:66). The lack memory of something is not only symptomatic of forgetting, however, it is also the case that one cannot recall what one has never experienced, or never yet experienced. One cannot base one's actions upon only the imagination, no matter how "vivid." This term can be taken in the same sense as when we might think to ourselves that a dream appeared to us to somehow be "more than a dream," the so-called "vivid dreaming" where we seem to be truly inhabiting another world and not merely that of the unconscious. Or perhaps we do not yet understand that the unconscious can create other worlds that also in some other manner exist in our cosmos. This is entirely a speculation, and in many ways does not "make sense." The fact that it does not, given our cultural druthers, is itself suggestive. But vividness associated with the lack of experience is something that we almost never speak of. It is always about what we have been through or, in the realm of ideas, what may have occurred to us after a long period of study or the reading of a diversity of texts. This kind of image does make sense, because it "figures" that something like this would occur to us. A figure appears in our mind's eye, perhaps, or, in the social world, someone is able to "cut a figure" because his abilities have been honed by experience or study. At the same time, for reflective thought, that which attempts to make sense of everything, there is something odd about these kinds of figures, something that we cannot "figure out": "These figures are not even true figures. Philosophy cannot speak directly, whether in the mode of vigilance or of truth (true or probable), about what these figures approach. The dream is between the two, neither one nor the other" (Derrida 1995:126 [1993]). Merleau-Ponty's "vigilance" regarding his "definition" of philosophy is well taken here. Not only does it cut a dashing figure—philosophy not being either a body of knowledge nor a way of ordering or making sense of things—it is also noble in that it does not stoop to clerical activity in the realm of the mind. In this it soars above the sense-making apparatus of mere discourses—as Foucault reminds us, both inventing the point where it supposedly enters our world, and thence putting up the pretense, cutting the figure of the life of the party line: "Itself marked by that deployment, exerts enough charm on everyone for them to accept hearing the grumble of death within it" (op. cit:156)—vigilance has within it the ability to note its own trajectory. It calls the point of entry of its work into discourse at the moment where it moves on to some other task. Sometimes, as we have seen, these tasks are what is at hand, or before us, but as well, they could be world-historical or ethical in the form of principled reflection. Philosophical vigilance also casts itself as its own critic. It cannot abide the artificial division of things that are in reality unified, or at least, running on together. In this it can "see" the future, its vision somewhere "in between" that of a dream of what is present, the one, and what is to come, the other: "If occidental man decides to follow to its normal conclusion the philosophy implied in the contemporary sciences, he will of necessity tend to reach a perspective where the antinomy which sets the objective world over against subjectivity is wiped out" (R. Godel, in Sorokin, op. cit:294). As Nietzsche suggested, these are not so much truths of any kind, but instead values to which we are kinds, they thus exhibit kindness in return. But this kindness cuts a double figure: one the one hand it protects us from seeing the truth of our condition in the Nietzs-chean "existential" sense, a kind of anti-promethean starkness that has been said to promote nihilism while in fact it can do precisely the opposite, and on the other hand, it also allows us to evaluate the world, place a value upon it that it otherwise would not have. If these are true obverses, we would see in them both object and subject at once. For we also object to the idea that the world is without value, and we subject others to this faith, this "error" of sense, simply because it makes sense to *do* something while we are alive and while we are "here." But vigilance forces us to ask the question: "What beliefs of ours would we give up last if we were compelled to?" (Barrett, op. cit:108). Quite possibly it would be the simple faith in our ability to value things, or perhaps our ability to think at all. But as far as our ability to ask questions in the absence of formal faith, this appears to have cut and run, not merely figuratively, in the face of the configuration of political and other discourses, including those sexual and having to do with popular culture. At the same time, such incisions, such entry points into the corpus of knowledge we have valued as not only our own but also as "the best" way of making sense of things, cannot do without their own insights, however partial or "subjective" they must remain. Our attempt at valuing them is kindred with our ability to use them to evaluate things. They attain their value by not only being valuable to us as elements of our "beliefs," but in their action in the world at large, where they take on the task of becoming vigilant, a task that is always that of a sometimes lonely philosophy: "The language of rights is only one part of the wide repertoire of moral language that we have at our disposal. Nothing compels us to use it in places where it clashes with other insights that seem more important" (Midgely, op. cit:162). And such insights as there may be enter into our consciousness from both the world and the world of dreams, whatever other worlds may or may not exist or that we potentially have access to. "Rights" aside for a moment—we have the right to ignore our values inasmuch as the world changes and we must adapt to these changes; at the same time, demanding that we change ourselves simply for the sake of change is often a dubious "proposition," the objective version of the lewd proposal that is suggestive to us of a scene that we may desire in general, but not with this or that particular "figure"—we do find in our moral language the evaluation of not only things and figures but the morality of the other and the history of morals, including, somewhat fortuitously, its "gene-alogy." This implies the arc that rears up "beyond good and evil," because we know that such values are historical, and their contents change over time. This is more a reason why we must alter our evaluation of things, perhaps including by-passing or ignoring what had been previously taken for "moral insights." There is enough factual diversity for any incision to have only a local effect. Our incisiveness in these cases may cut us a fine figure, but the cut and thrust of our vigilance cannot afford to lapse into mere vigil: "Evil, like good, belongs to the category of human values, and we are the authors of moral value judgments, but only to a limited degree are we authors of the facts submitted to our moral judgement. These facts are called by one person good and by another evil." (Jung, op., cit:47). If values propose to us, they are considered noble. If they proposition us, they are considered vulgar. Our values are enacted as well as acted out by real people, including ourselves. But a proposal may lead to a proposition as well as vice-versa, pending outcome and our evaluation of it. Perhaps it was the best thing that could have ever occurred to us at the time, and perhaps it only appeared to be. Perhaps, in the long run, there is little difference between the two of them, both of them "dreams" in the sense of us having lived them and now only submitted to a partial valuation because only partially recalled. Or further, perhaps in the longer term, they have no value at all because we either cannot recall them or their import has faded with the biographical and even the historical changes that have occurred around us and to us in the interim. This sounds ominous, but it is in fact common place. "Living" with the truth of things may be difficult—so much so that we engage in the usual evaluation of existence that confers values and concurs that things must have value in order for us to live at all; "These are basic errors, which have made it possible for the species to survive..." (Lingis, op. cit:84)—but it is not only not impossible but it is demanded by our vigilance, the very thinking that has also created the sense categories of making sense of this odd life, the life that thinks itself through to the end, bitter or fulfilled.

All of these ways of making sense do not, however, understand what it is about the human condition that *makes* itself make sense of things. We are indebted to Nietzsche and those after him for attempting to create a new sensibility regarding the sense-making apparatus of both historical discourses and tables of cultural value: "Of all the ideal types human culture has so far invented, Nietzsche finds that in not one has there been devised a way for man to affirm his own nature. It is as though the total man is impossible" (ibid:69). One of the themes of this book is both the idea of anything total, let alone the idea of achieving it, is a myth. Such a myth may be an error "necessary for life," but it remains an error nonetheless. Post-Nietzsche though, I think we can go a bit further and say that such ideas, even in their ideal form where everyone agrees that they cannot be actually attained, are in fact dangerous errors. They are a threat to the reality of the human condition, rather than just something that can be used to cover it over. Nietzsche felt that the human condition was an autochthonous threat to our very humanity. Perhaps instead we can begin to understand that the errors we have con-structed in order to mask that threat are indeed more threatening than the reality itself. This, I take to be a step toward human maturity, and also a step away from the "Nietzschean" concern that denuded of his basic errors of self-misrecognition, Man could not survive. No doubt this is true of "Man," a concept that Nietzsche himself stated must die given the death of God, but humans? Rather than this, the "total" vision of what we are and what we can become includes not only our mythic ideals—to be taken as cautionary tales as much as allegories of greatness—we can learn to understand our completeness in the acts and thoughts of how we work within the social reality of others and not merely the generalized otherness of either myth or "Society," an ill-conceived successor to "Man" and a replacement for "God."

When Taylor suggests that radical thoughts must still cleave to those of others around me, we are issued a dual challenge of staking claim to our own thoughts in the face of the resistance of what has been and the world that presents itself to us as an historical object and an imminent face of immanence as in the character of its "worlding," as well as the sense that I have that my insight may not be so insightful after all, that is, self-doubt. "And this challenge I can only meet by confronting my thought and language with the thought and reactions of others" (op. cit:37). Since no reaction, no matter how insightful, can ever be "total" in either the ideal sense of myth or divinity or yet in the Nietzschean sense of being "beyond" the morality of the day—in truth, truth in a non-moral sense is something that can be found beside any morality as its set of signifiers lying outside any system that cannot itself understand its whole from within itself; this is a key insight of Nietzsche's critique that was later formalized in Gödel—we must rely on the perspective of others to lend not only credence to our work and thought but to submit it to the necessary critique that yields something more than it would have been able to accomplish by itself. Certainly, given the absence of the fundamental responses that some may have expected of the Enlightenment and of science concerning existential questions, the polyglot character of a Nietzsche, romantic, psychoanalytic, structural and moral, to name a few aspects of his overall tone, could only try to cobble together some of the critiques of Enlightenment thought, amongst others previous, and attempt something seemingly utterly new, the "eternal recurrence of the same": "He was a great moralist and with this doctrine he wanted to show how in the face of absolute hopelessness we must learn to be resolute. What he demanded of us was genuine morality, something more than human" (Gadamer 1996:160 [1990). But neither human hope or hopelessness is ever absolute. Death removes us from either extreme, but so does life. The most extreme cases of hopelessness move us toward death, and indeed, death is a release from these states of utter despair. There is no indemnificatory finger pointing at us to remain resolute, say, if we were victims of the Holocaust, and Nietzsche himself would never have judged those who had recognized the hopelessness of their situation as somehow morally weak. Like all of the concepts we have been discussing, it may be that in order to "make sense" of them we have to posit or imagine their polar extremities as somehow being real to us. We have seen this is an error, and Nietzsche himself, interpreted in this way, reaches into one of these basic errors for his material regarding his metaphysical doctrine. In doing so, he bases his critical hermeneutics on something that cannot bear the weight of his interpretation; that is, does not have the moral gravity or even the reality he appears to think it does. Or perhaps, akin to the social psychological aspect of his thought, he is merely stating that it is our beliefs about it that give it an overcompensatory reality that cannot exist for humans, and his doctrine is simply a better metaphor for our condition. Interpreted in *this* way, he begins to stop making sense and starts to become more sensible.

It is more sensible to think of human life as itself an overcompensation for the absence of both instinct and nature. Culture is something that both rests atop the natural order and soars beyond it. Culture is, ironically, both the inventor of good and evil and the means to go beyond them. Nature has no such means because it has no such need. It is a human need to self-transcend and, as we have seen, we can accomplish this through the sleight of hand of taking myths as a too literal representation of reality, including that of God or the gods, where we are possessed of the idea of stamping a human life and death upon them. Nature overcompensates as well, but in a more basic evolutionary way, where those members of any species better equipped by chance for the environment they find themselves within survive longer and reproduce more of others like them. But things can always change, sometimes rapidly, as when a cosmic impact wiped out the large reptiles that had been the "masters" of this world for some one hundred million years. Our human version of this catastrophic alteration lies within our own apocalyptic hands, and it too represents an "excess of force" (cf. Lingis, op. cit:4). In our theories of life as well, there is this affirmation of the human will taken to the nth degree. To witness the Higg's boson in action or to witness the Big Bang "occurring," are current scientific examples of human curiosity and know-how combining in dramatic and perhaps even spiritual ways. Even if the cosmos cannot now be said to have a "plan," humans maintain and extend their various plans both in the face of this challenge and because we also have the necessary conceit that our planning might be just a little more interesting than anything the cosmos can come up with on its own. The resonance of the dead but still existing godhead of humanity can clearly be seen here as well. We can use our new plan to counter the fatigue found within those previous: "This plan turns into an order that counters all the dissolving powers of the exhausted state spirit with the resistance of a new cosmic dignity" (Gadamer 2001:101 [1935]). And it is also not bereft of mythic archetypes, their "gender" insignificant when compared to their force of compensation which is an overcompensation, both for real world gender relations in post-agrarian culture and for the lingering resonance of those agrarian in our customs and mores. But we have added something, going "beyond" the morality of the original myths in the exact way that Nietzsche would have approved of, perhaps not in detail, but in principle (cf. Neumann, op. cit:358). This "likeness" presents itself as its own self-overcoming, its self-affirmation of will that wills "all that it has been." In our contemporary understanding of the world systems of diverse cultures, this new force of will is both something human—its "all too human" status was grotesquely revealed in Nazism, for one—and something that seeks to overcome the aspects of its own humanity that make it unable to will itself with ever-renewed vigor. Some of these have to do with the very concepts we have been working through, the self, the idea of God, the faith in technology, the sense of home, concerns about our ability to be in love or the loss of love, and finally, and most importantly our compulsion regarding forms of freedom. Overcoming any of these by placing them back within the social reality from which they originated is a movement toward the self-overcoming affirmation of a humane will to power; power over oneself and over the problem of self-misrecognition that always attends our confrontation with the tradition. In doing so, we can continue the affirming and overcoming work of human thought in general (cf. Gadamer 1996:167 [1989] where he speaks of the "enigmatic" questions of human existence not being conducive to what we generally refer to as "knowledge"). Indeed, these kinds of questions require of us to stop "making sense" of them in the usual manner of discourse and knowledge of any formal and institutional kind. For there are other, more base responses to these questions and the Third Reich is hardly the only example of their manifestation. Perhaps the most important affirmation of self-overcoming we can will is that which goes beyond the stark and simple rationalizations of fundamental human questions, those that tell us things always make sense and that there is no need to question such a sense that is given by any official source or any customary presentation. For the "enigmatic" quality of human existence is what is covered over by the errors from which we draw a kind of subsistence. Realizing this is both an act of the will to power and an affirmation that how we think and what we do can go beyond what we have thought and what we have done. Given the constant and sometimes unexpected character of social and world change, the ability to step away from and over our current practices is one of the most sensible gifts that we humans possess.

START BEING SENSIBLE

We can begin by simply recognizing that there is never a human situation where what passes for the rules can simply be applied. We have seen that rules are the down to earth version of myths. They present responses to situations that have been typified into a kind of ideal form. Of course the vast majority of human situations do not represent anything heroic in the martial sense or "mythic" in the phantasmagorical sense. But what they do represent is a template for what most of us would agree would be the "ideal" setting or set of behaviors that persons would manifest or the ideal performance of this of that social role. So to follow a rule is to bend ourselves toward this phantasm of correct action or even thoughts, though we like to maintain, in spite of the fact that the source of all human thought is a combination of history, society and personal experience, that thoughts remain somehow "free" of all rules, or at least potentially so. Another necessary error, perhaps, but in relation to the formalities found in all human contexts, the "interaction rituals" of daily life, as Goffman has referred to them, we generally know what is expected of us at the same time as we also know how far we can bend the rules and suffer no great consequence for doing so. The ability that allows us to balance rule adherence and individual expression is simply called inter-pretation: "Understanding plays a role wherever rules cannot simply be ap-plied, and this includes the entire sphere of human collective life. Thus it transpires that we can prove incomprehensible to ourselves, that we can fail to understand ourselves, just as we can fail to understand others" (ibid:165). If it were only a matter of following rules, as within the circuits of a pro-grammed machine, then there could be neither understanding nor misunder-standing, let alone any morality of any kind. Simply correct and incorrect responses would do, input and output matching in each case, and no "sense" of what is either nonsense or what could make better sense for being more sensible given changing situations. Certainly this is not a human affair, and we can speculate whether or not our constructing of computers in the widest sense of the term represents both an aspiration toward perfect understanding that would be all-comprehending and comprehensive, as well as a response to the anxiety of Babel; the problem of not being able to communicate and understand each other and sometimes also ourselves. This anxiety produces a position in the world: "I stand this way before the world naming, name denying, attending, intending in love—a noesis that senses in its imperfection the possibility of perfection" (Lilburn 1999:31). This "sense" allows the play of meanings that coruscate across the rifts and ravines of thinking in action. It has little other merit, especially if harnessed to a formal ontology or yet worse, an ideology. The idea of perfection is a dangerous one, as history has shown, perhaps one the very most dangerous of human ideas. Embodied in the rituals and rules of every culture is the sense that if performed "correct-ly," perfection would be achieved. We still casually say today that where there are humans present, there will be mistakes, that humans are not perfect, or that error is something quintessentially human. It is true to say that no other creature "errs" in the same way as we. Animals might "misjudge" their leap, their prey, their own strength in the face of a competitor, but this is not real "judgement" in any meaningful sense. It is an error only in the broadest sense of something not going right from the human observer's standpoint, as when we take in a nature show and watch our distant relatives do what they do in their world. But to try to extend this notion that because we are free to choose our mistakes in some cases ahead of time, omit them and commit to them, reflect on them afterwards and learn from them, that there is a sense of perfection "in the air," is nonsense. But what Lilburn is getting across is not so much that we, in erring, foreshadow our own perfection, it is more simply the sense that in knowing that there is another way to do things, we think quite "naturally" that there exists the *best* way, given our current knowledge and circumstances, and that this, other things being equal, would qualify as "perfect," as in having a "perfect" day with one's lover on one's birthday, or some such sentimental experience. That "best" ways are practiced—in managerial language, there is a stock phrase that dully states "best practices," seemingly as if these could be ultimately known—reflects the previous collective experience of human beings working together. That practices are also shrouded in other meanings, mythic and biographical alike, sometimes aids their being "the best," and sometimes hampers their sensibility from attaining any pitch of relevance to the situation before us. In either case, we are aware, through a kind of knowledge that has an existential import, that we must make ourselves at home with what we *do* know and how we *do* live: "Knowledge is the generosity of being to the homeless mind" (ibid:32).

But there is no knowledge without first being interpretation. It is more correct to frame the humanity of our consciousness by way of this process than of either possessing knowledge, the sense of perfection, or even our ability to make mistakes. For "interpreting is itself a possible and distinctive how of the character of being of facticity. Interpreting is a being which belongs to the being of factical life itself" (Heidegger, op. cit:12). It is the mode of being-able-to-know inasmuch as it also centers the corresponding mode of being able to live in the world. And this knowledge is merely a model of organized and sometimes highly formalized understanding that itself has no more permanent a hold over us as it does have a permanent relation to the world. Just as "prominent ideas cannot die until the problems that arise within them have been resolved" (Midgely, op. cit:4), it is also quite correct to say that the tasks before us that are defined as problematic are so because of the presence of many of these big ideas, as we have seen throughout this book. Sometimes it is the case that with the passing of ideas real human problems also pass away. If we were to abandon the self-centered rationalizations associated with material inequality—the work ethic, the idea of individuated value based on marketable skills alone, the naturalization of what we imagine in nature also being applied to us in a form of neo-Spencerism, etc.—surely the reality of a just system of equity and quality of life would soon emerge, due to our sense of disgust at the formerly "prominent," one would like to say today, preeminent, ideas. But subjecting our cherished ideals to analysis is not only risky from a business point of view—how many customers are there who desire to dismantle their own way of comfortable and comforting life?—it is also something that seems to depart from the "way things are," the common sense view of making sense of the world as it is. But this kind of sense, as we began to see in the previous section is reactive, sometimes even reactionary. It observes things as they are and then describes them without a view that, unlike our vaunted "sense of perfection" above, to changing them so that they more closely mirror other, more humane ideas about how we live and how we live together on one world. It struggles with the fact that any analytic or critical sensibility comes from the same source as it does: "To say that analysis is suspect means that common sense has intuitively located an internal threat, for philosophy originates in the soil of the mundane." (Natanson, op. cit:152). And indeed, such thinking, *all* thinking, if what we have argued in the above is correct, can be a serious threat to the social order and as well to our general peace of mind. It tends to bring abstractions down to earth, relativize "sacred" truths, and untruths, and boldly call out the confidence trickery associated with propaganda, marketing, certain aspects of the "sorcery" of the social sciences, as Andreski has slyly written about, and disturb our general good feeling about how we choose to live. It is never a nice thing to think about the world as it is within the boundaries of certain "issues," such as geopolitics, poverty, ideology, ethnic and gender bigotries and the indentured servitude of "wage slavery." It is quite preferable even to think about crime or domestic political scandal, sexual innuendo and personality disorders. For this latter list includes things that seem to effect the few, the outliers, and to a certain extent, the outcast. We also can feel, smugly or no, that most of these persons have chosen their lot quite freely, not unlike the philosopher who rails against society while at the same time gaining his full sustenance from it. The so-called "structural" problems of our time also seem too big to tackle on one's own, or to even engage in thinking about. The ideals put forward by those who do make a habit, or a career, of publicly thinking about them seem too grand to be applied in a realistic manner. We *do* know ourselves, after all. This should not cause any astonishment to the culture critic. After all, even when we refuse to think about much of anything at all we remain human. As Jung intones, "Only a ruthless self-knowledge on the widest scale, which sees good and evil in correct perspective and can weigh up the motives of human action, offers some guarantee that the end-result will not turn out too badly" (op. cit:166).

It is also all too easy to practice the "blame game" for its own sake. It gratifies the fragile ego of those who feel that their place in the world is either not well enough acknowledged, their notoriety is lacking in some way, or yet perhaps they are not notorious enough. Analysis of any critical kind must also unmask these motives, which rarely can be categorized by the grand moral terms such as good and evil. They are petty and can easily be recognized as such. They are, in this way, much more common and also historically human because, as we saw above, neither "good" nor "evil" in any ultimately pure form exists in the human condition. There is certainly relative good and bad, positive and negative, and alas, an ongoing and developing prevalence of "correct" and "incorrect," as if life were a kind of sophisticated mathematics exercise. No, analysis subverts common sense, this much is true, but it does not do so from outside of common sense reality. It springs form the same "soil," but it grows a rather different plant. Nonetheless, it also seeks the light, just as do all forms of vegetation, and it has its moments as well where it can be caught "vegetating"; that is, stalling, resting on its sometimes dilapidated laurels—for some decades Marxism struggled with this problem—or simply pretending that it, having shown the world its own truths, can stand aloof to further question and introspection. This last form of the vegetative life of critique can probably describe almost all forms of "*KulturKritik*" over the past two centuries or more. At best, some suites of ideas, becoming enthralled to the very discourses they have sought to sabotage, can become mere names for historical constructs (cf. Foucault, op. cit:105ff). In this, other possible or even actual historical meanings begin to slip away, and we think we have finally grasped the "value" of a home truth concerning our situatedness of being in the world. But "in order to be understood as expressions of thought the words must be grasped in terms of both their original meanings and their respective contexts" (Gadamer 2000:86). The key dynamic that we have been speaking about throughout this section, understanding, is not only a hermeneutic "axiom," but an existential quality. It does not turn on the dime of currency, whether this be discursive fashion, state-sponsored research, or what "most people" think about things, though this last is likely a shill of marketing and politics combined, based on no serious ethnographic work. Indeed, in order to understand something, anything at all, we must not merely know what it has meant—though Gadamer is quite correct that this is absolutely necessary—but what it means today, and whether indeed it can even have a sensible meaning in our world. If so, according to who, what sources, and allaying what motives? (cf. Midgely's conception of self-understanding to this regard, op. cit:73-4). It is this self-understanding that could be experienced as the most serious threat, not only because most of us do not care for politics all that much, nor do we seek fame at the expense of our "ordinary" lives because we are aware that those who are famous, or yet infamous, must forsake both privacy and the sense that they are a real person instead of a series of popular personas. But self-knowledge is something that rest within the home and hearth of the soul. It does not speak to us from afar, nor does it claim any fame or fortune. It simply is with us as we are in the world. Its presence may well obtrude on our public lives, as well as intrude on our innermost thoughts. If self-concealing is part of our vanity, then it interferes with the process of being able to remake ourselves in a more formally acceptable image. All of us have rough edges that we might rather see burnished away. But we cannot lead ourselves to imagine that even if we succeeded in doing so, some other person would still see them in their former places. People get used to knowing us in a way in which they feel comfortable. So, once again, it is self-knowledge, or better, self-understanding, that cleaves to the soul of being-present. It can do so even when we are young, when our experience of the world and of ourselves is nascent, as long as our elders are circumspect in their demands of us and realistically pragmatic in their imagination of what we can do with any acumen. Most especially, education itself must understand that the world is not a mechanical forum for the application of rules bereft of the process of interpretation. In addition, "We cannot and should not lead young people to believe that they will inherit a future of satisfying comfort and increasing ease. Rather, we should convey to them a pleasure in collective responsibility and in a genuinely shared existence both with and for one another" (Gadamer 1996:82 [1986]). It may seem odd to refer to such a daunting task as "pleasurable" in any way, but it should be immediately recalled that when something is "figured out" by a number of persons working together that in fact there occurs an intense pleasure, almost akin to that erotic or that filial—the realization of the other's love or the recognition of a friend in the street—and this can be seen as a kind of human reward for taking on the very challenge of being human. This has always been the case, as far as we can speculate about our primordial ancestry, for we see a consistent, if not constant or rapid, movement from the most simple forms of life to those much more sophisticated. This movement is remarkable in itself, even when it appears to stagnate over geologic time periods, because in it we can see ourselves as historical beings. We are beings who have a history. This is unique to our form of life. That it is a shared history presents to us its homiletic: we must continue to share it and thus work together with others. In our contemporary world, this means others of all kinds and stripes. For those who were present at the origins of this world-historical dynamic, it was enough to confront the world itself without also having to deal with cultural diversity: "However much the world forced early man to face reality, it was with the greatest reluctance that he consciously entered this reality" (Neumann, op. cit:16). Although the analogy has been consistently made between "primitives" and children in a great deal of sentimental variants, from cognitive development and forms of logic, to art and fantasy, to the conceptions surrounding the functions of sexuality, it is clear that none of these has any merit other than to point up the fact that all of us, as human beings in all time periods, recognize the difference between becoming conscious and being fully conscious of our surrounding world. Much more importantly for contemporary life is the ability, once conscious, to submit this world and our place in it to both an inner scrutiny in the manner that can produce self-understanding and as well the cultural critique that enlightens what is greater than ourselves. We often feel, very much due to the problem of becoming conscious of the world, that what is sensible about it can never be made our own. But the "bigger picture" is in fact incomplete without our consent. Society as a whole does not function without members, and its conventions are agreed to by those who appear to be imprisoned by them. Even so, calling it out requires a whistle-blower of courageous tenor, for many of the reasons already discussed: "It takes a much higher emotional investment to admit to oneself that things are wrong than it takes to consent to conventional truths" (Portelli 1990:151). On top of this subjectivity, "intensified" by some slight of status or something more serious such that it is felt as an existential threat, "Doubt and dissent can only surface when they possess a high degree of intensity; and then those who express them are often also partly speaking for the majority who dare not admit their doubts even to themselves" (ibid). Just like the student in a large classroom who has a question, she neither realizes that half the class has the same or related question or that she herself as an individual has a right to ask. There is the peer pressure of having to conform to the ideal student who supposedly already knows everything—why then take any class at all?—as well as the pride of the specific ego involved; that it should not have to ask anything. In reality, the ideal student is the one who queries, not out of spite or vanity, but out of curiosity and a sense that things are not always "right," at least not for everyone and not all the time. There is, side by side with human curiosity, the sensibility associated with human justice and thus injustice, of which there is a surfeit in our modern world, and of which there has been plenty in all historically known time periods. Justice "herself" is said to be blind, akin to the cosmos. But this is sometimes a fatal metaphor. At best, the human dispensation of justice can only look both ways before crossing the stygian divide. And for it to do so it needs the very opposite of blindness. It needs be possessed of the same inspiration and wonder as are we ourselves when we consider how we feel when we must take justice as our collective responsibility to one another in lieu of anything the cosmos can produce. It is something akin to how we feel being in love or being aware that one is dying, "but we also feel it before the extraordinary fact that out of this vast blind silence, thought, vision, speech can evolve" (Taylor, op. cit:347). This "communicative life" acts as a beacon in the surrounding darkness. Not that the darkness is itself an evil thing, but it does seem always ready to engulf us and extinguish our light. Science, as Sagan has famously stated, is one of these sources of human light just as it is a source of contemporary consciousness, but it is not, as we have seen above, the only one. But this light itself is not a solid thing, and indeed, somewhat paradoxically, it too participates, and must participate, in the darkness in order to provide for its own justification of being lit. Human consciousness does not entirely source itself, following only from its own logic or even the supposedly more objective logic of argument, philosophical or historical, and this experience "reveals something deeply rooted in human nature: that even in a state of perfect enlightenment we cannot ground everything we hold to be true through strict proof of conclusive deduction. Rather, we must permanently rely on something, and ultimately on someone, in whom we have trust. Our entire communicative life rests on this" (Gadamer 1996:121 [1983]). These relationships also rest on the fact that our presence as a flickering point both as a planet in the spatial void and as a consciously reflective species in the panoply of a nature that "does its own thing" around us and beside us, presents us with something that can only be self-fulfilling, even while at the same time it cannot afford to be only self-referencing. In the midst of nature but yet outside of it, we might be forgiven for imagining that we had, at some point become outcast from it. In the face of its natural self-reproduction, its seemingly endless cycle and its also apparent nonchalance at being able to exist in this way, we might begin to feel a little inferior. This inferiority can be felt at the level of culture or that of the individual. Since we can do nothing to annul the effect of nature in the cosmos, or for that matter, the very presence of an anonymous and infinite universe that does not seem to have a consciousness with which we can relate let alone anything in mind for us, we often turn to ourselves for both support but also on ourselves for a scapegoat: "The bottom is then knocked out of the human relationship, for, like megalomania, a feeling of inferiority makes mutual recognition impossible, and without this there is no relationship" (Jung, op. cit:17). To avoid this catastrophe, one that we today seem always to be dancing on the edge of, we must recognize that we share the most basic and common feature of consciousness that we imagine must be shared with any species, however alien to our own, everywhere and anywhere conscious-ness is to be found within the envelope of the non-conscious, the void of meaning and the utterly anonymous. If there is something that all of us share as human beings, it is the bare fact of both having to become conscious, like the primordial ancestor that has been the child in all of us, and once attained, of consciously practicing this unique ability against the shroud of our self-made darkness which is, by definition, the truer threat to existence: "The collective unconscious of mankind must be experienced and apprehended by the consciousness of mankind as the ground common to all men" (Neumann, op. cit:418). That this commonality can make meaning in general, and not just that specific set of meanings that make life fulfilling, is the place where each of us begins. This, as Nietzsche said of "man," cannot be "over-stepped." That all human languages rely on metaphor for their art of making meaning is clear (cf. Barrett, op. cit:186). That our language of the human sciences and of the sciences of nature as well are then constructed from and on this basis tells us of the demand we must place on ourselves and is also placed before us by the history of the species: living is at once both life and art. The latter may seem obscure, but the daily use of language, even in the most quotidian of contexts, requires that we be at least a competent artist, as well as a competent judge. Blindness in either realm produces only the loosely connected if not the randomness of chance that is more akin to the origins of what we take to be our natural substrates. Confusion can only result from the misapplication of the arts of being human, but that said, we must remember that the only source and recipient of such confusion can be ourselves (cf. Jung, op. cit:x). The communicative life then though it rests on the competent understanding of language and its internal grammar and play of metaphor, rests as well on its goals; that is, to ultimately come to some working and sensible understanding of one another, our most intimate companions and the farthest flung strangers alike. To do this, we need to be able to hear what they are saying to us: "We are listening to how people relate their lives—*what is of value to them*" (Ben Mayor 19990:198, italics the text's). This kind of subjectivity makes things more objective *for us*. We cannot know more than our own space, the circle of light thrown by our own version of the lighted space of the species. But now we begin, peering into the surrounding velvet void, to observe other pinpricks of light, moving to and fro, some toward us and some away. We begin to understand that we are not alone, either here or if we travel somewhere else, and that all of us is in the same situation regarding existence and being conscious of being in the world. The shadows that seem to envelope us and threaten our existence are really just as likely to be the distances necessary between beings like us to create a difference and diversity that we can learn from, for the identical twin of our consciousness cannot enlighten us. These shadows also present to us the presence of our own, in which we find there to be as much that is rational and sensible as mysterious (cf. Jung, op. cit:266). The sensibility of the light which we hold and see in the hands of others is mostly *ad hoc*. This is what it needs to be for a finite species conscious of its own capabilities to extinguish itself. One light goes out and another must replace it in some way. We cannot, and should not, strive to be the *same* thing, but we must strive to know that what animates our similarities makes us nevertheless the same *kind* of thing. There is both a kind of revulsion in this, but also the kind kindred of a kindness. This latter is done for us, while the former is done to us. To concentrate on the latter is one of the great human tasks, but it no more departs from the specific context than does any task that requires a set of sensible instruments and stocks of knowledge at hand: "What great philosophers do for us is not to hand out an all-purpose system. It is to light up and clarify some special aspect of life, to supply conceptual tools which will do a certain necessary kind of work" (Midgely, op. cit:156). One of the great lessons in becoming conscious is the realization that all human tasks have this specific quality to them. Even those whose scope suggests the largest questions must hone their particular abilities in order to approach them, and this approach must also be from a set of specific angles, not all angles at once, even if we flattered ourselves in thinking that we could know all of these, we could never embrace all of them at the same time. Perhaps over the life course, some of them can be explored in some detail. That we can do this, resting on the shoulders of our collective cultural history as well as upon the broader body of nature in its entirety, is a tribute not to hubris or vanity, but to patient sensibility and the courageous persistence of a poetry that more resembles a dogged doggerel than any great epic (cf. Neumann's conception of the species' "genius", op. cit:208). This "genius" includes all that is also in between reality and the irreality of uncanny semi-consciousness states. Therein lies the ability to learn almost by a kind of osmosis, the primary socialization of every culture. And even in the face of the most suffocating and disingenuous discourses, we have learned to adapt and create new experiences: "It is often said that we have been incapable of imagining any new pleasures. We have at least invented a different kind of pleasure: pleasure in the truth of pleasure" (Foucault, op. cit:71). This may be considered something quite secondary, but even so, such appendices, footnotes, and loose threads often hold within them the germ of something radically and world-historically new. Over time, this has been the case with a number of aspects of conscious thought, and for all we know, also that now buttressing part of the architecture of the unconscious, vast and deep to our usual senses. Here the challenge is not to lose conscious culture altogether in its depths, after all of the eons of working ourselves out of their pure and constant influence over us as the transition from animal instinct to culture (cf. Neumann, op. cit:339). Even today, it is an ongoing challenge to think ourselves through not only the problems of the mundane world, but towards some fulfilling and generative response to existential questions about which the collective psyche of the species has been orbiting for countless generations. These possibilities, though within each of us, are themselves ambiguous enough on their own to become brittle with any further ambiguation placed upon them by the resistance of formative and systemic institutionalization, the rationalization of workplaces and even families, and the God of wealth and its minions of financial "security." Such sacrifices as there have been have created the idea that culture comes from and also somehow belongs to elites. Ambiguity is at the heart of what we are, but as such it requires of us patience and vigilance, an alertness to precisely the possibility and not the plausible, as we saw in the previous section, nor even the probable, in which the discourses of science are interested. We have seen throughout this book that oppositional logic sabotages the reality of both human consciousness and its synthetic "soul" hosted as its conscience: "The present age must come to terms drastically with the facts as they are, with the absolute opposition that is not only tearing the world asunder politically but has planted a schism in the human heart." (Jung, op. cit:86). Typification alone, as we have also seen, is no antidote for opposition. It tends to view the world from far above it, and while it is handy to have a sense of the abstract whole—and no more profound than the first views of the entire earth from space—this vista cannot impress upon us the essential conflicts that are held within such a whole. The problem with the understanding that we are in fact one world is that images of this mask the equally stunning fact that we remain divided in numerous serious ways. We need, along with a story of how we have attained a perspective of the abstraction, a story that delineates in detail the history of our distanciation, and our self-distanciation, from this apparent ideal. Even here, there are important limits: "The story can at best utilize what may be known about actual persons; it cannot transcend the limits of hypothesis. And this is because daily life has no heroes" (Natanson, op. cit:93). This is so not because we generally do not recognize the courage it takes to live on in the face of loss, poverty, disability, disdain or outright persecution, the total effects of which take into account the vast majority of human lives, but because heroism occurs when one is taken precisely out of the mundane world and one is faced with the confrontation of remaking it in the face of what is standard and unquestioned. It is not nature itself that has blemished culture with these problems—they are not additional elements that have taken us unawares—but all that lies within culture and cultures globally by which some persons benefit and others do not. It is an insult to our own unique achievement, culture itself, that we continue to prevaricate, often with the most transparently cynical "justifications," such things against our human fellows. At the same time, we are stuck with culture unless or until some other species comes along, whether from the far reaches of the stars or developed out of the organic creatures we are today: "We should not forget: it is nature itself that has impelled us toward culture. Thus, the fact that we cannot survive without culture continues to be true as well" (Gadamer 2001:140 [1994]). That the concept of the present also has a history, though a briefer one that certain other concepts we have encountered, is also something that cannot be forgotten. Throughout its recent vintage, new vantage points were being discovered and organized into our thoughts. The concept of ecology, for instance, is so new that we are still struggling with understanding that our actions, even at the personal level, have effects that "impel" us away from the symbiosis that mechanical cultures had—though this by virtue of their population load and their means of resource extraction and *not* through any Rousseauistic romance—and thereby force us to reckon with a more and more precise date of reckoning with the environmental crisis. But even this current concern did not occur overnight: "Western man was gradually learning what it meant to be a living species in a living world, to have a body, conditions of existence, probabilities of life, an individual and collective welfare, forces that could be modified, and a space in which they could be distributed in an optimal manner" (Foucault, op. cit:142). Modification and organization, distribution and condition all speak to us of order and sense, both of which we have learned to impose upon the often apparently irrational aspects of the world and also of our own social world. Some formality is always necessary. After all, one must become something from nothing. No human skill, idea, art or wisdom is innate in any detailed and sophisticated way. There may be predilections, even prescience, but never the ability itself. We are not chaotic creatures, acting on the command of chance. Such a conception is both "unworthy" and "dangerous": "Unworthy because there is also a reality of reason upon which incomparably more depends in the long run than upon the reality of the factual. Dangerous because our idea of reality is one of the factors that shape the future" (Lösch, op. cit:219). Like the reality of the consequences of any seriously held belief, the future as preconceived in the present order can only run down the rails that our imagination has provided for it. So what is fatal in our present is fated for our future? The moral theme of this book as part of a lengthy discourse of critique and questioning is rather the opposite. Factuality and even facticity by themselves do not paint the future in any detail. They provide a framework within which we are still more or less free to act, but it is this framework, whatever it may consist of, that can also be called into question by each generation. In doing so, we generate another kind of belief; a belief in the ability of the imagination and conscience to shape the way in which we live rather than accept the way in which we supposedly have to live based only on the facts of having had to live in this way: "This belief is based on nature and reason when it can no longer depend on the facts. From them it creates the model for an order that may originate only as a result of it" (ibid). Such beliefs as may be generated by going "beyond" the facts of any specific case are what drives the process and progress of the sciences as well as what allows individual humans to learn from their experiences. Factuality within the enactmental complex of the factical life-being is the occurrence of the exceptional of consciousness within the ambit of the world order. That it has itself constructed this order can be a grand distraction to the work needed to make it something vital and viable. It needs these much more and even instead of merely reproducing the adoration it receives in its maintenance. And this is no task for the technician who knows only this mechanical genuflection as his stock in trade: "No outward tinkering with the world and no social amelioration can give quietus to the daemon, to the gods and devils of the human soul, or prevent them from tearing down again and again what consciousness has built" (Neumann, op. cit:393). The essence of human life is an historical one. It is not, in other words, "essential" in any other sense but that given by the time and place into which we are thrown as incomplete and incompletable projects. Even the idea of the soul, whatever the rationalist might refer to it as, the gestalt of an evolutionary mechanism that winks on and off with the deterioration of its organic envelope, or the subjugation of its cognitive faculties by chemical or ideological propaganda, can serve as a decoy from the pressing and serious task of working within that historical life and thus constructing a livable future for ourselves: "We must rigorously deny the possibility that human life can be lived without a future. For, as I see it, it is a distinctively human fact that we must always keep the future open and with it new possibilities" (Gadamer 1996:80 [1986]).

If possibility is too vague to "make sense," it is in fact in spite of its vagueness the most sensible understanding we can come to regarding our presence in this world. We can calculate all the probabilities we need to make certain kinds of decisions, or invest in outcomes that can be constructed as more or less likely. We must also live in this way, for to avoid the crises and abysses that are by definition part of the human future in its possibility, we cannot entirely forego planning in favor of the Dionysian exuberance that is itself too often suppressed by over-planning. But in essence we do not actually live in this controlled and rationalized manner. It remains, in spite of its voracious appetite for global domination and docimological calculus, a way in which we cover over the reality of existence. Its desire for the infinite, which it inherits from mythic thought, its narrative of progress and civilization, which it borrows from soteriological doctrine, and its simple convenience for those at the helm, make it an implacable companion in our contemporary travels. But it is a companion that we cannot ultimately trust. We must throw ourselves back onto our own wit, bend ourselves toward the world as it is, and recall to ourselves the intensity of emotion that accompanied our first experiences of everything that was new to us in order to stride forward together into the possibility of our collective future.

Notes

INTRODUCTION

1. One of the perennial examples in modern life is the rationalization of the problem of wealth, most of which is inherited. As the value of the self-made individual has hardly lapsed since the Protestant reformation, the source and therefore the moral authority of wealth needs to be given a fictive but respectable cosmogony: "The myth of a poor childhood can be found in almost all better-off sections of society. The sociologist meets it as soon as, for example, he asks shopkeepers, up-and-coming artisans, or rich farmers for their life story. You will find everywhere the same theme with only a few small variations" (Peneff, 19990:37).

2. There are of course exceptions to this, such as the current state of affairs in Kurdistan and neighboring environs where the so-called ISIS operates and has made it clear that someone such as myself, a Western intellectual no less, would be executed if I trespassed in their territory, or even if I go to a North American mall, though this latter is most unlikely due to geographic distances and security arrangements. The astonishing thing about what Jung referred to as an "enantiodromian" process is always the extremity to which fellow human beings feel they must go to in order to off-set the presence of the thesis of this or that cultural suasion. Of course, it may be that in a dictatorship, violence is the only means out (cf. Jung 1959:95 where he notes that the schism of Western Christendom had been accurately predicted simply due to the sense that the thesis, in this case, the Roman church, had become too much of a dominant force in people's everyday lives, especially the peoples whose cultures had originally not given birth to these beliefs).

3. Cf. Lösch for a comment on the relationships between organization and production, input and output, and the problem of what is superfluous if things become "too efficient" (1967:239 [1945]).

4. The anxiety of reality is ironically stronger the more intimate and personal the issue. Intercourse with the dead is likened to that sexual, and necrophilia is generally a crime cross-culturally: "How does one account for the displacement which, while claiming to free us from the sinful nature of sex, taxes us with a great historical wrong which consists precisely in imagining that nature to be blameworthy and in drawing disastrous consequences from that belief?" (Foucault 1980:9).

1. THE SINGULAR SELF

1. Nor can we assume that where general to particular analogic models are warranted do they in turn warrant us to attempt to count ourselves automatically in league with their contents. (cf. Lösch 1967:235-6 [1945]) for an excellent example of a reasonable analogue, and ibid:347 for a more dubious one. The former list only objective considerations; the latter contains a few elements that were in vogue during the Third Reich and may be viewed as somewhat suspicious on those grounds).

2. THE MACHINE MESSIAH

1. Foucault has charted this historical dynamic with detailed aplomb: "From the direction of conscience to psychoanalysis, the deployments of alliance and sexuality were involved in a slow process that had them turning into one another until, more than three centuries later, their positions were reversed." (1980:113 [1978]). One can now desire the alliance that before had limited the very desire that was its most shunned object, the most objectionable thing about it, and thus constructed as the most abject absence of solace—"sex without love" even today is stigmatized, but what is love without sex but a return to the doctrine of "Platonic" forms, aptly given its vernacular metaphor and suasion through the abstinence which supposedly directs us to a higher form of desire.

2. So far, its most patent and overweening "achievement" seems to be the measurement of intelligence insofar as it has developed complex rubrics for testing and defending the results of such tests across cultures and creed, ethnicities and genders (cf. Sorokin 1956:52ff for the most complete critical list to date of such "achievements" and their objects).

3. Indeed, this compulsion might actually benefit us less while claiming to give us more: "Through their mistesting and misselection they would likely aggravate rather than alleviate the defects of the existing selection and distribution." (Sorokin, op. cit:100).

3. WANTED DEAD OR ALIVE: GOD

1. Thus Neumann almost immediately gives the example of the Greek Gods who, though they no longer exist as a pantheon either literally or figuratively—though they keep showing up in contemporary advertising and, in a very Nazi like way, as "models" for hygiene and aesthetics—or as "living forces," they have been "broken down" into other facets of society: "They exist as contents of consciousness, and no longer—or only in special cases—as symbols of the unconscious" (op.cit:328).

2. See also 114 for a list of the major tropes of Christian mythic narrative as encapsulated in the fish symbol; we are also told that the age of Pisces has about 135 years left to in terms of the astrological procession of the "Great Year." Perhaps at that time a new religion will also have appeared and Christianity will be marginalized in the way the Judaism, the belief system of the age of the Ram, eventually was.

4. NO PLACE LIKE HOME

1. This would include Midgely, where, though she takes Marx to task for believing in the "infinite" of natural resources, the ethnocentrism of his European examples—capital in his time had not spread outside of Europe, for the most part—or quasi-Darwinist factors "outside the

human species" though it is unclear why such factors would be relevant in any case (cf. op. cit:78-9). Her point that we began to use the terms of natural history in a loaded manner is deadpan to this regard (cf. ibid:81).

6. "FREEDOM OF THOUGHT," THOUGHT FREEDOM

1. Examples from all areas of human behavior and history abound, but one of the most disconcerting and omnipresent developments for us today has to be that of the models and templates for sexuality and intimacy, as these impinge particularly on our sense of human freedom including private expression of the idiosyncrasies of passion: "This scheme for transforming sex into discourse had been devised long before in an ascetic and monastic setting, The seventeenth century made it into a rule for everyone" (Foucault, op. cit:20).

References

Adorno, Theodor. *Critical Models: interventions and catchwords.* Columbia University Press, New York. 1998 [1969].

Ash, Marinell. "William Wallace and Robert the Bruce; the life and death of a national myth," in *The Myths We Live By,* edited by Raphael Samuel and Paul Thompson. Routledge, London. Pages 83-94. 1990

Bachelard, Gaston. *The Poetics of Space.* Beacon Press, Boston. 1969 [1958].

———. *The Psychoanalysis of Fire.* Beacon Press, Boston. 1964 [1938].

Barrett, William. *The Illusion of Technique: a search for meaning in a technological civilization.* Anchors Books, New York. 1979.

Basso, Rosanna. "Myths in contemporary oral transmission: a children's strike," in *The Myths We Live By,* edited by Raphael Samuel and Paul Thompson. Routledge, London. Pages 61-70. 1990.

Bravo, Anna, Lilia Davite, and Daniele Jalla. "Myth, impotence, and survival in the concentration camps," in *the Myths We Live By,* edited by Raphael Samuel and Paul Thompson. Routledge, London. Pages 95-110. 1990.

Benmayor, Rina, Blanca Vázquez, Ana Juarbe and Celia Alvarez. "Stories to live by: continuity and change in three generations of Puerto Rican women," in *The Myths We Live By,* edited by Raphael Samuel and Paul Thompson. Routledge, London. Pages 184-200. 1990.

Burchardt, Natasha. "Stepchildren's memories: myth, understanding, and forgiveness," in *The Myths We Live By,* edited by Raphael Samuel and Paul Thompson. Routledge, London. Pages 239-251. 1990.

Byng-Hall, John, interviewed by Paul Thompson "The power of family myths," in *The Myths We Live By,* edited by Raphael Samuel and Paul Thompson. Routledge, London. Pages 216-224. 1990.

Cabezali, Elena, Matilde Cuevas and Maria Teresa Chicote. "Myth as suppression: motherhood and the historical consciousness of the women of Madrid, 1936-9," in *The Myths We Live By,* edited by Raphael Samuel and Paul Thompson. Routledge, London. Pages 161-173. 1990.

Champigny, Robert. *Sense, Antisense, Nonsense.* University of Florida Press, Gainesville. 1986.

Cruikshank, Julie. "Myth as a framework for life stories: Athapaskan women making sense of social change in northern Canada," in *The Myths We Live By,* edited by Raphael Samuel and Paul Thompson. Routledge, London. Pages 174-183. 1990.

Derrida, Jacques. *On the Name.* Stanford University Press, Stanford. 1995 [1993].

Foucault, Michel. *The History of Sexuality Volume One: Introduction.* Vintage Books, New York 1980 [1978].

Gadamer, Hans-Georg. *The Beginning of Philosophy.* Continuum, New York 1998 [1996].
———. "Natural Science and the Concept of Nature," in *The Beginning of Knowledge.* Continuum. New York 2001. Pages 127-140. [1995].
———. "On the Enigmatic Character of Health," in *The Enigma of Health: The Art of healing in a Scientific Age.* Stanford University Press, Stanford. 1996. Pages 103-116. [1993].
———. "Anxiety and Anxieties," in *The Enigma of Health: The Art of healing in a Scientific Age.* Stanford University Press, Stanford. 1996. Pages 152-162. [1990].
———. "Philosophy and Practical Medicine," in *The Enigma of Health: The Art of healing in a Scientific Age.* Stanford University Press, Stanford. 1996. Pages 92-102. [1990].
———. "Heraclitus Studies," in *The Beginning of Knowledge.* Continuum. New York 2001. Pages 33-81. [1990].
———. "Hermeneutics and Psychiatry," in *The Enigma of Health: The Art of healing in a Scientific Age.* Stanford University Press, Stanford. 1996. Pages 163-173. [1989].
———. "Between Nature and Art," in *The Enigma of Health: The Art of healing in a Scientific Age.* Stanford University Press, Stanford. 1996. Pages 83-91. [1987].
———. "Life and Soul," in *The Enigma of Health: The Art of healing in a Scientific Age.* Stanford University Press, Stanford. 1996. Pages 141-151. [1987].
———. "Bodily Experience and the Limits of Objectification," in *The Enigma of Health: The Art of healing in a Scientific Age.* Stanford University Press, Stanford.
———. "Greek Philosophy and Modern Thought," in *The Beginning of Knowledge.* Continuum. New York, 2001. Pages 119-126. [1978].
———. "On the Tradition of Heraclitus," in *The Beginning of Knowledge.* Continuum. New York, 2001. Pages 21-34. [1974].
———. "Theory, Technology, Praxis," in *The Enigma of Health: The Art of healing in a Scientific Age.* Stanford University Press, Stanford. 1996. Pages 1-30. [1972].
———. "Apologia for the Art of Healing," in *The Enigma of Health: The Art of healing in a Scientific Age.* Stanford University Press, Stanford. 1996. Pages 31-44. [1967].
———. "Plato and Presocratic Cosmology," in *The Beginning of Knowledge.* Continuum. New York 2001. Pages 102-118. [1964].
———. "The Problem of Intelligence," in *The Enigma of Health: The Art of healing in a Scientific Age.* Stanford University Press, Stanford. 1996. Pages 45-60. [1964].
———. "Ancient Atomic Theory," in *The Beginning of Knowledge.* Continuum. New York 2001. Pages 82-101. [1935].
Hall, John A. *How Homogenous Must We Be? Reflections on the Theory of Nationalism.* University of Saskatchewan, Saskatoon, Saskatchewan. 2005.
Heidegger, Martin. *Ontology—The Hermeneutics of Facticity.* Indiana University Press, Bloomington. 1999 [1988].
Henkes, Barbara. "Changing images of German maids during the inter-war period in the Netherlands: from trusted help to traitor in the nest," in *The Myths We Live By,* edited by Raphael Samuel and Paul Thompson. Routledge, London. Pages 225-236. 1990.
Johansson, Ella. "Free sons of the forest: storytelling and the construction of identity among Swedish lumberjacks," in *The Myths We Live By,* edited by Raphael Samuel and Paul Thompson. Routledge, London. Pages 129-142. 1990.
Jung, Carl G. *Aion: Researches into the Phenomenology of the Self.* Bollingen, Princeton University Press, Princeton. 1959 [1951].
Lilburn, Tim. *The Larger Conversation: the ethical significance of the human relationship to place.* STM College, Saskatoon, Saskatchewan. 2010.
———. *Living in the World as if it were Home: Essays.* Cormorant Books, Dunvegen, Ontario. 1999.
Lingis, Alphonso. *Deathbound Subjectivity.* Indiana University Press, Bloomington. 1989.
Lösch, August. *The Economics of Location.* Wiley Science Editions, John Wiley and Sons, New York. 1967 [1945].
Midgely, Mary. *The Myths We Live By.* Routledge, London. 2004.
Nasson, Bill. "Abraham Esau's war, 1899-1901: martyrdom, myth, and folk memory in Calvinia, South Africa," in *The Myths We Live By,* edited by Raphael Samuel and Paul Thompson. Routledge, London. Pages 111-126. 1990.

Natanson, Maurice. *The Journeying Self: a study in philosophy and social role.* Addison-Wesley Publishing Company, Reading, MA. 1990.

Neumann, Erich. *The Origins and History of Consciousness.* Bollingen, Princeton University Press, Princeton. 1970 [1949].

Nietzsche, Friedrich. *The Portable Nietzsche.* Edited by Walter Kaufman, Viking, Penguin, New York. 1954.

Passerini, Luisa. "Mythbiography in oral history," in *The Myths We Live By,* edited by Raphael Samuel and Paul Thompson. Routledge, London. Pages 49-60. 1990.

Peneff, Jean. "Myths in life stores," in *The Myths We Live By,* edited by Raphael Samuel and Paul Thompson. Routledge, London. Pages 36-48. 1990.

Portelli, Alessandro. "Uchronic dreams: working-class memory and possible worlds," in *The Myths We Live By,* edited by Raphael Samuel and Paul Thompson. Routledge, London. Pages 143-160. 1990.

Samuel, Raphael, and Paul Thompson, eds. *The Myths We Live By.* Routledge, London. 1990.

———. "Introduction," in *The Myths We Live By,* edited by Raphael Samuel and Paul Thompson. Routledge, London. Pages 1-22. 1990.

Schutz, Alfred. *The Phenomenology of the Social World.* Northwestern University Press, Evanston, Illinois. 1967 [1932].

Simmel, Georg. *The View of Life: four metaphysical essays with journal aphorisms.* The University of Chicago press, Chicago 2010 [1918].

Sorokin, Pitirim. *Fads and Foibles in Modern Sociology and Related Sciences.* Henry Regnery Company, Chicago. 1956.

Taylor, Charles. *Sources of the Self: The Making of Modern Identity.* Harvard University Press, Cambridge, MA. 1989.

Thomas, Rosalind. "Ancient Greek family tradition and democracy: from oral history to myth," in *The Myths We Live By,* edited by Raphael Samuel and Paul Thompson. Routledge, London. Pages 203-215. 1990.

Thomson, Alistair. "The Anzac legend: exploring national myth and memory in Australia," in *The Myths We Live By,* edited by Raphael Samuel and Paul Thompson. Routledge, London. Pages 73-82. 1990.

Tonkin, Elizabeth. "History and the myth of realism," in *The Myths We Live By,* edited by Raphael Samuel and Paul Thompson. Routledge, London. Pages 25-35. 1990.